CASE OF VENEZUELA

IN THE QUESTION OF
BOUNDARY BETWEEN VENEZUELA
AND BRITISH GUIANA.

PRESENTED BY VENEZUELA TO THE ARBITRATORS,
IN CONFORMITY WITH THE TREATY OF
FEBRUARY 2, 1897.

Part II.

(Translated from the Spanish.)

OFFICIAL EDITION.

WASHINGTON, D. C.
PRESS OF MCGILL & WALLACE.
1898.

CONTENTS OF PART II.

CARACAS, November 10, 1897.

Arbitration Treaty.

Her Majesty the Queen of the United Kingdom of Great Britain and Ireland, and the United States of Venezuela, being desirous to provide for an amicable settlement of the question which has arisen between their respective governments concerning the boundary between the Colony of British Guiana and the United States of Venezuela, have resolved to submit to arbitration the question involved, and to the end of concluding a treaty for that purpose have appointed as their respective Plenipotentiaries:

Her Majesty the Queen of the United Kingdom of Great Britain and Ireland, the Right Honorable Sir Julian Pauncefote, a member of Her Majesty's Most Honorable Privy Council, Knight Grand Cross of the Most Honorable Order of the Bath and of the Most Distinguished Order of St. Michael and St. George, and Her Majesty's Ambassador Extraordinary and Plenipotentiary to the United States;

And the President of the United States of Venezuela, Señor José Andrade, Envoy Extraordinary and Minister Plenipotentiary of Vene-

Los Estados Unidos de Venezuela y Su Majestad la Reina del Reino Unido de la Gran Bretaña é Irlanda, deseando estipular el arreglo amistoso de la cuestión que se ha suscitado entre sus respectivos Gobiernos acerca del límite de los Estados Unidos de Venezuela y la Colonia de la Guayana Británica, han resuelto someter dicha cuestión á arbitramento, y á fin de concluir con ese objeto un tratado, han elegido por sus respectivos Plenipotenciarios:

El Presidente de los Estados Unidos de Venezuela, al Señor José Andrade, Enviado Extraordinario y Ministro Plenipotenciario de Venezuela en los Estados Unidos de América:

Y Su Majestad la Reina del Reino Unido de la Gran Bretaña é Irlanda al Muy Honorable Sir Julian Pauncefote, Miembro del Muy Honorable Consejo Privado de Su Majestad, Caballero Gran Cruz de la Muy Honorable Orden del Baño y de la Muy Distinguida Orden de San Miguel y San Jorge, y Embajador Extraordinario y Plenipotenciario de Su Majestad en los Estados Unidos:

Quienes, habiéndose com-

zuela to the United States of America:

Who, having communicated to each other their respective full powers which were found to be in due and proper form, have agreed to and concluded the following articles:

unicado sus respectivos plenos poderes que fueron hallados en propia y debida forma, han acordado y concluido los artículos siguientes:

ARTICLE I.

An arbitral tribunal shall be immediately appointed to determine the boundary line between the Colony of British Guiana and the United States of Venezuela.

ARTÍCULO I.

Se nombrará inmediatamente un Tribunal arbitral para determinar la línea divisoria entre los Estados Unidos de Venezuela y la Colonia de la Guayana Británica.

ARTICLE II.

The tribunal shall consist of five jurists: Two on the part of Great Britain, nominated by the members of the Judicial Committee of Her Majesty's Privy Council, namely, the Right Honorable Baron Herschell, Knight Grand Cross of the Most Honorable Order of the Bath; and the Honorable Sir Richard Henn Collins, Knight, one of the Justices of Her Britannic Majesty's Supreme Court of Judicature; two on the part of Venezuela nominated, one by the President of the United States of Venezuela, namely, the Honorable Melville Weston Fuller, Chief Justice of the United States of America, and one nomi-

ARTÍCULO II.

El Tribunal se compondrá de cinco Juristas; dos de parte de Venezuela, nombrados, uno por el Presidente de los Estados Unidos de Venezuela, á saber, el Honorable Melville Weston Fuller, Justicia Mayor de los Estados Unidos de América, y uno por los Justicias de la Corte Suprema de los Estados Unidos de América, á saber, el Honorable David Josiah Brewer, Justicia de la Corte Suprema de los Estados Unidos de América; dos de parte de la Gran Bretaña nombrados por los miembros de la Comisión Judicial del Consejo Privado de Su Majestad, á saber, el Muy Honorable Barón

nated by the Justices of the Supreme Court of the United States of America, namely, the Honorable David Josiah Brewer, a Justice of the Supreme Court of the United States of America; and of a fifth jurist to be selected by the four persons so nominated, or, in the event of their failure to agree within three months from the date of the exchange of ratifications of the present treaty, to be selected by His Majesty the King of Sweden and Norway. The jurist so selected shall be president of the tribunal.

In case of the death, absence or incapacity to serve of any of the four arbitrators above named, or in the event of any such arbitrator omitting or declining or ceasing to act as such, another jurist of repute shall be forthwith substituted in his place. If such vacancy shall occur among those nominated on the part of Great Britain the substitute shall be appointed by the members for the time being of the Judicial Committee of Her Majesty's Privy Council, acting by a majority, and if among those nominated on the part of Venezuela he shall be appointed by the Justices of the Supreme Court of the United States, acting by a majority. If such vacancy

Herschell, Caballero Gran Cruz de la Muy Honorable Orden del Baño, y el Honorable Sir Richard Henn Collins, Caballero, uno de los Justicias de la Corte Suprema de Judícatura de Su Majestad; y de un quinto Jurista, que será elegido por las cuatro personas así nombradas, ó, en el evento de no lograr ellas acordarse en la designación dentro de los tres meses contados desde la fecha del canje de las ratificaciones del presente Tratado, por Su Majestad el Rey de Suecia y Noruega. El Jurista á quien así se elija será Presidente del Tribunal.

En caso de muerte, ausencia ó incapacidad para servir de cualquiera de los cuatro Arbitros arriba mencionados, ó en el evento de que alguno de ellos no llegue á ejercer las funciones de tal por omisión, renuncia ó cesación, se sustituirá inmediatamente por otro Jurista de reputación. Si tal vacante ocurre entre los nombrados por parte de Venezuela, el sustituto será elegido por los Justicias de la Corte Suprema de los Estados Unidos, de América por mayoria; y si ocurriere entre los nombrados por parte de la Gran Bretaña, elegirán al sustituto, por mayoría, los que fueren

shall occur in the case of the fifth arbitrator, a substitute shall be selected in the manner herein provided for with regard to the original appointment.

entonces miembros de la Comisión Judicial del Consejo Privado de Su Majestad. Si vacare el puésto de quinto Arbitro, se le elegirá sustituto del modo aqui estipulado en cuanto al nombramiento primitivo.

Article III.

The tribunal shall investigate and ascertain the extent of the territories belonging to or that might lawfully be claimed by the United Netherlands or by the Kingdom of Spain, respectively, at the time of the acquisition by Great Britain of the Colony of British Guiana—and shall determine the boundary line between the Colony of British Guiana and the United States of Venezuela.

Artículo III.

El Tribunal investigará y se cerciorará de la extensión de los territorios pertenecientes á las Provincias Unidas de los Países Bajos ó al Reino de España respectivamente, ó que pudieran ser legítimamente reclamados por aquéllas ó éste, al tiempo de la adquisición de la Colonia de la Guayana Británica por la Gran Bretaña, y determinará la línea divisoria entre los Estados Unidos de Venezuela y la Colonia de la Guayana Británica.

Article IV.

In deciding the matters submitted, the arbitrators shall ascertain all facts which they deem necessary to a decision of the controversy, and shall be governed by the following rules, which are agreed upon by the high contracting parties as rules to be taken as applicable to the case, and by such principles of international law not in-

Artículo IV.

Al decidir los asuntos sometidos á los Arbitros, estos se cerciorarán de todos los hechos que estimen necesarios para la decisión de la controversia, y se gobernarán por las siguientes reglas en que están convenidas las Altas Partes contratantes como reglas que han de considerarse aplicables al caso, y por los principios de de-

consistent therewith as the arbitrators shall determine to be applicable to the case.

Rules.

(*a*) Adverse holding or prescription during a period of fifty years shall make a good title. The arbitrators may deem exclusive political control of a district as well as actual settlement thereof sufficient to constitute adverse holding or to make title by prescription.

(*b*) The arbitrators may recognize and give effect to rights and claims resting on any other ground whatever valid according to international law and on any principles of international law which the arbitrators may deem to be applicable to the case and which are not in contravention of the foregoing rule.

(*c*) In determining the boundary line, if territory of one party be found by the tribunal to have been at the date of this treaty in the occupation of the subjects or citizens of the other party, such effect shall be given to such occupation as reason, justice, the principles of international law and the equities of the case shall, in the opinion of the tribunal, require.

recho internacional no incompatibles con ellas, que los Arbitros juzgaren aplicables al mismo:

Reglas:

(*a*) Una posesión adversa ó prescripción por el término de cincuenta años constituirá un buen título. Los Arbitros podrán estimar que la dominación política exclusiva de un distrito, asi como la efectiva colonización de él, son suficientes para constituir una posesión adversa ó crear título de prescripción.

(*b*) Los Arbitros podrán reconocer y hacer efectivos derechos y reivindicaciones que se apoyen en cualquier otro fundamento válido conforme al derecho internacional, y en cualesquiera principios de derecho internacional, que los Arbitros estimen aplicables al caso y que no contravengan á la regla precedente.

(*c*) Al determinar la línea divisoria, si el Tribunal hallare que territorio de una parte ha estado en la fecha de este Tratado ocupado por los ciudadanos ó súbditos de la otra parte, se dará á tal ocupación el efecto que, en opinión del Tribunal, requieran la razón, la justicia, los principios del derecho internacional, y la equidad del caso.

Article V.

The arbitrators shall meet at Paris, within sixty days after the delivery of the printed arguments mentioned in Article VIII, and shall proceed impartially and carefully to examine and decide the questions that have been or shall be laid before them as herein provided on the part of the Governments of Her Britannic Majesty and the United States of Venezuela respectively.

Provided always that the arbitrators may, if they shall think fit, hold their meetings or any of them at any other place which they may determine.

All questions considered by the tribunal, including the final decision, shall be determined by a majority of all the arbitrators.

Each of the high contracting parties shall name one person as its agent to attend the tribunal and to represent it generally in all matters connected with the tribunal.

Artículo V.

Los Arbitros se reunirán en Paris dentro de los sesenta días después de la entrega de los argumentos impresos mencionados en el Artículo VIII, y procederán á examinar y decidir imparcial y cuidadosamente las cuestiones que se les hayan sometido ó se les presentaren, según aquí se estipula, por parte de los Gobiernos de los Estados Unidos de Venezuela y de Su Majestad Británica respectivamente.

Pero queda siempre entendido que los Arbitros, si lo juzgan conveniente, podrán celebrar sus reuniones, ó algunas de ellas, en cualquier otro lugar que determinen.

Todas las cuestiones consideradas por el Tribunal, inclusive la decisión definitiva, serán resueltas por mayoría de todos los Arbitros.

Cada una de las Altas Partes Contratantes nombrará como su Agente una persona que asista al Tribunal y la represente generalmente en todos los asuntos conexos con el Tribunal.

Article VI.

The printed case of each of the two parties, accom-

Artículo VI.

Tan pronto como sea posible después de nombrados

panied by the documents, the official correspondence, and other evidence on which each relies, shall be delivered in duplicate to each of the arbitrators and to the agent of the other party as soon as may be after the appointment of the members of the tribunal, but within a period not exceeding eight months from the date of the exchange of the ratifications of this treaty.

los miembros del Tribunal, pero dentro de un plazo que no excederá de ocho meses contados desde la fecha del canje de las ratificaciones de este Tratado, se entregará por duplicado á cada uno de los Arbitros y al Agente de la otra parte, el Alegato impreso de cada una de las dos partes, acompañado de los documentos, la correspondencia oficial y las demás pruebas, en que cada una se apoye.

Article VII.

Within four months after the delivery on both sides of the printed case, either party may in like manner deliver in duplicate to each of the said arbitrators, and to the agent of the other party, a counter case, and additional documents, correspondence, and evidence, in reply to the case, documents, correspondence, and evidence so presented by the other party.

If, in the case submitted to the arbitrators, either party shall have specified or alluded to any report or document in its own exclusive possession, without annexing a copy, such party shall be bound, if the other party thinks proper to apply for it, to furnish that party with a copy thereof, and either party may call upon

Artículo VII.

Dentro de los cuatro meses siguientes á la entrega por ambas partes del Alegato impreso, una ú otra podrá del mismo modo entregar por duplicado á cada uno de dichos Arbitros, y al Agente de la otra parte, un contra-Alegato y nuevos documentos, correspondencia y pruebas, para contestar al Alegato, documentos, correspondencia y pruebas presentados por la otra parte.

Si en el Alegato sometido á los Arbitros una ú otra parte hubiere especificado ó citado algún informe ó documento que esté en su exclusiva posesión, sin agregar copia, tal parte quedará obligada, si la otra cree conveniente pedirla, á suministrarle copia de élá y una ú otra parte podra

the other, through the arbitrators, to produce the originals or certified copies of any papers adduced as evidence, giving in each instance notice thereof within thirty days after delivery of the case; and the original or copy so requested shall be delivered as soon as may be and within a period not exceeding forty days after receipt of notice.

excitar á la otra, por medio de los Arbitros, á producir los originales ó copias certificadas de los papeles aducidos como pruebas, dando en cada caso aviso de esto dentro de los treinta días después de la presentación del Alegato; y el original ó la copia pedidos se entregarán tan pronto como sea posible y dentro de un plazo que no exceda de cuarenta días después del recibo del aviso.

Article VIII.

It shall be the duty of the agent of each party, within three months after the expiration of the time limited for the delivery of the counter case on both sides, to deliver in duplicate to each of the said arbitrators and to the agent of the other party a printed argument showing the points and referring to the evidence upon which his Government relies, and either party may also support the same before the arbitrators by oral argument of counsel; and the arbitrators may, if they desire further elucidation with regard to any point, require a written or printed statement or argument, or oral argument by counsel, upon it; but in such case the other party shall be entitled to reply either or-

Artículo VIII.

El Agente de cada parte, dentro de los tres meses después de la expiración del tiempo señalado para la entrega del contra-Alegato por ambas partes, deberá entregar por duplicado á cada uno de dichos Arbitros y al Agente de la otra parte un argumento impreso que señale los puntos y cite las pruebas en que se funda su Gobierno, y cualquiera de las dos partes podrá también apoyarlo ante los Arbitros con argumentos orales de su Abogado; y los Arbitros podrán, si desean mayor esclarecimiento con respecto á algún punto, requerir sobre él una exposición ó argumento escritos ó impresos, ó argumentos orales del Abogado; pero en tal caso la otra parte

ally or in writing, as the case may be.

tendrá derecho á contestar oralmente ó por escrito, según fuere el caso.

ARTICLE IX.

The arbitrators may, for any cause deemed by them sufficient, enlarge either of the periods fixed by Articles VI, VII, and VIII by the allowance of thirty days additional.

ARTÍCULO IX.

Los Arbitros por cualquier causa que juzguen suficiente podrán prorrogar uno ú otro de los plazos fijados en los Artículos VI, VII y VIII, concediendo treinta días adicionales.

ARTICLE X.

The decision of the tribunal shall, if possible, be made within three months from the close of the argument on both sides.

It shall be made in writing and dated, and shall be signed by the arbitrators who may assent to it.

The decision shall be in duplicate, one copy whereof shall be delivered to the agent of Great Britain for his Government, and the other copy shall be delivered to the agent of the United States of Venezuela for his Government.

ARTÍCULO X.

Si fuere posible, el Tribunal dará su decisión dentro de tres meses contados desde que termine la argumentación por ambos lados.

La decisión se dará por escríto, llevará fecha y se firmará por los Arbitros que asientan á ella.

La decisión se extenderá por duplicado; de ella se entregará un ejemplar al Agente de los Estados Unidos de Venezuela para su Gobierno, y el otro se entregará al Agente de la Gran Bretaña para su Gobierno.

ARTICLE XI.

The arbitrators shall keep an accurate record of their proceedings and may appoint and employ the necessary officers to assist them.

ARTÍCULO XI.

Los Arbitros llevarán un registro exacto de sus procedimientos y podrán elegir y emplear las personas que necesiten para su ayuda.

ARTICLE XII.

Each Government shall pay its own agent and provide for the proper remuneration of the counsel employed by it and of the arbitrators appointed by it or in its behalf, and for the expense of preparing and submitting its case to the tribunal. All other expenses connected with the arbitration shall be defrayed by the two Governments, in equal moieties.

ARTÍCULO XII.

Cada Gobierno pagará á su propio Agente y proveerá la remuneración conveniente para el Abogado que emplee y para los Arbitros elegidos por él ó en su nombre, y costeará los gastos de la preparación y sometimiento de su causa al Tribunal. Los dos Gobiernos satisfarán por partes iguales todos los demás gastos relativos al arbitramento.

ARTICLE XIII.

The high contracting parties engage to consider the result of the proceedings of the tribunal of arbitration as a full, perfect, and final settlement of all the questions referred to the arbitrators.

ARTÍCULO XIII.

Las altas Partes Contratantes se obligan á considerar el resultado de los procedimientos del Tribunal de Arbitramento como arreglo pleno, perfecto y definitivo de todas las cuestiones sometidas á los árbitros.

ARTICLE XIV.

The present treaty shall be duly ratified by Her Britannic Majesty and by the President of the United States of Venezuela, by and with the approval of the Congress thereof; and the ratifications shall be exchanged in London or in Washington within six months from the date hereof.

ARTÍCULO XIV.

El presente Tratado será debidamente ratificado por el Presidente de los Estados Unidos de Venezuela con la aprobación del Congreso de ellos, y por Su Majestad Británica: y las ratificaciones se canjearán en Washington ó en Londres dentro de los seis meses contados desde la fecha del presente tratado.

In faith whereof, we, the respective Plenipotentiaries, have signed this treaty and have hereunto affixed our seals.

Done in duplicate at Washington, the second day of February, one thousand eight hundred and ninety-seven.

JULIAN PAUNCEFOTE. [SEAL.]
JOSÉ ANDRADE. [SEAL.]

En fé de lo cual los respectivos Plenipotenciarios hemos firmado este tratado y le hemos puesto nuestros sellos.

Hecho por duplicado en Washington, a dos de Febrero, de mil ochocientos noventa y siete.

JOSÉ ANDRADE. [SELLO.]
JULIAN PAUNCEFOTE. [SELLO.]

INTRODUCTION.

Through the generous interposition of the United States of America in favor of the United States of Venezuela, in the long-standing question about limits between the latter and the Colony of British Guiana, a Treaty of Arbitration was concluded between the two countries on the 2d of February, 1897. A copy of that Treaty, as it was signed, ratified, and the ratifications exchanged, is reproduced on the preceding pages. It was negotiated and signed on the part of Venezuela by Mr. José Andrade, Envoy Extraordinary and Minister Plenipotentiary of that Republic, and on the part of Great Britain by Sir Julian Pauncefote, Ambassador Extraordinary and Plenipotentiary of Her Britannic Majesty.

The Treaty consists of fourteen articles, most of which relate to the proceedings that must be followed in the arbitration. The articles of greatest importance, namely, I, II, III, and IV, provide for the creation of an Arbitral Tribunal, consisting of five jurists, which shall decide the controversy and fix the rules to be followed in determining the question. Their provisions are the same that were previously agreed upon between the United States of America and Great Britain, and subsequently submitted to Venezuela, as the basis for a direct convention between the two contending parties. Venezuela accepted them, although suggesting that she herself should choose, directly, one of the arbitrators, which was agreed to. The selection of the other was entrusted to the Supreme Court of the United States. Venezuela selected the Hon. Melville Weston Fuller, Chief Justice of the Supreme Court of the United States of America, and that high court selected the Hon. David Josiah Brewer one of its Associate Justices, who had been also the President of the Commission appointed by the United States to "Investigate and report upon the true divisional line between Venezuela and British Guiana."

Great Britain is represented in the Arbitral Tribunal by the Right Hon. Baron Herschell, Knight, Grand Cross of the most Honorable Order of the Bath, and the Hon. Sir Richard Henn Collins, Knight, one of the Justices of the Supreme Court of Judicature of Her Britannic Majesty. The fifth arbitrator was to be a jurist of repute, selected by the other four, and in the event of their failure to agree, by His Majesty the King of Sweden and Norway; the jurist so selected to be the president of the Tribunal.

The decision is to be made by a majority of all the arbitrators, and shall be signed by those who agree to it.

It is to be noticed, therefore, that the arbitrators shall be five jurists of high standing, three of whom are members of the Supreme Courts of the United States and of Great Britain. The fact that they hold such high and honorable positions, sufficiently attests their exalted character and the value of their services to their respective countries; countries so eminently civilized, in which the science of the law has made such great progress. And if due consideration be given to the fact that their judicial positions are for life; that they, in the fulfillment of their duties, have acquired, together with great experience, that perfection of judgment which comes by familiarity with numerous and grave questions of diverse nature; and that they have a reputation, the preservation of which is a matter of extreme interest to them, we can not fail to conclude that they are in all respects eminently well fitted to command the confidence of both the contending parties.

It was not, therefore, too much for Venezuela to consent to entrust to such hands the determination of an affair of the most transcendent importance to her, and upon the result of which her political future, her domestic tranquillity, her aggrandizement, and her standing among the nations of the world shall, in a great measure, depend.

This arbitration is no ordinary one. It is *sui generis.* It has been entrusted to jurists more than to diplomatists, and to jurists of recognized ability, conversant as well with theory as practice; jurists who are going to decide an intricate, long-standing controversy, of essentially a judicial character; and surely none could have been found better qualified by learning and experience to adjust it properly than those who have been selected. They place themselves in a position of perfect impartiality, without remembering that they were chosen by this or that party; without losing sight of their character as *sacerdotes justitiæ,* and without permitting themselves to be influenced in their decision by the relative feebleness or strength of the parties to the contention. They will doubtless realize the august functions which they have been called upon to exercise: namely, the removal, finally and forever, of such a prolific source of dispute between two neighboring States, as is the unsettlement of their frontiers, and the promotion thereby of the holy cause of peace and friendship between the two nations. The just and final decision to be expected from them will also increase the prestige of international arbitration, as a substitute for war—a barbarous remedy which still disgraces the human race. It is for this reason that the eyes of the whole world are fixed upon them.

Undoubtedly the United States of America are prominent among those who trust that the convention negotiated by them with Great Britain for a just, peaceful and honorable settlement of the boundary line between the Venezuelan and British Guiana should prove a success. The services which they have rendered Venezuela ever since 1877, throughout all the various stages of this controversy, have been magnanimous. They have made this question their own by considering the Monroe Doctrine to be affected by it. They conceived the idea, forming the essential basis of the compact, which put an end to the diplomatic discussion of the case. Their chief executive, His Excellency Grover Cleveland, in his letter to His Excellency General Joaquin Crespo, constitutional President of the United States of Venezuela, dated at Washington, the 12th of November, 1896, recommending that the Treaty should be accepted by Venezuela, used the following significant language: "I wish to congratulate myself and congratulate you also on the prospect of a speedy settlement of the controversy between your country and Great Britain. If the proposed Treaty shall deserve the approval of your Government, you will have the satisfaction to look at it in the future as a most happy incident of your wise Administration. I regard as something especially fortunate for me to have been able to contribute in some way to the favorable result thus far obtained."

The United States are continuing still to render Venezuela their generous assistance, by publishing the results of the work entrusted by them to the Commission established in the latter part of 1895, to investigate and report upon the true dividing line between the Republic of Venezuela and the Colony of British Guiana; a Commission composed of men of great learning, untiring industry, and special aptitude for this duty, and which called to its assistance cartographers, historians, polyglots, and other experts, who made for it the most patient and scrupulous examination of ancient documents and geographical charts in both the Dutch and the British archives. That Commission has now given to the public, in printed form, the result of their investigations, and collected no less than seventy-six maps to illustrate the points under debate. Fifteen of these maps are entirely new, and especially prepared for this case, the others being *fac-simile* reproductions of ancient maps. So that the United States, for the benefit of the contending parties, have placed at their disposal all the great elements, in the shape of individual learning—libraries, documents, and maps which they possess—and all the treasures accumulated in their museums and archives. They are as follows:

Among the printed documents of the Commission is a report on the meaning of Articles V and VI of the Treaty of Munster, and another on the territorial rights of the Dutch West India Company, by Prof. George Lincoln Burr; a report on the Spanish and Dutch settlements prior to 1648, by Prof. J. Franklin Jameson; another on the geographers' cartographic testimony, by the Secretary of the Commission; another on the maps of the Orinoco and Essequibo regions, by Prof. Justin Winsor; another on the maps coming from official sources, by Professor Burr; and another on the so-called historical maps. In addition to these papers, the Notes of Prof. Marcus Baker, on the geography of the Orinoco and the Essequibo regions, have been printed, together with a list of part of the maps of those regions, giving, in each case, the name of the author, size of the map, date of its publication, different editions, the boundary, if any, given by it, etc.

The collection of ancient Dutch and other documents gathered by the Commission forms a thick volume, and includes, in addition to the manuscript papers of a miscellaneous character, filed by Venezuela, not less than 353 extracts, in the original Dutch language, with parallel translations into English, page by page, of manuscript documents in the archives of The Hague. All these papers have been selected with great care, and contain very important data.

In addition to the above, various studies of Professor Burr form part of Volume I. Their interest is increased to a great extent by the fact that they contain a digest of the Dutch documents, made upon severe critical examination, and a synopsis of the conclusions to be drawn from them, from the standpoint furnished by the analysis of all the facts and evidence relating to the question. The simple indication of the titles of these studies will suffice to show their importance.

The first relates to "The evidence furnished by the Dutch archives in regard to the European occupation and claims in Western Guiana."

The second is entitled "The Dutch on the Essequibo."

The third, "The Dutch on the Pomarón."

The fourth, "The Dutch on the Moroco."

The fifth, "The Dutch on the Guaima."

The sixth, "The Dutch on the Barima."

The seventh, "The Dutch on and beyond the Amacuro."

The eighth, "The Dutch on the Guyuni."

The ninth, "The Dutch on the Mazaruni."

The tenth, "Dutch claims in Guiana."

And the eleventh, "Spanish occupation and claims in Guiana."

These studies, occupying from page 119 to page 406 of the volume, are illustrated by two plates, one of which represents a certain section of a wall of Fort Kykoveral, as sketched by General Netscher in 1845, and the other showing the site on which, according to a sketch, the same fort stood.

CHAPTER I.

ORIGIN AND CAUSE OF THE QUESTION.

By the treaty concluded at Washington February 2, 1897, between the Republic of the United States of Venezuela and Her Britannic Majesty, it was agreed that the long-standing question of boundary between this Republic and the Colony of British Guiana should be submitted for decision to an Arbitral Tribunal.

Article VI is as follows:

"The printed case of each of the two parties, accompanied by the documents, the official correspondence, and other evidence on which each relies shall be delivered in duplicate to each of the arbitrators and to the agent of the other party as soon as may be after the appointment of the members of the Tribunal, but within a period not exceeding eight months from the date of the exchange of the ratifications of this Treaty."

In compliance with this agreement, an explanation shall be made herein of the origin of the controversy, the course which it has followed, and the rights which Venezuela claims to have in contraposition to those alleged by Great Britain in behalf of her Colony.

As everybody knows, Spain was the European nation which, in the latter part of the fifteenth century, accomplished the wonderful feat of discovering the New World, through her agent, the eminent navigator, Christopher Columbus, who had been provided by her for that purpose with all the necessary authority and given all the assistance which he, in vain, had asked from other powers.

The discovery having been made, some other powers made an effort to take advantage of it and acquire territory on this continent, although the Supreme Pontiff of the Roman Church, in exercise of the sovereignty recognized in him at that time by the Christian world, had vested exclusively the ownership thereof in the Catholic kings. Later on, the same ecclesiastical power drew a line of demarcation between the discoveries and acquisitions of the crowns of Spain and Portugal, which those nations somewhat changed afterwards by the Treaty of Tordesillas, and was confirmed by the Pope, as amended.

The struggle against Spain, in which the Dutch, the British, and the French engaged, gave as a result the establishment by the latter of different settlements in both Americas; but Spain always retained and occupied a larger portion of the northern continent and almost all the southern, with no other exception of importance than Brazil, which fell into the hands of Portugal. All the rest, from north to south, including the adjacent islands, remained in the possession of the Spanish crown.

The Captaincy-General of Caracas or Venezuela (now the Republic of Venezuela), was a province bounded on the sea side by the coast between the Essequibo and Cape Vela, and on the land side by Portugal and by the new Kingdom of Granada, afterwards successively known as New Granada, United States of Colombia (or, as it is now designated, Republic of Colombia). Holland had succeeded in taking possession, on the Atlantic coast, of the mouth of the Essequibo river, and had established there, near the seashore, certain settlements, which she called by the same name as the river. This happened at a time when a state of war existed between Spain and Holland, which finally resulted in Holland's independence of Spain and her establishment as a sovereign nation. By the Treaty of Munster, of January 30, 1648, when Spain recognized her as an independent State, it was stipulated that the new Republic (known as the United Netherlands) should remain in the possession and enjoyment of the sovereign rights, cities, castles, fortresses, commerce and countries in the East and West Indies, and also in Brazil and on the coasts of Asia, Africa and America, which she held and possessed at that date; also the localities and places which the Portuguese had taken from the Dutch and occupied since 1641, and such localities and places as the Republic might thereafter conquer and possess, without violating the Treaty, being included in the agreement.

No determination was made by that Treaty of the limits of the places ceded, nor were they designated by name, or in any other manner. But, in the agreement signed at Aranjuez, on the 23d of June, 1791, the establishments of San Eustaquio, Curaçao, Essequibo, Demerara, Berbice and Surinam, situated opposite to the Spanish possessions of Puerto Rico, Coro and Orinoco, were designated as Dutch colonies.

Later on, under a convention signed in London, on the 13th of August, 1814, the Colonies of Essequibo, Demerara and Berbice became the property of Great Britain. Nothing was said, however, as to the extent of the ceded territory, or the determination of its limits; and the matter therefore remained in the same condition in which it had been up to that time, and in which it has continued to be up to the present.

On the 19th of April, 1810, a movement in favor of independence was started in the Capitancy-General of Venezuela, and the example was promptly followed by the other Spanish Colonies in the New World. A Congress representing the revolted provinces declared them, on the 5th of July, 1811, to be independent from Spain. The war which then ensued between the Colony and the mother country, was waged with varying fortune under the leadership of the Liberator, Simón Bolivar; but in 1820, the cause of the Republic had made such great progress, that a virtual recognition of her independence, by means of two treaties signed on the one side by the patriot leader, and on the other by the Spanish General, who conducted the military operations, had been secured. One of those treaties provided for an armistice between the belligerents, and the other established some rules for the conduct of the war, so as to make it conform to the principles of modern civilization. In the following year the victory of Carabobo crowned the work of the patriots.

A Congress, which had met at Angostura in 1819, had proclaimed the consolidation of the provinces of Venezuela and New Granada into one great commonwealth, to be called the Republic of Colombia, and this decision was solemnly ratified by another Congress, representing the two provinces, which met at Rosario de Cucuta, on the 12th of July, 1821.

Venezuela and New Granada, so united, under the express condition that their Government would be and remain ever after, popular and representative, were recognized as a sovereign nation by the United States of America on the 3d of October, 1824, and by Great Britain on the 18th of April, 1825. At that time the Presidency of Quito (thence called the Republic of Ecuador) had already at its own request, united itself with Colombia.

"Gran Colombia" (as it is known in history) lasted only ten years. The three political entities which had combined to form a common nationality separated from each other in 1830. Venezuela resumed her individual sovereignty, and became a separate and independent Republic.

The same was done, in their turn, by the other two sections of the former Union—one becoming "The Republic of New Granada," the other "The Republic of Ecuador."

On the 20th of October, 1834, Venezuela renewed, word for word, with Great Britain, the Treaty which Colombia had concluded with the latter in 1825.

Spain did not formally acknowledge the independence of Venezuela until the 30th of March, 1845, when a Treaty to that effect was signed at Madrid. The first and second articles of that Treaty are as follows:

"ARTICLE I. Her Catholic Majesty, using the power vested in her by the Decree of the General Cortes of the Kingdom of December 4, 1836, renounces for herself, her heirs and successors, the sovereignty, rights, and claims belonging to her, in and to the American Territory, known by the ancient name of Captaincy-General of Venezuela, now Republic of Venezuela."

"ARTICLE II. In consequence of this renunciation and cession, Her Majesty recognizes as a free, sovereign, and independent nation the Republic of Venezuela, consisting of the provinces and territories set forth in her Constitution and subsequent laws, namely: Margarita, Guayana, Cumana, Barcelona, Caracas, Carabobo, Barquisimeto, Barinas, Apure, Merida, Trujillo, Coro, and Maracaibo, and all the other territories and islands whatsoever which may belong to her."

The ratifications of this Treaty (negotiated and signed on the part of Venezuela by Dr. Alejo Fortique, on the part of Spain by Don Francisco Martinez de la Rosa) were exchanged at Madrid on the 22d of June, 1846.

A Treaty to the same effect had been concluded with the Republic of Ecuador since the 16th of February, 1840.

No Treaty of recognition by Spain was made with New Granada until the 20th of January, 1881, when that Republic had changed its name to that of the United States of Colombia.

Under the cession by Spain, above referred to, Venezuela succeeded the Spanish Crown in all its rights and claims in and to the territory of the Province of Guayana which bordered upon the Dutch Colony—which had become British since 1814.

It was in this way that the question of limits between Spain and Holland was transmitted by inheritance to Venezuela and Great Britain.

During the short existence of Gran Colombia, in whose territory Guayana was included, no negotiation appears to have been initiated for the settlement of the boundary line, although Señor José Rafael Revenga, when sent to London in 1822, as Colombian Diplomatic Agent, received from Dr. Pedro Gual, the Colombian Secretary of Foreign Relations, the following instruction:

"I wish to be permitted to call your attention particularly to the second article of the draft of Treaty, which refers to limits. The English are now in possession of the Dutch Guiana, and are our neighbors on that side. Do as much as you can to fix as exactly as possible the dividing line between the two territories according to the last Treaties between Spain and Holland. The colonists of Demerara and Berbice have usurped a great portion of land on this side of the Essequibo river, which, according to those Treaties, belongs to us. It is absolutely indispensable that said colonists be caused to place themselves under the protection and sway of our laws, or to withdraw to their former possessions, they being given, of course, in the latter case, sufficient time to do so, as set forth in the draft."

The language of this instruction shows, that Colombia had noticed, from the very beginning of her existence as a nation, the encroachment made upon her territory by the colonists of Demerara and Berbice; that she had devised some means of putting an end to that wrong, and suggested that the said colonists should either be compelled to place themselves under the rule of the sovereign of the territory in which they had settled without right, or to withdraw from that territory; and, also, that in the opinion of the Government of Colombia the boundary line was on the Essequibo river.

In the work entitled "Anales Diplomáticos de Colombia," officially published at Bogotá by Don Pedro Ignacio Cadena, in 1870, nothing is said of the result, if any, secured by Señor Revenga in this part of his mission; but as so many other questions, of different nature, principally financial, had presented themselves at that time, and as the compliance with the instructions aforesaid had been left to the diplomatist's discretion, it is to be presumed that he could not find any favorable opportunity to present the subject.

The fact is, that for many years thereafter the question of demarcation of limits between the bordering territories was left untouched.

But in the early part of 1841 it was taken up, with peculiar energy, by the British Government, through her Consul-General at Caracas. That official gave notice to the Government of Venezuela that Sir Robert Herman Schomburgk had been appointed commissioner to survey and determine the limits between Venezuela and British Guiana, and that the Governor of the latter Colony had been authorized to resist any aggression on the territories adjacent to the frontier until now occupied by independent tribes.

The Venezuelan executive considered such a course of action to be novel, since, as it thought, the negotiation of a Treaty should have preceded the survey, and that the survey itself should in all cases be made by commissioners from both countries. When it gave expression to these sentiments and proposed the negotiation of a Treaty, the answer given was that the surveyor appointed was probably at that time in the actual fulfillment of his duties, that the action taken was in conformity with the established practice, and was calculated to facilitate the work of any other commission which might be agreed upon in the future.

It has already been stated in behalf of Venezuela in the argument submitted to the Investigating Commission at Washington (and printed in Vol. IX of the Documents) that, as shown by the British Blue Book* No. 1, from pages 133 to 184, Mr. Schomburgk had, as far back as July 1, 1839, given his opinion to Governor Light, and urgently recommended the necessity of a prompt demarcation of the boundary line, with the concurrence of all the parties in interest; that thereupon the Minister, Lord Palmerston, recommended, on the 18th of March, 1840, the preparation of a map on which the boundary, as suggested by Schomburgk, should be marked or drawn, and the communication of that map, with an explanatory report, to all the bordering countries, namely, Venezuela, Holland, and Brazil, so as to enable them to set forth their objections, if any, and explain the reasons on which their opposition was based. The Blue Book also shows that in the meantime British commissioners were sent to the disputed territory to mark out the frontier claimed by Great Britain; that Schomburgk was chosen to do this, and that he did it without either the map or the report having ever been communicated to Venezuela.

While Schomburgk was going on with his work notwithstanding the objections of Venezuela, the fact became known, in the month of August, that he had encroached upon the territory of the Republic and planted posts and other marks of British ownership at Amacuro, Barima, and other places.

Such an extraordinary proceeding caused a profound impression, both on the public and on the Government of the Republic. The latter did not lose any time in sending to Demerara two special commissioners to ask the Governor of that Colony for an explanation of what had passed. The Venezuelan Minister in London, Señor

Fortique, was instructed to ask for such explanation from the Cabinet of Her Britannic Majesty. The answer received from the latter was that Mr. Schomburgk had planted monuments on certain places in the country which he had surveyed; that, as the Cabinet perfectly knew, the *demarcation thus made was merely preliminary, and open to future discussion between the Governments of Great Britain and Venezuela;* and that no evidence existed of the surveyor having left behind him any military post, custom-house or any other building, over which the British flag should have been hoisted. This was written on the 21st of October, 1841. On the 18th of November following, the Venezuelan Minister assured Lord Aberdeen, on the authority of his Government, that Commissioner Schomburgk, in excess, no doubt, of his orders, had actually planted, at a certain place on the mouth of the Orinoco, several posts with Her Majesty's initials on them, and had also hoisted at the place, with some military display, the British flag.

The Venezuelan Minister complained in that note, not only of the fact that no answer had been given to his proposition to make a Treaty, to be followed by the survey, but also of the survey having been made unilaterally. He said:

"If the mere fact of planting posts in the territory of the Republic is an open violation of the rights of the latter, the undersigned leaves it to the consideration of Her Majesty's Government, to their clear intelligence, and to their feelings of delicacy, to judge of the impression received in Venezuela on learning that the planting of said posts had been accompanied by all the signs of true possession. The dissatisfaction caused by this unmerited offense was indeed great. Suffice it to say that it gave occasion to some charges against the executive power on the ground of its alleged negligence in preserving the dignity as well as the proper rights of the Republic—charges, however, which had no other foundation than the unlimited confidence in the righteousness of Her Majesty's Government, always shown by the executive during the discussion of this affair."

The Venezuelan Plenipotentiary took note also of the threat involved in the notice that power had been granted to the Governor of British Guiana "to resist any aggression on the territories adjacent to the frontier, until now occupied by free Indian tribes," and asked for an explanation of that language; because his Government had not been able to persuade itself that Her Majesty's Government was desirous either to assume a protectorate over Indians who lived outside of the British frontier and inhabited Venezuelan territory, or to pretend to recognize in those savage tribes the character which, under the law of nations, belongs only to countries politically organized and constituted as nations, or to attempt to deprive Venezuela of the rights which, in America, have always been recognized as belonging to discoverers.

Before receiving any answer from Lord Aberdeen, the Venezuelan Minister, acting in obedience to new instructions sent him, insisted upon negotiating at once a Treaty of limits, and more particularly upon the removal of the boundary posts which Schomburgk had placed, contrary to all law, at Barima and other places on Venezuelan territory; a fact which had produced among the people of Venezuela a feeling of great dissatisfaction which, far from decreasing, was growing more and more intense, as was natural, since time passed without redress being made.

In the same communication the Venezuelan Minister complained of the course, which he found contradictory, pursued by the Governor of British Guiana while dealing with the Venezuelan Commissioners. The Governor had said to them that he could not change the demarcation made by Schomburgk, but, at the same time, he had acknowledged that the true limits between the two Guianas were then undefined and in dispute. According to him, what had been done by the surveyor was not, nor could it be, done with the desire of taking possession of anything, but merely to locate the line *claimed* as true by British Guiana; and that, therefore, as long as the boundary line should remain undetermined, the Government of Venezuela could trust that no fort would be built on the territory in question, nor would any military or other force be sent there. He further stated that, although the Governor and Mr. Schomburgk had said, for the purpose of justifying their action, that the boundary posts had no more value than mere lines drawn with ink upon the map might have, the determination of the former not to remove them excited a suspicion not at all calculated to calm the dissatisfaction of the nation, or to inspire the Government with that confidence which was necessary to enter into an arrangement about limits.

He represented finally that everybody was able to distinguish between the action, generally timid and hesitating, of subaltern authorities and the pure and righteous intentions of the Government of Her Majesty, and that no one feared that the latter, for the sake of backing or supporting Commissioner Schomburgk, would approve, in regard to Venezuela, what it had refused to approve in regard to the United States of North America.

Upon these and other cogent reasons Señor Fortique based his insistance on the speedy removal of boundary marks of all kinds placed by Commissioner Schomburgk, and on the immediate negotiation of a final arrangement about limits between the Venezuelan and the British Guianas.

On the 11th of December, Lord Aberdeen repeated that the *boundary marks placed by Mr. Schomburgk at some places of the country which he has explored were merely a preliminary step, subject to future discussion between the two Governments*, and that a treaty of limits would be premature before the exploration of the land would be completed. The British Minister ended his reply with the following words:

"The undersigned has only further to state that much unnecessary inconvenience would result from the removal of the posts fixed by Mr. Schomburgk, as they will afford the only tangible means by which Her Majesty's Government can be prepared to discuss the question of the boundaries with the Government of Venezuela. Those posts were erected for that express purpose, and not as the Venezuelan Government appears to apprehend, as indication of dominion and empire on the part of Great Britain. And the undersigned is glad to learn from Señor Fortique's note of the 8th instant that the two Venezuelan gentlemen who have been sent by their Government to British Guiana have had the means of ascertaining from the Governor of that Colony that the British authorities have not occupied Punta Barima."

By note of the 10th of January, 1842, Señor Fortique replied, asking again for the removal of the posts, earnestly representing the uneasiness which the operations of Mr. Schomburgk produced in Venezuela, the apprehension that the safety of British subjects residing in this Republic would be thereby impaired, the excitement which such a state of things would create in the Venezuelan Congress, which was about to meet, the increase of the smuggling already carried on from the Island of Trinidad, and the fatal consequences which the anticipation of a disagreement between the two nations was apt to produce. As to the advantages alleged by Lord Aberdeen of preserving the posts, Señor Fortique remarked that the line such as drawn by Mr. Schomburgk was not the one believed by the Government of Her Majesty to be the boundary of British Guiana; but a different line which Commissioner Schomburgk had thought it advisable to describe, as the map which he had been entrusted to draw upon actual survey of the ground had not even been received in London. He said further, that, in his opinion, in such a state of uncertainty the initial operation should properly be the demarcation of points; that the fact of one of the parties beginning by itself, without the concurrence of the other, to mark the ground which it believed to be its property was not in any manner calculated to inspire such confidence as was necessary to all negotiations; that when the points to be touched by the boundary line are already agreed upon, and when, as had been the case with the United States of America, there being a pre-existing Treaty of limits in force, then the commissioners whom both parties might appoint could very well proceed to actually locate the line, and should they disagree each one could then fix the marks as he understood them until a settlement should be reached, said settlement to depend only upon the proper understanding or construction of the compact; that Venezuela was ready to enter into an agreement of that kind, and had fully authorized him to negotiate for that purpose; and that if, as was to be hoped, a real disposition in the Government of Her Majesty to enter into a friendly arrangement, the removal of the posts were not only useful, but absolutely necessary.

On the 31st of January of the same year Lord Aberdeen replied to the Venezuelan Minister, after acknowledging the receipt of his communication, in the following language:

"The undersigned begs to inform Señor Fortique, in reply, that in order to meet *the wishes of the Government of Venezuela, Her Majesty's Government will send instructions to the Governor of British Guiana, directing him to remove the posts which have been placed by Mr. Schomburgk near the Orinoco.*

"But the undersigned feels it his duty distinctly to declare to Señor Fortique, that, although, in order to put an end to the misapprehension which appears to prevail in Venezuela in regard to the object of Mr. Schomburgk's survey, the undersigned has consented to comply with the renewed representations of Señor Fortique, upon this affair, Her Majesty's Government must not be understood to abandon any right of Great Britain over the territory which was formerly held by the Dutch in Guiana."

Mr. Henry Light, Governor of British Guiana, wrote, on the 9th of March, 1842, to Mr. D. F. O'Leary, British Consul-General at Caracas, informing him for the satisfaction of the Government of Venezuela, that he had received instruction from the Right Honorable the Secretary of State for the Colonies, to remove the marks placed upon the ground by Mr. Schomburgk, on the Barima and elsewhere, in his survey of the assumed limits of British Guiana, and that he trusted that this step would be received by Venezuela as a token of the friendly intentions of the Government of Her Majesty.

A copy of this communication was enclosed by Mr. O'Leary in a note addressed by him on the 8th of April following to Señor Aranda, Minister of Foreign Relations of Venezuela, informing him of the order from the Secretary of the Colonies directing the removal of the posts.

So the incident ended for the time being; and it should not be forgotten, because during the discussion thereof it was clearly shown that the British Government did *not* claim any indisputable rights to Barima, and much less to Amacuro; that the work entrusted to Mr. Schomburgk was merely an attempt to make *ex parte* a temporary survey, subject to future discussion between the interested Governments; that Schomburgk had not occupied Punta Barima, as positively stated by Governor

Light to Señor Rodriguez and Señor Romero, Commissioners of Venezuela, and as repeated by Lord Aberdeen to Señor Fortique in his note of the 11th of December, 1841; and that the British Government did not believe it had other rights in or to the territory of Guiana than those which were conveyed by the Dutch, nor did that Government claim to have any right or claim in virtue of any arrangements made with the Indians.

This matter, then, having been set at rest, Señor Fortique insisted with vigor on entering at once into the negotiation of a Treaty of limits which Venezuela ardently desired because of her belief that it was the best way to prevent such unpleasant events as those before described. He at last succeeded in formally initiating the negotiation by means of a long note dated on the 31st of January, 1844, in which he explained the rights of the Republic. That note ended with the following words:

"But in drawing this line the future must not be lost sight of, and such points must be selected as will allow such a division to be made as will obviate all causes of future misunderstanding. There is no doubt that the Essequibo seems to be a river purposely made by nature to fulfill this object, and as the British colonists at present occupy nothing or almost nothing of the land between this river and the Orinoco, their plantations being on the other side, a settlement of this question upon this basis would suit the purpose, and would insure to Great Britain even the most extreme rights which she may claim as the successor to Holland."

On the 30th of March following, Lord Aberdeen gave his answer to this, and after making an effort to refute the arguments of Señor Fortique, went on to declare what he called the "concessions" which Great Britain was ready to make through her friendly consideration for Venezuela and her desire to remove all ground of serious differences between the two countries.

"Being convinced," he said, "that the most important object for the interests of Venezuela is the exclusive possession of Orinoco, Her Majesty's Government is ready to yield to the Republic of Venezuela a portion of the coast sufficient to insure her the free control of the mouth of this, her principal river, and prevent its being under the control of any foreign power. With this end in view, and being persuaded that a concession of the greatest importance has been made to Venezuela, Her Majesty's Government is disposed to lay aside its rights on the Amacuro as the western limit of the British territory, and to consider the mouth of the Guaima river as the boundary of Her Majesty's possession on the coast side. Her Majesty's Government will consent that the boundary in the interior be fixed by a line from the mouth of the Moroco to the point where the rivers Barama and Guaima meet; continuing from this point, the line follows up the Barama as far as the Aunama, whose upward course will be followed until this stream approaches the point nearest the Acarabisi; then following the downward course of the Acarabisi as far as its confluence with the Cuyuni, it will pursue the upward course of the latter as far as the high lands contiguous to the Roraima mountain, where its waters are divided between the Essequibo and the River Branco.

"Great Britain is, then, disposed to cede to Venezuela all the territory lying between the above-mentioned line and the Amacuro river, and the chain of mountains where it has its head, upon condition that the Government of Venezuela shall engage itself not to alienate any portion of said territory to any foreign power, and also upon condition that the tribes of Indians, now living in said territory, shall be protected against all ill treatment and oppression."

When this proposal was received by Señor Fortique, he transmitted it through the Department of Foreign Relations to the President of the Republic, who thought that, as it involved a matter of such great importance, the opinion of the Council of Government ought to be heard about it. The Council of Government gave the subject the proper consideration, and reported that, without admitting that the true line did not start *de jure* from the Essequibo, but, on the contrary, strongly refuting the ideas maintained to that effect by Lord Aberdeen, it felt inclined to accept, as a compromise, the Moroco frontier; not following, however, the line suggested by Lord Aberdeen, because that line encroached too much, without reason, upon the national territory. The Council then suggested another line, which should run from the initial point above named to the Imataca, and thence follow directly along the meridian of that place as far as the Cuyuni, then crossing this river and continuing farther on until reaching the Pacaraima mountains. It was also of the opinion that a stipulation should be made in regard to the Indians, binding both parties not to take any steps calculated to cause the tribes of one territory to migrate to the other. As to the condition binding Venezuela not to alienate the territory, the Council thought it derogatory of the national sovereignty, as such a condition could only have been acceptable in case of a true cession of territory made by Great Britain, as a matter of favor to Venezuela, without the latter understanding, as she does, that the territory is hers by right.

Matters remained in this condition for a long time, until through special circumstances the question was taken up again by the Council, and its former opinion somewhat modified. The Council now agreed to the non-alienation clause, provided it should be made reciprocal, indicating, however, that it would not withhold its assent to that clause, even if it were written in such a way as to allow Great Britain to dispose in any way whatever and for whatever reason, of the whole territory of her Colony in favor of a foreign power. The

Executive, after endorsing the opinion of the Council, sent to London the necessary instructions to carry its suggestions into effect.

But the Venezuelan Minister, Señor Fortique, was at that time in Sweden, where he had gone on a special mission of the Government; and when he came back he fell sick, and died on the 28th of October, 1845. The instruction given him could not thus be complied with, and the course of the negotiation was again stopped.

It is well to note here, before proceeding farther, that Lord Aberdeen hastened to recognize the importance of the Orinoco to the Republic, and to suggest a line which left to Venezuela the exclusive control of its mouth.

Such was the status of the case when, on the 18th of November, 1850, Mr. Belford Hinton Wilson, Chargé d'Affaires of Great Britain at Caracas, wrote to Señor Vincente Lecuna, Minister of Foreign Relations, recapitulating the steps he had taken to contradict the rumors mischievously spread in Venezuela, namely, that Great Britain intended to claim the province of Venezuelan Guiana—stating that he had communicated to his Government extracts of letters which the British vice-consul had addressed to him from Ciudad Bolivar, saying that orders had been communicated to the authorities of the Province of Guiana to place it in a state of defense, and to repair and arm the dismantled and abandoned forts, and that the Governor of that province, Señor José Tomás Machado, had spoken of raising a fort at Punta Barima, the right of possession to which, Señor Wilson said, "is in dispute between Great Britain and Venezuela;" announcing, further, that he had reported to his Government the introduction in the Venezuelan House of Representatives of a bill authorizing the Executive to construct at once a fort on a point to serve as boundary between Venezuela and British Guiana, without, however, naming this point, thus authorizing the executive to commit, *de facto*, an aggression and usurpation of the territory in dispute between the two countries, by the construction of a fort on any point which Venezuela may claim, although Great Britain may also claim their lawful possession of that point—and informing the Venezuelan Government that Viscount Palmerston had addressed the Lords Commissioners of the Admiralty, notifying them of the Queen's injunctions in regard to the orders to be given to the vice-admiral commanding Her Majesty's naval forces in the West Indies as to the course he should pursue if the Venezuelan authorities should construct fortifications in the territory in dispute between Great Britain and Venezuela.

Mr. Wilson announced, also, that he had been instructed to call the serious attention of the President of Venezuela to this question, and to declare that, while, on the one hand, Her Majesty's Government had no intention to occupy or encroach upon the territory in dispute, they would not, on the other hand, view with indifference any aggressions by Venezuela upon that territory. He had been instructed, furthermore, to say that under these circumstances Her Majesty's Government expected that positive instructions would be sent to the Venezuelan authorities in Guiana to refrain from taking measures which the British authorities might justly regard as aggressive; for such measures, if taken, would perforce lead to a collision, which Her Majesty's Government would deeply regret, but for the consequences of which, whatever they might be, Her Majesty's Government would hold that of Venezuela entirely responsible.

"The Venezuelan Government," Mr. Wilson said, "in justice to Great Britain, can not mistrust for a moment the sincerity of the formal declaration which is now made, in the name and by the express order of Her Majesty's Government, that Great Britain has no intention to occupy or encroach upon the territory in dispute; therefore the Venezuelan Government, in an equal spirit of good faith and friendship, can not refuse to make a similar declaration to Her Majesty's Government, namely, that Venezuela herself has no intention to occupy or encroach upon the territory in dispute."

"The systematic persistence with which, since 1843, the propaganda has fabricated and circulated false rumors in regard to the conduct and policy of Her Majesty's Government in what concerns the Venezuelan Guiana, among other mischievous effects, has produced that of serving the ends of that propaganda and keeping alive an insane spirit of distrust and puerile credulity as to all the frivolous rumors respecting this boundary question, thus exposing the amicable relations between Great Britain and Venezuela to be at any moment interrupted by a collision between both countries, arising out of any sudden and, perhaps, authorized aggression on the part of the local authorities of Venezuela, whether committed by constructing forts, or by occupying and encroaching upon the territory in dispute."

"Her Majesty's Government, as above stated, will not order or sanction such occupations or encroachments on the part of the British authorities; and if, at any time, there should be any error about their determination in this respect, the undersigned is persuaded that they would willingly renew their orders on the subject. He is then satisfied that, in accordance with the friendly suggestions of Her Majesty's Government, the Government of Venezuela will not hesitate to send to the Venezuelan authorities positive orders to refrain from taking measures which the British authorities may justly consider as aggressions."

The language of this note from the British legation at Caracas clearly shows that Her Majesty's Government took the initiative in the work of contradicting the rumors which had been set afloat, attributing to Great Britain an intention to take possession of Venezuelan Guiana under this or the other pretext; that in order to prevent Venezuela from exercising acts of jurisdiction in places believed by her to belong to her national domain, Her Majesty's Government had resorted to the means of threatening Venezuela with the naval forces of Her Majesty stationed in the West Indies; that Her Majesty's Government said, and reiterated over and over again, that Great Britain had "no intention" to occupy or encroach upon the territory in dispute, and that no steps in that direction or on the part of the British authorities would be taken or sanctioned, the order to that effect, if an error should happen to have been committed, to be willingly renewed; that Her Majesty's Government desired that friendly relations between the two countries should not be interrupted by the construction of forts, or by the occupation of or encroachment upon, any part of the territory in dispute; and that in return for this declaration a similar one should be made by Venezuela, namely, that Venezuela had "no intention" to occupy or encroach upon the territory in dispute, and that orders should be sent to the authorities of Guayana not to take any measure which might justly be considered by the British authorities as aggressive. The Minister of Foreign Relations, Señor Vicente Lacuna, under date of September 20, 1850, replied as follows:

"The undersigned has been instructed by His Excellency the President of the Republic, to give the following answer:

"The Government could never be persuaded that Great Britain, in contempt of the negotiation opened on the subject, and of the alleged rights in the question of limits pending between the two countries, would desire to use force in order to occupy the land which each party claims; much less after Mr. Wilson's repeated assurance, which the Executive believes to have been most sincere, that these imputations had no foundation whatever, they being, on the contrary, quite the reverse of the truth. Fully confident of this, and fortified by the declaration contained in the note herein referred to, the Government has no difficulty in declaring, as it hereby does, that

Venezuela has no intention to occupy or encroach upon any part of the territory the possession of which is the matter of this controversy; neither will she look with indifference upon a contrary proceeding on the part of Great Britain. The Venezuelan Government will, furthermore, send instructions to the authorities in Guayana to refrain from taking any step conflicting with the obligation herein contracted by the Government, and giving rise possibly to fatal consequences, all in the same manner, as Mr. Wilson says, have been done, and will be willingly repeated, if necessary, by the British Government, with the authorities in British Guiana. In conclusion, the undersigned may add that the Venezuelan Government fully appreciates the motives which have led Mr. Wilson to abstain from at once carrying out the instructions which he has received on the subject."

The foregoing correspondence shows that the English Government has given to that of Venezuela, over and over again, spontaneously, the solemn assurance that Great Britain did not intend to occupy or encroach upon any part of the territory in dispute; that such an occupation or encroachment by the British authorities would not be ordered or sanctioned, and that orders to that effect would be willingly repeated, should any error about the Government's determination in this respect be found; that upon these grounds a declaration similar to the one made in the name and by express orders of Her Majesty's Government, namely, that Great Britain had "no intention" to occupy or encroach upon the territory in dispute, was asked and obtained from Venezuela, after invoking her spirit of faith and friendship, as well as her sentiments of justice; that Venezuela, relying upon these repeated assurances, assented to all that was asked of her, and instructed her authorities in Guayana to refrain from taking measures which the British authorities might consider aggressive; and that the Department of Foreign Relations expressed to the British Foreign Office the full confidence of Venezuela in the fulfillment by Great Britain of her promise; namely, that force should not be employed to take possession of the territory in dispute, in regard to which negotiations were pending.

Out of all this the fact comes out prominently, that n the territory of Guayana there were certain portions not occupied by either party to the contention; and that, as explicitly said by Mr. Wilson, Punta Barima was a place the right to which was a matter of dispute between Great Britain and Venezuela.

It will be seen further on, that in spite of such declarations, and what is more, in spite of the agreement entered into by means of the interchange of notes between Venezuela and Great Britain, the latter did, in 1884, occupy, and has continued to occupy up to the present time, several places within the territory in dispute; among them, Punta Barima itself, and that she has moreover advanced her posts westwardly as far as the right bank of the Amacuro, an affluent of the Orinoco, and also on the side of the Cuyuni as far as the confluence of the latter river with the Yuruán.

In 1856, the matter was again discussed, although indirectly, owing to the discovery of the Carratal gold mines, and to the attempt by colonists of Demerara to reach them from their own side of their territory. The Executive had objected to this, on the ground that the laws of Venezuela do not allow foreigners to enter the Venezuelan territory, except through such ports as are granted this privilege; and that, furthermore, the building of a road, as attempted, constituted an act of jurisdiction which could not be exercised by any one, except the sovereign, within the territory belonging to the latter.

The Venezuelan Government, nevertheless, took steps to facilitate the access of foreigners to these mines, and permitted them to be started from Puerto de Las Tablas, thereby relieving them from the necessity of going as far up as Ciudad Bolivar.

The next step taken on the part of the Republic in this negotiation was the sending, directly to the British court, of a note written by Doctor Eduardo Calcaño, then Venezuelan Minister of Foreign Relations, dated November 14, 1876, in which the speedy settlement of the question of limits was earnestly urged, "so as to avoid the risk of any dangerous contingency which might disturb, in the future, the peace and sincere friendship, which up to this time have been happily preserved between the two nations."

Reference was made therein to the past record of the case, and new arguments presented tending to strengthen the claim of Venezuela to the line of the Essequibo, pursuant to the proposition which Dr. Alejo Fortique, as Minister, had submitted, January 31, 1844. No answer was given to this, except that the British Cabinet would take the subject into consideration, when Señor Rojas, who had then been appointed Minister at London, and received as such, would make representations in regard to it, or when the attention of the Cabinet should be called to it through the British legation at Caracas.

Some communications having been exchanged between the Plenipotentiary and the St. James Cabinet, the suggestion was made by the former of a new line, "starting from a point on the coast one mile to the north of the mouth of the Moroco, where a post or land-mark, should be placed, in order to indicate the true limit between the two countries, on the seashore. From this point a line should be drawn westward along the parallel marking the latitude of the land-mark until reaching the place where that parallel crosses the meridian of longitude 60° west of Greenwich. From this point the dividing line should go southward, following the direction of the same meridian, until reaching the southern terminus of both countries. This proposed demarcation of limits had the advantage of being precise and unchangeable, it being also the most which Venezuela could do in the way of concessions in order to secure a friendly compromise."

In submitting this proposition, Dr. Rojas made reference to the former one made in 1844, by Lord Aberdeen, which, as he had already said to Lord Salisbury, explaining the reasons therefor, had not been accepted by Venezuela.

It is to be observed that although Dr. Rojas had shown his desire, since his arrival in London, of entering at once into the negotiation, nothing was done at that time, because of the wish of the British Government to await the arrival of the Attorney-General, and of the Governor of British Guiana.

Lord Granville, Minister of Foreign Relations, declined, September 15, 1881, the proposition of Dr. Rojas; the reasons which determined this action having been explained in the note of Lord Salisbury to Sir Julian Pauncefote, dated November 26, 1895, with the contents of which the latter was instructed to acquaint the Secretary of State of the United States. The passage of that note bearing on this point is as follows:

> "Señor Rojas' proposal was referred to the Lieutenant-Governor and Attorney-General of British Guiana, who were then in England, and they presented an elaborate report showing that in the thirty-five years which had elapsed since Lord Aberdeen's proposed concession, natives and others had settled in the territory, under the belief that they would enjoy the benefits of British rule, and that it was impossible to assent to any such concessions as Señor Rojas' line would involve. They, however, proposed an alternate line, which involved considerable reductions of that laid down by Sir R. Schomburgk. This boundary was proposed to the Venezuelan Government by Lord Granville in September, 1881, but no answer was ever returned by that Government to the proposal."

The "proposal" here alluded to was this:

"The initial point to be fixed at a spot on the seashore twenty-nine miles of longitude due east from the right bank of the River Barima, and to be carried thence south over the mountain or hill called on Schomburgk's original map the Yarikita Hill, to the eighth parallel of north latitude; thence west along the same parallel of latitude until it cuts the boundary line proposed by Schomburgk and laid down on the map before mentioned; thence to follow such boundary along its course to the Acarabisi, following the Acarabisi to its junction with the Cuyuni; thence along the left bank of the River Cuyuni to its source, and thence in a southeasterly direction to the line as proposed by Schomburgk to the Essequibo and Corentyne."

In 1883, Mr. Mansfield, Minister Resident of Her Britannic Majesty at Caracas, pressed upon the attention of the Government of Venezuela, by order of his Government, the three questions which were then pending between the two countries, namely: that of limits between Venezuela and British Guiana; that of differential duties on the imports from the British Colonies; and that of claims of British creditors of the Republic. Mr. Mansfield said that these three questions should be dealt with as a whole, and that great importance was attached to their simultaneous settlement.

As a preliminary to negotiations, Lord Granville considered it indispensable that an answer should be given to the proposals of Her Majesty's Government in regard to the boundary; should that answer be in the affirmative, and should the other questions be satisfactorily settled, the wishes of the Venezuelan Government in regard to the cession of the Island of Patos would receive favorable consideration.

On the 15th of November of the same year the Department of Foreign Relations of Venezuela manifested a strong desire to have the three points at issue, thus combined with each other, amicably terminated; but taking up, above all, the question of boundary, gave the answer which Lord Salisbury in the passage of his note, above quoted, charges Venezuela with having failed to give.

This answer was as follows:

"For one year the President has been consulting the opinion of jurists and public men of high standing, in order to be enlightened as to the proper solution of the question of the Guiana boundary by means of a Treaty. But as all the men of reputation who have been consulted have confirmed more and more the belief that the limit *de jure* inherited by the Republic, between her and the old Dutch Colony (now British Guiana), is the Essequibo River, the impossibility has become self-evident of settling this affair by other means than the decision of an arbitrator, who, being chosen voluntarily by unanimous consent of both Governments, should adjudge and finally decide the matter.

"This is the obstacle which His Excellency the President has found in meeting the wishes of Lord Granville (as he would otherwise like to do), of putting an end, by means of a treaty, to all causes of dispute between the two governments.

"A judicial decision of the point under controversy would put at rest, finally and happily, the question of limits; and so I am directed by His Excellency to recommend, through the worthy channel of Your Excellency, to Lord Granville's attention, the urgency of appointing, by common consent, an arbitrator, so as to secure between now and next February the satisfaction of the friendly purposes of the two Governments, as it certainly can be done, if the Government of Her Majesty shall be pleased to instruct its legation at Caracas to agree, without delay, with the Venezuelan Government in selecting such an arbitrator."

The words just quoted were plainly equivalent to a rejection of Lord Granville's proposition, in substitution whereof a new one was made. Lord Granville's tended to a direct agreement between the two governments. Señor Seijas suggested the submission of the question to arbitral decision.

The British Government, as stated by Mr. Mansfield, in his note to the Secretary of Foreign Relations of Venezuela, dated March 29, 1884, was not willing to refer the question to arbitration, but expressed at the same time the hope that some other means might be devised for bringing this long-standing matter to an issue satisfactory to both powers.

On the 2d of April following, the Venezuelan Department of Foreign Relations, after entering into different considerations in favor of a settlement by arbitration, requested the British Government to kindly suggest, without losing sight of the Venezuelan constitutional aspect of the case, such other acceptable manner of settling this difficulty as might respond to the earnest wishes of the Republic in regard to this point.

No agreement was ever reached, as the British Government tenaciously adhered to the opinion that arbitration was not a proper or desirable method for settling this question.

The proposal that the Arbitral decision should be made by a friendly nation having been rejected, the Venezuelan Legation at London made another one in December, 1884, namely, to create a Tribunal or commission of jurists, appointed by both parties, whose decision should be final.

Lord Granville replied, on the 13th of February, 1885, that the proposal presented constitutional difficulties which prevented Her Majesty's Government from acceding to it, and that they were not prepared to depart from the arrangement proposed by the Venezuelan Government in 1877, and accepted by Her Majesty's Government, to decide the question by adopting a conventional boundary to be fixed by mutual consent of the two Governments.

In the negotiation of a new treaty of commerce, undertaken in London in 1885, between Venezuela and Great Britain, the Venezuelan negotiator and Lord Granville had agreed to embody in that instrument an article providing in general that "all differences" whatsoever between the two nations which could not be adjusted by direct friendly negotiation should be submitted to arbitration, and referred for settlement to one or to more than one power friendly to the two parties, and that war should never be resorted to between them.

When this Treaty was about to be signed a change in the British Cabinet took place, and Lord Granville, Minister of Foreign Affairs, was replaced by Lord Salisbury.

The new functionary informed the representative of Venezuela that Her Majesty's Government were unable to concur in the assent given by their predecessors in office to the general arbitration clause proposed by Venezuela, or to agree to the inclusion of matters other than those arising out of the interpretation or alleged violation of this particular Treaty. To engage to refer to arbitration, he said, all disputes and controversies whatsoever would be without precedent in the Treaties made by Great Britain. Questions might arise, he said, involving the title of the British Crown to territory or other sovereign right which her Majesty's Government could not pledge themselves beforehand to refer to arbitration.

The Venezuelan Legation refuted (on the 5th of August and the 17th of December, 1885) the arguments on which Lord Salisbury had based his withdrawal of the consent by his predecessor to the general arbitration article of the Treaty, and declined to recognize his authority to abrogate that consent by his sole action, much more so after his own declaration in the House of Lords (speaking of another and similar case), that he would respect the engagements which might have been entered into by the preceding administration. His attention was called particularly to the fact that questions of limits are precisely the questions most naturally called to be settled by the decision of an impartial third party; and that such an opinion had been entertained by Great Britain herself in 1829 and 1871, when she agreed to refer two territorial controversies, one to the decision of the King of the Netherlands, and another to the decision of the Emperor of Germany; the particular fact being noticeable that in the latter case, according to the argument of the United States, the proposal to submit to arbitration the question whether the boundary between them and the British Dominion was or was not to pass along the Haro Canal, was made six times in succession by the Government of Her Majesty, and was not accepted by the United States until it was made a seventh time. Reference was made also to the fact that a proposition of the same character to put an end to the Guiana dispute had been made orally to Señor Fortique.

The precedent established by Lord Salisbury himself, in an analogous case concerning the Afghanistan boundary, was also invoked. The Cabinet presided over by him had approved what the preceding one had done, although the individual opinion of the Minister in charge of the matter was adverse to the demarcation agreed upon with the Russian Empire.

All these arguments having proved useless, the negotiation was interrupted.

But in the middle of 1886, the Cabinet presided over by Mr. Gladstone, with which the arrangement had been initiated and almost terminated, came back into power. The opportunity, therefore, seemed favorable to consummate what had been promised in its time and in its name by Lord Granville. In the new administration, however, Lord Granville did not hold the same position he had before, his Department being now that of the Colonies. Lord Rosebery had succeeded him in the Department of Foreign Affairs, and he it was who answered the Venezuelan Legation, by submitting the following proposal:

"It is proposed that the two Governments shall agree upon considering as territory disputed between the two countries the line situated between the two boundary lines indicated respectively in the eighteenth paragraph of Señor Rojas' note of February 21, 1881, and Lord

Granville's note of September 15, 1881, and to draw a dividing line within the limits of this territory, either by arbitration or by a mixed commission, on the principle of equal division of said territory and in due regard to natural boundaries. The Government of Her Majesty gives special importance to the possession of the River Guaima by British Guiana, and wishes, therefore, to make the stipulation that the boundary line is to begin at the coast point, and a proper compensation to be found in any other part of the disputed territory, for this deviation of the principle of equal division. In connection with the boundary there shall be considered the cession of the Island of *Patos* to Venezuela.

" The River Orinoco shall be entirely free to commerce navigation.

"In case of a satisfactory arrangement of the other pending questions, the Government of Her Majesty will be disposed to accept the 'most favored nation' clause proposed by Venezuela, instead of the absolute clause which, until now, this Government had insisted upon.

" It will likewise be convenient to add in the Treaty the clause 'by arbitration' proposed by Venezuela, limited to those differences that may arise after the Treaty is signed, with exclusion of the questions of the boundary and the Island of *Patos*, which the Government of Her Majesty is ready to consider separately in the manner before indicated."

So it was that the Cabinet of Mr. Gladstone did not adhere to the agreement which the negotiators had reached in 1885 as to the arbitration article, although suggesting an arrangement which admitted that method, or the similar one of a mixed commission, to be resorted to, upon the basis of an equal division of the disputed territory.

The Venezuelan representative hastened to declare that the plan devised by Lord Roseberry was unacceptable, this declaration being based on the ground that the question of limits for the settlement of which no other or better means had been found than arbitration, had been nevertheless left out or excluded from the plan of the latter. Furthermore, the restriction of this means of adjustment to only a part of the contention, as suggested by the British Cabinet, was in opposition to a provision of the Venezuelan Constitution, which required the adoption of that method absolutely, as had been agreed upon with Italy, Spain, Belgium, Colombia, etc.

The efforts which had been made to secure in London the adjustment of the outstanding questions between Venezuela and Great Britain thus proved to be a failure.

In July 28, 1886, the Venezuelan Legation at London addressed a final note to the Cabinet of Her Britannic Majesty, setting forth the complaints and claims of the Government of Venezuela for repeated acts of violation of the National Territory by Colonial authorities—complaints and claims which had not been presented before because of the confidence which had been entertained that, upon proper consideration of each case, such redress for the offenses committed as was just and proper would be granted. The wrongs referred to consisted in violations of the agreement of 1850 (proposed by England herself), not to occupy any part of the territory then in dispute, which Venezuela had respected faithfully.

In October, 1884, some English functionaries asked that they might be furnished with pilots to go up the Orinoco river: and although none was furnished, because those functionaries were not bound in their trip for any Venezuelan port of entry, they, however, continued their voyage, penetrating into places which always had been considered as belonging to Venezuela, placing posts or land-marks, affixing notices, by which it was announced that the British laws were in force there; removing the employés of the Republic and appointing in their stead others of their own choice; attempting to enlist the services of Venezuelan officials, and threatening to come back later on with a larger number of men, as they did, to enforce their demands. They arrested and carried away an officer of the Republic, Señor Roberto Wells, commissioner for Amacuro, whom they wanted to try and punish for some alleged ill-treatment in that place of a Portuguese subject. All of this was ascertained on investigation entrusted to General Federico Puga, and conducted by him on the spot. In answer to a communication written by him at Morajuana to Mr. Michael McTurk (who called himself "Special Magistrate *pro tem.* and Superintendent of the Crown Lands and Forests in the District of the River Pomaroon"), the latter said, on April 4, 1885, that he had been on Rivers Amacuro, Barima, Morajuana, and Guaima, and placed notices in English at the principal points thereon, as he had been ordered to do by his Excellency the Governor of British Guiana. He added that he had been several times on the aforesaid rivers after the placing of the notices, and that he had done so in the discharge of his duties as magistrate in charge of the district of which they form a part, and that he had not needed a pilot for the Amacuro, nor had he asked for the services of one for the Orinoco.

It was pointed out that such action was in violation of the declaration made in 1850, in the name and by express order of Her Majesty's Government, namely, that "Great Britain has no inteition to occupy or encroach upon the territory in dispute," and also of the orders repeatedly transmitted to the Governor of British Guiana, not to permit such occupation or encroachment, because of the promise made by the Government of Her Majesty not to order or sanction such action on the part of the British authorities, and to willingly renew such orders, whenever any error about its determination in this respect should be committed.

The point was duly insisted upon that if the agreement

aforesaid applied to such portions of the territory as were then in dispute, much more did it apply to other places not hitherto in dispute, but had always remained in the quiet and peaceful possession of Venezuela, their lawful owner.

Attention was also called to the fact that Mr. McTurk exposed himself to the risk if force were resorted to for preventing the consummation of an act so much in derogation of the rights of the Republic; whose laws did not permit any one to enter the Venezuelan territory except through such ports as were properly authorized for that purpose, or foreign ships of war to enter ports not open to foreign commerce, except for scientific purposes, and upon previous permission from the Executive.

The fact was brought out forcibly of the insult offered to the majesty of the Republic by arresting, through artful means, its Commissioner duly appointed, who, even if guilty of any offense, was amenable only before the Venezuelan courts and the judges of competent jurisdiction of his own country, and not before tribunals of a foreign country, to which he was not a subject—it being understood in all cases that the Government making the appointment should assume, and assumed, all the consequences of his acts. It was urged, on the other hand, that even in the case of offences committed by private individuals having no official character whatsoever, the power to try and punish said individuals belongs exclusively to the sovereign of the territory where the acts were committed, and not to the British Judiciary of Demerara, which had tried and punished Señor Wells.

As to the functionary who had entered the Orinoco on board a British man-of-war and ascended that river, it was known that he, when reaching the light-ship, had asked for a pilot to continue his voyage, and that, when his request was denied, he went on without any pilot as far as Amacuro, proceeding the next day to Guaima by the channel Barima, and leaving at all the places he touched the following notification:

"[SEAL.] GOVERNMENT NOTICE.

"Notice is hereby given that any persons infringing the right of Her Majesty, or acting in contravention of the laws of British Guiana, will be prosecuted according to law. By command

"FRANCIS VILLIERS,
"Acting Government Secretary.

"Georgetown, Demerara, October 16, 1884."

After the date of this notice the invasions of the Venezuelan territory, having for their object the violent removal of the authorities constituted by the Governor of the Delta territory at the mouths of the Amacuro and the Morajuana, began to take place, and the proposition was then made by the British to Señor Roberto Lizo, the Venezuelan Commissioner, at the place first named, that he be vested with authority, paid a fixed salary, and provided with such forces as were necessary, if he would undertake to preserve and defend that place under British jurisdiction!

On the 22d of November following, Mr. McTurk wrote to Señor Tomas Kelly, president and manager of the Manoa Company, that he had received information that the company was contemplating the establishment of a saw-mill at the mouth of the Barima, and said:

"I deem it my duty, as the officer now in charge of the Pomarón River Judicial District, which extends to the limits of the Colony on its Venezuelan or western side, to notify you that the Barima river is in the County of Essequibo, and Colony of British Guiana, and forms part of the Judicial District over which I exercise jurisdiction.

"No settlement of any kind, whether for the purpose of trade or any other purposes, can be made within the limits of the Colony, unless in accordance with its existing laws, and those who may become residents thereof shall be required to obey them.

"I desire to call your attention to the notices posted on the trees at the Amacuro, Barima, and Guaima rivers, one of which I am told is in your possession. I enclose, nevertheless, a manuscript copy of that notice. All of them were affixed, as above said, by order of His Excellency the Governor."

In another communication of the same date Mr. McTurk said to Señor Kelly:

"I have the honor to inform you that you are now within the limits of the Colony of British Guiana, and within those of the district under my jurisdiction, as Special Magistrate and Superintendent of the Crown Lands and Forests of this Colony, and therefore outside your own jurisdiction as a functionary of Venezuela. Whatever notifications you should make to the inhabitants will be void, and all persons residing in this or any other part of this Colony, or visiting it, will have to conduct themselves in accordance to its laws. I must likewise call your attention to the notices affixed on the trees, on the banks of this river, and of the Waini and Barima. These notices were placed where they are by order of the Governor of British Guiana."

On the 25th of October, 1884, the Secretary *pro tem.* of the Government of that Colony wrote to Mr. C. C. Fitzgerald as follows:

"British Guiana,
"Government Secretary's Office,
"Georgetown, Demerara, *25th October, 1884.*

"Sir: I am directed by His Excellency the Governor of British Guiana to acknowledge the receipt of your three letters, noted on the margin, relating to the Manoa Company and to the concession granted by the Venezuelan Government, and transmitting some documents, and to convey to you the expressions of His Excellency's thanks for the information therein contained and the documents supplied.

"With regard to the British Guiana boundary, I am directed by His Excellency to intimate to you that the Colonial Government exercise authority and jurisdiction within the limits laid down in the map hereto accompanied, starting from the right bank of the Amacuro river, and that within these limits the Colonial Government will enforce the laws of British Guiana.

"I have further to intimate to you that any person disregarding the laws of British Guiana, or acting in contravention of them within these limits, will be liable to be prosecuted according to the laws of the Colony.

"The whole of the territory between the Amacuro and the Moruca rivers is part of the Colony of Barima, British Guiana, and the Colonial Government will maintain jurisdiction over it and prevent the rights of Her Majesty, or of the inhabitants of the Colony, from being in any way infringed."

All that has been stated thus far only shows that Great Britain had unduly assumed jurisdiction both over disputed territories and over territories which had not been in dispute, thereby contradicting the formal assurances and promises which she had given, and violating the agreement she had made, in 1850, through her Chargé d'Affaires in Caracas; promises voluntarily given, whereby Venezuela's reciprocal assurances and promises were obtained to the same effect. She also showed herself inconsistent and hasty by the peculiar manner of her committing such infringements.

This is proven by the following abstracts of a note of January 8, 1885, from the British Legation at Caracas to the Secretary of Foreign Relations of Venezuela:

"In a despatch dated London, the 28th November, I am directed by Her Majesty's Government to draw the attention of that of Venezuela to the proceedings of the agents of the Manoa Company *in certain districts, the sovereignty of which is equally claimed by Her Majesty's Government and that of Venezuela.*

"Earl Granville further instructs me to request the Venezuelan Government to take steps to prevent the agents of the Manoa Company, or of Mr. H. Gordon, who has also a concession for colonization from the Venezuelan Government, from asserting claims to, or interfering with any of the territory claimed by Great Britain

"Her Majesty's Government, in the event of Venezuela's declining to move in this matter, would, to their great regret, feel themselves under the necessity of adopting measures for preventing the encroachment of the Manoa Company, and the Governor of British Guiana would even be instructed to employ an adequate police force for the prevention of such encroachment and the maintenance of order.

"Lord Granville further informs me, however, that no steps will be taken by the Governor of British Guiana pending this reference to the Venezuelan Government.

"I need hardly remind your Excellency that the question of the boundary of British Guiana is one of long standing, and that communications upon the subject are at the present moment taking place between Her Majesty's Government and the Venezuelan Minister in London. It is, therefore, all the more important that incidents calculated to produce grave inconvenience should be prevented. The territories, irrespective of those disputed by Venezuela and Great Britain, conceded to the Manoa Company, are enormous in extent; but without entering into that feature of the question, I feel certain that His Excellency, the President of the Republic, will duly appreciate the immense importance of obviating the possibility of any collision between the agents of that Company and the British authorities *in the territories, the sovereignty of which is still a disputed question.*"

The above shows, beyond doubt, that while, according to the express declaration of the British Government, the question was concerning territories, the sovereignty over which was a matter of *dispute* between Venezuela and Great Britain, the latter thought it proper to assert her claims as if they were *acknowledged rights*, and to threaten to take the law in her own hands and resort to force if the Venezuelan Government did not acquiesce in such *ex parte* measures—promising, however, that no such action would be taken pending the reference to Venezuela of the complaints made by the British Government against the so-called encroachments of the Manoa Government.

On the 26th of the same month the British Minister informed the Venezuelan Government that the Governor of British Guiana had been authorized to send Magistrate McTurk, with an adequate police force, to the district situated on the right bank of the Amacuro river, to investigate the acts of the Manoa Company, and more especially those of Mr. Robert Wells and others, who had been charged with torturing people by hanging them from their ankles and keeping them for a long time in that position, etc.

He also said that Commissioner McTurk would act in the premises in the manner provided by the laws in force in the other sections of British Guiana, and reminded the Venezuelan Government that in the contract with the Manoa Company the words "as far as British Guiana" were to be found textually. In connection with this circumstance the British Minister remarked that Mr. C. C. Fitzgerald, in his report on the territorial concession of the great Delta of the Orinoco to the Manoa Company, had said that "at about ten miles to the southwest of Punta Barima is the mouth of the Amacuro river, which, in 1800, formed the frontier between British Guiana and Venezuela," wherefrom it would result that the place, notice of which was taken, was not even claimed by the Manoa Company; and, finally, that the Governor of the Colony had reported to London the removal, presumably by order of the Venezuelan Government, of the posts which had been erected by order of the Government of the Colony on the eastern bank of the Amacuro river and other places, for the purpose of warning the people against encroaching upon that territory, the sovereignty of which was claimed by the British Crown—which posts, he added, had been taken to Ciudad Bolivar. This incident, the Minister remarked, might lead to correspondence of rather an unsatisfactory character, if not to serious troubles in the future.

The Venezuelan Minister in London took particular

pains in refuting Mr. Fitzgerald's assertion in regard to the location of the boundary between Venezuela and British Guiana in 1800. Although at that time the Dutch Colonies in Guiana were under military occupation by Great Britain, the sovereignty thereof was not vested as yet in that nation; for sovereignty was not acquired by Great Britain until Holland transferred it to her by the Treaty of London, of August 13th, 1814. It was only then, but not before, that she became legitimately the lawful owner of the "establishments" of Essequibo, Demerara, and Berbice. They were not even called "British Guiana" until 1831, when they were consolidated so as to form one single Colony. In 1800 the Captaincy-General of Venezuela was a dependency of Spain, and neither Spain nor Holland, as we have seen, had ever defined the boundary between their respective possessions in Guayana.

In regard to the removal of the posts, the Venezuelan Minister stated, that, if the removal had really taken place, it should be considered as a protest by Venezuela, intended to dispel the remotest inference of her assent, or of her acquiescence in the fact of their erection as evidence of British occupation of a territory which Her Majesty's Government had spontaneously bound itself "not to occupy or encroach upon." That even in case Venezuela had, in her turn, violated the agreement of 1850 (which was denied), no other action could be taken properly, except representing to her in a friendly manner what would be necessary to secure the righting of the wrong done; as the resorting at once to coercive *ex parte* measures would only serve the purpose of wounding the dignity of a sovereign State, who saw, then more than ever, the national integrity threatened, especially in such an important part of her domain as the Orinoco river, which carries to the ocean the waters of the numerous streams which run through the soil of the Republic, as also that of the neighboring countries.

That river forms the principal avenue of communication, not only between Venezuelan centers of population, but also between them and the neighboring nations, thus forestalling in the natural progress of the young nations of America the most splendent future.

In the answer given to Mr. Mansfield by the Department of Foreign Relations of Venezuela, the former was assured that, in accordance with the words, "as far as British Guiana" used in the Manoa contract, the area embraced in that grant did not, in any manner, encroach upon the disputed territory; but Mr. Mansfield was promised, nevertheless, frankly and sincerely, that as the Manoa Company had been charged with such encroachments, the proper investigation should be made. Advantage was taken of the occasion to reiterate that on October 18, 1884, a British war steamer had entered the Orinoco, as before stated, leaving, at all the places where she touched, marks and declarations of British dominion, which the Venezuelan Government had contemplated with astonishment and even refused to believe.

In another note addressed to Mr. Mansfield, the Secretary of Foreign Relations of Venezuela expressed the great surprise of the Executive at the contents of the communication of the 26th of January, both as to the part which referred to the acts attributed to Señor Roberto Wells, and those relating to the orders given to the Governor of British Guiana to send Mr. McTurk, with an adequate police force, to investigate the action of the Company on the eastern side of the Amacuro river, notwithstanding the fact that said company was doing its work upon a territory that indisputably belonged to Venezuela. "This surprise of the Government," the Secretary said, "reached its climax when a telegram was received yesterday from the Governor of the Delta territory, giving the information that an armed force, sent by the Governor of British Guiana, had actually invaded

Venezuelan territory; and had, by violence, placed under arrest the Venezuelan Commissioner for the mouth of Amacuro, and carrying him away by force, leaving a body of British police at that place." "This incident," wrote the Minister of Foreign Affairs, "even if considered independently of all the others of which Your Excellency has full knowledge, would be sufficient in itself to cause Venezuela to feel that she has been attacked in her most sacred rights of sovereignty, and to justify her urgent appeal to Your Excellency to take such measures as are required by the nature of the case, for the reparation of the harm done, and for the restoration of the *status quo* of 1859; neither nation having the right to exercise jurisdiction over the territory in dispute. And this is the more indispensable, since negotiations are now pending between Venezuela and Great Britain looking to the settlement of this long-standing question of limits. The Plenipotentiary of the Republic has been instructed to hasten that negotiation; and, no doubt, the two nations would promptly reach the so-much desired conciliation but for inadequate proceedings, having all the appearances of being high-handed, and entirely at variance with that respect due to the principles of territorial dominion and with the feeling of justice which should regulate the relations between civilized countries, should be avoided."

The Venezuelan Minister in London, in compliance with instructions from his Government, and on the grounds already stated, respectfully urged the British Government to direct—

"First. The removal of all marks of sovereignty placed on the disputed territories by order of the Governor of British Guiana.

"Second. The recall of all the functionaries, and of the armed force stationed in those territories.

"Third. Satisfactory explanations and assurances for future compliance with the agreement proposed to Venezuela by Great Britain, and for the violation of the laws of the Republic in regard to ports not open to foreign ships.

"Fourth. The annulment of the proceedings taken against Señor Roberto Wells, his release from imprisonment, and the payment to him of an indemnity for the personal injuries, trial, conviction, and punishment for alleged offenses committed in Venezuelan territory.

"Fifth. The complete re-establishment of the *status quo* of 1850, and the issuing of stringent orders to the Governor of British Guiana to scrupulously preserve and maintain that status until the question of limits shall be finally settled by the two Governments."

No attention whatever was paid to any of these demands presented by Venezuela to Lord Rosebery, Minister of Foreign Affairs of the British Government. Neither he nor his immediate or any other successor ever took any notice of them.

The encroachments which had provoked these demands, and the wrongs done to Venezuela, became thereafter more and more aggravated every day by the action of the authorities of the British Colony.

In December of the same year the President of the Republic had a conference with the Minister Resident of Her Britannic Majesty in Caracas, in which, after making a brief recapitulation of the events which had taken place, he acquainted the Minister with his purpose of sending an engineer to Punta Barima to re-establish there a light-house, as had been asked by Sir Robert Ker Porter, as far back as 1836, and of appointing new officials who should exercise authority in behalf of Venezuela at the same place and at others between the Barima and the Amacuro rivers, and to give notice to the foreign occupants of these localities that they must withdraw. The President added that if the Government of Her Britannic Majesty should occupy such a place as Barima, and become thereby a joint owner of the Orinoco, thus deciding *ex parte* and in its favor a question of such extreme gravity for Venezuela, taking from her by force the exclusive control of that river, he would be reluctantly compelled by the necessities of the case and by the duties of his office, to suspend diplomatic relations between the two countries.

When the substance of this interview was reduced to writing by the proper official and communicated to the British Minister, the latter was requested to furnish whatever information might be found in his possession touching the unprecedented and almost incredible events which had taken place at the mouth of the Orinoco.

Mr. St. John (the British Minister), in view of the fact that the President had refused to postpone the projected occupation of the disputed territory until he could learn the result of his reference of these intentions to the Government of His Majesty, declined to continue the discussion, and confined his reply to the contradiction of some statements made by Doctor Urbaneja.

The Executive carried out its purpose, conferring upon Doctor Jesus Muñoz Tebar the announced Commission. Señor Juan Bautista Dalla Costa, Santiago Rodil, and others were made his associates, but Señor Dalla Costa fell sick and was unable to accompany the other two Commissioners on their trip.

Before explaining the conclusions which they reached, it will be well to remember that in the month of January, 1887, Lord Salisbury authorized Mr. St. John (the British Minister at Caracas) to inform Venezuela that the petition of the British Consul, made in 1836, asking for the establishment of a light-house at Punta Barima had been neither known nor authorized by the British Government; that the attempt to establish that light-house without the consent of the Government of Her Majesty would be a violation of the reciprocal engagement contracted by Venezuela and Great Britain in 1850, namely: not to occupy or encroach upon any territory in dispute between the two countries; and that the Government of Her Majesty would have the right to resist such an action as an aggressive step on the part of Venezuela.

It was a matter of no small surprise to the Government, then, that after the lapse of fifty years and eight months since the petition of Sir Robert Ker Porter, such a statement could be made, namely, that that petition had not been known or authorized by the British Government; that the said official referred to being merely a Consul, as if for the purpose of weakening the weight of his action, in spite of the fact that Sir Robert Ker Porter had been promoted from his position of Consul to that of Chargé d'Affaires of Great Britain immediately after the exchange of the ratifications of the Treaty of 1834, and that in 1836 he was in the actual exercise of his functions as Chargé d'Affaires.

It may be seen, also, in the British Blue Book, page 243, that Mr. Daniel F. O'Leary, British Consul, had sent in September 1, 1842, to the Foreign Office at London, the identical correspondence of Sir Robert Ker Porter with the Secretary of Foreign Relations of Venezuela, relating to the establishment of the light house at Punta Barima.

It will be noticed with surprise that, although all the facts alleged by Lord Rosebery in 1893, in his communication to Señor Michelena, for the purpose of showing that the agreement of 1850 between Venezuela and Great Britain had fallen to the ground and had no validity whatsoever, had happened before January, 1887, no notice was taken of them at that date by Lord Salisbury, who, on the contrary, and in spite of the alleged violations of the agreement, explicitly maintained that *it was in force.*

The Commissioners sent by Venezuela, as above stated, to investigate the subject, returned from their trip and reported the result of their labors.

They found that on the right bank of the Amacuro there were two Commissioners, appointed by British authority, one in 1885 and the other in 1886, entrusted with the duty of preventing Venezuelan ships touching there from selling rum or any spirituous liquors, without a license from the Governor of Demerara, under penalty of seizure of the vessel. They also saw a frame house used as a "Government Office" over which the British flag was hoisted. They ascertained that the British revenue cutter "Transfer" had made several trips to that place, carrying on board a magistrate, accompanied by armed police, who came there to hear and decide criminal cases and others of minor importance. They discovered that at Amacuro and at Barima, ships legally cleared from Ciudad Bolivar, had been searched by British officers and forbidden to sell their cargoes of merchandise, or to continue to the Barima Caño except in ballast. They were informed that another Commissioner had been stationed in the Aruca settlement, and that a magistrate had come there about three months be fore to try a case of murder, in which the defendant, charged with the killing of a coolie, was condemned to five years imprisonment at hard labor. At Cuabana he found a Protestant Church, which served at the same time as a school-house, and in which a marriage registry was kept, wherein it was stated that that locality belonged to "the County of Essequibo." They learned that the Colonial Government had appointed another Commissioner for the town of Guaramuri, on the bank of the Moroco river, and that some gold mines were being worked, under British authority, on the Venezuelan territory situated between the Cuyuni, the Mazaruni and the Puruni rivers, a large portion of the mineral having been already exported through the Demerara customhouse.

The Commissioners then went to Georgetown, and through the Venezuelan Consul there made the Governor acquainted with the purposes and object of their visit, with the work already done by them in discharge of their duties, and with the encroachments upon the Venezuelan territory which they had discovered. The

Government Secretary replied, on the 6th of January, referring to the "notice" published in the *London Gazette* of October 22, 1886, stating that the places referred to in the official communication of the Commissioners were within the limits described in that "notice," and "*formed part of British Guiana!*"

The aforesaid notice proclaims that—

> "Whereas the boundary line between Her Majesty's Colony of British Guiana and the Republic of Venezuela is in dispute between Her Majesty's Government and the Government of Venezuela; and
>
> "Whereas it has come to the knowledge of Her Majesty's Government that grants of land within the territory claimed by Her Majesty's Government as part of the said Colony have been made, or purport to have been made, by or in the name of the Government of Venezuela;
>
> "Notice is hereby given that no title to land or to any right in or over or affecting any land within the territory claimed by Her Majesty's Government * * * will be admitted or recognized by Her Majesty or by the Government of British Guiana; and that any person taking possession of or exercising any right over any such land, under color of any such title, or pretended title, will be liable to be treated as a trespasser under the laws of the said Colony."

The notice ends by stating that a "map" showing the "boundary between British Guiana and Venezuela," as claimed by Her Majesty's Government, could be seen "in the Library of the Colonial Office, Downing street, or at the office of the Government Secretary, at Georgetown, British Guiana."

In the note of February 20, 1887, from Dr. Urbaneja to Mr. St. John, which contains a statement of the rights of Venezuela, and a recapitulation of the stages through which the question had passed down to that date, including what had been done by the Commissioners sent to the disputed territory, the British Minister's attention was called to the fact that the Venezuelan Government (as shown by the previous note sent him on January 26, reiterating its willingness to have the controversy settled by arbitration), had demanded from Her Majesty's Government the evacuation of the Venezuelan territory from the mouth of the Orinoco to the mouth of the Pomarón, which territory had been unduly encroached upon, with the understanding that if, on the 20th of February, no answer should be received, all diplomatic relations between the two countries would be at once suspended.

On the 31st of January, the Venezuelan Government gave its answer to the conditions upon which the British Government said that it would consent to the establishment of the light-house at Punta Barima, and reiterated the demands above alluded to, coupling them with the suggestion of arbitration.

On the 11th of February following, Mr. St. John stated that he had communicated by cable to Her Majesty's Government the Venezuelan despatch of the 25th of January, and had received instructions to say in reply, that, while the said Government was still prepared to enter into friendly negotiations for the settlement of the boundary question, it was unable to accede to the present demand of the Government of Venezuela, much as it would regret the action indicated in said despatch.

It was for this reason that Venezuela renewed and ratified in all their parts her notes of the 26th and the 31st of January, as the Executive was not allowed to enter into any new discussion until Great Britain should have evacuated the territory, recently taken into possession by her; that is to say, as far westward as the Pomarón river as Venezuela was perfectly entitled to demand under the agreement of 1850.

On the 20th of February, 1887, the date designated for that purpose in the Venezuelan communications, the anticipated refusal by Great Britain of the Venezuelan demands having been received, the Venezuelan Minister of Foreign Relations, after making a recapitulation of the wrongs done by Great Britain to the Republic in this matter of the Guiana boundary, explicitly declared:

That Venezuela could not any longer maintain friendly intercourse with a nation which had thus offended her; that from that day she suspended her relations with Great Britain; that she protested before Her Majesty's Government and before the civilized world against the acts of spoliation which, to Venezuela's detriment, had been committed by the Government of Great Britain; that Venezuela, at no time and for no reason whatsoever, would ever consider such acts as capable in any way of abridging or changing the rights which she had inherited from Spain; and that, notwithstanding all this, she would always be ready to abide by the decision of a third power, to whom the question should be referred for settlement.

The note closes by stating that it had been already written, when Mr. St. John's communication of the 19th of the same month was received, in which he stated, by order of Her Majesty's Government, that the latter had been informed of the visit made by two Venezuelan Commissioners to the portion of the territory claimed by Great Britain as belonging to British Guiana, and of what the said Commissioners had done there, and that he had instructed him to say that Her Majesty's Government would not permit any one to interfere with the British subjects at those places.

This gave the Venezuelan Minister of Foreign Relations an opportunity to add that the communication just referred to, showed still more clearly than all other proofs that Great Britain openly asserted jurisdiction over a part of the territory of the Republic, upon which she had encroached, and which she now claimed to be hers, and that she acted on it as if she were the true and lawful owner of the land, without any regard whatever to the rights of Venezuela, who looked upon it as her own property. This was a further reason for the Venezuelan Government to ratify, as it did thereby, all the complaints and protests which had been made in the preceding part of the note, against the action of Great Britain, as arbitrary as it was inexcusable, and that Venezuela would always deem those acts by Great Britain to be illegal and without valid effect.

A few days afterwards Mr. St. John left Caracas, under the circumstances described in the British Blue Book, No. 1 (1896).

In the latter part of 1889 the Venezuelan Government being desirous to re-establish diplomatic relations with the Government of Great Britain, sent to London its Minister in France, Doctor Modesto Urbaneja, who was given full powers in the premises.

As soon as he reached London he put himself in communication with the Foreign Office, and received from the Under-Secretary, Mr. Th. Sanderson, the following statement:

"*Pro Memoria.*

"Her Majesty's Government have received with satisfaction the communication from Señor Urbaneja that he has been empowered by the President of Venezuela to negotiate for a renewal of diplomatic relations between the two countries, which were interrupted in 1887 by the Venezuelan Government then in office. Her Majesty's Government have, on their side, always had every desire to cultivate friendly relations with the Republic of Venezuela.

"In accordance with Señor Urbaneja's request, the following statement has been prepared of the conditions which Her Majesty's Government consider to be necessary for a satisfactory settlement of the questions pending between the two countries:

"I. As regards the frontier between Venezuela and the Colony of British Guiana, Her Majesty's Government could not accept as satisfactory any arrangement which did not admit the British *title*[1] to the territory comprised within the line laid down by Sir R. Schomburgk in 1841. They would be ready to refer to arbitration the claim of Great Britain to certain territories to the west of that line.

"II. Her Majesty's Government consider that they are entitled to expect that the differential duties now levied on imports from British Colonies, in violation of article IV of the Commercial Treaty of 1825, shall be repealed.

"III. They would propose that all outstanding claims on the part of subjects of either country against the Government of the other should be referred to a Mixed Commission."

Doctor Urbaneja replied in reference to article I of the foregoing memorandum that, according to the record of the case, the British Government had proposed, through the Right Honorable Sir Andrew Clark, Lieutenant-General, and the Right Honorable Captain Lowther, in exchange of the renewal of diplomatic relations between the two countries, to evacuate the invaded territory and to submit the question to the decision of a friendly power, and that it was with this understanding that he had been appointed confidential agent for Venezuela to negotiate a preliminary arrangement for the renewal of such relations. He added that the propositions now made in that part of the memorandum were much more unfavorable to Venezuela than those which had been formerly made; and that Venezuela, notwithstanding the unquestionable character of her rights, had then proposed, as she proposed now, to refer to arbitration the title to the whole territory in dispute west of the Essequibo, and to evacuate the invaded country from the Pomarón to the lands which border upon the Orinoco.

As to the second point Dr. Urbaneja said that, although the levying of the differential duty referred to was not in violation of Article IV of the Commercial Treaty of 1825, he did not see any difficulty in arranging the matter by means of another treaty.

[1] Italics are ours. The *claim* of 1841 had grown, it seems, into a "title," but *when* or *how*? (Editor.)

The rejoinder of the British Government, dated March 19, 1890, was, that

"Her Majesty's Government have given their careful attention to Señor Urbaneja's memorandum of the 13th of February.

"The following observations are forwarded in reply:

"I. As regards the boundary of British Guiana, Her Majesty's Government have carefully studied all the documents, historical data, maps and other information which have been communicated or referred to by the Venezuelan Government in the course of the discussion.

"They have also recently made further investigations which have resulted in the acquisition of much information, of which they believe that the Venezuelan Government is not aware.

"After examination of all this evidence they can say without hesitation that the claim of the Venezuelan Government to the Essequibo is one which Spain never asserted, and which Her Majesty's Government must regard as absolutely untenable. The claim of Great Britain, on the other hand, to the whole basin of the Cuyuni and Yuruary is shown to be solidly founded, and the greater part of the district has been for three centuries[1] under continuous settlement by the Dutch, and by the British as their successors.

"In these circumstances Her Majesty's Government must decline, as they have repeatedly declined before, to entertain any proposal for bringing into an arbitration claims on the part of Venezuela which in their full extent involve the title of the larger half of the British colony.

"They can not admit that there is any foundation for the assertion that any Government of Her Majesty ever recognized Point Barima as Venezuelan territory. Her Majesty's Government have constantly maintained that, of strict right, they are entitled to the whole country within the line described in Lord Salisbury's note to Señor Rojas of the 10th of January, 1880; that is, as far as the Highlands of Upata, if not up to the Orinoco itself, and that all settlements by Venezuela to the east of that line are in the nature of encroachments on the

[1] Not true. Part only of that region was occupied, and that part only about *six years*.

rights of Great Britain, whose desire has been throughout to pursue a conciliatory course and to effect a solution by means of friendly compromise and concession.

"Her Majesty's Government must repeat that they can not admit any question as to their title to territory within the line surveyed by Sir R. Schomburgk in 1841 and laid down on Hebert's map inclosed herewith; on the other hand, Her Majesty's Government do not wish to insist on the extreme limit of their claim, which is indicated by a green line on the map marked "A" and attached hereto, and which they are prepared to submit to the arbitration of a third party.

"Her Majesty's Government have never in any way authorized either Sir Andrew Clark or Captain Lowther to present any proposals to the Government of Venezuela, and they must now, while regretting that Señor Urbaneja should have been misled, state their entire inability to adopt such proposals as he mentions.

"II. As regards the question of the differential duties, Her Majesty's Government have the highest legal opinion in support of their view, that these duties are an infraction of the Treaty of 1825. They consider themselves therefore justified in claiming the repeal of the duties quite apart from the question of a fresh commercial Treaty.

"Her Majesty's Government have, on their part, always endeavored, to the best of their ability, to prevent all illicit traffic between Her Majesty's colonies and Venezuela, but it would not be reasonable to hold Great Britain or her Colonies responsible for the conduct of Venezuelan officials or for the administration of law outside Her Majesty's Colonial waters.

"Her Majesty's Government do not doubt that if the other questions at issue between the two Governments were satisfactorily adjusted means could be found for arranging on an equitable basis the claims of the two nations against each other on behalf of their respective subjects.

"Her Majesty's Government can not conclude this expression of their views without calling Señor Urbaneja's attention to the annexed notice, which appeared in the 'Opinion Nacional,' of Caracas, of the 24th of January last. A large part of the district therein granted by contract to Monsieur le Mye is within the Schomburgk line above alluded to, and therefore within British territory. The contract can not be recognized by Her Majesty's Government, and any attempt to put the conclusion in force within that line would entail the risk of a collision with the British authorities."

Dr. Urbaneja was prevented from making any reply to this second memorandum of Lord Salisbury, because as he was getting ready to prepare it, his successor, as representative of Venezuela in Great Britain, arrived in London.

That reply would, no doubt, have been facilitated considerably by Lord Roseberry's declaration that no arrangement would be satisfactory to Great Britain if it were to refer to territory different from that included within the line marked by Mr. Schomburgk in 1841, and by the additional fact that this so-called "Schomburgk Line" was a new capricious line, of recent date, and different from the real one, which had been given to the public and had been made the subject of diplomatic discussion. The original Schomburgk line is the one which appears on the map which Mr. Schomburgk attached to his pamphlet, printed in London in 1840, with the title of "Geographical and Statistical Description of British Guiana, showing the resources and capabilities, as well as the present and future condition of the Colony,"—on the map, identical to the above, forming a part of the chart of Guiana, intended to illustrate the "Travels through Guiana and the Orinoco, from 1835 to 1839, according to his reports and communications to the London Geographical Society, by Robert Herman Schomburgk;" a book published in Leipsic, in 1841, in the German language, by O. A. Schomburgk, and having a preface from Alexander Von Humboldt, and the dessertation of the same Mr. R. H. Schombugrk on certain important astronomical positions in Guiana; or the map, also identical, accompanying Mr. Schomburgk's report, published with other papers of the British Parliament in 1840.

That the line drawn on those maps was thereafter considerably deviated, so as to make it embrace a larger portion of Territory, has been shown beyond doubt in another brief.[1]

The new line, by which the British claim was enlarged, had never been known to the Venezuelan Government until the moment in which the latter received the Herbert map, which had been delivered to Doctor Modesto Urbaneja, and against which the latter had at once commenced to set forth his objections.

The Venezuelan Government had been greatly surprised when the Government of Great Britain insistently declared that no arrangement could ever be satisfactory for the latter nation if the British *title* to the territory limited by the "Schomburgk Line" was not admitted. But that feeling was now carried to its utmost limit, through the further information transmitted to it, that even that line itself was not to be the one originally drawn by Mr. Schomburgk, but another line, which Venezuela had never before known. The conditions imposed in the reply involved a loss to Venezuela of a part of her territory, and the complete nullification, by British action exclusively, of the agreement of 1850, by which Great Britain promised not to occupy or encroach upon any part of the disputed territory, or allow her authorities to act in contravention of that agreement.

The claims of Spain to the Essequibo line, as recognized by even British maps as late as 1838–9, will be explained elsewhere; but the fact can now be stated that General P. M. Netscher, author of a History of the Colonies of Essequibo, Demerara, and Berbice, pubin 1888, positively maintained (page 419) that "the Spaniards in their time used to fix in their maps the

[1] See "Notes on the Schomburgk Line," Part I, of "Case of Venezuela."

western limit of their Guiana on the coast side, on the Moruco or Moroco, and also on the Pomarón, and sometimes on the Essequibo river, and that the Republic of Venezuela has continued in her claims the same traditions."

The exorbitant pretensions of Great Britain were not sufficient to deter Venezuela from pursuing her conciliatory course, or from sending for that purpose another confidential agent to London, instructed to continue the negotiations initiated by Doctor Urbaneja. The Venezuelan Congress repealed its resolution of May 12, 1887, forbidding the Executive to enter into negotiations with Great Britain, except in case she should evacuate the territory upon which she had unjustly encroached, and the Executive appointed Doctor Lucio Pulido to renew the efforts looking to a just settlement.

The legislative body, which, by its resolution aforesaid, restored the President of the Republic to the full possession of all his constitutional powers in diplomatic matters, and left his action untrammeled, entertained the hope that by this measure and others taken to the same effect, a settlement of the conflict, honorable and satisfactory, would be facilitated.

On the 24th of June following, Señor Pulido delivered to Mr. Th. Sanderson, Under-Secretary of the Foreign Office, a memorandum, in which, after stating his Government's desire to renew diplomatic relations (for which purpose he had been provided with full authority), and being animated personally by the most concilatory feelings, said that the communications exchanged between Dr. Urbaneja and the Foreign Office, especially those containing the conditions, peremptorily set forth, upon which Her Majesty's Government would not consent to an adjustment of the pending contention by arbitration, had produced in his Government a sentiment of deep sorrow, and that he had been instructed to say in answer that his Government was unable to take such proposals into formal consideration.

He expressed his readiness to agree to the holding of an informal conference, as suggested by Mr. Blaine, Secretary of State of the United States, between the United States representative in London, a representative of Great Britain, and himself as representative of Venezuela, with a view to reaching, through friendly discussion of the pending difficulties, a final settlement, permitting both Governments to renew their friendly relations.

Dr. Pulido said, furthermore, that as soon as these relations should be re-established, all pending questions could be easily arranged, as he had received instructions in this regard of the most cordial and satisfactory character. And, in conclusion, he said that the only real outstanding difficulty between the two Governments, in regard to which public opinion in Venezuela was very much excited (for which reason the Government was desirous to act with the greatest prudence), was the one growing out of the question of limits between the Venezuelan and British Guiana. To obviate that difficulty and bring about a final settlement, Dr. Pulido suggested a preliminary arrangement to be made between the two Governments on the following basis:

"1st. The Government of the United States of Venezuela should formally declare that the Essequibo, its banks, and the lands covering it belong to British Guiana; and Her Majesty's Government should formally declare that the Orinoco river, its banks, and the lands covering it, belong exclusively to the United States of Venezuela.

"2d. Considering that the region of the west and northwest of the Essequibo river toward the Orinoco river is not officially well known, and considering that the surveys made by the explorer, Schomburgk, can not be invoked as a title of property against the United States of Venezuela in the same manner in which the surveys made by several Venezuelan explorers, can not be invoked as a title of property against Her Majesty's Colony of British Guiana, both Governments should at once agree to appoint a mixed Commission, composed of two chief engineers and their respective staffs, to proceed to make, without any delay, and in the course of one year, the chorographical, geographical, and hydrographical maps and charts of the said region, in order to officially determine the exact course of the rivers and streams, the precise position and situation of the mountains and hills, and all other valuable details which would afford to both Governments a reliable official knowledge of the territory which is actually in dispute.

"3d. The said official maps and charts would enable both Governments to determine, with a mutual feeling of friendship and good will, a boundary with perfect knowledge of the case, and a natural boundary between British Guiana and the United States of Venezuela should in all cases be preferred and determined.

"4th. But, if in view of such official maps and charts both Governments do not agree upon a friendly boundary, it should, from the present moment, be agreed that, in such event, the final decision and settlement of the boundary question shall be submitted to two arbitrators appointed, one by each Government, and a third elected by the two arbitrators to decide the question, having in view the original titles and documents which both Governments would then submit in supporting their claims to the lands or territories in dispute, the said arbitrators should be authorized to fix a boundary line, which being in accordance with the respective rights and titles should have the advantage of constituting as far as possible a natural boundary.

"5th. In order to arrive at this desirable result and to prevent any chance of international discord, both Governments should agree to withdraw or to remove all posts or any other indications or signs of presumptive possession and dominion from the said region, until the final boundary shall have been fixed in the manner aforesaid, and therefore that neither Government exercise any jurisdiction upon the disputed region pending the final arrangement."

In answer to this memorandum, Mr. Sanderson transmitted to Dr. Pulido, on July 24th following, an extra, memorandum as follows:

"Señor Pulido's memorandum of the 24th ultimo has received the careful consideration of Her Majesty's Government, who have been desirous of examining in the most friendly and impartial spirit any proposals which the Venezuelan Government may wish to offer for the resumption of diplomatic relations and the settlement of pending differences.

"In Señor Pulido's opinion the only matter which presents real difficulties is the question of the frontier between Venezuela and British Guiana, upon which he states that public opinion in Venezuela is greatly excited. He thinks that it is materially impossible to settle this question in a short time, but as a step towards its final solution he proposes a preliminary agreement to the following effect:

"Venezuela to recognize the title of British Guiana to the exclusive possession of the River Essequibo, with its banks and the lands covering it, while Her Majesty's Government would similarly recognize the title of Venezuela to the exclusive possession of the River Orinoco, its banks, and the lands covering it. A mixed commission of engineers, appointed by the two Governments, to survey, in the course of a year, the country to the west and northwest of the Essequibo river and the two Governments then to proceed, with the information thus obtained, to lay down a frontier between their respective territories, giving the preference to a natural boundary. In case of their being unable to agree on a line the decision of the boundary to be referred to two arbitrators to be appointed, one by each Government, and if they should disagree, to a third arbitrator to be chosen by the other two; pending these discussions both Governments to withdraw all posts and signs of presumptive possession or dominion from the territory in dispute.

"Her Majesty's Government regret that this proposal is not such as they would feel justified in accepting. The proposed declaration, if it be correctly understood, would recognize the right of Great Britian to the main stream only of the Essequibo and the land immediately upon its banks, without including its tributaries, in exchange for a similar recognition of the right of Venezuela to the main stream of the Orinoco and the lands upon its banks and in the neighborhood of its mouth, including Point Barima and the adjacent district, while the whole intervening country would remain subject to discussion, and at last resort to arbitration. Such a transaction is clearly inadmissible. For in this manner

Venezuela would maintain her full claim, surrendering nothing to which she can hope to show any legitimate title, while Great Britain would not only admit the discussion of claims upon the part of Venezuela for which she has constantly maintained that there is no serious foundation, but would at once and unconditionally abandon a considerable portion of territory of which she is in actual occupation. That territory, and by far the greater portion of the large tract of country which the Venezuelan Government seeks to put in question, accrued to the Netherlands under the Treaty of Munster of 1648 by right of previous occupation. It was constantly held and claimed by the States-General in succeeding years. It was publicly and effectively occupied by Great Britain during the wars at the close of the last century, and the formal transfer of the country so occupied was effected by the Treaty of peace with the Netherlands of August 13th, 1814, and was in no way questioned by Spain in the conclusion of peace with her in the same year.

"Her Majesty's Government would have no object in joining in such a survey, as is proposed by Señor Pulido, of country which is already sufficiently well known to them and which has been scientifically surveyed by British engineers. For many years past the British administration has been familiar with the greater part of the districts watered by the Cuyuni and Masaruni rivers. There is, therefore, already at the disposal of the two Governments ample information for the purpose of settling a general line of frontier, although the decision of any minor points of detail might be properly left to a mixed commission of delimitation.

"Her Majesty's Government have indicated, in previous statements, the extent of the full territorial claim which they believe themselves entitled to make. They have also defined the line within which they consider the British title to be unquestionable. In offering that certain portions of their claim beyond that line should be submitted to arbitration, they expressed their willingness to exclude from the proposed reference those valuable districts in the neighborhood of Guacipati which, although falling within their claim, have for some time been in Venezuelan occupation, and in regard to which an arbitral decision adverse to Venezuela might have caused her considerable embarrassment, and would have involved heavy pecuniary claims on the part of Great Britain on account of revenue received during the past years.

"They regret to see that this offer on their part does not appear to have been appreciated or to have met with any response on the part of Venezuela. Her Majesty's Government would not object to receive for examination and possible discussion any suggestion for modification of their proposal in points where the Government of Venezuela consider that the interests of the Republic are seriously involved; but they are unable to depart from the general principle on which those proposals are based, or to accept an eventual reference to arbitration of a character so extensive as the method of procedure suggested by Señor Pulido would not improbably involve.

"Her Majesty's Government have more than once explained that they can not consent to submit to arbitration what they regard as their indisputable title to districts in the possession of the British Colony.

"Every fresh investigation tends only to enforce and enlarge that title, and to make it more incumbent on them to maintain it, as an act of justice to the rights and interests of the Colony."

To palliate this refusal to accept Dr. Pulido's proposal, Her Majesty's Government alleged that Great Britain, through the compromise, now suggested by them, would not only consent to discuss unfounded claims of Venezuela, but would, at once and unconditionally, abandon to the latter a considerable portion of the territory of which she (Great Britain) was then in actual possession; that that territory, as well as the greater portion of the large tract of country which the Venezuelan Government seeks to put in question, *accrued to Holland under the Treaty of Munster of 1648 by right of previous occupation;* that it was constantly held and claimed as Dutch by the States-General in the succeeding years; that it was publicly and effectively occupied by Great Britain during the wars at the close of the last century; that the formal transfer of the country so occupied was effected by the Treaty of peace with the Netherlands of August 13,

1814, and that it was in no way questioned by Spain when the peace with her was signed in that year.

Against all these assertions there is much to say. Conquest, confirmed by the Treaty of peace of 1648, was the only title Holland ever had to any territory in Guayana. It has been shown by the Washington Investigating Commision, that Holland far from having acquired that territory by right of occupation, previous to the Treaty of Munster of 1648, only held, on that territory, and at that date, the post of Kykoveral, which had previously belonged to Spain.

On the other hand, the fact should be remembered that neither that Treaty, nor the subsequent one of August 13, 1814, defined the territory to which they referred, except very vaguely. The Treaty of Munster, indeed, did not even mention it by its name, but referred to it by such a general expression as the one which it used, namely, the "places," etc., which the Dutch *then* held on the *coast* of America. As to the second Treaty, it scarcely did anything else than express the cession to Great Britain of the establishments of Demerara, Essequibo and Berbice, without determining in the least the extent of area embraced by them.

It is to be observed also that the United Netherlands were ignorant of the limits of the territory of that Colony, and that for this reason the Government of that Republic, when presenting to the Court of Madrid a complaint against the action of the Spaniards of the Orinoco in regard to the Cuyuni, in the year 1759, demanded the restoration of the "post" that had been destroyed by the Spaniards the year before, and proposed that an authoritive and correct demarcation between the Colony of Essequibo and Orinoco should be made. To this fact Lord Salisbury referred in his note of the 26th of November, 1895, addressed to Sir Julian Pauncefote, and so it is read in the claim ordered to be presented to the Minister of State in Spain, and printed in the Blue Book, No. 1 (1896), page 105.

It has been proved also by documents taken from the Dutch archives that when, in 1666, the British took possession of the Dutch Colonies in Guiana, the latter did not extend west of the Moroco, and that therefore the British could not take it from them through conquest. When the British and the Dutch made the Treaty of Peace of 1667, the mutual restitution of all the places occupied by either party was agreed upon, and from there it resulted that things were re-established to the condition in which they were before the war.

As to the subsequent occupations of 1781, 1796, and 1803, it must be said that the latter was the only one which permanently affected the territory of the Colonies, because it was sanctioned by the Treaty of 1814, which, as has been stated, ceded to Great Britain the establishments of Demerara, Essequibo, and Berbice and no more. But the limits of these Colonies, which never embraced the territory now claimed for them, were not defined. So undetermined they have been always for Great Britain herself, that under the Treaty of the 2d of February, 1897, she has agreed with Venezuela to refer their demarcation to an Arbitral Tribunal of jurists.

It was not in 1814, but in 1809 (January 14), when the peace was signed in London between Spain and the United Kingdom of Great Britain and Ireland. And that Treaty, besides declaring that friendship was re-established between the two nations, provided for an alliance between them, which bound Great Britain to continue to assist Spain in her struggle against French tyranny and usurpation; to recognize no other King of Spain and the Indies than Ferdinand VII. and his heirs and legitimate successors, recognized as such by the Spanish nation; and which bound Spain, in return, not to transfer to France, in any case, any portion whatever of the Spanish territories.

True it is that in Madrid, on the 5th of July, 1814, a new Treaty, called a Treaty of Peace, Friendship and Alliance, was concluded between Great Britain and

Spain. But this Treaty was concluded, not for the purpose of putting an end to any preceding war, but to preserve the peace of 1809 and to render closer the alliance and intimate union which existed between the two nations. As stated in its preamble, its negotiation had been deemed to be conducive to the proper re-establishment of the balance of power in Europe, and for thus insuring the peace of Europe. So that, even this Treaty of July 5, 1814, preceded the one by which the cession of three of the Dutch Colonies of Guiana was made; and that therefore Spain could not have then raised any difficulty at all against the said transfer, because at that time it had not yet been made. On the other hand, Spain would never have had anything to urge against a transfer, which, owing to the indefinite character of its terms, did not inflict upon her any apparent injury.

Lord Salisbury repeated to Dr. Pulido that Her Majesty's Government had defined the line within which they considered the British title to be unquestionable; but that in consenting to certain portions of their claim beyond that line being referred to arbitration they had expressed their willingness to exclude from the proposed reference, although falling within the British claim, certain valuable districts in the neighborhood of Guacipati, occupied by Venezuela, because an arbitral decision in regard to them, adverse to Venezuela, might cause her considerable embarrassment and render her liable to heavy pecuniary claims on the part of Great Britain on account of revenue received in past years.

This was to adhere tenaciously to the plan of circumscribing, to the benefit of the British Government, the territory in dispute, by means of a boundary line which the Republic never heard of until the 19th of March, 1890, when for the first time it was made known to Señor Urbaneja.

In regard to the liabilities which an arbitral decision might have accrued to one of the parties, on account of benefits derived by unlawful occupation, it is important, in this connection, to take notice of the opinion set forth by Lord Salisbury.

In the letter with which Sir Thomas Sanderson transmitted to Señor Pulido the above inserted memorandum, the British Minister of Foreign Affairs declared that he could not but regard the establishment of Venezuelan administrations in the district between Punta Barima and the Pomarón river and in the neighborhood thereof, where the Cuyuni debouches into the Essequibo, as entirely inconsistent with the professed desire of the Venezuelan Government to come to a settlement of pending differences by means of friendly discussion; that such measures could have no practical effect, and that, if attempted to be put into execution, they could be regarded only as an invasion of the Colony, and be dealt with accordingly. He said that it would be useless to continue the present negotiations unless Venezuela should show a more conciliatory disposition and expunge, with the proper explanations, the two decrees referred to.

To which Señor Pulido answered: "I have no information from my Government in reference to this new incident; but I think it opportune to suggest that this makes more apparent the necessity of adjusting, in the manner adopted by civilized nations, the frontiers between Venezuela and the British Colony of Guiana; and it shows, at the same time, how much it is to be regretted that Her Majesty's Government should persist in refusing to submit them to the study and decision of impartial arbitrators, as Venezuela has been proposing for the last ten years, and as other nations have been doing who have possessions in Guayana.

"In effect, these frontiers, which are more or less uncertain or indefinite, from Her Majesty's Government's point of view, as they have been successively extending them solely on their own authority during the last fifty years, can not but give rise to conflicts upon the rights of authority and territorial jurisdiction. If, in 1884, Her Majesty's Government occupied those territories, declared as disputable and neutral by both Governments in 1850, and took measures looking to a permanent establishment therein, there is, in reality, no reason to be surprised that Venezuela refuses to abandon her rights and her jurisdiction there while the question is not settled in the customary form, or while said territories are not taken from her by force, which, unhappily, is still imposed upon them as an inexorable necessity."

Señor Pulido reported, also, an interview which he had, on the 31st of July, with Mr. Sanderson, of whom he asked the meaning of the last paragraph of the memorandum transmitted to him, and that Mr. Sanderson answered that Her Majesty's Government was disposed to listen to and take into consideration the propositions of Venezuela to draw a line reciprocally advantageous, not far removed from the Schomburgk line; and that, in reference to the mouth of the Orinoco and Punta Barima, these places would be abandoned to Venezuela on condition that, in compensation therefor, there should be given to Great Britain a certain tract of land, to be agreed upon, between the Uruan (Yuruan) river and the mouth of the Cuyuni, west of the Schomburgk line, which tract of land Mr. Sanderson showed to him on the map at the time of this interview. At Dr. Pulido's request that Mr. Sanderson should write down his ideas, he did so, with his own hand, upon the paper which he attached to his report, and which is as follows:

"A line starting from Point Mocomoco between Point Barima and the River Guaima, and touching the Amacuro river at the southwest."

"In exchange or compensation, the boundary line will follow the course of the river Uruan (Yuruan) from its junction with the Cuyuni river, and might be extended to the Usupamo range or to the Rinocoto range of mountains."

Mr. Sanderson said afterwards to Dr. Pulido that what he had written upon that paper was a personal suggestion, and added that Great Britain, in case of an adjustment, would withdraw her claims upon the territories not actually occupied by her outside of the original Schomburgk line, although those claims might be pressed with probable success before an arbitrator. When the remark was made to him that there is no occasion for compensation when the thing given up is one upon which no right at all can be claimed, as was the case with the mouth of the Orinoco, for which reason the proper word to be used here was restitution, instead of compensation, and also, that the territory asked for by him seemed to be too large, he replied that the territory asked for had no real value on account of its remote situation, while that one at the mouth of the Orinoco was of a great political and commercial importance, and that in case of negotiation all of this would be taken into consideration to make the agreement really compensatory. He added that he looked at this subject from the standpoint of accomplished facts.

Dr. Pulido then informed Mr. Sanderson that he was bound by his duty to merely listen to what was said, not without protesting, however, against the injustice done to Venezuela, and against any abuse of might on the part of Her Majesty's Government; that he had no authority to discuss the question on the ground now suggested; and that, while all the declarations he had made up to that time, either orally or in writing, should be considered to be in force, he now had no authority to do anything more than take note of his proposals. He recognized the fact that the exclusive possession of the mouths of the Orinoco was a capital question for Venezuela, and that for that reason the promise of Her Majesty's Government in regard to its restitution would be duly appreciated by the Venezuelan Government. Due information of his suggestions and of the conference in which they were made, would be properly transmitted by him to his Government, whose answer would, also in due time, be communicated to Mr. Sanderson.

In regard to the decrees complained of by Lord Salisbury, Dr. Pulido said he had no official knowledge of them, that they had been issued before the beginning of the negotiations; and that, in his private opinion, they should be considered only as a manifestation on the part of Venezuela of her determination not to abandon her right to the territory so long as the question of the frontier was not settled in proper form—an assertion of her rights which Venezuela had been constantly making by all means within her power for a great number of years.

It has been noticed elsewhere that the British Blue Book does not say a word about this new proposal of Mr. Sanderson.

On the 30th of September, 1890, Dr. Pulido, who was then in Paris, wrote to Mr. Sanderson informing him that he had to return to Venezuela, and that his Government was considering his note of the 24th of July, and the memorandum annexed thereto; that in due time the result would be communicated to him; that the Government of Venezuela was anxious to find some acceptable basis for the arrangement of the frontier dispute and was animated by that spirit of conciliation which is indispensable to carry any negotiation to success; that, if Her Majesty's Government was animated by corresponding feelings, and desired to give Venezuela that share of justice to which she was entitled, he had no doubt that an agreement could be reached; but that in case his expectations should be disappointed, he had instructions from his Government to tell Mr. Sanderson that *Venezuela would never recognize the occupation of the Territories of Guayana,* which, since 1850, had been declared neutral and in dispute, nor would she recognize the measures which the Colonial authorities of Her Majesty's Government should take to permanently occupy them, reserving for all time her rights to recover them.

Early in the spring of 1893, Señor Tomàs Michelena arrived at London in the character of confidential agent of Venezuela, entrusted with the mission of settling the pending question with Her Majesty's Government and renewal of diplomatic relations.

In compliance with the intimation made to him by Lord Rosebery at their first conference, Señor Michelena transmitted to him the following *Pro Memoria:*

"Bases for the conclusion of a preliminary agreement between Her Majesty's Government and the Government of the United States of Venezuela, with the object of re-establishing diplomatic relations and of amicably adjusting the various questions now pending between them:

1st. "The Government of Great Britain claiming certain territory in Guayana as successor to the rights of the Netherlands, and the Government of Venezuela claiming a portion of said territory as heir of Spain, prompted by an amicable spirit, and being desirous of putting an end to all differences respecting the titles, jurisdiction, and dominion of each to and over said territory in dispute, do hereby agree and stipulate that after official relations shall have been re-established between the two countries in consequence of the ratification of this preliminary agreement by the respective Governments, each party shall appoint one or more delegates invested with full powers to conclude a treaty of limits, based upon the conscientious examination which they may make of the documents, titles, and antecedents which may prove the respective claims; it being understood that the decision of doubtful points, or the demarcation of a frontier line, upon which the delegates so appointed may not be able to agree, shall be submitted to the final and unappealable decision of a judicial arbiter, to be appointed by common consent of both Governments.

2d. "The Government of Venezuela, with the object of re-establishing relations with Her Britannic Majesty's Government upon a footing of a greater cordiality, shall immediately proceed to conclude a new treaty of commerce, abrogating the additional duty of thirty per cent. and substituting therefor another of a definite duration, as proposed by Lord Granville, in 1884.

3d. "All claims by subjects of Her Britannic Majesty's Government against Venezuela, and those of the citizens of the Republic of Venezuela against Her Majesty's Government, shall be examined by a Commission appointed *ad hoc;* Venezuela agreeing thereto in this special case, adjudication of all foreign claims being, by a decree of the Republic, placed under the jurisdiction of the High Federal Court. It will therefore be of record that in all future claims Great Britain accepts said provision.

4th. "The preliminary agreement shall stipulate that both Her Britannic Majesty's Government and that of Venezuela recognize and declare to be the *status quo* of the boundary question that which existed in the year 1850, when the Honorable Sir Belford H. Wilson, Her Britannic Majesty's Chargé d'Affaires at Caracas, made the formal declaration on behalf, and at the express command of Her Britannic Majesty's Government, namely, that no portion of the territory in dispute should be occupied, and requesting a similar declaration by the Government of Venezuela, which was made by the latter, said *status quo* to be maintained until the Treaty of Boundaries mentioned in basis 1st shall be concluded.

5th. "The agreement made on the basis herein proposed, which shall be signed by the confidential agent of Venezuela, by virtue of the powers vested in him, and by the person duly authorized thereto by Her Britannic Majesty's Government, shall also be immediately submitted to the direct ratification of both Governments, and after the exchange of ratifications shall have been made, the diplomatic relations shall be *ipso facto* re-established between the two countries."

In his answer Lord Rosebery confined himself to the point relating to the boundary question. In the first place, he said the fact that the proposal involved a reference to arbitration in case of difference between the two Governments, practically reduced it to the form which had been several times declined by Her Majesty's Government, for which reason he suggested an amendment to article 1st of the memorandum in the terms which will be seen hereafter.

With regard to clause 4th of the same document, relating to the re-establishment of the agreement of 1850 and the evacuation of what he said constituted for some years an "integral part" of British Guiana, he regretted to be unable to accept it. He alleged that Venezuela had disturbed that arrangement on several successive occasions, the first one having been the establishment by the Venezuelan Government, in the same year, 1850, of new positions to the east of Tumuremo; that in 1858 she had allowed the town of Nueva Providencia to be founded on the south side of the river Yuruary; that in 1876 she had granted licenses to trade and cut wood in the district of Barima and to eastward of that district; that in 1881 she had made a grant of a large part of the territory in dispute to General Pulgar; and that in 1884 she had made concessions to the Manoa Company and others, which were followed by actual attempts to settle the territory. He contrasted this action with that of the British Government, which had been, he said, marked by great forbearance and a strong desire to execute the arrangement in good faith; in proof of which he mentioned that, when applied to in 1881, to grant a concession in the disputed territory, Her Majesty's Government had distinctly declined to entertain the proposal on the ground that negotiations were pending with Venezuela, and that it was not until the encroachments of the Manoa Company began to interfere with the peace and good order of the Colony that Her Majesty's Government decided that an effective occupation of the territory could no longer be deferred, and steps were taken for publicly asserting what they believe to be the incontestable rights of Great Britain. These rights Her Majesty's Government could not now abandon by consenting to any *status quo* except that "now existing," which must remain in force during the progress of the negotiations.

The following is the amendment suggested in place of article 1st of Señor Michelena's memorandum, above referred to:

"Whereas the Government of Great Britain claims certain territory in Guiana, as successor in title of the Netherlands, and the Government of Venezuela as heir to Spain claims the same territory, both Governments being inspired by friendly intentions, and being desirous of putting an end to the differences which have arisen on this matter, and both Governments wishing to pay all deference to the titles alleged by either to prove its jurisdiction and proprietary rights over the territory in question, do agree and stipulate that as soon as official relations shall have been re-established between the two countries, and after the ratification of the present preliminary convention by both Governments, one or more delegates shall be named by each party with full power to conclude a frontier Treaty founded on a conscientious and full examination by the said delegates of the documents, titles, and past events supporting the claims of either party; it being agreed *that the said territory in dispute lies to the west of the line laid down in the map communicated to the Government of Venezuela on the 19th of March, 1890, and to the east of a line to be marked on the same map running from the source of the River Cumano down that stream and up the Aima, and so along the Sierra Usapamo;* and that the decision of doubtful points and the laying down of a frontier on the line of which the delegates may be unable to agree shall be submitted to the final decision, from which there shall be no appeal, of a judicial arbitrator to be appointed should the case arise, by common agreement between the two Governments."

Señor Michelena could but decline to accept the proposal of Lord Rosebery, which implied the consent by Venezuela, in the very same text of the Treaty, to the loss of the territories which the British Government claimed, without reason, and reduced the scope of the arbitration to the mere consideration of absolutely unfounded *new* claims to territory, situated to the west of the Schomburgk line, thus taking it for granted that said line has been finally adopted. Señor Michelena, therefore, confined himself to refute one by one the allegations of the British note, devoting his attention chiefly to the exclusion from discussion of the lands which Great Britain had occupied, in spite of the fact that she herself had declared in 1850 that they were in dispute.

The Venezuelan agent supplemented this refutation by examining the reasons alleged by Lord Rosebery, in support of his statement that the arrangement of 1850 was not in force, and maintaining that such statement was untenable. Even if the violations of that arrangement, with which Venezuela was charged, were ever committed, as alleged, that was not a reason for one party to the arrangement, by its own act, to ignore the obligations which the arrangement imposed upon it, much less when nothing had been said by it against the alleged violations. To make things still worse, the fact stands out that Great Britain herself, in 1887 (a date far subsequent to the alleged committal of all the wrongs charged to Venezuela), invoked, through her legation at Caracas, the agreement of 1850, which she then considered to be in force, and upon which she maintained that Venezuela would ignore her engagement under that compact, if, by her sole action, without the assent of Great Britain, she should undertake, as announced, to construct a light-house at Punta Barima.

Señor Michelena inquired what territory was declared to be in dispute in 1850? It was not then defined, as it ought to have been, in order to show clearly the extent of the obligation which each party contracted and to avoid further difficulties. It is most natural to suppose, he said, in answer to his query, that the agreement had no other line in contemplation than the one proposed nine years before by Lord Aberdeen, which, on the coast side, began at the Moroco; and neither that line nor the one suggested in 1886 by Lord Rosebery himself, left within territory claimed by the British Government the Yuruary river or its southern bank, on which the town of *Nueva Providencia* was founded. Neither did either of the said two lines include in the alleged British claim to the Barima district, wherein the licenses granted to trade and cut wood were to be operated. As to the concessions granted to General Pulgar, to the Manoa Company, and to others, Señor Michelena remarked that they had had no effect, and had no reference to territory not belonging to Venezuela. In conclusion, he said that the theory that accomplished facts have the force of law, can not be applied to diplomatic negotiations intended to bring about a cordial and friendly settlement, much less when those facts have no foundation other than disputed rights, unsupported by proof, not defined by any authority, never consented to or accepted under the public law of nations, and when the purpose in view was to avoid serious apprehensions of future danger and to restore confidence among the capitalists who had, in Venezuela, important commercial undertakings of great magnitude.

Lord Rosebery did not deign to reply to the arguments which had been submitted for his consideration, but confined himself to an acknowledgment of the receipt of Señor Michelena's note, and to stating that the contents of said note did not open the way to any agreement which the British Government could accept.

When, shortly afterwards, the attention of Lord Rosebery was called to the new acts of jurisdiction which were being exercised by the Government of Demerara in the so-called "district of the northwest," which reached the mouth of the Orinoco, he said that those acts were no more than part of the necessary administration of a territory which Her Majesty's Government "consider to be indisputably a portion of the Colony of British Guiana," and to which, as stated more than once, that Government could not "admit any claim on the part of Venezuela."

When Señor Michelena wrote again to Lord Rosebery in regard to the boundary question, he vigorously refuted the reasons upon which the British Government had declined to submit to arbitration, as suggested by Venezuela, the said question in its entirety, consenting to that reference only in case it should be limited to the claim to certain portions of the territory *which had never been disputed before*, and upon condition that Venezuela should admit once and forever the validity of the acts by which the British Government, without right and by merely an abuse of its power, had encroached upon territories which the very same Government itself had previously declared to be in dispute.

In making a brief synopsis of all the stages of the negotiation, he found himself unable to forget the offer made by Sir Th. Sanderson to Dr. Pulido, on July 30, 1890, that Great Britain would abandon her pretensions to the mouth of the Orinoco and agree to fix a limit on that side " by means of a line which, starting from Point Mocomoco, between Point Barima and the River Guaima, should reach the River Amacuro on the southwest." This assertion was not contradicted in the least by Lord Rosebery, and therefore it entered into the category of indubitable truths, and constituted an additional manifestation of inconsistency to increase the number of those already incurred in this matter by the British Ministers.

Such inconsistency appears in the most striking manner from the comparison of the different lines suggested in the course of time by Her Majesty's Government. They all show the area of the British claim to have been previously enlarged to such an extent as to have added to the original claim, in only one year, from 1886 to 1887, as remarked by the United States Foreign Office, not less than 33,000 square miles, *the reason for such an extraordinary increase having never been given.*

It appears, furthermore, that during the discussion Venezuela has always shown her sincere desire to put an end to this question, even at the cost (as she suggested once by the way of comparison) of losing something which up to that time, and thereafter, she considered to be her territory; and that, far from unflinchingly adhering to her own views, she has been ready always to refer the whole matter (not a mere fragment thereof) to the decision of an impartial arbitrator.

In 1890 Venezuela began to send envoys to the other American Republics for the purpose of making them acquainted with the grave events which were then taking place, and which could not fail to excite their interest, particularly the interest of the greatest part of those situated in South America. They are more directly concerned with the possible consequences of the British control of the mouth of the Orinoco, this river being one of the principal arteries of intercommunication in the continent, owing to the system of waterways which cross its whole area. The object was to secure the opinion and enlist the moral support of the sister Republics, and even of holding, if possible, at the proper place, an American Congress in which those Republics should be represented by lawfully constituted delegates, wherein this matter, deemed to be of common interest to all, should be duly considered.

It is but just to say that the plans of Venezuela were everywhere received with the kindest attention, and that some of those nations made an urgent appeal to Great Britain in favor of referring the question to the decision of a friendly power. But their efforts were frustrated by the tenacious refusal by Great Britain to recede from her proposals to Señors Urbaneja, Pulido, and Michelena; in other words, her determination to hold as her own the territory she had so unjustly seized, and to refer to arbitration no other question than that relating to the land situated outside of that territory, and not included in any of her claims prior to 1890.

Spain, who, through her generosity and friendship for , had taken part in the question, and offered her mediation to Great Britain to bring the matter to a settlement, had no better success.

Some years afterward Venezuela requested the interposition of the Pope, so as to secure through him a peaceable, just, and honorable settlement of the grave question of limits between the two countries. His Holiness went as far as to send to London a special envoy, His Excellency Julio Fonti, who had resided at Caracas for some time, as Papal Nuncio. The circumstance that this envoy had lived in Venezuela, and that he had made a special study of the case, rendered him eminently qualified for his mission. But although he displayed in this business the greatest patience and skill, and had frequent conferences with the British Minister of Foreign Affairs, and took many other steps which might have been conducive to success, he had, nevertheless, to undergo the disappointment of seeing his efforts to put an end to such a deplorable situation prove a complete failure.

Since 1876 the Venezuelan Government had persistently endeavored to secure the assistance of the United States of America, in the hope that their efforts, which began at once to be made, would be conducive to the arrangement so much wished for.

It is unnecessary to explain all that the United States have done in this matter, as it appears in full in the several publications already made, which the Arbitral Tribunal will have before it. But perhaps it will not be useless to recommend, earnestly and particularly, to the consideration of this Tribunal what was stated in the printed memorandum of the Venezuelan Department of Foreign Relations, of March 24, 1896, intended to refute the second note of Lord Salisbury, of November 26, 1895, in reply to the despatch of Mr. Olney on the subject of Guayana.

CHAPTER II.

The Essequibo.

In his note of January 31, 1844, Señor Fortique said to Lord Aberdeen that the Essequibo seems to be a river purposely made by nature to serve as a boundary between Venezuela and the British Colony of Demerara, and that a settlement upon this basis would avoid any possible contention on the subject, and insure to Great Britain even the most extreme rights which she may possess as the successor of Holland.

Some years afterwards Dr. José Maria Rojas, Venezuelan Minister, suggested as a compromise, another line, "starting from a point on the coast one mile northwards from the mouth of the Moroco, where a post or landmark should be placed. He said that at that point a parallel of latitude could be drawn westward until it reached the meridian of longitude 60° west of Greenwich, and that thence the line could be continued southward along the said meridian until it reached the southern boundaries of both countries."

This proposition was not accepted, and the Government of Venezuela came back to its original position, namely: The maintenance of the *de jure* frontier, which it had marked in its memorandum of July 15th, 1882, in the following language:

"The boundary of Venezuela begins at the mouth of the Essequibo river; thence it continues along the same river, southward, until reaching the parallel of 4° 12′ north latitude, at middle distance from the mouths of the Sibarona and the Rupumuni rivers; thence it crosses the Essequibo and continues toward the east and the east quarter southeast, over the Tumucuraque mountains, and turning thence towards the southeast until reaching a point situated 2° 11′ south latitude, and 56° 4′ west longitude, where it joins the line of the Aracay mountains in a region inhabited by the Chiñguana Indians."

This is the limit described by Mr. Manuel Montenegro in his geography, published in 1837. It is also the limit marked in the chart of the Republic of Colombia, divided into departments, to be found in the atlas published in Paris by Cadazzi in 1840; a chart which shows two spaces marked with red ink, situated, one between the Moroco, the Barama, the Cuyuni, and the Essequibo rivers, and the other on that portion of the territory which begins at the mouth of the Rupunini river, continues along the line of the boundary above described, and ends at the Aracay mountains. Both spaces marked: "Territory deemed to have been usurped by the British."

It is likewise the boundary given in the map published in 1879 and 1880 by M. Miguel Tejera, which seems to be the same Codazzi map with a number of additions.

It is also the limit given in the map of Bianconi published in Paris in 1888.

It is also the line marked in the map attached to the official publication of the Government of Venezuela, entitled "Anuario Estadístico," as published in 1884, and continued ever since in all the yearly subsequent editions.

It is also the boundary marked in the official map of Venezuela, and attached to the "Official History" of the discussions, published in the United States of America in 1896, a map which exhibits all the other lines suggested by either party.

Excepting only some difference as to the starting point of the line, it is also the boundary marked in the maps of Cruz Caño and Olmedilla, in 1775, of Surville in 1788, and of Don Francisco Requena, a Spanish Engineer and Commissioner for the determination of the boundary, in 1796.

It is more or less the same line that is marked in many other maps presented by Venezuela to the Washington Investigating Commission.

In the argument by the Commission at Caracas, which

was put on file before the Washington Commission, the original title of Spain, not only to Guayana, but, in general, to the whole of America, was abundantly established.

That title was shown to be derived from discovery by Commissioners duly appointed by the Kings of Spain, from bulls of the Popes, from the Treaty of Tordesillas concluded between Spain and Portugal; from the occupation, colonization, and civilization of this continent; from the necessity of applying to the case the principles which prevailed at the time in which those events took place, and at that time the recognized right of the Supreme Pontiff to distribute among the Christian Princes the lands discovered, or to be discovered by them, but inhabited by heathens.

Among the proofs produced to show that the Essequibo river is the *de jure* boundary between Venezuela and British Guiana, the following can be cited:

1st. The instructions given in 1822 by the Governor of Colombia to Señor José Rafael Revenga, when appointed agent to England.

2d. The words written by Señor José Manual Restrepo, Secretary of the Interior of the same Republic in 1827, when he published a History of the Revolution, together with an atlas.

3d. The assertions to be found in the record of the proceedings for the organization of the Province of Guayana, in 1761, under which it became, July 5th, 1762, an individual commandery, put in charge of Col. Don Joaquin Moreno de Mendoza.

4th. The Royal Ordinance of May 5th, 1768, in which it was positively stated that the Province of Guayana bordered on the south by the Amazon river and on the east by the Atlantic ocean.

5th. Article 1 of the Treaty of Extradition between Spain and Holland, concluded in 1791, in which Porto Rico, Coro and Orinoco are described as Spanish possessions, and San Eustaquio, and Curaçao, and Essequibo, Demerary, Berbice, and Surinam as Dutch.

6th. The appointment of a Royal Commission in 1781 to occupy and settle the localities specified in Don José Felipe de Inciarte's report of November 27, 1779, and to build the two small, temporary forts which he deemed necessary—one to protect against any insult attempted *by the Dutch of Essequibo*, the town to be in the neighborhood of the inlet formed by the Moroco, at about a quarter of a mile from the advanced outpost kept by the Dutch, some eighteen leagues from the Essequibo, in the direction of the Orinoco, and the other, provided with four or six guns, on the same inlet of the Moroco, to prevent enemies passing there, and to eject the Dutch from the advanced post which they had built there. It was said, it was well understood, that if the Director-General or Governor of *Essequibo* should complain of such action, the answer to be given would be that it had been taken and would continue to be taken " in obedience to general laws and instructions made and provided for the good government of *our* Indies, *which do not permit such intrusions* on the part of foreigners into the Spanish dominions."

7th. The remarks made by the same Inciarte, that with four or five towns the banks of the Essequibo could be reached, and the Dutch should be deprived thereby of communication, not only with certain Indian tribes on the south of that river, but with any of the inland waterways to the Orinoco, etc.

8th. The opinions of Father Caulin, of Herera, of Father Murillo, of Velarde Alcedo, Governor Digujo of Cumaná, Governor and Commandant General Centurion of Guayana, Governor Marmion, Governor Gil, Engineer and Boundary Commissioner Reguejo, etc.

9th. The work published by Messrs. James Rodway and Thomas Watt, entitled "Annals of Guiana, Chronological History of the Discovery and Colonization of Guiana," wherein it is stated that the Essequibo River, so named after Don Juan Essequivel, an officer in the service of Diego Colón, was discovered by Ojeda, in 1499; that the country watered by it was overrun by the people of Margarita; that a party of these people penetrated into the interior of the country as far as the river itself; that the Spaniards attempted to found there a town; that they made frequent incursions in the territory between the Orinoco and the Essequibo; that in 1596, in union with the Arnacas, they destroyed the establishments of the Dutch on the latter river, and that in the same year, 1596, Berrio heard that three hundred Spaniards were in Essequibo.

10th. The letter written by the Duke of Lerma to the President of the Council of the Indies, dated February 2, 1615, wherein he informed the Council that the Dutchman William Uselinex was fitting vessels to establish colonies on the banks of three or four rivers of America or the West India, one in Wiapa, another in Cayena, and another in Surinam, where he said positively that there were some settlers, from twelve to fifteen Spaniards, engaged in the cultivation of the soil and the raising of the cassave root, of which they make bread for the Governor of Trinidad and Orinoco, Don Fernando de Berrio.

11th. The statement of Mr. James Rodway, in his "History of Guiana," Vol. I, Introduction, supported by Netscher, to the effect that the Kykoveral fort was built upon a structure said to have been erected by the Spaniards in 1591.

12th. The opinions and writings of Señor Alejo Fortique, of Ministers Dr. Eduardo Calcaño, and Diego Bautista Urbaneja, and of Señores Santos Michelena, Francisco Aranda, General José Felix Blanco, Doctor Diego Bautista Urbaneja, Sr. General Rafael Urdaneta, Doctor Mariano Talavera, the Bishop of Tricalca, Tomás José Sanavria, and Juan Manuel Manrique, members of the Council of Government.

13th. The studies of General José Felix Blanco, Doctor Francisco Xavier Yanes, Señor Rafael Maria Baralt, and Doctor Francisco J. Marmol, three of which (namely, the first, the second, and the fourth) were published in the book of Señor R. F. Seijas on the "British Limits of Guiana."

14th. The opinions of newspapers of different times and countries, and of many foreign geographers, as inserted in the book above named and in some others.

15th. Some other works and maps of different origin, a list embracing fourteen of the latter, some of them British, was then made and given to the public.

16th. A document from the General Archives of Simancas, being an opinion of the Spanish Council of State, explaining to His Majesty the advisability of looking into the movements of the Dutch in making establishments windward of the Orinoco river, at 5° north latitude, and scarcely 225° of longitude, according to Delisle, under shelter of the Cayena Island, and at 6° north latitude, and 220° 40′ of longitude, where they had built two forts between the Surinam and the Compenan rivers—acts manifesting an intention which could not be other than to come near the mouth and the banks of said river, and establish thereon some plantations to facilitate their trade with the New Kingdom of Granada, so as to allow ingress from that side into the interior of the country and take possession of such places as their interests might suggest, and to make them masters of the mouth of the river and of the nations who inhabited that region. The opinion ends by saying that, it being necessary for the defence of the New Kingdom to retain possession of the mouth of that river, it was not less imperative for Spain to prevent the Dutch from coming near its banks, whether by sea or land; that upon consideration of Articles 5 and 6 of the Treaty of Peace of 1648, between Spain and Holland, and of the fact *that the mouth of the Essequibo afforded favorable opportunities for the purpose aforesaid, because the situation of the river permitted a body of land to be formed capable of being converted into a province, under its own special government, separate from the Government of Cumana, having within its limits many nations to be reduced, which might be used as an efficient obstacle to prevent the Dutch from coming to the west; the council was of the opinion that it was advisable to occupy the mouth of the river with a fort, and to found there, under shelter of that fort, a city, which in time should become the capital of that region.*

This opinion was given by the Council when consulted on the dispute then going on between Spain and Portugal. It is dated August 7th, 1743.

Other proofs can be now added in corroboration of the claim of Venezuela. The first one will be what Prof. George Lincoln Burr reported to the Washington Investigating Commission in regard to the historical maps. In page 201, Vol. 3d, he says:

"To begin with those farthest to the east, our knowledge of the existence of that 'IN QUERIBURA, UP IN MAZARUNI,' of that 'AT MAWAKKEN, UP SIPARUNI,' and of that 'IN WENAMU, A BRANCH OF CUYUNI,' rests on a somewhat hysterical letter of a Dutch postholder in Arinda to the Essequibo Governor in 1756. Had this worthy spoken merely of the presence of missionaries at these points, one might have believed them engaged in mere *entradas*, for the purpose of recruiting Indians for the missions. But he speaks of the Spaniards as here strongly fortified; and the fact that Governor Storm van's Gravesande himself was inclined to lend credence to the report, makes it impossible for me to treat it lightly. As to that in Mazaruni, there is, moreover, the concurrent testimony of the Colonist Couvreur. (See Extracts, p. 196, Vol. II.) It is on the basis of the latter's testimony that the strangers were only two or three days' journey (which the Governor interprets 'by ten to twelve Dutch hours') up the river, that I have connected Queribura with Curabiri, the name of the fall of the Mazaruni, at its junction with the Puruni. Of all recorded names of localities on the Mazaruni, it is this whose name most closely resembles Queribura; though, but for Couvreur's testimony, the mouth of the Carubung, much higher up, where a recruiting party of Spanish priests made a sojourn early in the present century (authorities cited), might be a serious competitor for the conjectural location. Either name might easily sound like Queribura to an imperfectly trained ear. As to the mission 'at Mawakken' there is no such clew. I can find in the region of the Siparuni no Indian name resembling this, and have, therefore, conjecturally placed the mission at a point high up toward the source of that river, which seemed to me to fall on the natural route of the Spaniards on their way to the savannas of the Rupumuni—an objective point which they are known to have had in view."

Now, if the Mawakken Mission was on the Siparuni, which is one of the affluents of the Essequibo on the left bank, and on the road which the Spaniards used to go to the prairies of the Rupununi, it is clear that the territory west of the Essequibo belonged to them. It is precisely at the point of its junction with the Rupununi, where the boundary running from north to south ends, turning at that point towards the east, and passing to the south of Surinam and French Guiana.

The missions were thus left within the territory assigned to them under the agreement between the missionaries of the Orinoco, signed March 20th, 1734, and confirmed by Royal letters of September 16th, 1736. In that agreement the Rev. Observant Fathers were given, in order that they should found as many towns as they could, the territories extending *from Angostura del Orinoco, upwards the stream, to the banks of the lower* part of the *Cuchivero river, drawing a straight line from the banks of the Orinoco up to the Marañon or Amazonas, while the Reverend Capuchin Fathers were to have the territory and district extending from Angostura down the river* to the great *mouth* of the *Orinoco*, and the Reverend Jesuit Fathers, that other portion lying *between the banks* of the *upper part* of the *Cuchivero river* and *forming the balance of the Orinoco* region ; *all these lines and demarcations always running upward* and in *straight line from* the *Orinoco* to the *Marañon* or *Amazonas river*.

This is another proof of the fact that the province of Guayana bordered on the Amazonas, and that out of that intervening territory situated between that river and the Orinoco, only that portion which was left to the east of the Essequibo ceased to belong to that province by virtue of the Treaty of Munster of 1648.

Mention must be made here, furthermore (as it tends to the same purpose), of the map, or draft of map of the missions of the Capuchins in Guayana, made about 1779, by Fray Carlos de Barcelona, a copy of which has been obtained from the congregation *De Propaganda Fide* of of the Capuchins at Rome.

In that map the lands situated east of the Essequibo are marked as "Lands of the Colonies of the Dutch," while those situated southwest of the foregoing are designated as "Lands belonging to the conquest of the Reverend Catalonian Capuchin Fathers of Guayana, form the Orinoco to the equinoctial line."

North of the lands last mentioned there is another lettering, which reads : "Deserted lands." And on the West, after a line of points, the words appear written, "Land belonging to the conquest of the Reverend Observant Fathers," so that the map represents the whole tract adjudicated to the Capuchins and a portion of the tract alloted to the Observants. Doubtless the word "conquest" in connection with the work of the two religious communities is intended to signify the entering by them in those territories to recruit Indians and form them into missions.

Another map of 1771, made by the same Father, besides locating the missions, explains the distances separating one from another, according to the general opinion of those who had travelled them, and mentions the missions which had been left either deserted or with little population, because of their being abandoned by the Indians, who had gone back to the forests. It also gives the names of the Presidents of each mission, and of the Indian nations which furnished their population.

A third map, bearing the title of "Province of Catalonian Capuchins, at Guayana," gives the names and places of thirty-three missions, some of them in the immediate neighborhood of the Caroni river and near its mouth, some others on the Yuruan river, and the rest on the banks of the Paraoa and some of its affluents.

In the first of the above-mentioned maps, namely, that of 1779, its author explains that his information had been derived from the Right Reverend Father Prefect, Benito de la Garriga, from the Indians themselves, and from new expeditionists of Centurion, and others.

In the report on the Chartographic testimony of Geographers, prepared by the secretary of the investigating commission, at Washington, reference is made to the Cruz Caño line and to the possible grounds on which the determination therein made of the Dutch rights might have been based. The report suggests that this was possibly due, either to considering those settlements as anterior to 1648, and therefore confirmed by the Treaty of Munster; to deeming them subsequent to that date, but confirmed by prescription or adverse possession for a long period of time, or to looking at them as merely *de facto* establishments, created and maintained without authority.

In the latter case, the line drawn indicates an implied recognition of the fact and nothing else. Be it as it may, the Secretary deems it very probable that the author of the map, being a Spaniard, should believe Spain to have been the original discoverer of Guayana, and the Dutch as intruders, who had not been able to acquire rights there without abridging the paramount and pre-existent title of Spain.

He then says that Cruz Caño followed a number of

map makers—namely, Bonne, Russell, Reid, Poirson, Myers, and others—all of whom denied to the Dutch any right on the west of the Essequibo, many of them going as far as to place under Spanish jurisdiction the region to the east of that river. He has no doubt that those boundaries were drawn to mark political divisions, but he thinks that the discussion of their respective merits would exceed the limits and scope of his report.

In the Cruz Caño map, a copy of which is No. 50 in the collection of the American Commission, in the map made by Surville, No. 71 of the same, and in the Requena map, which is not found in that collection, the boundary begins at Cape Nassau, and for this reason the said maps were included in the list attached to the Venezuelan argument, indicative of those which exhibit that boundary. The maps of Cruz Caño and Almedilla make the line start from the mouth of the "Moruga River," which is a very short distance from the Pomarón, and which is not the Moroco marked on the map more towards the north. So it seems to be beyond doubt that none of these three maps gives the Moroco River to the Dutch.

In the "History of the Colonies of the Essequibo, Demerara, and Bérbice, from the establishment there of the Dutch to our own times," by P. M. Netscher, published in 1888, it is said, with reference to the boundary question between Venezuela and British Guiana, that the Spaniards used to fix in their time the western limit on the coast side of the Spanish Guayana at the Moruca, and sometimes also at the Pomarón, and on some occasions even at the Essequibo river; and that the Republic of Venezuela, if the author was well informed, has continued these traditions in the discussion of her claims.

In 1750 Spain and Portugal concluded a treaty by which the limits between their respective possessions in South America were determined, but the actual demarcation of the boundary, as agreed, could not be carried into effect owing to many differences of opinion between the Commissioners appointed by each party to make the survey. Matters went so far in 1761 as to practically nullify the arrangement; but on October 1, 1771, a new treaty was concluded at San Ildefonso, by which it was agreed that from the very moment in which the point of the line on the Rio Negro and on the others which flow into it should be located, it would not be permissible for the Spaniards to enter the Portuguese establishments and ways of communication, or to navigate any streams running through places beyond the western mouth of the Tapura; nor would it be lawful for the Portuguese to navigate the said Rio Negro and the others flowing into it, following an upward direction, for the purpose of entering the Spanish possessions and ways of communication, or to extend themselves toward the Orinoco, or to provinces, whether populated or unpopulated, belonging to Spain under the provisions of the same Treaty. It was further provided that the surveyors to be appointed for the actual location of the boundary should look for the lakes and rivers joining the Tapura and the Negro, which should be found to run northward, or more northward than others, and fix there the point which was to be the limit for use and navigation on the part of each nation. As to the line to be continued, after leaving the rivers, through the mountains between the Orinoco and the Marañon, they should also draw it as much as possible toward the north without paying attention to the fact that either nation might thus be given a little more or a little less of the territory really belonging to it, provided that the purposes of the treaty, in clearly defining the limits of each monarchy, should be accomplished thereby.

Under this demarcation, a part of the Amazonas and the whole territory, whether settled or unsettled, to the north of the mountains between the Orinoco and the Amazonas, belonged to Spain.

Article 25 of the Treaty of 1750, above referred to, provided that Spain and Portugal guaranteed each to the other, respectively, the title to the whole territory of their dominions in South America, together with the islands adjacent thereto, as defined and separated by the boundaries agreed upon. The two nations bound themselves to come to the assistance of each other whenever their rights on this subject might be attacked or invaded by third parties; this assistance to continue until the lawful sovereign of the territory encroached upon should recover full possession of it. The territory which Portugal had thus to defend extended on the side of the seacoast and the territories in the neighborhood, *as far as the banks of the Orinoco, on both sides,* and from Castillas to the Straights of Magellan. And the territory which Spain, in her turn, was bound to defend extended as far as the banks of the Amazonas (Marañon) river, on both sides, and from Castillas to the port of Santos. As to the interior of South America, the obligation was undefined; but in all cases of invasion or uprising, each Crown was to assist the other until securing the restoration of peace.

These guarantees were renewed by Article III of the Treaty, concluded between the same nations at the Royal site of El Pardo, on the 11th of March, 1778.

The title of Spain to the two banks of the Orinoco and the neighborhood thereof was therefore fully recognized and established.

Naturally, all these acts were well known by the Dutch Government, especially after the arrival of the Commissioners, who came with a considerable retinue of subalterns and troops to make the survey. Not a word of protest was ever raised against the determination of these limits and guarantees.

A silence not less signficant was kept by Great Britain when the treaty of limits between Venezuela and Portugal, concluded May 5, 1859, was promulgated, although in fixing there the frontier between the two countries, it was stipulated that the dividing line would, after leaving the island of San José, run along the top of Sierra Parima as far as the place where this chain of mountains meets the Sierra de Pacaraima and forms an angle with it, so as to cause all the waters running into the Rio Blanco to belong to Brazil, and all those going to the Orinoco to belong to Venezuela; thence the line to be continued along the highest points of Sierra Pacaraima, so as to cause the waters going to the Rio Blanco to belong to Brazil, and those going to *the Essequibo, the Cuyuni, and the Caroni rivers* to belong to Venezuela, until finally reaching the limit of the territories of the two nations on their eastern part.

It appears from this delineation that the territories watered by the streams which run into the Essequibo, the Cuyuni, and the Caroni rivers form part of the jurisdiction of Venezuela.

The following abstract from the work published in Stuttgardt, in 1857, by Mr. Carl Klunsinger, under the title of "Part taken by the Germans in the discovery of South America," it being the first paragraph of the first section of the work, should be quoted in this connection. It reads as follows:

"One year after the discovery by Christopher Columbus of the coast of Cumaná, and therefore of what was called Tierra Firme, or, in other words, the mainland of South America, the Spaniard Alonso de Ojeda, accompanied by the learned navigator, Juan de la Cosa, and by Amerigo Vespucci, discovered the whole coast of Venezuela this side of the meridian of Maracaibo lake, *from the Essequibo river* to Cape Vela. This voyage took from May 20, 1499, to some time in June, 1500. The above-named Juan de la Cosa and Rodrigo de Bastidas continued their voyages of discovery in a westward direction as far as the port of Retrete."

This question of the limits between Venezuela and British Guiana was skillfully discussed by General José Felix Blanco, an illustrious veteran of the War of Independence, in the papers published by him in May, 1844, in three issues of the journal called "El Venezolano." After a brief explanation of the discovery and the explorations made by Vicente Yañez Pinzon, Alonso Ojeda, Diego de Ordáz, as well as the expeditions of Sir Walter Raleigh and Captain Keymis, the writer made abundant use of historical quotations, which are undoubtedly of great weight for the purposes of the present discussion. A portion of those papers was republished in 1888 in a book entitled "Limites de Guayana."

One of the quotations aforesaid is from Monsieur de la Condamine, in the following words: "Dutch Guiana begins at the River Marowine, *and ends at the Essequibo. All the country between the Essequibo, where the Dutch Colony ends, and the Orinoco, has been left to Spanish Guiana.*"

Another is from Father Caulin, in his *Historia Corografica de Nueva Andalucia,* stating positively that "the Dutch, in violation of the provisions of Articles V and VI of the Treaty of Munster, *possessed themselves of the Essequibo river,* established their colonies and settlements, founded cities or towns, as well as large estates or plantations, and engaged a good deal in unlawful trade, remaining there until they were expelled; but they came back some time afterwards and extended their encroachments upon the Spanish territory as far as the Pomarón river, on the banks of which they founded New Middelburg."

A further quotation from the Philosophical History of the two Indies, vol. VI, book 12, No. 25, page 282, of the Paris edition of 1820, reads as follows:

"The Colony of Essequibo, situated in the near proximity of the river of this name, is twenty leagues distant from Berbice. The Dutch, who, as many other Europeans overran Guiana in the latter part of the sixteenth century in search of gold, first settled there. The time of their arrival at the Essequibo is not known, *but it is a proven fact that the Spaniards ejected them from there in*

1595. They came back afterwards to the same place, but they were ejected anew by the English in 1666. This establishment was one of scarce importance, and in 1740, after its having been recovered, scarcely yielded what was necessary to make the cargo of a ship. Two or three years afterwards some colonists of Essequibo turned their eyes towards the neighboring lands of Demarara, which were more fertile, and this movement brought about very favorable consequences. Some time afterwards all work at Surinam was suspended on account of the bloody and devastating war which had to be waged against the negroes who had taken refuge in the forests. Berbice was at that time agitated by an uprising of its slaves. Such was the origin of the three colonies which the Dutch established one after another at Guiana."

Another quotation from the Geographical Dictionary, prepared in accordance with the universal geography of Malte-Brun, reads as follows:

"Guiana borders on the north and the northwest upon the Orinoco; on the west, upon New Granada; on the south, upon the River of the Amazonas, and on the east, upon the ocean. The Spanish Guiana is bounded on the south by the Portuguese Guiana; on the east by the ocean, and on the north and the west by the Orinoco. The limits of the Dutch Guiana are: *On the north, the Essequibo;* on the east, the ocean; on the south, the Maroni, and on the west, the Spanish Guiana."

A further passage taken from the "Derrotero" of the coast of Guiana and Island of Trinidad, compiled upon the most recent observations and the best authorities, by J. William Norie, hydrographer, and the author of a new and complete "Epitome" of navigation, printed in London in 1828, reads as follows:

"The land which stretches towards the northwest, along the coast of South America, from the mouth of the Amazonas to the mouth of the Orinoco, is generally called Guayana, Guyana or Guayne. This large territory is divided into separate districts, occupied by the Portuguese, the French, the Dutch the English and the Colombians, from whose respective Governments they depend politically. *British Guiana extends itself from the Corentin river towards the northwest, up to reaching the Essequibo.* This territory formerly belonged to the Dutch, but it was ceded by the Netherlands to Great Britain by the Treaty of 1814. That was the real area of the Colony as arranged between Spaniards and Dutch by the Treaty of Munster of 1648, which was never abrogated; but as some British and Dutch colonists planted establishments north of the said limits, on the banks of the Pomarón, on Cape Nassua and even beyond the latter place, the boundary now claimed by the British is found as far as the meridian of Cape Barima, *although in reality that region constitutes a part of what must be called Spanish or Colombian Guayana.*"

General Blanco quoted also from a Spanish royal order issued in consequence of the report made by Don José Felipe de Inciarte, who some time afterwards became Governor of the Province of Guayana, the passages to which reference has been made already.

The "Geographical and Historical Dictionary of the West Indies or America," by Colonel Don Antonio Alcedo, says, *in verbo* ESEQUIVO, that such is the name of a large river in the Province and Government of Guayana, having its source, according to the discoveries and surveys made in 1745 on the great Parima lake, and receiving in its course the waters of many great rivers, among which the Mazaruni and the Cuyuni are the most notable—both affluent, joining it at a point about ten leagues before it reaches the sea, into which it empties through five large mouths, of depth enough to admit minor ships, but not sufficient for large vessels. On two islands on this river the Dutch have planted establishments, consisting of some houses for negroes and Indians, and these settlements are part of the Dutch Colony which stands on the banks and stretches itself for more than thirty leagues, this area being occupied by large plantations for the cultivation of the sugar cane and the manufacture of sugar. Sugar and rum are the staple productions of the Colony, and as each colonist lives in his own plantation, and the plantations are separated from each other, sometimes by a distance of two or three leagues, there is no town or center of population in the whole territory, except on an island towards the east, where about a dozen houses have been erected in addition to the buildings occupied by the Governor of the Colony, the Commander of the troops, the surgeon, the secretary in charge of the interests of the Company of commerce, two inns or lodging houses, two stores, one church, and the negro quarters. On the highest point of that island, near the Governor's house, a fort was built which is called Zeeland Fort, and is in communication with a battery of twelve cannon of twenty-four caliber, which commands the waters of the stream at that place.

In Verbo Guayana, Alcedo's Dictionary says that such is the name of "a great province of the Government of Cumaná, forming a part of New Andalucia, and being one of the largest in America, as it embraces the whole country lying between the Orinoco on the nórth and the Marañon on the south. It is bounded on the east by the seacoast, where the Dutch have several colonies, and where the French, more to the east, have Cayena; on the north, by the banks of the Orinoco, which divide it from the Provinces of Cumaná, Barcelona, Caracas, Barinas, Santa Fé, and Popayan, and turns to the east, as if looking again for its source, on the Parima lake, and describing a kind of semi-circle; on the south, by the dominions of the King of Portugal in Brazil, the dividing line on this side being not known." After explaining the geography of the province and enumerating the best known Indian nations to be found on its territory, Alcedo says that the Jesuits Ignacio Llauri and Julian de Vergara went there, in 1596, as missionaries for the conversion of those Indians; that three years afterwards they had to go away because of the invasion by Captain Janson, and that in 1687 the Catalonian Capuccin Fathers, who had been successful to the extreme of founding twenty-eight towns, whose names are given in the dictionary, in addition to those of Guirior and Barceloneta de Españoles, went there to do their work. Alcedo gives the names of all the Governors of Guayana and Cumaná from Don Diego Fernandez de Serpa, who was sent, in 1568, with men, arms, and provisions, as Governor of whatever territory he might be able to conquer, to Don Miguel Marmión, who was appointed in 1786, the year before the publication of the dictionary, and summarily describes the principal events which took place during the time of their respective administrations, and how long each one of them remained in office."

In recapitulating the conclusions of his report to the Washington Investigating Commission, on the Spanish and Dutch establishment previous to 1648, Mr. J. Franklin Jameson says: "The results of the investigation can be shortly summarized as follows: I have found no evidence whatever of any Dutch occupation in 1648, to the north or to the west of Essequibo and Kykoveral, unless it may be deemed advisable to place confidence on the translation of Document No. 12 and enclosure, printed on page 56 of the British Blue Book. I have not found any evidence of occupation of Punta Barima previous to 1648."

This Mr. Jameson is referred to in the report of the Commission as a professor of history in Brown University. Mr. George L. Burr is also professor of the same branch of knowledge in Cornell University. And both Mr. Jameson and Mr. Burr are acknowledged to be authorities on historical matters.

On the other hand, the same Mr. Burr, upon inquiring into the meaning of articles V and VI of the Treaty of Munster, reached the following conclusions:

"1st. It is improbable that, in the intent of its framers and its ratifiers, the Treaty of Munster conceded to the

the Dutch a right to win from the natives any land claimed by Spain.

"2d. It does not appear that it was ever interpreted in this sense by either Spain or the Dutch."

This being so, and the Dutch having held nothing in 1648 except Kykoveral and Essequibo, that, and nothing else, was confirmed by that Treaty, which gave the Dutch no authority to extend the limits of their possessions farther. They could win or conquer new places on the Brazilian side; but even this power given them was conditioned upon the fact that the conquest should not be in violation of the Treaty.

This is therefore a further proof of the fact that the Dutch ought not to have gone beyond the posts occupied by them in 1648, and of the incorrectness of the British Blue Book No. 1, when it states that previous to the Treaty of Munster the Dutch establishments extended, with the knowledge of the Spanish Government, the area of their occupation on the coast side up to the neighborhood of Barima and the Amacuro rivers, and also when it says that the Treaty, besides confirming the title of the Dutch to all the possessions thus far acquired by them in South America, gave them liberty to make new acquisitions wherever the Spaniards were not already established.

In the British Blue Book, herein specially referred to, not less than in many others of the same description, the inconsistency is clearly incurred of denying to Spain any right in Guayana, except in so far as Santo Tomé was concerned, this being the only possession acknowledged to be theirs, and of alleging, nevertheless, that she granted the Dutch the right to make new acquisitions on territories not already occupied by her.

In fact, if it be true, as claimed, that occupation constitutes the only source of the right of ownership, and that Spain occupied only the place above named, the conclusion can not be escaped that she was granting what did not belong to her, and that such a concession was absolutely unnecessary, because land which has no owner is subject to occupation by the first who comes and takes possession of it with the purpose and intent of making it his own property.

The same must be said in regard to the acceptance by Holland of the establishments which she had planted up to 1648, because to ask from Spain the concession thereof, and to receive them from her hands was tantamount to recognizing in her the rights and powers of lawful ownership. If Spain in 1648 occupied only the city of Santo Tomé de Guayana, and her rights did not go beyond that city, the Dutch were not in need of any concession from Spain to consider themselves owners of whatever they had taken in the province, provided it was not situated within the limits of the special place over which the Spanish jurisdiction was exercised. The fact, nevertheless, is singular in the extreme, that while Spain was the nation which made the discovery, and the right of the Dutch to share in the ownership of the territories so discovered had come to them from her and through her as members, as they were at the time of the Spanish Empire, they have, nevertheless, sometimes pretended to possess in their own right the powers and advantages which belong only to Spain.

Among the "Extracts from Dutch documents," collected by Mr. Burr, there is one marked No. 172, taken from the minutes of a meeting held in 1750 by the West India Company (Chamber of Zeeland), to which a report personally submitted by Commandeur Storm van 's Gravesande, on June 22, 1750, had been ordered to be attached. It appears from a foot note of this report that it had been referred for opinion and advice to a committee of the Chamber, and that the report of this committee was approved and accepted.

The extract herein referred to reads as follows:

"That, furthermore, they the members of the Committee, were of opinion, that the Company's shop there should again be started, especially if some new colonists were to be sent thither, because not only would it in that case be extremely necessary for supplying the needs of those colonists, but also in view of the increasing Spanish trade, it was not unlikely that a reasonable profit might be made by it; especially so, if it could be brought about that the Spaniards no longer, as heretofore has usually happened, tarry with their wares and articles of trade among the private settlers living up the river, but come with them farther down and as far as to the fort. To attain this end, a resolution might be passed that no one whosoever be allowed to come into the river, much less make a stay there, unless he beforehand address himself in person to the Commandeur there, to ask from him a permit to stay in the Colony for a stipulated period, and at the same time all inhabitants be also forbidden without the aforesaid permit or consent of the Commandeur to lodge or shelter for more than one night any strangers, on penalty of a certain fine to be imposed for violation of either rule."

Mr. Burr finds this passage embarrassing, as it seems, on the one hand, to imply that Spanish traders used to come from the upper Essequibo, while on the other, it is possible that it merely refers to a trade made by way of the Cuyuni, and he refers to the fact, stated by him elsewhere in his work, that in the early part of the eighteenth century the Dutch used to trade in horses by the way of the Cuyuni, and that many have been led by that fact into the belief that that trade was with the Spaniards.

This fact harmonizes perfectly with the existence of the Spanish Mission of Mawakken on the Siparuni river, which is an affluent of the Essequibo. Mr. Burr speaks of this Mission, which he locates near the Siparuni, considering that it must have been situated on the road naturally followed by the Spaniards when going to the prairies of the Rupunini, which were for them an objective point.

Perhaps the difficulty depends only upon the fact, perfectly well known by all, that the Dutch settlements were planted exclusively on those parts of the banks of the rivers which were near the seacoast, while the upper part of the same rivers continued to be Spanish, it resulting therefrom that the ownership of the stream was divided between the two nations.

Be it as it may, the extract alluded to proves that the trade on the Essequibo or its affluents was not exclusively carried on by the Dutch, but was shared by the Spaniards.

In a letter from Director Gravesande to the West India Company, dated July 31, the following appears:

"Three excellent slaves of John Liot, carpenters, have run away to Orinoco; he has been in pursuit, but was compelled to return, the Spaniards (so he says) having followed to beyond Pomeroon. The man whom Vulskow had sent in pursuit of his slaves, and who, as I had the honor to inform you in my preceding letter, had been seized and put in chains by the Spaniards, has come back.

"He told me that he had been treated very badly as soon as he arrived in Orinoco; that the Governor had sold the slaves, and, as he sustained, had put the money in his pocket, and in order that this [might not become known] had sent him to Martinique, from where Mr. Bedu, who had land in Demerara, had brought him along to here, without any charge, which is really very courteous. That Governor bragged considerably to this man, and said that the land belonged to His Catholic Majesty as far as to the bank of the Oene, and that he would come and seize those plantations which lay on Spanish territory. The bank of Oene lies along the western coast of this river and there are several plantations below it. It therefore is very well that the militia-captain Tierens has been so prompt in executing the regulations, the inspection of that company having been completed and the roll thereof already handed in; it consists of nineteen men." [Extracts from Dutch Archives, pages 467 and 468.]

On page 495 of the same volume the following letter of Mr. Buisson, a counsellor at Essequibo, to the Director-

General of the same Colony, dated December 3, 1769, can be found:

"I can not fail to inform Your Excellency that Pedro Sanchez has come from Orinoco with the bad news that within a month or six weeks two boats with about 50 or 60 men will come here to kidnap the Indians as far as in Pomarón and then, I fear, plantations will surely be plundered, *for this Governor fixes his boundary on the bank of the Oene,* where James Fenning lives. I do not doubt that many slaves, black and red, will go over to them. And then who will make them come back here?"

Professor Burr, in his article, "Dutch Claims in Guiana," to be found in volume I, pages from 364 to 366, says that,

"Unfortunately for the importance of these claims of the Chamber of Zeeland, that Chamber then, and even before the date of its memoir of 1751, had lost the right to speak, as a whole, in so far as Guiana was concerned, in behalf of the West India Company. The quarrels and dissensions among the members of the Chamber, in regard to Zeeland's monopolizing the official inspection of the Essequibo, a struggle which had been growing up for a long time, had turned to be, in 1750, an open contest; and as the question had been submitted for decision to the States-General, the members of the Chamber who held views antagonistic to Zeeland's pretensions, had washed their hands of everything concerning the Colony, and gone so far as to refuse this subject to be taken up, as a proper matter for discussion, at the meetings of the board of Ten. Furthermore, the contra-memorials sent to the States-General by the Chamber of Amsterdam controverted the assertions of the Zeelanders, *without excepting what they had said about the limits of the Colony. They went as far as to deny that 'the Colony of Essequibo, and river pertaining thereto,' should be entitled to anything in addition to the Essequibo river and its tributaries, not failing to indicate that several statements made by the Chamber of Zeeland were conflicting with each other, in so far as the determination of the limits was concerned.* However untenable the position of the Chamber of Amsterdam may be historically, it certainly has to contribute largely, especially in view of the fact that the decision of the case was in favor of the official inspection by the Colony itself, to neutralize the effect of the assertions of Zeeland in regard to the claims of the West India Company."

The fact must be added that, as it appears from the Spanish Document, published in the British Blue Book, No. 1, pages 68 and 69, Marquis de Torre Nueva advised the Government of Her Catholic Majesty to occupy with a fort the mouth of the Essequibo, so as to prevent the Orinoco from being approached by the Dutch, as they otherwise could do very easily. He founded his advice upon the additional ground that the Essequibo river watered a large tract of land, where a separate province, with a government of itself, independent from that of Cumaná, could be established, the said province containing within its limits numberless Indian tribes to be reduced to Christian civilization, which could be used also as a barrier to prevent the Dutch from passing to the west of the Essequibo river.

CHAPTER III.

THE POMARÓN RIVER.

What was said in the Venezuelan argument of 1896, in relation to the Pomarón river, can now be supplemented by some facts, stated in the report of Mr. Burr, about the settlements of the Dutch on its banks.

The first Dutch Colony thereon established began its existence in 1658; but in 1665–66, when it was still in its infancy, the British came and destroyed it. In 1686, after having been abandoned for twenty years, the Colony was reinstated; but the French came soon after and caused it to be abandoned a second time. Subsequently to that date no further attempt was made to colonize that region until the very last days of the Dutch occupation. The abandoned settlement was left all the time in the possession of the Essequibo Colony, under the custody of a post-holder, and allowed to be crossed and recrossed in search of dyewoods, as well as timber and straw.

During the British invasion, the forts which had been built on the right bank of this river, and had been given the names of New Zeeland and New Middleburg, were demolished, never to be raised again.

Rodway, in his History of British Guiana (Vol. III, page 279) makes a significant admission relative to this point. He says, in effect, that prior to the year 1882 the English Government appears to have made no claim to the Pomarón; that it had no representative there, although the Dutch had maintained a "post" there or on the Moroco from a remote period; that in 1882, however, when Mr. E. F. im Thurn was appointed magistrate for the western district, steps were taken to gradually recover the lost territory, which had already come to be looked upon as *terra nullius*, and which, unfortunately for the present claim, gave color to the idea that Great Britain was in doubt as to her rights there.

The rule must be applied here, which is derived from Mr. Burr's opinion, in regard to the construction to be placed upon articles 5th and 6th of the Treaty of Munster, namely, that it is improbable that those who signed that treaty and those who ratified it would have ever had the intention of granting to the Dutch the right to acquire from the natives any lands claimed by Spain, there being nothing to show that such a construction was ever placed on that compact by either Spain or the Dutch. On the other hand, as the report of Mr. J. Franklin Jameson leaves it absolutely beyond doubt that in 1648 the Dutch occupation did not extend, on the north and on the west, beyond the Essequibo and the Kykoveral, the conclusion is to be drawn, without any effort whatever, that the Dutch ought not to have trespassed upon these limits and gone to the Pomarón river, or to any other point north or west of the territory occupied by them.

The Pomarón river is situated almost exactly on the north of the Essequibo, and falls, therefore, under this rule.

This reasoning must be applied also to all the lands situated beyond the limits of the actual possessions of the Dutch in 1648, and in order to avoid repetitions the argument is here made once for all.

The colony which the Dutch, unduly trespassing the limits of their territory, established on the Pomarón was constantly threatened by Spanish invasions. Mr. Burr refers to the fact that, in 1769, the Spanish Governor of Orinoco declared that the Spanish territory reached as far as the right bank of the Oene, on the mouth of the Essequibo. Mr. Burr further says, that in subsequent years, and notwithstanding the fact that Spain and Holland were at peace, more than one Spanish incursion was made there, as for instance, those of 1769, 1775, 1786, and 1794. He also says that, although some harm was done on the side of the seashore, and some Indians were taken from the interior of the country, no real attempt to take possession of the river was ever made; that, as it seems, the Dutch knew nothing of the instructions given by the Intendant-General of Venezuela, in February, 1789, for the occupation and settlement of Guayana up to the boundary of the Dutch Colony on the Essequibo, but were, nevertheless, acquainted with the survey made the latter part of the year 1779 by the Spanish official, Señor Inciarte, who not only inspected carefully the Pomarón river and all the streams on the west, but went as far as to select a site for the construction of a fort on the banks of the Pomarón; that the post-holder on the Moroco reported the arrival of the Spaniards at that place, and that the Indians had heard them say that within three months they would come back to build there a fort; that the Director-General, having ascertained that all the Spaniards had left without doing harm, either to the post or to the Indians, did not feel any uneasiness on account of that visit, nor did he take any steps either to protest against it or to continue his investigations in that respect; and that the latest incursion known, namely, that of 1794, was repelled by the Indians, who were then under the command of a Dutch colonist.

Be it as it may, the fact is that these reiterated threats of the Spaniards against the Pomarón Colony, as well as invasions of them, and the orders given Don Felipe de Inciarte, with the approval of the Spanish Crown, prove beyond doubt that Spain considered at all times these encroachments by the Dutch, both on the side of the coast and on the interior of the country, as usurpations of her sovereignty.

That the Dutch themselves did not feel aggrieved by such action on the part of Spain is fully demonstrated by the fact that they kept silent, without ever making a complaint or uttering a single word in protest against the multiplied incursions, which have been referred to. So that the consent by Spain can never be alleged to justify the enlargement of the Dutch Colonies.

The fact is well known that several geographers and historians have located the boundary either on the mouth of this river or at Cape Nassau, on the right side of that mouth. But by doing so these geographers and historians have only meant to represent the condition of things *de facto* existing at the time of the publication of their work.

The Venezuelan argument of 1896 contains an enumeration of official documents of British Guiana, by which it is shown that the Colony never exercised authority this side of the Pomarón river. This fact is proven by the various measures which were taken for the reward of captors of runaway slaves; by orders given in relation to the payment of judicial fees; by the list of the farms or estates situated on the western coast; by the law then enacted regarding the militia; by some provisions made in regard to journeys and to services rendered in the Colony; by a statement of the ecclesiastical establishments in British Guiana, arranged by parishes; by a recapitulation of the census of 1841; by a report on the state of the Colony made by a committee, appointed for that purpose, in 1850; by a census of the Essequibo county in 1881, and by the census of the province of Essequibo in 1891.

Many other proofs might be given to the same effect.

Mr. Burr, after refuting successfully all assertions to the contrary, has proved that the earliest occupation on the Pomarón river by the Dutch, as far as can be ascertained from historical archives, took place, as has been stated, in 1658, when the three Walcheren cities—the colonization of the coast of Guiana having been taken out of the hands of the West India Company—sent an engineer by the name of Cornelius Goliat to survey the locality, draw a map thereof, and submit his plan for the new Colony. Goliat's idea was to build a city to be called New Middleburg, on the right bank of the Pomarón river, some fifteen or twenty miles from its mouth; to build also a strong fort, to be called New Zeeland, at some distance from the city above named towards the interior; and to erect, at some place between the city and the mouth of the river, on the same right bank of the stream, what was to be designated by the name of "The House of the Heights," which doubtless was intended to be a kind of fortified lookout or advanced port. Steps had been taken to carry these plans into practical effect, and the hope was entertained that the Colony would reach a flourishing condition, when twelve years thereafter, namely, in 1665–66, the British, who had taken possession of the Essequibo, came down the Pomarón and left the settlement in ruins. Whatever was spared by the British was devoured by the French in an incursion made by them soon after, and the colonists were dispersed. But in spite of the fact that this city—the only one attempted to be built by the Essequibo Colony up to the time, in the latter part of the last century, in which the city of Stabrock was founded—was completely destroyed, New Middleburg continued to appear upon the maps. In 1679 an effort was again made to build it, and Commander Beekman sent one of his soldiers there to buy annatto dye. This continued to be done up to 1686, when the Colony was declared independent and De Jonge was appointed commander. The latter went there and began his operations in 1686. He was followed by several colonists, and the settlement seemed to be in a fair way to success, when, on the 30th of April, 1689, the French, guided by the Carib Indians, and coming through the inland pass on the side of the Barima, fell upon it at night and totally destroyed it.

No attempt was ever made thereafter to re-establish it. When the West India Company was fully informed of the event its action was confined to authorizing the Commander of Essequibo to cause the flag of the Company to be kept hoisted at that place, under the custody of three men, so as to retain possession. The post, however, was established and preserved; two men only, and not three, as previously directed, were assigned to that duty. In 1700 it was still there and in the same condition, but in that year it was removed to the place called Wacupo, on the affluent of the Pomarón, known by the same name, which flows into it on the left bank, a short distance above its mouth. That affluent has considerable importance, commercial as well as military, because it affords navigable communication, at least during the season of the rising of its waters, with the Moroco river on the west, and through it with the system of waterways navigated by canoes up to the Guaima, the Barima, and the Orinoco.

So the West India Company abandoned the Pomarón post; and even in case the existence of the latter could have given the Company any rights as an occupant, such rights disappeared when the removal was accomplished. No one can say that a flag, accompanied by two or three men serving it as a guard, is sufficient to constitute possession or retain any right over the spot. Occupation must be permanent, and when it is not permanent, but only temporary, no legal effects can be ascribed to it.

Spain in former times had colonists at Essequibo. It is shown by even Dutch testimony that the Dutch fort at Kykoveral was built upon structures which the

Spaniards had raised there, and vestiges of which can still be distinguished among the ruins of that fort. She also had colonies at Surinam, and it is proven that she destroyed the barracks which the Dutch had erected at Corentin. But, as at the time of the Treaty of Munster, 1648, the Dutch were not in Pumaron, and Spain, on her part, gave up by that instrument all her rights only to what had passed to the hands of her enemies, the conclusion is clear that no attention can be paid to any temporary occupation of the Pumaron on the part of the Dutch.

CHAPTER IV.

The Moroco.

We shall begin by calling attention to the remarks made in regard to this river in the Venezuelan argument of 1896. The first one was to the effect that the existence of a Dutch post at the Moroco, for the purpose of preventing the escape of the runaway slaves, did not properly constitute occupation, it being merely the result of a friendly favor rendered the Dutch by a good neighbor, and that the attacks, which from time to time were made against those posts by the Spaniards, indicated, at least, that they were not disposed to continue indefinitely their toleration thereof, and thus prevent their inaction from being construed into an abandonment of the Spanish rights. In proof that these favors were not of rare occurrence between neighboring nations, reference was made to Article VI, of the Treaty between Spain and Great Britain, of 1790, by which their respective subjects were granted the privilege of landing on the eastern and western coasts of South America and the adjacent islands, for fishing purposes, and also of building there sheds and cabins and other temporary constructions. Mention was made also of the fact that Commissioner Don José Felipe Inciarte, who visited the Moroco in 1779, reported that the post was reduced to a miserable house, with two unmounted guns and some *pedreros.* The same official wrote, in 1783, that the Dutch had abandoned that post, owing to the invasion of the French. It was remarked, furthermore, that all this agreed with what had been said by Governor Light in 1838, when he affirmed that the one hundred miles of territory, lying between the Orinoco and the Pomarón rivers were unoccupied, under no authority whatever, and considered *nullius.* Therefore, the new occupation accomplished in 1882, when the agreement of 1850—that no part of the disputed territory should be occupied or encroached upon by any of the contending parties—was in full operation, had only fourteen years of existence, instead of being an uninterrupted possession for more than two centuries, as assured in the preliminary remarks, in the British Blue Book No. 1. Now, we see that this river empties into the sea at a distance west of the Pomarón river no greater than two or three miles; but it comes from a very different point of the compass. It has its source in the lowlands of the coast, towards the west, in the middle of the way to Guaima. It runs thence to the southeast, through two-thirds of its course, almost parallel to the seashore; then, after receiving two small affluents, called Haimara and Mannawuarima, it makes its junction with the latter, and turns at right angles towards the northeast, and from there it goes to the sea. Its importance is due to the sudden change of its course, and to the circumstance that it affords in its upper part a water communication, navigable by canoes, at least during the rainy season, with the rivers of the west, which form a part of the great fluvial system of the Orinoco. The powerful ocean current westward, along the coast of Guayana, renders the trip impossible to sailing vessels, from the Orinoco eastward along the coast. So that the Moroco became, and, to a certain extent, still is, the regular route for the coastwise commerce with the Orinoco, the Essequibo, and all the other Colonies of Guayana.

According to a letter written by Don José Iturriaga, Chief Commissioner in the Spanish-Portuguese Boundary Commission, to Don José Ricardo Wall, Spanish Secretary of State, published in the Blue Book No. 1, page 89, together with the report given by the Capuchin fathers of Guayana, stating that the Dutch were building a fort on the Moroco river, the commanding officer of Guayana was asked to send there a barge, with pilots, to investigate what the situation really was. Don Juan de Dios Valdés was commissioned for that purpose, and he, under date of the 2d of December, 1757, reported that he had fulfilled the duty entrusted to him, of examining the waters of the Moroco river, and the fortification said to be in course of construction on its banks, and that the rumors transmitted to this effect had no foundation in fact, because neither on that river, nor on any other communicating with it, were any fortifications of any kind, and that the only thing which might have given occasion for the rumor was that the Dutch were trying to move the post which they had on the Moroco river to a place at a distance of about six leagues from its mouth, and had made for that purpose preparations to cultivate that part of the territory. That the purpose which the Dutch had had in view was only to prevent the escape of the negro slaves from their Colonies and taking easy refuge in the Spanish dominion, and that they had thought that by moving the post to the mouth of the Moroco they would be able to command the surrounding country and discover any vessel which, without entering the river, should pass along the coast in the direction of the great mouth of the Orinoco.

In a communication dated March 30, 1758, the same Commissioner reported to Señor Iturriaga that the intended removal of the Moroco post had not taken place, and that on the mouth of the said river only a house fifteen yards long, surrounded by a stockade, was intended, as it was said, for the use of those engaged in the trade of the Colony of Essequibo, and also to serve as a place of rest during the rising of the river; that the post had been maintained for the reasons aforesaid, without increasing either its artillery, which consisted only of three unmounted guns of caliber three, or its force, merely reduced to a corporal with two soldiers; that the Aruaca Indians, who lived there for the purposes of commerce, were divided into three villages or settlements, each having from ten to twelve small houses occupied by Indian families, separated from each other by distances of more than a league, and all situated on the banks of the Moroco.

On his part Señor Iturriaga reported that he had understood by the report that an attempt was being made to found some plantations for the cultivation of the sugar cane, and for that purpose to effect a union of the owners of the estates and their slaves, with a certain number of Aruaca Indians who had for them great friendship, and prevent in this way the soldiers and the Indian slaves from deserting that region; that it was possible that, in order to secure that result, and that of protecting the sugar mills against any uprising of slaves of either race, they should build a fort, and arm it with some small guns and garrison it with four or six soldiers.

He took advantage of the occasion to inform the Minister that he had seen a passport or patent, written in Latin, granted by the Governor of Essequibo to a Caribbean chief, who lived at a certain distance from the river toward the interior, and that upon inquiry in regard to the meaning of this step, he learned that the States-General in their commissions to the Governors of the Essequibo, gave them also the title of Governors of the Orinoco, and that the Governors also gave themselves that second title in the licenses which they issued. In regard to this point Señor Iturriaga said that if the Dutch were then permitted to remain at the Moroco, they would soon go also to the Barima, which empties into the very same mouth of the Orinoco, and a little later they would go also to the Rio Aquiare, which empties into the body of the Orinoco at a place distant a few leagues from the sea.

In regard to this point an investigation was made subsequently which gave for its result that the Dutch could not adduce any legal reason for the possession of the post they had established on the river Moroco, because the Treaty of Munster forbade them to erect fortifications for any purpose under any pretext whatever, and that they could only allege that the authorities of Guayana had said nothing against its encroachment upon the Spanish territory. The existence of this post on the right banks of the Moroco was due only to toleration by the Spaniards, the Dutch not having been there from "immemorial time," because nothing in the Colony, which was not established until 1658, was old enough to have that character.

The foregoing shows that the Spaniards believed the Moroco to belong to them, and that they, therefore, had the right, whenever advisable, to visit it; to examine the extent of its waters; to watch the operations of the Dutch; to take away the Indians found there; either to reduce them to a condition of civilization or to recover possession of them as runaway slaves; and to exercise there all other acts of dominion and jurisdiction.

On the 12th of January, 1793, Captain José Sarol, with his pilot, Manuel Col, and eight sailors of the crew of the Spanish merchant ship *Nuestra Señora de la Concepción*, left Cartagena, and on the 23d of March, one hundred miles to the east of Cape St. Vincent, they were captured and carried to Cayena by the French frigate *La Blonde*. After three months of detention there, they succeeded in escaping in a canoe, and reached Surinam on the 14th of July. The Dutch Governor treated them with the greatest kindness and generosity, and on the 24th of the same month caused them to be transported to the Moroco on the ship *Esnola Gloria*. In reference to this and to the payment of the bill of expenses for those services, Duke de la Alcudia, Spanish Secretary of State, wrote, on the 9th of July, 1794, that the Governor of Surinam had caused the above-mentioned individuals to "be placed on Spanish territory;" thus showing that he considered as such that part of the Moroco, whatever it was, where the men had been transported. (Documents presented by Venezuela, vol. 2, No. 20, pages 53 to 57.)

The Dutch did not know at all where to locate the boundary between their possessions and those of the Spaniards, and the opinions in regard to this point were various. For instance, in 1737, the Governor of Essequibo informed the Dutch West India Company that the post of Wacupo and Moroco, heretofore the commercial point of greatest importance for the annatto trade of the Company, had declined during the last years; that he had taken the trouble to investigate the cause of this decline and had found out that it was due, not to any fault of the postholder, but to the competition of the Surinam slave-traders, because the business of the slave trade was much more profitable than all others and had caused the Indians to become negligent in cutting dye-woods. "While I do not see any way to change this," he said, "I consider, however, that it is necessary for us to retain this post, *because it was established for the preservation of your frontiers, which extend towards the Orinoco.*"

In a copy of the minutes of the Court of Policy of Essequibo, dated November 11, 1777, to be found as No. 301 of the extracts from the Dutch archives, made by Mr. Burr, page 539, the following passage occurs:

"That, furthermore, in so far as preventing the slaves from escaping to the interior is concerned, there is no practical remedy against it, because the ways of exit from these estates are forests inaccessible to white men; that, nevertheless, on the frontiers towards the side of the Orinoco, there is a post on the Moroco and Wacupo which, in the opinion of this Council, would be infinitely more useful, if transferred to the seashore, to the angle of the mouth of said river, and if entrusted to a commander of ability, accompanied by an assistant and a good number of Indians."

General P. M. Netscher wrote, in 1888, a "History of the Colonies of Essequibo, Demerara and Berbice from the Establishment There of the Dutch up to Our Days." An appendix to his book relates to the boundary question between Venezuela and British Guiana, and gives the writer's conclusions as to the dividing line between both countries. He says that the Spaniards used to fix in their charts the western limit of the coast of Spanish Guayana either on the Moroco, the Pomarón, or even the Essequibo rivers, and that the Republic of Venezuela, if he is well informed, has continued in her claims the Spanish tradition; that England, on the contrary, claims for British Guiana a boundary situated much more toward the west, along the Amacuro, near the Barima, probably basing her claim upon the ground that, according to the chart of Bouchenroeder (1798), to that of Mr. Robert Schomburgk (1841), and to other charts and ancient information, a Dutch post appears to have existed, in the seventeenth century, near the mouth of the Barima or the Amacuro. The British Government derives from this fact the conclusion that the territory of the Colony—formerly Dutch, now British—extends itself to the Orinoco."

He remarks that in the seventeenth and eighteenth centuries the commanding officers of all the Dutch Colonies in Guayana used always to establish small trading posts in places distant from their own territory, and carried on by this means the commerce of the Colony with the native races. These trading posts have been, in some maps, unjustly exaggerated into forts. "These trading posts," he says, "only had, as a general rule, a master or chief of the post, called the *uitlegger* (post-holder or 'outlier') and one or two soldiers, generally Europeans, besides some slaves, Indian or negro. The house or lodge was sometimes surrounded, either by a kind of earthwork or by a palisade, such defenses being intended as a protection against any attack from Indian enemies."

It seemed to him certain that in the second half of the seventeenth century a trading post was situated on the mouth of the Barima, independently from the Essequibo. Hartsinck speaks of it, but Mr. Burr, having carefully investigated the matter in the royal archives, says that such a trading post did *not* exist in 1683 or 1684, and that therefore it had been either destroyed by enemies or abandoned. He examined the correspondence of the commanding officer of Essequibo and Pomarón, which is complete and without break after the year 1680, as found in the royal archives, but failed to find any mention of a trading post at Barima, although he found references to establishments of the same kind in other parts. In this way he saw that in the first letter of the commanding officer of Essequibo, dated September 8, 1691, in speaking of the state of the Colony, mention is made of two post-holders at Demerara and Pomarón, and that in another letter of June 14, 1703, the same officer reported to have increased the number of trading posts by establishing one at the Mahaicony and another at the Cuyuni. But the trading post of Barima is not mentioned, which is not strange, because in 1685 the West India Company had decided not to trade any longer with the Orinoco. He states, furthermore, that in the first half of the eighteenth century a trading post was established at the Pomarón, it being situated probably at the mouth of that river, near the one established east of the Moroco river, and that mention is made of this in some recent documents and old letters.

Mr. Burr does not understand the reason why Bouchenroeder, in 1798, fixed with so much certainty near the Barima the boundary of what was then called Essequibo. The only explanation he finds for it is the desire of that cartographer to gratify the national pride of his sovereign, the Executive power of the Batavian Republic. He did not believe that the action of the said cartographer was the result of a correct investigation, as he was convinced that the latter had never personally visited the territory, as shown by the circumstance of his having given in his map the name of Amacuro to the Barima river and the name of Barima to the Amacuro. For these and similar reasons Mr. Burr believes that the pretension of the British to locate their frontier on the Barima or the Amacuro, and those of Venezuela to extend her territory up to the Pomarón or the Essequibo are both incorrect, and that the Moroco, where during the greater part of the eighteenth century a Dutch-kept trading post on the east bank of that river must be accepted impartially as the limit on that part of the seashore between Venezuela and British Guiana.

He understands that before 1680, perhaps for a short time, a trading post existed at the mouth of the Barima river, said post being a dependency of Essequibo; but that this fact can not, in his opinion, justify any territorial claim on the part of British Guiana in regard to the disputed territory, because said post was never occupied in the name of the Dutch, and that if such an argument as this were admitted the maps of many countries, especially those in far distant regions, would be very different from what they are.

From recent investigations in the archives of London by agents of the British Government and by Prof. Burr in behalf of the Investigating Commission of Washington, the results of which have been printed respectively in the British Blue Book, No. 3, and in the volumes published by the Commission, the facts relating to the Dutch trading post on the Barima have been clearly explained.

It happened, according to that data, that on the 25th of December, 1683, the commanding officer of the Essequibo, Mr. Abraham Beekman, reported to the West India Company that he had ordered one of its servants to reside there to protect a great quantity of annatto dye and hard woods found there, chiefly against a man named Gabriel Bishop, who largely traded in both articles, with great success for himself and corresponding loss to the Company. He expressed the "hope" that the Company would approve his action and appreciate his desire that the Company should "take possession" of the rivers, as he himself had done *temporarily* for the purpose of finding out the revenues which they could yield; yet he was of the opinion that the Company, so the Blue Book says, has as much *right* to trade there in "an open river" as private individuals. It has been objected that the Dutch text does not contain the word "right," and that the true meaning of the Dutch words used in the report, is *that the Company could make there as successful a trade in an open river as private individuals.* But such an interpretation is hardly admissible.

On the 31st of March, 1684, the same commanding officer of Essequibo communicated to the Company that, in order to stop the annatto trade which was being made at Barima by the same Gabriel Bishop and other traders from Surinam, who not only had injured that commerce, but had purchased all the hard wood to be found in that locality, which was good and abundant, he had ordered the construction at Barima, of a "small shelter," not a *station*, which Abraham Baudarte, the post-holder at the Pomarón, would visit from time to time.

The Company never gave its approval of this action of their subordinate officer.

Although in the second half of the following century, during the command of Storm van 's Gravesande, the latter was granted permission to establish a trading post at Barima; the truth is, that this was never done, this being the reason why the name of that post is not found in the list of the four which were allowed to remain for a period of time, and are mentioned in several pages of the British Blue Book, No. 3.

Mr. Burr has also explained what was the meaning at that time of the Dutch word now mistranslated into English by the word "station." It consisted merely in a kind of shed formed by some posts and covered with a thatched roof, which could be erected and put down in an hour or so.

There is no possibility for pretending that such a shelter can be considered as a house or dwelling place, much less when it is considered that it was *never occupied* except by one person, and this rarely and temporarily.

We know that the existence of a trading post at Barima was never mentioned in the Dutch documents; that in the incursion ordered by Centurión, in 1769, a house and some cultivated fields belonging to Dutch subjects, on or near that place, were burnt and destroyed; and that in 1785 the Commissioner, ordered by Marmion to travel through those localities, found in or about them nothing but Indians.

In subsequent time no mention at all is made of any attempt by the Dutch to occupy Barima; and from the assurances given by Lord Aberdeen to Señor Fortique, to the Commissioners of Venezuela sent to Guayana, namely, José Santiago Rodriguez and Juan José Romero, stating that he (Schomburgk) had not occupied the Barima, it appears that such an occupation was not a fact, even in 1841.

A similar conclusion is to be drawn from the inclusion of this place, by Mr. Wilson, in the list of places which could not be occupied, either by Venezuela or Great Britain, as long as the boundary should remain undecided, as agreed upon in the arrangement suggested by him under instructions of Great Britain, and accepted by Venezuela.

If Great Britain has occupied Barima ever since 1884 it has been in spite of numerous protests on the part of the Republic, and in open and manifest violation of the engagement mutually contracted by the two nations in 1850, as demonstrated in other chapters of this argument.

It appears from the foregoing that if there is any

reason to locate on the Barima the frontier between Venezuela and British Guiana, as is now pretended, in spite of all the arguments set forth, and against all the proposals made in the name of the British Government by Lord Aberdeen in 1844, by Lord Granville in 1881, by Lord Rosebery in 1886, and by Lord Salisbury himself, through the Under-Secretary, Mr. Thomas Sanderson, in 1891, in conference held by the latter with the Venezuelan agent, Señor Pulido, there are also many other reasons which are sufficient to refute the idea that the Moroco was the eastern limit of the Spanish Possessions, as suggested by Mr. Netscher, Mr. im Thurn, Mr. Codazzi, and others.

It is important not to lose sight of the fact that if Venezuela has sometimes shown herself inclined to accept this line as an amicable compromise between the lines called "of the Council" and "of Dr. Rojas," it has been with the understanding that the line would not extend to the interior of the country in the direction suggested by Lord Aberdeen, who included in the British territory most of the land watered by the Cuyuni, the right margin of which is lost for Venezuela, in the line of Lord Aberdeen, from the moment in which it is reached by the proposed boundary. The most that Venezuela could possibly do was to draw a line along the meridian of 60° of longitude, so as to be sure that the British territory should not go beyond the lower rapids of the Cuyuni, below which there seems to have been some Dutch estates founded in far remote times, but which were afterwards abandoned.

In the map accompanying his description of British Guiana, published by Mr. Schomburgk, in 1840, the claim of Venezuela is designated by a green line. Its initial point is the mouth of the Moroco. The Government of Venezuela had not claimed that line. The one which the Government of Colombia claimed in 1822 was the line of the Essequibo. Between that time and 1881 the question remained dormant. Probably Mr. Schomburgk considered the frontier described by Codazzi in his *Resumen de la Geografía de Venezuela*, page 3, to be sufficiently established. But neither the latter work, nor the maps attached to it, has ever had official character; it represented nothing more than the private opinions of the authors, and so repeatedly declared by the Executive power of Venezuela.

Codazzi, nevertheless, as remarked by Schomburgk himself, says that the territory between the Essequibo, the Tupuro and the Moroco, was usurped by the English. In addition to this usurpation, they also encroached upon the territory situated south of the Rupumuni, and between the river and the Acarai mountains, but Mr. Schomburgk did not take notice of this fact. (See map No. 10, of the Codazzi atlas.)

CHAPTER V.

The Guaima River.

Alcedo's Dictionary calls it Waini and sometimes Guainy, stating that it is one of the rivers of the Province and Government of Cumaná, the sources of which are found to spring from the ridges of the Imataca mountains, running northward, and reaching the seacoast at a place by the side of the point and river Barima.

Mr. Burr, in his article on this river, says that within the space of a hundred miles, more or less, to the west of the Moroco river, no other river reaches the sea, and that the Guaima (or Waini), notwithstanding the fact that it follows its way to the seashore, runs, however, for a length of about half the distance of its whole course, in a direction almost parallel with the coast, and that at a point where, after winding southward, it turns towards the northwest, there is no more than twenty leagues distance from the Moroco river, with which it is connected, through a navigable pass at high water.

He affirms that there never was, to the west of the Moroco river, any Dutch post, nor even a Dutch concession of colonial lands, and that, therefore, the occupation that may be pointed out, in regard to the Guaima river, is of an unwritten character.

He observes that, before the eighteenth century, this river is hardly mentioned in the Dutch archives, and that in regard to the first period, this may be explained as being the resort of the docile Aruaca Indians, and not of the Caribs, frequenting the rivers towards the east.

The first time that the Waini river is mentioned in the Dutch archives is in connection with the arrival of the hostile Caribs, expelled by the Hollanders from Surinam, and whose presence seems to have interrupted for some time the traffic of the Hollanders beyond the Moroco river. That was so in 1685. The name of that river does not appear again until the year 1700, when the Governor of Essequibo reports having sent the colonial vessel to the Guaima river, in order to salt fish and get provisions. In the following year a military force was detached, in order to find out the designs of the Frenchmen and to threaten the Carib Indians, near the Guaima river, with the revenge that the Christians and Aruacas of the Dutch Colonies would take if they rendered assistance to the enemy.

In 1703 the Essequibo Hollanders watched, as if they were in their own home, adds Mr. Burr, all the way from the Mora pass, and arrested those deserters who ran away. In 1711 an expedition started from Surinam to Orinoco, through an inland pass, and crossed and recrossed the Guaima river, without hindrance; but they did not find there any lodgings or landing places of Indians. In 1717 the Surinam merchants were trading in that river.

The Professor notices other acts of the authorities of Essequibo, by which they arrogated to themselves the ownership of the Guaima river, but that they had no assurance of the fact, is indicated by some of their own measures; as, for instance, when Governor Storm van 's Gravesande, in 1746, sent there the post-holder from the Moroco river to make a survey, he instructed him not to set foot on Spanish ground, nor even at any place below the Guaima river. In the answer approving his conduct, the Company wrote to him inquiring about the region under the name of "the Wacupo and Moroco;" and, when mention was again made of the subject, the Governor adopted this phrase without mentioning the Guaima (or Waini) river.

In 1749, when the colonist, van Rosen, tried to induce the King of Sweden to take possession of the territory between the Essequibo and Orinoco rivers, he represented the Guaima river as uninhabited and savage, as well as the Barima river.

It is alleged that in 1754 the same Governor ordered the manning of revenue cutters to watch the coast, in the expectation of a Spanish invasion from the Orinoco river, with instructions to go as far as the Guaima river. This is an ambiguous phrase, which does not express whether the cruisers included or excluded the Guaima river.

It is likewise adduced that when, in 1758, the Spaniards made an incursion on the Dutch post of the Cuyuni, the West India Company decided to inquire about their title to that river, and the Governor answered that the situation of the Cuyuni, "up to that side of the Guaima river (said to be the limit, although I believe that it should be extended as far as Barima)" left no doubt as to its property. It is seen that this way of reasoning is a vicious circle, as, instead of pointing out legal facts constituting the origin of the ownership, nothing else is done than to merely assert it.

The Company asked to be informed as to the reasons of this alleged title to Barima, and for the "inference that, as the Cuyuni river is situated on this side of the Guaima, it ought of necessity to belong to the Colony," as no conventions, as far as they knew, existed by which it was established "that the boundary lines in South America were run in a straight line from the seacoast to the interior." This does not call for any remark touching its pretension over the Guaima river. Nothing is found in this silence to show any title, although the wording of the Company's statement, "on this side of the Cuyuni, on this side of the Guaima river," is not without significance.

In 1761, in consequence of the seizure of several fishing boats belonging to Hollanders near the mouth of the Guaima river, the Colonial Secretary, Spoors, protested to the Company that whatever the difference of opinion might be as to limits, "the Guaima river indisputably belongs to the Company," and although the Company again inquired of the Governor what "reasons" he had for thus claiming the Barima as a frontier, he left the question unanswered.

The seizure made by the Spaniards at the mouth of the Guaima river, shows only that they considered it (the right of fishery) their own, as in time of peace no nation may effect captures outside the waters of that fishery ; while with regard to the Spoors protest, it is a mere repetition of what Gravesande had stated having no foundation.

In August, 1762, the Spaniards made a new seizure of another fishing boat at the mouth of the Guaima river, and the Governor again asserted that that river was "indisputably the territory of the Company." The Company applauded the Governor's zeal, although without reproducing the terms of his pretension. Before ascertaining the facts complained of, the Company asked the Governor of Demerara for a map in which all the rivers between the Essequibo and the Orinoco rivers were accurately marked out.

It is therefore strange that Governor van 's Gravesande, in his letter of protest addressed to the Governor of Trinidad, in regard to the seizure of the fishing boats, should state that passports were only given to "boats going from one country (or Colony) to another," notwithstanding the two boats seized at the mouth of the Guaima river "were both provided with passports in due form." In order not to find the conduct of the Governor contradictory, it must be assumed that he considered the Guaima a part of a Colony different from the Dutch one; that is to say, Spanish.

Mr. Burr notices that in 1764 is found the first explicit claim to the Guaima, in behalf of the West India Company. It was as follows: The stockholders of Zealand, in a report to the States-General, in which they defend their administration of Essequibo, describe it as "crossed, not only by that river, but likewise by various smaller streams, such as the Barima, the Guaima, the Moroco, the Pomarón, and the Demerara." But the West India Company had a struggle within itself, and a counter report was submitted, in 1767, by the representative of the Staudholder and the Director of the Chamber of Amsterdam, whose rival pretensions to the Colony in the name of the Company, as a whole, won at last, before the States-General impugned the pretensions, claiming that the adjacent rivers were a part of the Colony of Essequibo. Even the critics alleged that the Chamber of Zealand was not in harmony within itself in point of limit.

It is true that a fact so significant as discord among the same members of the West India Company, some of whom limited the Colony of Essequibo to said river, and others aggregated the various neighboring rivers, such as the Barima, the Guaima, the Moroco, the Pomarón, and the Demerara, can not be presented as an argument in favor of their ownership of the Guaima river, much less while having in mind the assertion that the followers of the first opinion were triumphant in the contest.

It is likewise alleged that the Spanish attempt to seize another fishing boat, off the mouth of the Guaima river, prompted the Dutch Governor to reiterate to the Company his belief that this river was "indisputably the Company's territory," and this time his words had their result, in the shape of a formal representation, addressed by the States-General to the Spanish Court, at the instance of the Company, containing a definite pretension to limits on the coast of Guayana. Indeed it was stated there that the territory of the Low Countries was extended "from the Marowin up to a point beyond the Guaima river."

It is known that Spain ignored these claims, considering that Holland, after failing to press the subject for fifteen years, must have become convinced of the injustice of its claim and had given up their pretensions.

This silence, and the fact of the continued advance of the Spaniards on the Guaima river, show that Spain considered her right thereto incontrovertible.

This conclusion is confirmed by the fact that in 1775 a Spanish expedition came, by way of the Guaima river, as far as the Moroco post, informed the post-holder there that a Spanish garrison was soon to be stationed at the junction of the Guaima and the Barinani rivers as a mark of the beginning of the waterway to Moroco. The Dutch post-holder claimed, in his reply, that not only the Guaima, but the Barima likewise, belonged to the Hollanders. This was contradicted by the Spanish captain. It is not known (as the Dutch archives are silent, as well as the Spanish officer Inciarte) whether the threat of the Spanish garrison in the Guaima river was carried out; but it is known that this same officer, four years later, led another party through this route as far as the interior of the Pomarón. Thus Spain reinstated its pretensions to all the rivers on the coast, with the exception of the Essequibo.

Mr. Burr reports the following conclusions as the result of his investigations:

1. "There never was any settlement in the Guaima river at any time."

2. "The Hollanders never made any effective use of the Guaima, except for the purpose of commerce and fishing at its mouth."

3. "Notwithstanding these facts, the Essequibo police court repeatedly granted, on behalf of the West India Company, formal permits to cut timber there. These permits, however, were useless, as the entrance to the river was not navigable."

4. "The Dutch pretension to ownership of the Guaima was officially announced to Spain in the representation of 1769, and, although forgotten at the time, yet served as a basis for the acts of the Dutch Colonial authorities at the time immediately preceding the final loss of the Colony."

In note 49, found in the famous history of General Netscher, after inserting part of a communication written by Governor Gravesande, on the 20th of November, 1849, to a high officer of the Netherlands, that is presumed to have been the representative of the Staudholder, in the Council of the Ten, an account is given of the discovery made by the Spaniards, in the year 1748, in the vicinity of the Colony, of which they made a map, and he obtained a copy, notwithstanding that the penalty of death was established against the allowance of such a copy. That officer adds that the information he had subsequently obtained from free Indians had convinced him that the said map had been really made by Jesuits, who had been in that expedition, under an officer and forty soldiers. The historian narrates, on his individual account, that, in order to reach an accurate understanding of this last point, he observed that the Governor of Spanish Guayana, in the eighteenth century, had established as missionaries a number of Jesuits and Capuchins, at various points, to the southwest of the Orinoco, sometimes directly into Dutch territory, as for instance, at the *Guaima*, Moroco, and the Cuyuni.

In view of this confession by that officer, and by the historian just mentioned, as well as other considerations, already adduced, it seems clear that the Spaniards iards exercised, up to the last, acts of authority, on the Guaima river, even after having been claimed by the Dutch as their own, in 1769, and that therefore the allegation that the Hollanders had exclusive dominion there is groundless.

CHAPTER VI.

The Barima River.

The Venezuelan brief of the 31st of July, 1896, before the Washington Commission, adduces numerous facts to show that the British pretension to Barima Point would, if admitted, give them full control of the Orinoco and all its affluents (of which the Barima is one); or, in other words, it would give the British control over a quarter of the American continent. In order to avoid repetition, mention will be made only of what has since taken place.

In the correspondence had during the first six months of the year 1896, between the United States and Great Britain, there is a note of the President of the Boundary Commission calling for the documents, serving as a basis for the assertion contained in the British Blue Book No. 1 (1896), namely, " that in 1648 the Dutch establishments in Guayana extended all along the coast, from the Maroni river to that of Barima." He further observes that in the same part it is alleged that, in 1684, the Dutch Commandeur of the Essequibo ordered the establishment of a small fort in Barima, instead of the small police station already in existence there; that in 1767, the Spanish Commander of the Orinoco sent his complaint to the Dutch authorities of the disorders which had taken place at Barima, presenting this fact as an evidence of the jurisdiction which they were exercising then and there; that, in 1764, the Dutch West India Company stated that the Essequibo Colony was intersected, not only by the river of that name, but likewise by various other rivers, such as the Barima, the Guaima, etc. He noticed that these assertions were made on the general authority of " the Hague's archives," but without accompanying any documents or extracts of the same.

At the same time the Commission found that neither the historian, General P. N. Netscher, nor the later modern English historian of the Colony, Mr. Rodway, confirmed the Blue Book's assertions; as the former found no evidence of them in the Dutch archives, and much less the latter, who, on the contrary, places, in the mouth of the Company, not only its unwillingness to establish a post at the Barima Point, but the significant fact that "the Orinoco was too far away to be sure that if the Dutch went there the Spaniards would not desire to go to the Essequibo."

The English Government answered by an insertion of the memorandum of the Attorney-General of Her Majesty and Counsellor of the Cabinet on the question, wherein it is stated, that the three documents noticed as missing and all others adduced by the preliminary exposition of the first Blue Book were to be found in the appendix to the same.

The first document is an official note of the Commandeur of the Essequibo, dated December 25, 1683, in which he informs the West India Company that he had detached one of the servants of the Company to take up his abode in Barima, because there was an abundance of annatto dye and hard wood there, the trade in which had become very productive. He expresses his "hope" that the Company would approve this, and likewise his suggestion that the Company would "take possession" of the rivers, as he had already done provisionally, in order to find out the revenue they could yield, and at any rate he thought the Company had as good a right to trade on "an open river" as had private parties.

Granting the truth of the statement, one fact remains that the Commandeur acted, without any authority from his superior, on his individual account, in a provisional and transitory way, and that he acted in the like manner in regard to the rivers. The Company never approved his action in either case.

Professor Burr shows that the Company did not return any answer as to these particular acts and suggestions of Mr. Beekman, but that the Company's reply to his letter contained serious charges against his fiscal honor, his fairness, his mercantile common sense, and of having transcended his powers. As to the commerce with the Orinoco, supported until then by the Company, they wrote him to stop it; not to trade there himself, nor permit others to do so until the receipt of further orders, because the Company was charged with all the expenses and burdens, while other parties received the profits.

The fact is that in the pay-roll of the employés of the Company in Essequibo, during the years from 1691 up to 1701, there was no person whatever employed at any post in Barima.

A few years later Commandeur Gravesande suggested again to the Company the convenience of a post in Barima. They answered him that they were not opposed to establishing a post-holder at Barima in order to help commerce, but recommended him to be careful not to permit frauds in that district. No project of any post or other establishment, however, was carried out. Two years later, on the 19th of March, 1746, the Commandeur explained to the Company that he had not yet established any post at Barima, as he had not found any competent person to go there. He never again mentions the project, although from that time to the end of his administration he makes frequent allusions to Barima, and even goes as far, in 1749, as to assert that it was under his jurisdiction. Professor Burr adds, that in 1756 a party of colonists from Essequibo, remaining there under pretext of salting fish and carrying on the trade in timber, was dislodged by the Essequibo Government, which prohibited any residence whatever at Barima.

The Venezuelan Government obtained lately, from the archives of the Dutch Colony of Surinam, a certified copy of a letter written by L. Storm van 's Gravesande to the

Governor, W. Crommelin, dated at the Essequibo river, on the 18th of August, 1764, the translation of which is as follows :

" Having found a boat at the plantation of La Retraite, etc., several tramps from Surinam were found to be provided with passes from you to go and carry on a trade at Barima. Instead of obeying their directions they are indefinitely protracting their stay in this Colony, and are evidently endeavoring to disappoint their creditors at Surinam. I shall expel them all, and I have ordered a man by the name of Wood to return at once to Surinam, intending not to permit, in future, any one else to stay there unless he is in need of bread or something to eat.

" Since I am talking on the subject, I take the liberty to inform you that, by naming in those passes the Barima river, complaints are originated with the Spaniards, who are keeping that river as their own, and I believe they are right. They have sent several of those passes to the Spanish Court.

" In all passes granted by me, I give only a permit to pass through the post and carry on commerce with the Indians, without naming any place, it being well expressed in the instructions to our post-holders that they are enjoined to respect your passes, so that all that [trouble with the Spaniards] may be well avoided. And there is so much here to complain of on account of the Spaniards, who submit to the court by the Embassador of Holland, I should not wish to give them [the Spaniards] the least pretext, as things have reached already a point that, when I carry out the orders I have received (for which I am beginning to make the necessary preparations) apprehensions may, before long, very easily grow into facts."

" It agrees with the contents of the extract of the original letter."

" G. W. WITTCHOW,
" *Sworn Secretary.*"

This document is an authenticated proof that, in the opinion of the Essequibo Governor, who knew these things, and who was the best promoter of the interest of the Colony under his command, the Barima river did not belong to it, but to the Spaniards.

For this reason he had adopted the practice of not specifying in his commercial permits the names of the places they were intended for, and advised the Governor of Surinam to do the same thing on his part.

Although the correspondence of Gravesande with the Company, to which he rendered such signal service, contains, very often, phrases in which he avows his ignorance of the limits between the Dutch Colony and that of Spain, and insists in having them fixed in an official manner, it is known that at last he fixed the Waini river, thus confirming the assertion that Barima was not considered by him to be within the territory of his jurisdiction.

In another place we have noticed the vigilance kept by the Spanish authorities of Guayana all along the coast, by means of corsairs, to prevent and punish the entrance of foreign vessels into the Orinoco river.

In the Blue Book No. 3, marked No. 21, is a document which it calls "Judicial information upon the attack made by the Spaniards against the Hollanders established in Barima (1760)."

"The original is called proceedings instituted upon the seizure of a schooner, two launches, and two canoes from Essequibo by the lieutenant of infantry, Don Juan de Flores."

The captain of the Spanish fort San Francisco, Don Juan de Dios Valdez, received an exposition, transmitted by the Father Prefect of the Missions of the Guayana Province, where it is stated that at the mouth of the Barima river five Hollanders were established in cabins and carried on the inhuman and lucrative trade in the purchase and enslaving of Indians; that he was awaiting at the time a party of them bespoken to the Caribs; that he deemed it conducive to the service of God and His Catholic Majesty to prevent such an injurious commerce and to reduce the Hollanders, by means of a punishment, to their possessions; and that he had decided to commission Don Juan de Dios Gonzales de Flores, lieutenant of infantry and second officer of the fortress, to betake himself to the vessel of his present nation, in Puerto Real, manned by ten soldiers of the line and armed, in the usual manner, with two small cannons, furnished with stores for twenty days, and provided with Spanish pilots of the river and several Indian refugees, and proceed to the place where it was said that the Hollanders were. He was directed to navigate day and night, without loss of time, and, on reaching the place, to attack the cabin and seize as prisoners all the Hollanders, French, or Spaniards that he might find, as well as the Caribs, and to make use of force, if resistance was offered, or if they refused to surrender. He was directed to seize, likewise, all vessels he could find going up or down the river, whether Spanish or foreign, if they were navigating without the necessary papers, and those were to be carried to the fort, with their captains, crews and cargoes. That order was issued on the 7th of September, 1760.

The Commissioner returned, on the 20th, to the point of his departure, bringing one schooner and two boats belonging to the same schooner, besides two launches, all from Essequibo.

He reported that on the 11th he saw a vessel making for Guani Point and endeavoring to find the mouth of the Orinoco. He chased her and fired a shot. She surrendered, and, after a search, ten Aruaca Indians were found on board, who reported that they were coming from Essequibo to fish in this river. He continued his journey on the following day and entered the mouth of the Barima river. About three leagues above he saw a vessel, unable to reach the point, awaiting high tide. When he neared her the crew ran away, carrying along with them the sails and cutting the greater portion of her rigging. Through the Aruacas he ascertained that the schooner hailed from and belonged to Essequibo, and that it was likewise coming to fish. He seized her, and finding himself with few men, knowing that he was far from the place where he had to go, he decided to return. On his way up the river he spied another launch, the situation of which had been made known to him, and he sent Pedro de Salas, who, on a canoe, would board and capture her, as he did. The crew had all escaped and taken to the woods. The truth of the facts was confirmed by the affidavits of Pedro Salas, José de Sosa, a soldier, a mustee, and another Aruaca Indian. On the strength of those affidavits Captain Don Juan Valdez directed to have copies taken from the documents and have them deposited at the royal treasury, and the originals forwarded to the superior tribunal of the Government and Treasury. As to the cargo of fish, he gave directions to sell it for the benefit of the Royal Treasury, as this was an article that decays and loses in weight. Nothing is said of the final result of the seizure; but it is well known that at Cumaná, where the authorities resided, upon whom Guayana depended the forfeiture of the prizes was made for the benefit of the Royal Treasury.

Venezuela finds in this fact one of the many proofs that the Spaniards considered themselves as the lawful sovereigns over Barima, and as such expelled from there as intruders all who went there, whether Hollanders or French, or what not. One of the chief effects of dominion is the right to exclude anybody else from the use of our things. Now, this right was exercised by the Spaniards, as they had before expelled the Hollanders from their Cuyuni post, and afterwards, in 1768, they expelled them from Barima.

If the Blue Book intends to show by this quotation that the Hollanders occupied Barima at that time, it is a mistake, as the case of five men who took refuge in a cabin, for the purpose of a clandestine trade, and chiefly to enslave the poor Indians, does not constitute a nucleus of any permanent settlement. Towards 1768, when Centurión swept Barima clear of intruders, those five men had disappeared, and those who might have arrived afterwards ran away.

The passage above mentioned can not be brought up in support of the pretended right of fishing at the mouth of the Orinoco, because no such rights can be claimed by intruders who have been kicked out by those who consider themselves the owners. The witnesses summoned by Centurión to testify as to the complaints of Holland against the proceedings of the Spaniards of the Orinoco, in regard to Essequibo (document No. 9, of the Blue Book, No. 3), assert that never had they seen or heard that the Dutch had any fisheries at the mouth of the Orinoco river, or that the Spaniards would have had to oppose them; that they did not understand that the Hollanders were in any need of such fisheries at the mouth of the Orinoco, since they had places where to provide themselves with fish much nearer to the Essequibo; and they were persuaded, therefore, that fishing was only a pretext, in order to bring freely their vessels to the mouth of the Orinoco, and thus re-establish and facilitate the furtive shipments of mules from the Guaripiche and Guarapo rivers, and of Barimas tobacco, hides, and other products of the Spanish provinces, with which they were wont to supply their Colony, when it was not as well guarded as the Orinoco river and its creeks are now. The want of commerce was the true cause of the decadence of Essequibo and the resentment of Gravesande, who was always the most interested in the illicit commerce of the Colony.

It is further asserted that the affidavits of "the six witnesses were all agreed in every respect, and that they all attested that it was likewise false, the assertion that the fisheries had been prevented by the Spaniards, in the territory called of the same State by Gravesande, who claims that it extends from the Mariguini, to that side of the Guaima (Waini) river, very near the mouth of the Orinoco river, said supposition being an intolerable error."

We must bear in mind the acts of jurisdiction exercised by Venezuela in Barima, spontaneously acknowledged by Sir Robert Ker Porter, British representative at Caracas in 1836, evidence of which has been produced.

It is a fact that in 1768, when, by command of Centurión, the Hollanders were expelled from Barima, where they had entered only a short time before, the Dutch Governor did not complain of an act so significant, as he would have done had he considered it a violation of their rights of ownership and sovereignty.

In the British Blue Book No. 3 (1896) an insertion is made of all the papers on file by Centurión on that subject, besides a summary reference in the Preliminary Exposition, pages 5 and 6. It is there stated that Centurión, then Commander of the Spanish Guayana, prompted, seemingly, by hints from Dutch deserters, decided to dislodge several Dutch families established at that time in Barima, and for that purpose sent the captain of a revenue cutter with two more boats full of people; that the expedition was conducted with secrecy, so the men might not be aware of their object before the mouth of the Barima river was reached; that then a body of Carib Indians became aware of their arrival, and as soon as they gave the alarm to the Dutch they withdrew; that the Spaniards proceeded to seize every article of furniture which they found in the abandoned houses, and returned, carrying them to Santo Tomé, where formal confiscation proceedings were instituted, and that said articles were sold at public auction for the benefit of the Provincial Treasury.

The Blue Book, however, omits what was stated by all the witnesses of the event. They asserted that besides carrying on board all the utensils found, they had set fire to the houses and destroyed what they found already planted in the farms of the place so as to prevent the return of the intruders. Nor is any mention made of the order issued by Don Manuel Centurión, Don Andrés de Oleaga, Don José de Alogen, and Don Fernando Lareo, wherein they explain the grounds for their proceedings; nor of the papers on file in regard to the expedition under the captain of pioneers, Don Francisco Cierto, who was sent with two launches of the revenue service and the crew and men of their company against the Dutch squatters who had been illegally established there to carry on a clandestine trade in lumber and other products in the Barima river under the jurisdiction of the Guayana Province; nor of the manner of their flight without any attempt to defend themselves, leaving behind their utensils and other articles of furniture that were found in their settlements. The judges state, besides, as their reasons, that the Hollanders had unjustly tried to take possession of the territory of Barima, a part of the jurisdiction of the Guayana Province, where they had established some plantations and dwelling houses so as to carry out the export of lumber and other products in a clandestine way, and that the several laws and the latest *cedules* issued by His Majesty prohibited, under any pretext whatever, permission to foreigners to establish settlements or colonies in those dominions. In consideration, therefore, of the crime perpetrated by the Hollanders and the penalty they had incurred, it was found that the sentence of confiscation was to be pronounced against the utensils and other things found in their possession, which were brought by the captain of the revenue cutters.

Taking into account all these details, we may understand how well founded were Centurion's proceedings and how sure he was of the rights of Spain in Barima.

If, on the contrary, Barima had been Dutch the Government at the Hague would not have failed to demand restitution of the territory and indemnity for the injury done on account of the expulsion of its subjects, nor failed to demand the punishment of the officers who carried out the seizure.

The Blue Book No. 1 states that the Hollanders complained energetically of these incursions of the Spaniards, but omits to mention the result of their representations.

The Spanish Government, as it appears, did not pay any attention to them, and thus Governor Centurión's proceeding was virtually approved. In the Blue Book No. 3 the case is given more attention, as has just been noticed, but nothing is said there of the claim or what success it attained. It is true that in Centurión's answer mention is made that the expedition had exceeded his orders, which were only applicable to the Grand mouth of the Orinoco; but this has reference to another visit to the Guaima and the Moroco rivers, not to Barima, as was positively enjoined by Centurión, according to his own certificate and that of other witnesses concurring to the same fact.

On the other hand, in the Blue Book No. 1 two resolutions are copied that were issued by the high plenipotentiaries, the first bearing date July 31, 1759, and the second August 2, 1769. But only one of these makes mention of the Barima affair; the other, verified in 1768, makes not the least mention of it.

The same Gravesande, when communicating the affair to the Dutch Company of Zeeland, in 1768, does not give any importance to it, probably on account of his opinion that Barima was an appurtenance of Spain.

It is argued that the English, in 1781, when they seized the Dutch Colony in Guayana, marked out its limit on the coast as located to the west of the Barima Point. In support of this proposition the official notes of Don Fermin de Sancinenea, General Agent of the Guipuzcoana (an old Biscayan Company and confidential agent of the Spanish Government of Guayana), addressed a letter on the 15th of June, 1790, to the Count of Campo de Alange, and another to the King on the 9th of February, 1791. In one of these he states that the progress of Guayana was in imminent danger of becoming the chief object of an attack by the enemy during the first war; and for that purpose the English, when holding the Dutch Colonies, had twenty officers in their several boats make a survey of the coast from Essequibo down to the large mouth of the Orinoco, and ten leagues farther up the river, etc.

The other note recommends the importance of the Fort of Guayana, situated at a distance of over thirty leagues from Angostura, the capital, from the mouth of the Orinoco river, and near the Dutch Colonies of Essequibo and Demerara, settled mostly by British subjects, and contiguous to Guayana. Finally, it is asserted that these places were marked out by Great Britain when in possession of the Dutch Colonies during the last war.

As has been elsewhere observed, the English, having been military occupants in time of war (1781), could not by themselves mark out the limits of the Dutch possession; or more plainly, the argument presupposes that Barima was Dutch property, and that Great Britain, then at war with the Netherlands, had a right to seize it as a war measure. The same condition existed between Great Britain and Spain which, by the Treaty of 1789, had joined France against the former nation. Thus we may account, not for the demarcation to the west of Barima Point, but for the seizure of the same as the territory of an enemy. But this condition ceased after the Treaty of peace of 1883 between Spain and England, in which the restitution of all conquests was stipulated (Article 6 of the preliminary Treaty of February 20th, and article 8 of the final Treaty of September the 3d.)

Again, it is alleged that in 1796 when the English again seized the Dutch Colonies, they marked out their limits, as is found by the official note of March 4, 1797, addressed by Don Pedro Carbonell, Captain-General of Caracas, to the Prince de la Paz, Secretary of State of Spain, in which he informs him that the English had distributed all the lands extending from the Essequibo Colony to Barima Point, which lies to the windward, and which, with the Cangrejos Point, forms the mouth of the Orinoco river; and that, from one point to the other, they had fixed stakes and posted notices explaining to whom they belonged and giving the name of the owner. This case is analogous to that of 1781, or even more equivocal, since Spain, in 1796, had become not only a belligerent, but declared war against Great Britain, and on the 31st of March of the following year took upon itself to guarantee the Dutch possessions in South America against the aggresions of the common enemy, Great Britain, and to that end it concluded a Treaty with the Batavian Republic, placing at its disposal a military force with which to garrison the Surinam Colony.

But, on the 27th of March, 1802, Spain and the French and Batavian Republics on the one side, and the King of the United Kingdom of Great Britain and Ireland on the other, concluded a treaty of peace, and (in Article III) His Britannic Majesty made restitution to His Catholic Majesty and to the Republic of Batavia of all possessions and Colonies belonging to them, respectively, that had been seized or conquered by British forces during the continuance of the war, except the Island of Trinidad and the Dutch possessions in the Island of Zealand. It is plain, therefore, that by this act Great Britain surrendered any and all rights acquired by her in virtue of any temporary military occupation during the war.

If no merit is attached to the Spanish attack on Morocco in 1797, on account of the existence of the war at that time, then for the same reason no merit can attach to the acts of the English in 1781 and 1796.

In 1803 Great Britain again seized the Dutch Colonies. This time they were never recovered by the Netherlands; but none of the Blue Books show any pretense of occupation of Barima by Great Britain at that time.

Neither was it carried out in 1840, as shown in another chapter of this brief. They did so in 1884, with an evident infraction of the convention proposed and adjusted by their Government in 1850, and they have continued there since that time, in spite of the constant and energetic protests by Venezuela.

Before dismissing this point it will be proper to rectify several mistakes of the Blue Book in relation to Barima.

The first is, that in 1684 the Commandeur of the Essequibo recommended the establishment at Barima of a small fortified place instead of the little temporary "shelter" put there by Beekman, whose action was never approved by the Dutch authorities. The Commandeur had ordered one of the servants of the Company to sojourn in Barima, in the hope of meeting approval by the Company. He recommended also that the Company take possession of the river, so as to secure its annatto trade there. The Company. failed to approve this, and the consequence was the withdrawal of the man from that place. Many years afterwards (in 1746) Governor Gravesande stated that no "post" had been established at Barima. (Compare No. 76 of the Dutch documents copied in the Blue Book No. 3 with the extracts in Vol. II of the Washington Commission.)

The second is, that in 1757 the Spanish Commandant of the Orinoco sent a complaint to the Dutch authorities on account of the disorders in Barima, thus showing that the Dutch held jurisdiction there at the time. Document No. 127 does not include any Spanish complaint, but only a communication from the Director General of Essequibo to the agent of the West India Company, advising *him* of the many complaints made by the Commandant of the Orinoco on account of the misconduct in Barima of traders from Surinam and Essequibo, and that, in consequence, he had written circumstantially to the Governor *ad interim*, Mr. F. Nepvue, and was daily awaiting an answer. It was Gravesande himself and not the Spanish Governor who made the complaint.

The third allegation is, that "the Spaniards acknowledged the authority of the Dutch as extending to the right bank of the Barima."

What is said in document No. 182 (a work of the Director-General of Essequibo, Gravesande), is that he would write to the Governor of Orinoco in regard to the state of things in Barima, which was becoming a very "den of thieves," and *being on the western side of Barima in territory certainly Spanish*; and that therefore he could not take any violent measures to destroy that nest of thieves, because he did not wish to lay himself open to any complaints from the Spaniards, and thus he thought he would propose to the Spanish Governor to carry out this affair in common concert or *allow him* to do so, etc.

In another note of Gravesande to the West India Company, dated on the 20th of March, 1757, he tells them that "in regard to the affair of Barima and to the Rose case," he had the honor to inform them that "*we and the Spaniards look upon the Barima river equally as the limitative division line of the two jurisdictions, being on the eastern margin a territory of the Company and on the western margin of the Spaniards.*"

In order to show accuracy, the Blue Book ought to have stated, not that the Spaniards acknowlegded as Dutch the eastern margin of Barima, but that the Governor of Essequibo *said* that the Spaniards did so. A vast difference exists between the two statements, as the Dutch authorities were naturally interested in advancing their limit. But with all this hearsay and assertion there is one fact, namely, that of the authority of the Governor of Guayana, who, in 1768, as has been noticed, took the ground that Barima was part of the province of his command, so as to order the expulsion of the Hollanders who had come there for the purpose only of trading and farming. Upon that subject Gravesande wrote to the West India Company, on the 1st of June, 1768, that he certainly would have otherwise sent reinforcements to Morocco, because "our rascally deserters have entered into Barima, with several Spaniards, and have robbed the widow La Rivière of all her slaves and effects," *that was of little importance, because he had strictly forbidden Jan La Rivière to establish himself between Essequibo and the Orinoco*; and in order to be more positive, he had caused the fact to be inserted in his passport, and to settle in Barima was likewise prohibited by the Court, *but that they (the Spaniards) had threatened also to come and raid the Post of Moroco.*

Later on, about the 4th of April, 1769, speaking of Jan La Rivière, he writes, "that he was the same who, against the absolute prohibition of the Court of Policy, had removed with his slaves to live in Barima, and had died there; *the Spaniards had robbed his wife of everything they had, and she had returned to this Colony*" (that is, of Essequibo).

The Attorney-General of Her Britannic Majesty, on the 28th of May, 1896, sent to Lord Salisbury a memorandum on the Barima question, in which is quoted, as a proof of the ownership of Barima by Holland, a statement from Baron von Humboldt, in his travels through the equinoctial regions of the new continent, namely, that "The Hollanders, far from acknowledging the Pomarón or the Morocco rivers as the limit of their territory, located the same at the *Barima river*, and consequently near the mouth of the Orinoco itself, from where they draw a line of demarcation northwest and southwest to the Cuyuni river; *and that they have gone as far as to militarily occupy the eastern margin of the Barima river*, before the English, in 1666, destroyed the fort of New Zealand and that of New Middleburg, on the right margin of the Pomarón."

This act, if true, might mean a Dutch claim, but it is no evidence of their right of occupation. It seems that Humboldt merely gave a rumor that came to his ears, but he was himself far from attaching any great importance to it. This is shown by the fact he at the same time advances his opinion that the possession of the country lying west of the *Pomarón* would be some day disputed between England and the Republic of Colombia.

Humboldt elsewhere (in his chapter 26, relative to Colombia), asserts that the longitude at the mouth of the small Morocco river, situated near the Pomarón, *and that served as a frontier between the English Colony of Guayana and the territory of Colombia*, depended from the longitude of the Essequibo river.

Further on he says, "the actual limit of the Republic of Colombia commenced at Point Careta, the eastern frontier of the Province of Costa Rica, and extended up to the Morocco and Pomarón rivers to the east of Cape Nassau, and thence, following from that point, the frontier went through the plains, where several small granite rocks are elevated, first to the southwest and then to the southeast, towards the confluence of the Cuyuni river with that of the Mazaruni, and where formerly a Dutch detachment was quartered in front of the Tupuro creek."

Mr. Burr censures Humboldt for his evident mistake in affirming that the Hollanders had any military occupation on the eastern margin of the Barima river. Humboldt, fixing even twice the limit of Colombia on the Morocco and Pomarón rivers to the east of Cape Nassau, obviously does not accept the opinion of the Hollanders who, as he says, wanted to fix it on the Barima.

The same thing may be observed in regard to Hartsinck, quoted likewise by the Attorney-General of Great Britain, inasmuch as the Dutch historian asserts that some persons give the Barima river as the western limit of the Dutch Guiana, while others consider the same as limited on the west by the Guaima river; and such is the opinion adopted by the author, as it appears from his first passage, just quoted.

Among the collection of Extracts from Dutch documents prepared by Mr. Burr is found, under No. 345, a secret instruction by "the Council of the American Colonies and possessions of the Batavian Republic," in which, under date of December 15, 1801, Citizen G. A. W. Ruysch was appointed special delegate to the Batavian Minister at the Congress of Amiens, so as to hold a conference with him concerning all the affairs of interest to commerce and navigation of said Republic and its Colonies in the West Indies. Under Art. 10 ("Extracts," p. 644) he is instructed as follows:

> "In case the negotiations at the aforesaid Congress should also extend themselves to the regulation of the interests of this Republic with other Powers, and this should lead to a precise definition of the boundaries of one or another of their respective possessions, the Citizen Ruysch shall try to have the limits between the Batavian and Spanish possessions in South America irrevocably defined, whether by the eastern bank of the *Orinoco* or by the river *Barima*, lying to the east of the first-named."

In No. 346 the printed answer of the delegate is given, showing that the subject should not be dealt with, and therefore was not in that Congress. He thought it impossible to speak there secretly of the case, and that it was against their interests to favor any extension of the Dutch Colony towards the west, on account of the close vicinity of Trinidad, then a British possession; that in case of a new war, situated as it was to the windward, it might be attacked and captured by the Demerara and Essequibo garrisons. He added that if the Hollanders obtained permits to draw cattle, horses, mules, jerked beef, skins, and tallow from the Orinoco, they would enjoy, over the English, the advantage of carrying to market their common manufactures, while the English from Trinidad would furnish them with goods from their factories. He observes that the Spaniards purchased English goods, out of sheer necessity and not of choice, preferring always common cotton goods, drillings, quiltings, and harlem cotton goods. He gives besides his opinion, as follows:

"My opinion therefore is that this negotiation should take place direct with the Spanish Court, through our ambassador there; that he should be empowered with full authority (1) to fix the boundary fifteen or twenty (Dutch) miles below Bahima or Barima, Barima being held among us as the frontier line. In case this should not find favor then at Barima, and if this should not go, then, in order to obviate all cavil in future, to pay therefor a certain sum; thereafter to conclude a new cartel, and to enter into a private convention between Spain and the Republic about the trade of the Orinoco with our Guiana Colonies. At Madrid, this affair can be dealt with much more secretly and with more hope of success, and brought to an end more speedily than at the Congress here. I am also of opinion that this negotiation should be taken up, the sooner the better, inasmuch as the Spaniards not yet acquainted with that possession will be tractable; while, on the contrary, if we wait long, they will learn to know it through the maps which are now being engraved in London, and which will be ready in the coming May. The river Waini is by them regarded as a creek, and it is a river as large as Demerara, and just as well adapted for the cultivation of coffee, sugar, and other colonial products. Barima is another large river of much fertility."

Neither the author of these instructions nor the delegate explains the foundations of the right they might have had to fix their limit on the Orinoco, or at least on Barima. What is plainly seen is the advantage they would derive from a similar arrangement, from a military point of view as well as commercial. They had so much interest in that matter that the agent recommended the "purchase" of that frontier, so as to be transferred in any event to the Hollanders. If the delegate could have been able to show any title upon which to base his pretension, he would certainly never have advised the "purchase" of that territory, as this fact would imply an acknowledgment of the right of the Spaniards, who possessed it.

The fact is, that neither then nor at any future time did the suggestion take any practical shape, not even in 1814, when the transfer to Great Britain of all the Dutch establishments of Essequibo, Demerara and Berbice was made, notwithstanding that would have been the most opportune time to fix the quantity of territory ceded. Thus, the same indeterminate line continued which subsists at the present day.

CHAPTER VII.

The Amacuro.

Alcedo's Dictionary refers to Amacuro as a portion of the Province and Government of Cumaná, in the Kingdom of Tierra Firme (mainland), situated in the interior of the ridge of mountains; one of the missions attended to in that Province by the Capuchin Fathers from Aragon at Baria Point, in the interior coast of Golfa Triste. There is, he says, a river of the same name in that province, running northwardly, and coming to the Orinoco, in its large mouth, called *El Boco de Navios.*

Mr. Marcus Baker, in his geographical notes about the region extending from the Orinoco to the Essequibo, says that this (the Amacuro) is one of the delta rivers, eighty or ninety miles in length, and that it seems its head waters have never been visited even by the natives.

From its mouth, which is at the great mouth of the Orinoco, it assumes a direction generally S. E. ½ E. for a distance of forty miles, until it reaches the Wause mountain, a small hill on its western margin, and then, turning sharply, takes a southerly course for a distance of ten miles beyond the Yarikita mountain, which is two hundred and fifty feet high; thence turning westward and rapidly reducing its volume as it takes a W. by S. ½ S. direction up to its source at the Imataca mountains for an unknown distance, supposed to be thirty or forty miles. In all its lower course through the swamps of the Delta it continues to receive numerous tributaries, particularly on the side of its eastern margin. Shomburgk calls them by their native names, which were given him by an Aruaca Indian. Fifteen are received on that side and thirteen on the western side.

After giving other particulars in regard to its course and different dimensions, the nature of the vegetation covering its banks, and the existence of the Cuyurara cataract, sixty-five miles distant from its mouth, he asserts that, according to Dixon's map, near it and on its right-hand margin to the east, the *British frontier station* is situated, and on the opposite margin the *Venezuelan frontier station.* In 1883 instructions were given to a Pomarón magistrate to visit, now and then, the foreign districts to the northwest, a region where, by the Ordinance No. 20, of 1890, a Government agency was created, as a part of the county of Essequibo, called "District of the Northwest." In 1885 a covered structure was erected at Amacuro for the accommodation of the magistrate during his visits. In 1887 another structure of the kind was built at Barima and increased in 1888 with a small police detachment. These were the first resident (British) officers in that district of the northwest.

Mr. Burr, considering that the first mention of the Amacuro found among the papers of the Dutch West India Company is in 1681, finds very embarrassing that which is contained in the Spanish documents of 1637, of the same Amacuro, in connection with Essequibo and Berbice. He has no doubt that that is an error, as he esteems it to be inconceivable that such an important place would have been ignored in the official archives of the Netherlands, inasmuch as there are documents presented by him to the Commission showing that in the same year, 1637, the Spanish Governor of Guayana, as well as the executive Dutch officer in charge of the neighboring island of Tabago, considered the Fort of Essequibo as a Holland possession, the nearest to the Orinoco river. He argues furthermore in support of this opinion the contents of a Spanish document printed in the British Blue Book, Venezuela, No. 3, page 216, in which reference is made to an attack made against the Hollanders of Essequibo and Berbice, without any mention of Amacuro, which certainly should have been first attacked.

He thinks the error may be explained, either by the support rendered to the Dutch by the Caribs of Amacuro, or by some confusion with the Morocco, or simply by the strange mistakes generally found in Spanish reports in reference to Dutch settlements. What he has said about Barima at this period shows the improbability of the presence of any Hollanders in Amacuro towards the middle of the seventeenth century; and that they were not there in 1673 is deduced, seemingly, from the words of an English captain who, in that year, secured his provisions there, and those of the Treasury English Council, which, in the following year, consulted and advised the authorities of Barbadoes to return "to Amacuro river, in Guayana, eleven Indians who had been brought there by force, as they understood" (carried there, perhaps, by W. Ross), and that they should avail themselves of the occasion to gratify the neighboring Indians, so as to make them friendly to Her Majesty's subjects, who had noticed recently the help rendered by said Indians to the French, and how beneficial it would be to keep them so.

The Spanish document he alludes to is a letter addressed to the King by the Common Council of Trinidad, dated December 27, 1637, explaining the condition of the city of Santo Tomé de Guayana, taken, ransacked, and set on fire by the Hollanders and the Carib Indians, who likewise threatened the Island of Trinidad with a powerful fleet. Annexed to it is a rule by Don Juan Eulape, Governor and Captain-General of the Island of Margarita, by which, under date of the 4th of December of the same year, and after having received the same report he ordered an investigation to be made in order to discover the plans of the enemy and the present condition of the two cities, and suggested the adoption of proper measures for the benefit of the Royal Service. In consequence he summoned to his presence Captain San Miguel de Morillas, the Prefect of Trinidad and a resident of Margarita. In these proceedings a report of the event is made by the person named, which concludes as follows:

"An Indian by the name of Andres, in the employment of Captain Cristóbal de Vera, a resident of Guayana, was taken prisoner at the time of the retreat of the above-mentioned enemy. This Indian says that in the three colonies of Amacuro, Essequibo and Berbice there are a great number of enemies, particularly in the two last-mentioned places. He heard that they had a large force; the Indian could not give the number, but he said that they were in league with all the Carib and Aruaca Indian tribes. He said, besides, that every year they received from Holland articles brought down by two, three, or four vessels, bringing the same articles, and they carried back cargoes of annatto seed, cotton, hammocks, and some tobacco.

"That is all the witness knows and attests, under oath; that he is thirty years old, and has stated nothing but the truth in his affidavit."

After these words the following phrases are added: "His signature attested—Don Juan Eulape—Miguel de Morillas." And at the end: "In my presence—Francisco Gonzales de Barrionuevo—Notary."

Assuming the authenticity of this document, although it is not legalized, it is most strange that an Indian should speak of the three Colonies of Amacuro, Essequibo, and Berbice, when it is a notorious fact that there never was a Dutch Colony at the first of said rivers, either before or after the year 1637. About Berbice, Netscher says that the new Colony, from 1627 to 1666, was of a very short significance. Its first Commanders, according to the same historian, were Matthaijs Vergenaar, in 1666, and Cornelis Marinus, in 1671.

If the Hollanders never had any establishment, either in Guaima or in Barima, how could a colony of them exist in Amacuro, situated, as it is, to the west of the former river?

Schomburgk himself, who placed post-marks in the Amacuro in 1841, does not say that Her Britannic Majesty had any right to that river, and if he traced the limits through it, it was only to give a natural line of British Guayana.

He, indeed, in a memoir presented by him, on the 30th of November, 1841, pretends to prove, by inaccurate data, that the Dutch West India Company once had real possession of Barima Point. But, in regard to Amacuro, situated as it is miles further west, he asserts that the Commissioner of Her Britannic Majesty (*i. e.*, himself) pretended to hold it as a provisional limit, as undoubtedly it was the most natural one to the west of the old Dutch possessions, which, in his opinion, did not go beyond Barima.

The remonstrance by Señor Fortique, in 1842, which was, as we have seen, successful, was based upon the fact of the display of English colors and other marks with the royal initials, at the mouth of the *Amacuro* river and at Barima Point.

In 1875 a correspondence was had between the Minister of Foreign Affairs of Venezuela and the British Legation at Caracas, on account of the arrest at *Amacuro* of Mr. Thomas Garret, who was taken to British Guayana to be tried judicially, he having been arrested and taken away at night and by force by police agents, who entered the house of Robert Welsch, a citizen, where he was at the time. And although that place is *now* part of the disputed territory, this act of jurisdiction could not be exercised without a violation of the convention of 1850, whereby both parties were prohibited from occupying any portion of the disputed territory. Wherefore Venezuela held that fact to be a violation of its territory and demanded the restitution of Garret to the place where he had been arrested.

Mr. Burr, continuing in his researches about this river finds that towards the year 1681 the Hollanders of Essequibo were familiarly acquainted with it, as they sent their canoes to salt Manati and Baquira meat, and that in 1685 the Caribs of Copenan, being on bad terms with the Hollanders, were expelled from Surinam, and there were rumors that they had taken refuge at Amacuro and Barima as well as at Guaima. For a long time the names of these rivers never appeared in the Dutch archives, but in 1762 it is found at the head of the title page of the first directory of the Colony of Essequibo designed as its western limit. Mr. Burr thinks that the "Amacuro" spoken of there must lie east of Barima since Barima is not found among the rivers of the Colony. He thinks it probable that it may be the "Amacuro" of D'Anville's map, so much favored and consulted by Governor Gravesande, the author of the directory; a river placed in that map, *between* those called Barima and Guaima (Waini), and flowing into the Orinoco river, at a place in which the modern maps place the mouth of Barima. He is convinced that if it is an error to hold that when Gravesande spoke of Barima he meant Amacuro, it is no less certain that when he spoke here of "Amacuro" he did not designate Amacuro proper, but at best a river known now under the name of Barima.

It is said that there are reasons to doubt whether, in the seventeenth century, and on to the beginning of the eighteenth, the Hollanders did consider the Orinoco river as fully Spanish, as it is often supposed to be the case. It is likewise asserted that the old Spanish documents are full of complaints against the liberties that the Hollanders used to take in that river, and even above Santo Tomé; that from said place down the river the Hollanders traded freely for a long time, and very often in connivance with the Spanish authorities themselves; and that the Dutch trade with the Spaniards on the Orinoco was of course a matter of connivance.

The first proposition mentioned gives us to understand

that at the beginning of the eighteenth century the opinion of the Hollanders changed in regard to their pretensions to the Orinoco river. No matter what they had been before that period, it is beyond question that in 1769 they did not set any claim beyond the Guaima (Waini) river. Unquestionably, the convention of extradition of 1791, being a solemn international act, is of a stronger force than any other document, and it does recognize as Spanish all the establishments of Puerto Rico, Coro, and the Orinoco; and as Dutch all the establishments of Saint Eustace, Curaçao, Essequibo, Demerara, Berbice, and Surinam. This ought to fix the matter so as not to leave even a shade of doubt.

As to the Aquiere river, Alcedo's Dictionary calls it "a river of the Province and Government of Guayana in New Andalusia, coming from the Imataca mountains and entering with a great body of water into the Orinoco, where the latter empties into the sea, through its broader mouth called *El Boco de Navios*, 7° 16′ north latitude. It is figured in geographies and political divisions as the territory of Guayana.

As the Venezuelan-British dispute has never been extended to regions west of the Orinoco, nor east of the Essequibo, it never was in any case extended to the Aquiere, since even the extreme British claim has not been extended beyond the Amacuro to the east of the former river. Supposing the Aquiere could enter the controversy there would be no room for questions about the Amacuro, the Barima, the Morocco, or the Pomarón, for all these rivers would be absorbed in the claim of the Aquiere situated beyond the other rivers.

That the Hollanders traded on its waters, and therefore on the Orinoco, from Santo Tomé downwards, and even upwards, that could only be the effect of one of two causes, namely, escaping the vigilance of the Spaniards or by doing so with their connivance. In regard to the first, the secrecy of the movement excluded the possibility of the sanction of any Spanish authorities, and as to the second, the superior authorities would have punished the delinquents, as was the case with the friar in charge of the Palmar Mission, who connived at acts of commerce with the Hollanders and was removed.

When, in 1758, the Governor of Essequibo, *ad interim*, informed the West India Company that the Spaniards were organizing a Mission at Imataca, he added, after having been well posted: "That that river was situated far into the Orinoco, and that, in his opinion, it was entirely beyond the interests of the Company." Now, the Aquiere is very near and to the west of Imataca, and if the latter river was very far from the Dutch Colony, it is natural to conclude that it was similarly situated in regard to the former.

When judicial proceedings were instituted, as a consequence of the complaints from Holland against the proceedings of the Spaniards of Orinoco, in regard to the Hollanders of Essequibo, the duly sworn witnesses who made their affidavits asserted that: "If then the Hollanders were permitted to use the Moruca they would soon go over to Barima, emptying its waters through the same mouth, and later on would go to the *Aquiere*, the mouth of which is on the Orinoco itself, a few leagues distant from the ocean; that through this river they could reach the vicinity of the Palmar Missions, and thus secure a free communication with the other missions of the interior of the country, as has been done before, through the indifference of Father Fr. Bruno de Barcelona, who was for that reason removed by his Prefect and reduced to serve as a companion in another mission, deprived of any part, active or passive, in the Boards." Here is a proof that the Aquiere did not pertain to the Hollanders, even when they used to fish there and undertake other operations of illicit commerce; that when such acts were brought to the knowledge of the authorities they only became objects of reproval and punishment. That the neighbors of the Aquiere rendered their assistance to similar acts, unquestionably out of their own individual advantage, may constitute a charge against their patriotism, but it does not afford any valid argument to affect the rights of Spain to the territory in which those things happened, for in point of international ownership, whether anything is to be acquired or lost, only the nations have a juridical capacity.

Mr. Burr, in his report on the Amacuro, reaches the conclusion that the Hollanders in Guayana never had other relations with Amacuro beyond fishing and hunting in that river, and that fact is ascertained through only one illustration.

He deems of little value the novelty of the fort, that Bouchenroeder has a fancy to place (on paper) at the mouth of the Amacuro, and that never was built there, nor is there found any evidence that it was ever begun.

Schomburgk made no mention of it, though undoubtedly it would have served his purpose, to attribute to British Guiana the Amacuro limit. Thus he founded it only out of "convenience" to the Colony, so as to possess a natural frontier, and secure the importance of a strategic position, as he did in regard to Barima. That view is so evident that the compiler of the Blue Book has not ventured to carry that mark on the map accompanying Book No. 3. All the other places are there, whether right or wrong, and for a short or a long time held at the Cuyuni, Arinda, Morocco, and as far as Barima, but no post appears at Amacuro.

Bouchenroeder is of those who mistake the positions of Barima for those of Amacuro, giving the latter what belongs to the former, and per contra; and as he may have erroneously fancied that Holland had a post at Barima, he transferred the same to Amacuro without fixing it any where else.

It will not be amiss to recall to the attention of the

Arbitrators that in an official note, addressed to the Governor of Demerara (Mr. Henry Light), the Venezuelan Commissioners (Señores Romero and Rodríguez), said, among other things: "And besides the service of pilots Venezuela has exercised its police rights and vigilance against smugglers all along the southern shore of the mouth of the Boco de Navíos, and on both banks and mouths of its two affluents, the Barima and the Amacuro rivers."

CHAPTER VIII.

The Cuyuni.

Alcedo's Dictionary describes it, as follows: "Cuyune or Cuyuni is a large river of the Guayana Province under the Government of Cumaná. Its source has not been accurately ascertained, but, according to the reports of the Carib Indians, it comes from the Lake Parime, in the interior of the Province, to the northwest, running from north to south, and entering into the Essequibo, after various windings on its course. The Hollanders of this Colony ascend it, in order to enslave Indians, for the work of their plantations, with the help of the Caribs, and they have built two forts on both banks of its mouth near the seacoast."

We shall observe briefly, that Alcedo does not give Cuyuni and its branches to the Hollanders, saying that the traders on those rivers were protected by the Caribs, and that the fact is a Spanish acknowledgment that the Hollanders had not withdrawn to the interior, but they had withdrawn to the coast. He refers to the Cuyuni only, without including any of its branches, and, what he asserts, is that the Hollanders of Essequibo went up said river supported by the Caribs. That he did not recognize the Cuyuni as Dutch is clear when he says: "*It is a great river of the Province of Guayana and under the Government of Cumaná,*" that is to say, a Spanish property.

It is an indisputable fact that the Dutch Colony was in the proximity with the sea, and did not go far into the interior. The only reason alleged for the extension is the principle that whoever acquires the mouth of a river is made *ipso facto* the owner of all the territory drained by it and all affluence received in its course. But tested by all recognized legal authorities (some of them English), as well as by common sense, there is no such rule. It has on several occasions been asserted, it is true; but the general consensus of mankind is against its acceptance.

But, laying aside mere theory, let us examine the fact, occupation, and dominion.

Plenty of light has been thrown on this matter through the investigations of the Washington Commission after hearing the statements of several persons, very particularly the learned Professor Burr. From this investigation it is ascertained that the Hollanders had a "post" on the table lands of Cuyuni, first in 1703, from May to September, at an unknown point, but in the plain and very probably at Curunio; the second, from 1754 to 1758, at Cuiva (probably Quive-Kuru), three days' journey *up* the river; third, in 1766 to 1778, first in the Island of Tokoro, from 1766 to 1769, and afterwards in that of the Toenamoeto, in the rapids of Tonoma, from 1769 to 1772.

The first was of so short a duration, as it has been represented, on account of the brutal and bad conduct of the post-holder, who, as a consequence, was dismissed. Whatever may have been the cause, he was not replaced, so *that* "post" could not have produced any effects as to title.

As to the second one, it is known that after the report of its existence, the Spaniards decided to dislodge the Hollanders from it, as was done in 1758, sending, under instructions of Commander Ferrera of Guayana, an expedition of a hundred men, who captured and destroyed and brought as prisoners the post-holder and his assistant, and a Creole he found there with his Indian woman, carrying them all tô Santo Tomé. Thus the second post met the same fate as the first; that is to say, it was never re-established, but forever after remained abandoned.

The third, set up in 1767, was located at the Island

of Tokoro, where it remained for a short time, when the holder of it, on his own account, and in the interest of his health, or for his own personal safety (for he did not consider himself safe against the frequent Spanish attacks), moved down to the Toenamoeto Island. He died in 1772, and Gerrit von Leeuwen, his second, seems to have acted for another year, returning afterwards to the garrison. Thus ended *this* "post," and no further mention of it is found in the Colony's archives.

Every appearance of Dutch occupation in Cuyuni had now disappeared and with it every semblance of juridical title pretended to be derived from it.

This reasoning takes for granted that the Cuyuni was open to Dutch occupation; but having been demonstrated that the Hollanders, in 1648, the date of the Treaty of Munster, possessed only the Fort of Kykoveral and the mouth of the Essequibo, and that that Treaty did not license them to acquire any territories that Spain had reserved to itself, it seems to be beyond question that the Hollanders had no right to extend their occupations any further by the coast nor inland.

It is well known that the claims set up by Holland, in 1759, by reason of the second post, were not entertained by Spain, who, for a long time, did not deign to even answer them.

In 1769 a similar complaint was made by the States-General to the Court of Spain on account of similar acts by the Spanish Colonial authorities on the northwest coast region, but without any better result than that of 1759.

In the Blue Book No. 3, page 305, it appears that, on the 27th of May, 1789, and 6th of the following June, the report and resolution of His Catholic Majesty's Council was, "that the proceedings did not call for any decision, in so far as the lapse of fifteen years, without any call for an answer on the part of the Minister of Holland, led to the belief that the Republic, better informed of its want of fair grounds for the pretended claim, had desisted."

In short, nothing was done on the subject, by either of the two powers, and thus it was abandoned by common consent.

Such was the state of things when Great Britain seized Guayana, in 1796, and when, in 1814, it was definitely reacquired.

On the other hand, Spain had a fort at the mouth of the Curumo, and another at the Yuruan, both branches of the Cuyuni, as has been shown in the proper place.

Adding all these arguments to that of 1896 (which is a part of the present one, as everything else introduced before the Washington Investigating Commission on behalf of the Government of Venezuela), it is beyond question that the Hollanders did not own, did never occupy, much less exclusively, the Cuyuni; and therefore it can not be awarded by prescription, nor as privative dominion or colonization. It is located in the interior of the territory of the Republic of Venezuela, of which it forms an inseparable part.

The British station on the right bank of the Cuyuni, in front of the mouth of Turucu, was established in the year 1892, and can not change the juridical condition of things.

CHAPTER IX.

The Mazaruni.

Alcedo's Dictionary remarks: "The Mazaroni, Mazaruni or Ataparán, is a large and voluminous river of the Guayana Province and the Government of Cumaná; it comes from the interior of its territory and runs from south to north until it joins the Essequibo, very near where it empties its waters into the sea. That the Hollanders, protected by the Caribs, go up to kidnap the Indians of the province and enslave them for the benefit and work of their plantations, using every possible means suggested by covetousness and tyranny, captivating the poor Indians, and for the purpose of keeping close and friendly relations with the Caribs, who are a warlike and ferocious tribe."

In his description of the Guayana Province, in which he gives a report of the river and the communication of its territory, he said that the Governor, Don Miguel Marmion, in an official note of the 10th of July, 1788 transmitted to the Spanish Government as follows: "The Mazuruni, from its confluence with the Essequibo river, runs southwardly, and at a distance of ten or twelve leagues forms the figure of a half star, with three branches which, running in different directions, have their sources in the Essequibo and the Caroni Chico rivers."

In the affidavits taken for the purpose of investigating the complaints of Holland against the conduct of the Orinoco Spaniards, the witnesses stated: "As soon as we became acquainted with the news of the case (the establishment of a 'post' in the Cuyuni), in the year 1757, they were dislodged from there, so that the Hollanders hold no possession in Cuyuni, Maserony,

Apanoni, or any other rivers flowing into the Essequibo; nor is it tolerable that they should have, because said rivers are comprised within the territory of the Guayana Province from their sources (the western terminus) down to the eastern limits, in which they joined the Essequibo; and it would result that the supposed possession by the Hollanders would make them masters of the extensive Province of Guayana, and that the Spaniards would not hold anything but the margins of the Orinoco, which would be an absurdity; that they had been tolerated merely on the banks of the Essequibo River, running from southeast to north in a direction almost parallel to the ocean coast, the eastern terminus of the Guayana Province, keeping the inland free for the Spaniards, their lawful possessors." (Venezuelan Documents, vol. 2, p. 193).

From the extracts in the Dutch Archives, taken by Mr. Burr, to which reference is made in two of his reports, it appears that the Director-General of Essequibo, Storm van 's Gravesande, wrote to the West India Company on the 7th of July, 1756, as follows:

"The Colonist D. Couvreur, who has just now come from up in Mazaroni, where he lives, has given me information which confirms the report of the bylier in Essequibo, saying that various Indians from above have retreated to his place; that between two and three days' journey above his plantation, which is equal to about twelve or at most fifteen hours of travel, there live some whites who have there a great house and more than two hundred Indians with them, whom they make believe a lot of things and are able to keep under absolute command. He has proposed to me that, in the month of August, when the water at the falls is somewhat lower, he shall go himself with some other colonists and creoles of the Company and kidnap those whites and bring them here. This was very acceptable to me, as I know him to be a man capable of a daring deed; wherefore I have accepted this and shall, in the next session of the court, submit the matter for consideration."

The report alluded to by the Director-General is that of Mr. J. Steyner, post-holder at Arinda, dated the 28th of May, 1756. It is as follows:

Your Excellency, you still remember the rumors of those three Christians who are above in the savannah; now they have made themselves masters of the entire savannah. Your Excellency, I do not know what will come of this; they make themselves masters of all rivers. Your Excellency, I believe that they are Spanish folk; that they make themselves masters of all places; they come by way of Cuyuni. You must know that they have three fast places, one in Wenamu, a branch of Cuyuni; the second up in Mazaruni in Queribura; the third up in Siparuni, at Mawakken. Those places are all of them gruesomely strong. On May 3 they came to the Caribs and began to clear gardens; on May 17 they went with ten corials to Demerara to dwell. Your Excellency, much though I ask them whence they come, they give me this answer, that they have risen from the dead, and they say that as many more will come. They are Caribs, and Accoways, and Arawaks, and Warrows; all sorts of nations. One gives himself out as the grandfather; another as the father and brothers of their friends. All those who have been dead for twenty years have all arisen again, as they say. I may say to them what I please—all in vain. Your Excellency, on May 27 I heard from an Accoway from Demerara that those Accoways who did harm last year are again preparing to go down with slaves to cheat those Christians, but not knowing; and as for the post, it is still quiet, as long as God wills it. Your Excellency, I do not know what it means that Mushack does not come to the post; I am half frightened at these folk; they give themselves out to be God's folk."

The two documents show as a fact that the Spaniards had, at the upper Mazaruni, a station "*fearfully* well fortified." About this point, Mr. Burr observes: "That the Governor himself, although skeptical as to the report, found in its contents subject enough for his anxiety." And when he was writing to the Company about this affair, a colonist arrived from the upper Mazaruni, who seemed to confirm the statement of the post-holder at

Arinda. This colonist, Couvreur, proposed, with the approval of the Governor, to organize a party, and go to the upper river and "kidnap" all these men, and the Governor accepted the project provisionally. It seems that Couvreur's report indicates unequivocally the presence of a Spanish mission, and recalling the forts that they always needed, the post-holder may not mean anything else.

In their *entradas*, organized expeditions for the purpose of gathering (often by force) Indians for the settlements of the Missions, it was the time when the friars who themselves ventured upon their journeys in the neighboring country, and their permanence was often a long one. Such a party, entering the immediate neighborhood of the Dutch post, had undoubtedly fortified those places where they made a halt, but as to the "*fearfully* well-garrisoned" fort, the post-holder may indeed be believed, as implying something else than a mere *entrance.* Two or three things in the circumstances of the time make the history less surprising. In the first place, the presence at that time in Spanish Guayana of a great military force, intent upon ascertaining the limit between the Spanish and Portuguese dominions in South America, must, in itself, have animated the Missionaries to new enterprises. The panic created in the neighboring Dutch Colony by this Spanish force, and the chronic presentiment following, fill an important part of the Essequibo correspondence, and even that of the Dutch Government at that period; but what is more to the point is, that we now know that all that anxiety was justified. The secret correspondence between Spain and Portugal, recently published by Great Britain, contains not only full evidence of a Convention between the two Governments for expulsion of all Hollanders, from Guayana, but gives likewise details of the methods to be followed.

Professor Burr mentions other facts to justify the truth of the narrative of the post-holder at Arinda.

Schomburgk frequently found in the Barima region, as well as in that of Cuyuni, some Indians that still gave signs of the teachings of the Spanish fathers, which he praises, calling them an improved race. Hillhouse made the same remark with reference to the interior of Mazaruni.

Beyond what has been said, as the Mazaruni is situated on this side of the Essequibo, which is the line claimed by Venezuela as its frontier, we must consider it as included in its territory, in spite of the fact that it is one of the chief affluents of the Essequibo, the mouth of which belonged to Holland.

The Commission sent by the Venezuelan Government to Guayana, about the end of 1886, ascertained the fact that, under British authorities, several gold mines were operated in the Venezuelan territory, situated between the Cuyuni, Mazaruni, and Uruni rivers, and that a great quantity of the mineral had been exported through the Demarara custom-house. Thus, we recall the note of protest addressed on the 20th of February, of 1887, to the British legation at Caracas, comprising the territory of Mazaruni and its affluents.

The Mazaruni is included among the Venezuelan rivers, as may be seen in the list made of them by Codazzi in his atlas, locating it among those originating in the Barima system.

CHAPTER X.

PRESCRIPTION.

The prominent article of the Treaty of Arbitration is that which, anticipating the finding of the Tribunal, indicates the three Rules which are to serve as a standard for its judgment, since thereby a most important question is decided beforehand, which otherwise would have remained submitted to the decision of the Arbitrators themselves. It is as follows:

"Adverse holding or prescription during a period of fifty years shall make a good title. The Arbitrators may deem exclusive political control of a district as well as actual settlement thereof sufficient to constitute adverse holding or to make title by prescription."

Before explaining the sense in which Venezuela understands and has accepted such a principle, it is proper to present some remarks indicative of her views in accepting it and of the effort she has made to determine forever a question, as arduous as it is vexatious, otherwise capable of keeping apart two neighboring and hitherto friendly nations, called to cultivate the greatest harmony and develop the fruitful sources of progress and welfare which so greatly favor the Guayana region; that land of immense and numerous interlacing rivers, rich virgin forests, boundless plains, varied metal mines, other numberless rich products, and a wonderful future.

No preceding compact of the same nature is known. Indeed, there has never been one, if we accept the assurances in an article printed in the "Review of Public Law," published at Paris since the beginning of 1894 (third number of 1896), the author of which is the French jurist, Mr. Eugène Audinet, a professor of international law in the faculty of Aix. And "The London Times," of the 11th of November, 1896, said (as will be seen farther on), referring to the toast given by the British Prime Minister at the inaugural banquet of the present Lord Mayor of that city, that "the law of nations knows nothing of prescription." Even Lord Salisbury himself, at that time Prime Minister and Secretary for Foreign Affairs, stated, on the same occasion, that the compact of Great Britain with the United States of America on the question of Venezuela had transferred the doctrine of prescription from the civil to international law, in order to shelter the titles of ownership of the possessions of the Empire from litigations.

Venezuela, for her part, as well as the other Spanish American Republics, has proclaimed in her institutions, as did her predecessor, Colombia, in hers, the principle of the *uti possidetis* (of right in 1810) to determine the extent of her territory.

And, in virtue thereof, when, on the 14th of September, 1881, Venezuela and the present Colombia agreed to refer their controversy as to boundaries to the arbitral decision of the Government of the King of Spain, in the character of juridical arbiter, the compromise established was as follows:

"Article 1st. Said high contracting parties refer the point of controversy in the aforesaid boundary question to the decision of the Government of His Majesty the King of Spain, as juridical arbiter, in order to obtain a final and inappealable judgment, according to which *all the territory belonging to the jurisdiction of the old Captaincy-General of Caracas, by royal acts of the old sovereign, until 1810, remains the jurisdictional territory of the Republic of Venezuela, and all that, by like acts, and at that same date, belonged to the Viceroyalty of Santa Fé, remains the territory of the present Republic called of the United States of Colombia.*"

By the award which the Government of Spain pronounced on the 19th of March, 1891, and founded principally upon the royal order of May 5, 1768, wherein the Spanish Sovereign had declared that the limits of the Province of Guayana were—on the east, the Atlantic ocean; on the north, the Orinoco; on the west, the Orinoco and the Rio Negro; and on the south, the Amazon river (which documents, by the way, Lord Salisbury does not consider an authorized exposition of the territories of said Captaincy, because it completely ignores the Dutch settlements, which not only existed in fact, but had been formally recognized by the treaty of Munster), many places were given to Colombia, which are situated on the western part of the Orinoco, and had been in the possession of Venezuela for at least a century.

It is affirmed that, by this award, Venezuela lost not only the exclusive control of the Orinoco, Casiquiere, and Rio Negro, but also an area of 300,000 kilometers in which there are a hundred and twenty-three villages, and that it was pronounced by the Sovereign of Spain, in virtue of that Royal Order, which another (a predecessor of his) issued on May 5, 1768, and which he, far from considering an absurd document, has taken as the ground for decision of so transcendent consequences to Venezuela.

But Venezuela, notwithstanding, has had to submit to such a dismemberment of her territory in deference to the decision of the arbiter, to whose impartiality she referred the determination of her old controversy of boundaries with her sister and companion, the Republic of Colombia.

Let us glance at the subject of prescription, in order to take into consideration how the learned jurists, constituted arbitrators, will apply it to this case.

Among the modes of acquisition are found, from early times, those called by the Romans, *usucaption and prescription*, both of which, in the long run, have been included in the latter of those words.

By the former was meant the acquisition of such things

as had been possessed during a certain length of time and under limited conditions, of which just title and good faith were the principal ones.

The one consisted in the transfer of property in things by reason of translative dominion, the other in the fact that the acquirer should believe the transferrer to be the true owner of the thing transferred. For it sometimes happens that we are sold, bartered, given, bequeathed a property not belonging to the seller, barterer, giver, or testator, and hence find ourselves in the position of him who, without any guilt on his part, has been deceived.

Several reasons are adduced for confirming, after a possession, sometimes short, sometimes more or less long, the right of the new owner. The one alleged by many as plausible is, that the silence or inertness of the former owner, or his failure to make use of his advantages, induces the presumption of his willingness to abandon them for the benefit of another. Others consider the argument as of little weight, because every one has a right to be negligent, to use or not use, or even to abuse, what is his; that he does not injure anybody by his negligence; that if he claims against the possessor, it is because he can legally dispossess him; that when the possessor calls himself the owner, his allegation must not prevail against him who proves that he is the real owner, thus excluding the presumption of abandonment; that an expropriation is committed without its being justified by public utility and without the previous indemnification prescribed by fundamental law; that, if the possessor has worked, he has also enjoyed the fruits of his own labor; that in case he had made any improvement, he could claim the value thereof; and that the real foundation of prescription is to be sought in the social interest and in the importance of securing property and sheltering it from litigations which otherwise might multiply and become perpetual.

There is no doubt that this argument explains the principle, but that does not make it good in every case.

The French Civil Code, for instance, according to which he who acquires, *in good faith* and with a *just title*, an immovable property, fixes the period of prescription at ten years; provided the real owner resides in the district of the Court of Appeals, within the area of which the property is situate, and twenty years if his domicile be out of the district, especially if the fact be borne in mind that the title, if null for want of form, does not avail, and above all that, as provided in Article 2229, the possession should, in order to become efficient for the purpose of prescription, be *continual and uninterrupted, peaceable and unequivocal, and exercised in the belief of being the owner.*

Such is *acquisitive* prescription. But there is another prescription called *extinctive*, which exonerates a debtor from the liability only because the creditor has failed, for a certain length of time, to demand the fulfillment of the obligation. Efforts have been made also to give this prescription a decent appearance by arguing the negligence of the creditor, as if demanding or not the fulfillment were not a faculty of his own, which he can not lose for want of use, or as if his marks of consideration for the debtor should not rather deserve appreciation than punishment, or as if, through his neglectful conduct, he would cause any damage to the debtor upon whom he really confers a benefit. It is maintained also in this instance that prescription is indefensible by principles derived from private law, and that only in the public convenience can a justification be sought for it; that is, in the expediency of limiting judicial actions to a certain period rather than converting them into a hotbed of disturbances in the condition of fortunes. This prescription scarcely wants any requisite as its very nature excludes, above all, the just title. To this kind pertain those that are called short prescriptions, as that of six months, one year, two and five, and which comprise respectively: 1st, the action of teachers and tutors in sciences and arts for monthly lessons; that of inn-keepers and tavern-keepers for the lodging and board they give; that of laborers and agents for the payment of their wages, supplies, and salaries; 2d, the action of physicians, surgeons, and apothecaries for their visits, operations, and medicines; that of constables for their fees; that of merchants for the goods sold to private persons not being merchants; that of owners of boarding houses for the amount of the pension of their boarders; that of the other teachers for the price of their teaching; and that of servants who engage themselves for the year concerning the payment of their salaries; 3d, the action of solicitors for the payment of their expenses and salaries; and also the one relating to pensions for maintenance, house rent and lease of rural estates, the interest of lent moneys, and generally, to all that is paid yearly or at shorter periodical terms.

There is little justice in condemning a person to lose his dues who has taught, cured, boarded, served, or defended somebody, only because he has been tardy in demanding the price of his labor so beneficial to his ungrateful debtor. It is said, with a view to lessen the injustice of prescription in such cases, that the credits involved never appear in writing, so that the creditor, being in want of title, ought not to have waited so long a time before demanding payment, and the debtor, for the very reason of the non-existence of any title against him, may have paid without obtaining a receipt; hence that rule is not applied when the transaction has been made in writing, and that, moreover, the law provides that the creditor may tender the oath to the debtor himself or to his representatives. In the first case he ought, *on pain of condemnation*, to affirm that he has paid the debt; and if it is the widow or the heirs of the debtor, or the guardian of his heirs (minor or interdicted), they ought *to affirm that they do not know of the thing being owed.* But this meets with other obstacles. The debtor, by swearing that he has paid, remains free from responsibility, and tranquil if his affirmation is not mendacious or tormented by his conscience, if so be he has not spoken the truth with a view to reap the benefit of the law. Such will almost always be the case when he shall have resorted to prescription in order, above all, not to place himself in conflict with himself. Such a law is not worthy of praise as places a man in the alternative of sustaining a loss or of violating an obligation of conscience. The trend of modern progress is to avoid such dilemmas. Nobody can, for this reason, according to the Constitution of Venezuela, be compelled to make an oath or to submit to an interrogatory in criminal matters against himself, or his relations within the fourth degree of consanguinity and the second of affinity, or his consort. For, naturally, the interrogated party will desire to save himself and those with whom he is connected by close links; and he being placed in the dilemma of prescinding from them or of respecting the oath required of him, it is necessary that he should fail in one of the two duties, which, in most cases, is that of not lying on any account.

It is strange that so little should be required for prescription under said circumstances, while with respect to movables, good faith and just title are demanded, in addition to a three-years' possession.

It seems as though the legislator himself has acted with hesitation and timidity in this matter; for, while on the one hand, he authorized the disclaimer of accomplished prescription, he, on the other, ascribes no value to such means of defense, except when the defendant opposes it, prohibiting the judge to supply the same, by virtue of his own office, in civil cases.

Another proof hereof, and of the odious nature of prescription, is that the law provides the means to interrupt or suspend it; excludes in certain cases from the effects thereof each consort with regard to the other; those exercising paternal authority respecting those who are submitted thereto, the minor and the interdicted with regard to their guardian, as long as the accounts of the admin istration have not been presented and approved; the emancipated minor and the persons of age provided with a guardian, on the one hand, and the guardian on the other; the heir and the estate accepted with benefit of inventory; such persons as are subjected by law to the administration of another, and to those exercising that administration; and, generally, unemancipated minors and interdicted persons; conditional rights, as long as the condition is not complied with; the action for indemnification, as long as eviction has not been effected; the estates hypothecated by the husband for the execution of the matrimonial articles, so long as the matrimony lasts; and any other right, the exercise of which is suspended for a certain term, as long as that term has not become due.

Article 2262 of the French Civil Code is as follows:

"All actions, whether real or personal, are prescribed in thirty years, without any obligation on the part of the person alleging that prescription to produce any title, or without the possibility of the exception drawn from bad faith being opposed to him."

This provision is likewise found in the codes of other countries, because the influence of the French, established in their territory in the early part of the present century, has been as great as that of the Romans all over the civilized world.

It is important, therefore, to ascertain what is the construction of that article which fixes thirty years as the longest term for prescription and gives it validity, even though wanting good faith and just title.

There are commentators who affirm that this provision comprises two kinds of prescription, the one extinctive of actions, whether personal or real; the other acquisitive of property through a possession of thirty years without title or good faith.

The last, however, is not fixed by the wording of the article, which only speaks of extinctive prescription. It is true that actions constitute the means of giving efficacy to rights, and that for this very reason the want of the former is equivalent to the want of the latter. M. Baudry-Lacantinerie, a modern French author, shows that the action for recovery is prescribed in thirty years, and the preparatory works are formal in this sense; that it is so, even if he who for the time being possesses the estates had not, on some account, become proprietor by prescription; for instance, if it is a society having no civil personality, and therefore no legal existence; that this proposition is not contrary to the one set forth by the same author, that the right of ownership can not be lost by the mere effect of time; that in such a case the owner shall have retained his right of ownership, but will not then have the action for recovery, sanctions the same; that his right will not, on this account, be necessarily useless to him; that particularly the owner, who would have succeeded in recovering the possession of his estates, could invoke his right of ownership in order to be kept therein; for instance, to defend himself against the State that would claim them as vacant and *nullius.*

Even in the case of prescription from ten to twenty years, more favorable than that of thirty, Aubry and Rau believe that, notwithstanding the accomplishment of the *usucaption* and the extinction of the action for recovery, the true owner may, as creditor of him who has alienated the usucaptioned immovables, institute action for nullity or rescission, which would yet be open to the benefit of the latter, against the title of alienation, and thus obtain, in the form of a personal action, the restitution of those immovables.

Some have even affirmed that the mere lapse of thirty years confers ownership, although possession has been taken in bad faith, without title, and with other vices, as, for instance, that of violence.

This, however, is unmindful of what they themselves set forth. For instance, Marcadé, one of them, commenting on article 2223, of the French Civil Code, says "that the prescription of thirty years requires but three conditions, namely, *possession with the conditions required by law*, the lapse of time, and the positive and public invocation by the possessor of this mode of acquisition offered him by the law."

The same jurist, when explaining article 2269, which sanctions said prescription, says: "It is also very clear that the article does not mean that, even assuming the prescriptibility and then the want of interruption and suspension, the action will always be prescribed for the mere fact of thirty years having elapsed without the right being claimed. It is observed that the law supposes this circumstance to be accompanied by the conditions it requires; and while the fact of the inaction of the party having right during thirty years will be sufficient for personal actions, *it is for the rest understood that, in case of an action for the recovery of an immovable property, it shall not be prescribed unless the defendant has had, during all that time, a possession provided with the necessary conditions for acquiring by prescription.* "Possession," says article 2228 of the code cited, "is the detention or enjoyment of a thing or right which we have or exercise by ourselves or by means of another who has or exercises it in our name."

The commentator adds: "To possess a thing is to hold it in one's power; to keep in one's service; to have it seized under one's control. There is no real and property called possession but that implied by this idea of dominion and control of the thing." And article 2229: "To be able to prescribe, *it is necessary that possession should be continual and uninterrupted, peaceable, public, unequivocal, and had in the belief of being the owner.*"

Article 2232: "Acts of mere faculty and those of simple tolerance can not furnish ground for either possession or prescription."

Article 2233: "Acts of violence can neither furnish

ground for a possession capable of producing prescription. Useful possession only begins when violence has ceased."

From what commentators say on this point, it is important to bear in mind that by peaceable possession is understood that which is not vitiated by violence or disturbed by a rival claim. That such a condition not only necessarily results from article 2233, which declares that acts of violence can not furnish ground for prescription, but something else is required; that if, in order to be peaceable, possession must, above all, not be violent, this circumstance is not sufficient; so that a possession might well not be violent and yet not be peaceable. For instance, if a party violently takes possession of a piece of land that appeared to be abandoned, and the proprietor, instead of resorting to a court of justice to have him ousted, attacks him with open force and maintains his possession for one or several years, only by sustaining continual struggles with his rival; in such case his possession is not only violent, but is *violated*, for it is clear that nothing is less peaceable than a possession constantly disturbed, molested, and questioned by the continual attacks of a rival. This being so, it is affirmed that peaceable possession is one that is neither violent nor violated, and that this second condition, as well as the first, renders it ineffectual for prescription.

A jurist, commenting on the proposition that the thirty years' prescription does not require either title or good faith, writes: "This proposition can have been written in Article 2262, with reference only to acquisitive prescription, as for extinctive prescription, no title is ever required. *Thus, the usurper can prescribe in thirty years; even the thief can avail himself of this prescription.*"

It is believed that the writer has not taken into consideration that character of prescriptive possession, according to which, in order that the usurper and the thief might invoke that recourse, it would be necessary that their possession should have been *continual and uninterrupted, peaceable, public, unequivocal, and held in the belief of being the owner*, in accordance with the foregoing reasonings.

It seems difficult that such conditions could occur in a usurper or a thief, for, in case the subject should be discussed, the proof would be incumbent upon him, the more so if the question were between nations.

Only in the existing Spanish Code, article 1956, has so strange a disposition been inserted, although there only with respect to movables. "Movables," it says, "when stolen or robbed, can not be prescribed by those who stole or robbed them, or by the accomplices or concealers, unless they have prescribed the offense or fault, or the penalty therefor, and the action for claiming the civil responsibility arising from the offense or fault."

Also in that Code, article 1959, it has been established in a conclusive manner that the thirty years' prescription gives dominion and all the other real rights, for it says:

"Also the dominion and the other real rights to immovable estates are prescribed by a thirty years' uninterrupted possession, without necessity of title or good faith, and without distinction between present and absent parties, save the exception made in article 539."

That exception refers to continual unapparent servitudes and discontinued servitudes, whether apparent or not, which can be acquired only by virtue of a title, which disposition exists in the French Civil Code and the imitations thereof.

Against the other prescription, the objections of which it is generally susceptible, do not militate in so high a degree; that is to say, against that established by law in favor of him who acquires immovables in good faith and with just title, when ten years have elapsed between present and twenty years between absent parties. Good faith consists, according to Marcadé, of three elements: 1st, that the acquirer believed the alienor to be the owner of the immovable; 2d, that he believed him capable of alienating the same, and 3d, that, in his opinion, the title has been free from all kinds of vices.

Under such circumstances, the possessor can not in any way be blamed for his having acquired the thing, for there was nothing of an unlawful character in the transaction. If there exists any hidden vice, he who is ignorant of it does not become an accomplice.

But here another difficulty is met with, which is, that modern laws, as did the old Roman, consider good faith at the beginning of the acquisition sufficient, and do not oppose the fact that the acquirer, upon the error which he had committed being subsequently ascertained, may continue in the useful possession of what is found to belong to another owner. Troplong is of opinion that the *Code Napoleon* is not equitable in this point, and that it is always vexatious to place the law in contrast with morality.

Some endeavor to vindicate the maxim by saying that a party can not be blamed who has bought and conscientiously paid for the property, but subsequently learns that it did not belong to the vendor, then perhaps insolvent, for not having been as scrupulous as to notify the owner and return him the property, which may have cost the possessor his whole fortune. It is certain that the guilt is graver, if bad faith existed at the beginning; but he, notwithstanding, loses his innocence who retains a thing after having known that it was wrongfully acquired. What is necessary to qualify the action is not the time during which it is practiced, but the nature of the same. In the one case, as in the other, the possessor contributes to make the primitive owner lose his property by appropriating the same to himself, despite his being conscious of the dispossession committed by another, to the detriment of that owner.

According to the Penal Codes of civilized nations, the concealers of offenses are criminally responsible, and the same may be said of those who, without having had any participation in the offense, either as authors or as accomplices, but with knowledge thereof, subsequently intervene by availing themselves or helping the offenders to avail themselves of the effects of the offense. (See Venezuelan Penal Code, article 15; French Penal Code, Book II, sole chapter, article 62; Italian Penal Code, Chapter V, article 421.)

What else can we say of the possessor of a piece of stolen landed property, who, knowing it to have been stolen, keeps silence as to the theft with a view of acquiring it by prescription, and, by leaving the price demanded with the vendor, not only avails himself of the theft, but likewise becomes the means of profit to the thief? Another requisite of the prescription from ten to twenty years is just title; that is, a juridical and lawful cause of acquisition or a title which by its nature may transfer the right of property, and, on the other hand, be valid; for instance, the sale, the barter, the donation, the legacy, the dedition in payment.

The title is to be real and valid and not putative; as that of him who believes he has received such properties in the estate of his father and possesses the same, therefore, in the belief of his being the heir of what his father was never possessed, and for that reason could never transfer it to him.

If the putative title be no title, neither will the conditional title deserve that consideration; for he who obtains a thing on condition can not believe himself to be the present owner. He will be such only when the condition shall have been accomplished; and if he mistakenly deemed that it had been accomplished, the ten years' prescription would not avail, as no title would have existed, but only an opinion of its actual existence.

Finally, the title must be valid. Article 2267 of the French Code declares that the title void for imperfect form can not be invoked here, which, it is said, meets with no difficulty in case of solemn acts, the efficacy of which depends on forms without which they have no legal existence. For instance, when a property has been conveyed in a private document while the law prescribes that it should be done in a public, registered deed, or in case of documents which are void or voidable by vices differing from those of form, such as violence or dole, error, incapacity, want of cause or lawful object, infraction of the laws concerning public order or morality, nullities which are not spoken of in the code. Respecting these, the rule established and considered to be the most rational, is that which consists in distinguishing between such as are absolute, introduced in favor of public order, and which all may invoke, and such as are relative to the author of the act.

Now, if the doctrines of prescription are to be transferred from private to international law, the wiser course would be to adopt for the latter (excepting, of course, the increase of the terms of ten and twenty years), which is the least objectionable; and not that of thirty, of which the same thing can not be said, because, it being deprived of just title and good faith, appears in a character which destroys the universal notions of justice and the confraternity of men and nations.

Justice demands that every one should be given what is his, and that his property be respected, subject only to contributions and to expropriations for the benefit of the public, upon the indemnification of its value, and everyone left without restriction in the enjoyment of its advantages.

Accordingly, in the Penal Code of Venezuela, for instance, there exists a section (the fifth) on the offenses against property, which treats of piracy and sharpers, of robbery and theft, and of encroachment upon immovable property and real rights. This last offense is committed, first, when some one appropriates to himself such property or rights without any title or with a manifestly invalid title; second, when he appropriates the same to himself with a valid title, but understood and applied in a manifestly erroneous manner, to the detriment of a third party; and, third, when he uses this kind of property with the intention, not of appropriating the same to himself, but of enjoying the usufruct thereof during some time.

Let this law be compared with the following examples given by Marcadé. He supposes that the possessor of a ground presents himself to the owner, when the latter claims the same, and answers him thus: "It is very true that I have never had a just title; that, in bad faith and with the knowledge that it was another's, I have appropriated that ground to myself; but I have cultivated and managed it these forty, fifty, or sixty years, as its owner; and now, for this reason only, it belongs to me; I have prescribed it."

In the same way, the author adds that the usurper will then be declared to be the true owner, for the sole reason of his having possessed as such during thirty years, and in spite of his avowal. So will also be sanctioned the claim of the defendant who will say: "I know perfectly well that I owed you 50,000 francs, and that my debt has never been paid by me nor forgiven by you; but it was due over thirty years ago, without your having ever prosecuted me or exercised any act interruptive of my prescription; therefore, your claim is extinguished; now I owe you nothing." The author characterizes such means of defense as "impudent," but agrees to the necessity of ascribing to it juridical efficacy. It is the reverse of the rule: "*Capta a latronibus et piratis dominium non mutant.*"

Authors are far from agreeing as to the morality of prescription; they, however, go so far as to say that it must be a sacrifice to the convenience of society.

Eugeñe Ortolan reminds us that it is called "*patroness of mankind, and, notwithstanding, there is generally, on the other hand, a tendency to consider it as implying something contrary to equity, and to see with little favor him who invokes the benefit thereof.*"

Marcadé blames Troplong for having said that, when prescription civilly extinguishes a debt, it, for that reason, extinguishes it morally, considering such as a grave error in which the same jurist contradicts and condemns himself, and affirms that "*the extinction of a debt by prescription leaves untouched the question of the existence or non-existence of the moral obligation, and that it is evident that the debtor in this case, although free in the eyes of the law, may continue obligated in conscience.*"

He quotes another passage from M. Troplong, in which he says that " by the mere fact of the thirty years falling due the obligation would remain totally annihilated, both civilly and morally, and that by the fact only of the term having elapsed the original obligation would have ceased to be an obligation, and could no longer reappear among the recognized rights," and notes that " such a passage contains two mistakes, because prescription, besides its breaking only the civil bond of the obligation, and not the natural or moral, only produces effect when the defendant opposes it against the plaintiff; that despite the expiration of the thirty years, and even of forty and more, the original obligation may, as long as the defendant has not declared that he takes a stand behind prescription, always and at any time reappear among the recognized rights, and will reappear with all its full force and effect."

Objecting to another assertion of M. Troplong, he affirms that "*prescription is in many cases repugnant to self-respect and probity, and for this very reason it should always be expected and desired that the litigant should not resort to this extreme stand, which often is but an asylum for rascals.*"

And in another place, M. Troplong tells us that it is then well impossible to believe in scruples of conscience. It is very certain, and it is not either by this motive of the truly honest man that we explain the silence about prescription of him who is seen to exhaust efforts of all kinds, and even some times ridiculous, in his purpose not to yield. But in the absence of this motive of the truly honest man, is there not also the motive of those who, being rascals in reality, endeavor, however, not to appear as such? In the absence of the fear of God, does not the fear of the world very often remain? And will it not very often be for this salutary fear of public opinion that this litigant of bad faith, who in reality would desire but to avail himself of prescription, dare not speak of it? Now, it is evidently the duty of the legislator to avail this fear of the world, this conscience of those who have none, to make the judges apply prescription by virtue of their office in favor of the same would be satisfying their wishes by offering them an easy means to obtain the benefit of their bad faith without even having the courage therefor required. Certainly the legislator ought not to do so, and in reality the least is, that he who desires to use prescription should make, in a loud voice, a declaration thereof.

"On the contrary, an accomplished prescription may well be disclaimed, because that is but a question of private interest, and the disclaimer, far from being then imposed by the dependence on which a future debtor finds himself, is only *an act of self-respect and conscience, perfectly free, and by which society can not but profit.*"

"*Prescription being an extreme means to which he may be reluctant to resort even in support of a very lawful right* (*as it seldom fails to impair, in the opinion of the public, the esteem of him who makes use of it*)*, a means which, on this very account, a litigant will not be apt to employ, except when finding all his other resources insufficient, through the turn taken by the issue the law ought to allow it to be invoked in any stage of the case, and even at the last moment; that is to say, as long as a final sentence has not been pronounced.*"

Aubry and Rau, in their "Course of French Civil Law, after the method of Zacharie," Vol. I, paragraph 210, say:

"Usucapation is less a mode of acquisition, in the true sense of the word, than a means of strengthening by the aid of a possession provided with certain characters and continued for a determined length of time an acquisition submitted to eviction or yet simply persumptive. Thence the retroactive effect united to the accomplishment of the prescription."

In a note to this passage they write:

"Such appears to us to be the true character of *usucaption* considered on its rational principle. It may undoubtedly happen that *usucaption* results in the transformation into property of a possession, in support of which no title ever existed; *but it can not be admitted that, in instituting usucaption, the legislator has had the thought of sanctioning the encroachment or the dispossession.*"

The most strenuous supporters of prescription are bound to admit that its results are sometimes deplorable. G. Baudry-Lacantinerie, in his "Summary of Civil Law (Vol. I, par. 1578), says: "But all human institutions have their weak part. Prescription is no exception to this rule. Incidentally, it will secure the victory of the trespasser over the true owner, or will discharge a debtor who has not paid a debt, and the creditor shall be the sufferer."

* * * * * * *

"In any case, if on some rare hypotheses it seems that prescription leads to results which equity disapproves, it may well be pardoned in exchange for the immense services which it renders to society."

In short, prescription may be convenient; but in most cases it implies injustice, and, sometimes, deplorable consequences. It punishes the negligence or inaction of the owner, and by so doing rewards at the same time a blamable action in those who possess themselves of another's property and retain it by force. It is, therefore, odious, and, according to the most approved rules of ethics, ought to be restrictively understood.

Vattel shows that, in case of doubt, if favorable things are the question, it is safer to amplify the meaning of words; and if odious things, to restrict it. And to distinguish what is favorable from what is odious, he offers certain rules, which Zello, following him, summarizes.

One of them is, that everything that will change the present condition of things, causing the profit of one to consist in the loss of another, is odious: *Incommoda vitandis melior quam commoda petentis est causa.*

Such happens with prescription. If the possessor gains, it is because the owner loses. This loss may arise, not only from negligence, but also from inculpable ignorance, generous sentiments, justified fear, the abuse of force against debility, the confidence in the honesty of the debtors, or their gratitude, etc.

The title of "odious" is also given to everything containing a penalty.

By virtue of prescription the penalty is inflicted of the loss of a property, either movable or immovable, or of a debt only because it has not been demanded at terms more or less short, notwithstanding the debtor may have availed the lodging or the board at a kind hotel-keeper's, or recovered his health through the intelligent services of a physician, or with the medicines of an apothecary, or gained a process through the proper direction of a jurist or the agency of a solicitor, or constructed a building with the labor of a workman.

CHAPTER XI.

PRESCRIPTION ACCORDING TO THE LAWS OF SEVERAL COUNTRIES.

In order to see what prescription has been and is now, the laws of several countries relating to it will be briefly referred to, beginning with those of the Romans. It is well known that their legislation was adopted in all the civilized world, and is still the basis of some of the modern systems of jurisprudence.

Before Justinian, prescription and usucaption were considered separately, and since that time confounded with each other, and have so continued. *Usucaption* was a mode of acquiring property by possession during a certain prolonged period of time and under certain conditions. *Prescription* gave the possessor the right to defend himself against revindication, when possession was in good faith, was founded on a fair title, and had continued for a specific time. Thus, as has been observed, usucaption was a means of acquiring property, while prescription was intended mainly, but not wholly, for the liberation of debtors from their obligations.

The requisites of prescription were: 1. Just cause. 2. Good faith. 3. Actual possession. 4. A certain period of time. 5. A thing susceptible of prescription. 6. Possibility of usucaption against the owner.

Just cause consisted in a juridical act, indicating that the delivery of the thing was made with the intention of conveying it, and that he who received it intended to acquire it; such as the case of a sale, donation, legacy, endowment, the act of giving in payment, abandonment, and acquisition of an inheritance, etc. The cause had to be just according to law, and not forbidden by it; no error intervening about it.

Good faith is the belief of the possessor that he who delivered him the property was its owner. Bonjean and others hold that good faith consists (1) in the fact that he who conveys the property believes himself to be the owner; (2) capacity to convey; and (3) that the title be free from vice. Good faith is a different thing from just cause. This is the juridical fact showing the animus of conveying. And good faith is the belief that the conveyor is the owner, or has the power to convey the thing.

Possession requires the *animus domini*. Whoever possesses on behalf of another can not make good the usucaption. Besides a possession, capable of producing effect, must be invested with the character of being continuous and uninterrupted. It is considered interrupted, either by a voluntary act of the interested party, or by abandoning the thing, or by an involuntary act on his part, as in the case of his being made a captive; or, if the thing falls in possession of a third person, the time of possession is thus lost. If, later on, the possessor recovers the thing and retains it in good faith, he may begin a new term, not being credited, however, with any portion of the time of the former possession. As to the effect of the judicial claim the Roman rules were lately changed.

The time required for prescription was fixed by Justinian at five years for present parties, and twenty years among absentees.

Several things were not susceptible of prescription, such as those which were not in the commerce of men, as, for instance, personal liberty, sacred, religious, holy, and public things, such as those under public dominion of the people and of the cities, runaway slaves, gifts to a provincional Governor, things stolen or possessed by force. As to the latter it was claimed that the thief could not acquire them by usucaption, for he has no fair title nor good faith, and that the meaning of the rule is not for him, but for everybody else, as the stolen things remain *furtive*, even when purchased in good faith by anybody. The same thing is applicable to immovable things occupied by violence. Here it is observed that among the Romans theft was not only the surreptitious, fraudulent taking of a thing, but likewise of its use or possession, such as that of a tenant or lessee conveying his trusts and receiving the price of the same. The vice of theft or violence disappeared with the return of things to their owners.

In regard to the possibility of usucaption against the owner of the thing possessed, it is observed that there were certain persons whose things were not susceptible of usucaption. Such as: 1. Things belonging to the treasury, although they were subject to the thirty years' prescription. 2. When women were under perpetual guardianship there *res manicipi* (things of a slave) things delivered by them without the authority of their guardian. 3. The immovable endowments of women. 4. The properties of minors. Upon the later point the jurists were not all agreed, but Justinian enacted that prescription was not to be valid against minors.

Besides the ordinary prescription there was one of thirty years, called a very long duration, which Justinian kept in vigor. But it did not give the property to a possessor in bad faith, but it did afford the means to defend it and oppose an exception against the action of recovery by the owner, so that if he had lost possession of the thing he had no right to recover it.

Another prescription of forty years was in reference—first, to church property, for the prescription of which a hundred years was needed in olden times; second, the hypothecary actions; and third, property belonging to the patrimony of the Emperor.

[The above doctrines have been condensed from "Justinian's Institutes Methodical Explanation," by George Bonjean, who continued the work of de Lariche, one of the highest authorities among modern commentators of the Roman law.]

Immemorial prescription is added by others, which is not determined by any fixed time, since there is no memory against it. It is proved by the testimony of old witnesses, who are questioned as to whether they have seen the thing intended to be prescribed in thirty or less years; if they heard their predecessors state the same thing; and if they fail to remember having heard anything to the contrary. The affirmative answers are considered as an evidence of the prescription thus mentioned.

Good faith and just cause or title are the cardinal bases upon which prescription lies, and the same may be said to give a color of justice in certain cases to the loss of the thing when its primitive owner has neglected for a long time the use of his rights, knowing them, and through a voluntary and sheer ignorance. If he has ignored the circumstances during the time defined by law, just as in the cases of short prescriptions, there is no fault of his, and the penalty applied to him is only to the advantage of the possessor and to that of a slow debtor in the fulfillment of his obligations, all of which seems to be unjustifiable.

The Roman law, and that of some modern nations following its example, was satisfied with the existence of good faith at the beginning. The least reflection is sufficient, however, to show that once the possessor was sure that the thing did not belong to his conveyor, or that it was stolen, robbed, or usurped, he becomes an accessory to the theft or usurpation, and must, in conscience, return the thing to its lawful owner. On this point it is not permitted to trifle with pecuniary interest. The purchaser knowing that the thing is stolen or usurped is as guilty as the one who retains it, even if it was for a day after the bargain, since he discovered the fraud. It is true that he may lose the price of the thing if the seller, from whom he has a right to recover, is insolvent; but by his silence in order to avoid any harm, he profits by the bad action; he contributes to the injury of the person despoiled and to the reward of the offender.

It is generally claimed that good faith must continue during the whole time required for the prescription, and that the specious reason that supervening bad faith does not change its status is not admitted. Good faith must continue from the beginning. They say that time can not be shortened, but only in consideration of a color of title, and chiefly good faith, and that *sublata causa tollitur effectus.* They recall that the old French law had embraced a rule of the Canon law, in consideration of the fact of the power of conscience in an honest man, and how much he can oppose to the light doctrine of the Roman law, making good faith necessary during the whole course of the possession. It is claimed that Pothier found this preference to be in accord with equity, and that two letters of appeal from Bourges and Paris had requested that the new Code Napoleon should adopt it. The legislator thought otherwise, and Mr. Bigot, his official interpreter, did not give any plausible explanation. There is something else yet, says M. de Troplong, and that is, in view of the obscurity of his ideas and the confusion of his style, usually plain and clear, he is tempted to believe that he resented the abrogation of the system, and concludes, "definitively, I think, that this point of Code Napoleon fails in equity, it is always vexatious to place the law in opposition to morals." (§ 936, Commentary on Article 2269 of the French Code.)

He is not alone in that opinion. The well-known British jurist, Bentham, in his treatise of civil legislation (2d Part, Chapter I), speaking of titles for the conveyance of property, writes:

"Possession, after a certain period of time, determined by law, must be considered above any other title. * * * I have supposed possession to be in good faith. Otherwise, to confirm it would not be to favor safety, but to reward crime. Nestor's age (over 200 years) ought not to be enough to secure for the usurper the salary and price of his iniquity. And why allow the malefactor any period of rest? Why should he enjoy the fruits of his crime under the protection of the laws he has violated?

"In regard to his heirs it is to be distinguished, if they are possessors in good faith, the same reasons may be alleged in favor of the former owner, and besides they have possession, so as to incline the balance. If they are in bad faith, just as were their ancestors, they are their accessories, and impunity never ought to be a privilege of fraud."

In Spain it is sufficient to prove good faith at the beginning. Such is the law, but not the practice, as the Canon Law is observed, whereby good faith must last till the very completion of prescription. Don Juan Salas, in his "Illustration of the Royal Spanish Law," asserts the same under the authority of Gregorio Lopez.

Covarruvias and Molina go so far as to hold, with many other authorities quoted by them, that bad faith makes prescription impossible, even if it were immemorial, when it is constant and not presumptive. Don Joaquin Escriche, in his Dictionary of Legislation, is of the same opinion, and Don Eugenio de Tapia likewise in his Febrero Novísimo. It is well known that Spain has recently not only introduced a change in very positive terms, but has carried things beyond the rules of other nations, in its present Civil Code, since 1886.

In that of France, which has been taken as a model by some other countries, prescription is adopted in the same way in which it was established by the Roman law. It excludes dominion over things not within the commerce of men. It requires a continued and uninterrupted possession—peaceful, public, unequivocal, and the conscience of the possessor that he is the owner. No merit is given to acts of mere faculty or simple tolerance, nor to those of violence, but it makes the possession useful and valid after the violence has ceased. It makes prescription liable to natural and civil interruption, as, for instance, in case the possessor or debtor acknowledges the right of the person against whom he holds or to whom he is obligated. It makes mention of thirty years' prescription of all actions, whether real or personal, without need of a title from the possessors and making unavailable the exception of bad faith. It fixes in ten years among parties present, and twenty among absentees, the prescription of immovable property acquired in good faith and a fair title. The title must not be null for want of form. Good faith is always presumed, the burden of proof being with the party alleging it; and it is enough that at the beginning of the acquisition it may have existed. In regard to immovable property, it establishes that possession is equivalent to title, but he who has lost a thing, or from whom it has been stolen, may recover it within three years, reckoning from the day of the loss or the theft, against the party in whose hands he finds it, and who retains recourse against the person from whom he received it. According to the commentators, the possession need not be with the conscience of the holder to be the master, so that a pawner may reject him. The possession, however, needs be in good faith, certain, and material.

The Italian Civil Code of 1865, the Spanish Code, and the codes of other countries, as well as that of Venezuela, are almost like that of France.

In regard to prescription according to the British laws, Stephen's Commentaries of the Laws of England, partially based on Blackstone's doctrine, fifth edition of 1863, has been consulted, and also "Wharton's Juridical Lexicon," forming an epitome of the laws of England, seventh edition of 1883. From the last-named work, as more recent, the following article on prescription is taken:

"The prescription title emanates from a long possession, continued and uninterrupted, of a property, and which Sir Edward Coke defines, *præscriptio est titulus ex usu et tempore substantian capiens ab auctoritate legis.* Any kind of prescription, by which property is acquired or lost, is founded upon the presumption that he who has held it quietly and uninterruptedly for a long period of years is supposed to have a right to it, without which he could not have continued in the peaceable use of the same. A long possession may be considered as a better title than what may be generally produced, as it supposes the general acquiescence of all other claimants, and that acquiescence supposes, likewise, some kind of a reason for the omission to recover.

"There are two kinds of prescription, to wit, the positive prescription, in reference to immovable things or corporal hereditaments, by which an uninterrupted possession for a definite time on the part of the occupant makes a valid and unexceptionable title against every other claimant of any old right or deferred lawsuit, that is now governed by 3 and 4, Wm. IV., c. 27; negative prescription refers to incorporal hereditaments, and had its origin in the common law for immemorial use only.

* * * * * * *

"The position of prescription has been widely modified by statutes 2 and 3, Wm. IV., c. 71; 2 and 3, Wm. IV., c. 100, and 4 and 5, Wm. IV., c. 88."

* * * * * * *

"Common law has the following rules in regard to positive prescription:

1. "The only property liable to be claimed by positive prescription is an *incorporal hereditament.*

2. "It must be founded on actual use and enjoyment of a thing, as a mere recovery does not establish any right.

3. "The use and enjoyment must have been continuous and peaceful, although an interruption for a comparatively short time does not affect it.

4. "The use must have been, from time immemorial, or from a time of which there is no memory or criterion, and it is thought that its beginning was during the time of Richard I.

* * * * * * *

5. "Prescription must be certain and reasonable.

* * * * * * *

8. "Prescription can not affect a thing that can not originate by or be the subject of a concession.

* * * * * * *

10." No person can prescribe the commission of an injustice or anything injurious to anybody else; nor against an act of Parliament, as that is the highest evidence; nor a lawfully-recorded deed, or against somebody else's prescription."

The same doctrine is held by Stephen, [Book 2, chapter 27] adding that prescription is regulated by 2 and 3 Wm. IV., c. 71, the law intending to shorten its time in certain cases, and suppress the rule requiring the enjoyment for an immemorial time in every case as the basis of a prescriptive right.

That law establishes in regard to rights to land held in common, and to every other use or benefit that may be derived from land, with the exception of tithes, rents, and services, which remain as they were by common law, that when there has been an enjoyment of them by any person, who claims a right to the same, without interruption during thirty years, near the time of the beginning of any lawsuit about the subject, the prescriptive right will not be considered as already destroyed by showing proper evidence that the enjoyment began at a period subsequent to that of legal memory; but that it may be destroyed in any other way by which it might have been destroyed before the enactment of the law, so that it may be satisfactorily responded by proving that the enjoyment for thirty years was without the knowledge of the adverse party, or the effect of a mere license or permission, as either of these circumstances would have obstructed the presumptive right before the statutes.

It is likewise established that in the computation of this period of thirty years the time will be excluded in which the adverse party may have been an infant, an idiot, or an incapable person, *non compos mentis*, a married woman, or a lessee for life at the time in which an action at law may have been pending and diligently followed until its annulment by death of the parties. But when the enjoyment has been for as long a time as *sixty* years the recovery must be perfect and indestructible, except only on the evidence that such an enjoyment was accomplished in virtue of a deed or a written agreement or consent; while on the other hand, if the period of the enjoyment has been for less than thirty years it is entirely inoperative, even for the purpose of the lightest presumption of right.

What has been said will suffice to show that the English legislation requires alike for the prescription *an actual possession continuous, peaceful, certain, and reasonable, of a thing that is in the commerce of men; that it is held by the possessor in the character of an owner and not as a lessee or as a consequence of permission or consent of the owner, for then even the possession for thirty years might be destroyed; and that it does not run against minors, idiots, incapable persons, married women, or when interrupted by a lawsuit.* On the other hand, only the possession in good faith may be qualified as certain and reasonable, undoubtedly equivalent to that which the French Civil Code and the laws of other nations call *unequivocal;* that is to say, according to the authors, that possession where the conditions of continuity, publicity under the idea of ownership, etc., are manifest and subject to no doubt; not as in mere uses, which are exercised only intermittently, as, for instance, the right of way, which leave doubtful and uncertain the point whether they are really exercised *animo domini* or by tolerance of the neighbor, and therefore if possession becomes equivocal in this case, the law considers it as not susceptible of acquisition by prescription.

Nothing has been found in the article "Limitation of Actions," inserted in Wharton's Juridical Lexicon, to contradict the above conclusions. On the contrary, in explaining the reason for the introduction of limitation in those cases where the extinguishing *prescription* is applied in regard to immovable things after more than forty years of adverse possession, and even less time, a person must, according to every principle of justice, *except in case of fraud*, remain quietly and surely in his possession, as in such a long time his documents and proofs may have been lost and the property may have changed hands by inheritance, legacy, or conveyance of any other kind, and it would be unjust to exact from the different occupants the proof of their title on behalf of a client who has allowed his rights to be kept dormant.

So that, if there has been any fraud, prescription is not accomplished by the English laws, even after forty years.

From Giles, Jacob and T. E. Tomlin's Law Dictionary," in two volumes, London edition of 1809, the following passages on the subject of prescription are taken:

"*Prescription.* A title acquired by use and time and conferred by law, as when a man pretends to a thing because he himself, his ancestors, or those from whom he derives his rights have had it in use for a time, of which there is no memory to the contrary, or when the continuance of the time *ultra memorium hominis*, a particular person has a particular right against another person.

"Blackstone classifies the *title by prescription* among the means of acquiring immovable things by *purchase*, as when a man can not show another title as to what he claims as his own, but that he himself and those from whom he derives his claim have used it and enjoyed it immemorially.

"Prescription must be for a time of which there is no memory to the contrary, yet it is not a long or short time that engenders a right of prescription, time having no effect, though everything is done in time; but it is a presumption of right that a possession can not continue quietly if it is against right of or is prejudicial to anyone else.

"Things acquired by prescription are not transferable to heirs in general, as are other things acquired; they constitute an exception to the rule, as, properly speaking, prescription must be considered rather as a proof of a previous acquisition than as an acquisition *de novo.*

* * * * * * *

"Prescription must have a legitimate beginning, and peaceful possession as well as time, as both are inseparable incidents of it. Although a title earned by custom or prescription is not to be lost by the interruption of possession for ten or twenty years, it may be lost by an interruption of right."

CHAPTER XII.

INTERNATIONAL PRESCRIPTION.

Let it be borne in mind that the prescription dealt with by the internal laws of States is that which relates to private property, which consists in "enjoying and disposing of a thing without any other limitations than those established by law," as the Spanish Civil Code says, or is, according to Roman law, a right *in re*, from which arises the faculty to dispose of a thing and of vindicating it. Such property may belong to absent foreigners, even to sovereigns in respect to lands situated in another territory, and which remain subject to the laws and tribunals of the same, as also to the by-laws and taxes of the local police in all that concerns such property. The said proprietors are known under the name of foreign subjects.

States may have a private or public dominion, a sort of property by private statute, combined with the dispositions of the internal public laws of each country.

They have also what has been styled eminent dominion, though not to the extent attributed to it in ancient times, for they have only the right to regulate the conditions, the consequences, and the public charges relating to private property.

Eugene Ortolan, the advocate of this doctrine, adds "that in all cases, without any possible discussion, the nation, or the collective being which constitutes the State, has, so far as the properties of its subjects are concerned, a power, a supreme right of legislation, of jurisdiction and of taxation; a right inferred from the relations of a nation, as sovereign, over the members forming it, which, when applied to lands, is in short nothing else than a part of the internal territorial sovereignty, though not the property as between nations."

He further contends "that the State has not only got a right over the properties of its subjects, but also over the properties of foreigners, whom it allows to reside and to possess property on its territory; and that as this right comes from the relations of a nation with private individuals, it is subject to the internal sovereignty and is not yet the right of property as between nations."

For the idea of this right to arise, it is necessary to consider the State, not in its home relations with private individuals, but in its foreign relations with other nations, respecting the territory upon which it is established. It is necessary to consider the moral wants of action or of inaction that the rational common law, or use or custom, imposes upon nations as between themselves with regard to such territory. *Thus the actors who figure in this kind of right are well described; it is the nations in their relations to one another.* For this reason, in calling this a right of *domain* or *property*, it is necessary to qualify these words by the addition of *international* domain, or property as between *State* and *State*."

The said author proceeds to point out the legal distinction between *property* and *possession*, the first of which conveys an idea of how to act, of the moral necessity of action or inaction, respecting the thing subject of it; while the second consists in holding a thing in one's power to be in a position to derive from it every advantage, to guard it against the action of others who may attempt to appropriate it; an idea of power and of pretension.

After explaining the various names of *mancipium dominium* and *proprietas*, by which it was successively known in the Roman law, and showing that it was an *absolute*, not a *relative* right, a *positive* right, not a *personal* one, he goes on to define it by saying that "it is the right that belongs to a nation to use, to take the products, to dispose of a territory, to the exclusion of all other nations, *and to command over it as a sovereign power, independently of all foreign power;* a right that carries with it, as regards other States, the reciprocal obligation not to throw any obstacles in the way of using such territory by the nation which owns it, nor of arrogating to itself any right of command over the same territory."

The enormous difference that exists between private property and international property makes it evident that the rules governing the first can not be applied to the second; but that on the contrary, the greatest discretion must be used, in order not to extend from one to the other principles which would prove incompatible with the independence of nations. Nor is it admissible for one nation to prescribe to another the number of years that shall render an acquisition legitimate, nor to set aside the vouchers of just title and good faith; nor that a mere possession pacific though it be, and uninterrupted, should suffice, through the lapse of time agreed upon, to convert into property an illegitimate possesion. The rulings of several codes have been cited, fixing thirty years as the term limiting all royal and personal actions, without the necessity on the other side to adduce a good title and to show good faith. This refers to destructive prescription, however much the commentators will stretch the meaning to acquisition. It is only the Spanish Code, article 1959, that determines in unmistakable terms, "that dominion and all other royal rights upon lands are prescribed by an uninterrupted possession during thirty years, regardless of title or of good faith, and without distinction between present and absent parties, excepting the case of non-apparent continuous uses and of the non-continuous, whether apparent or not, that can only be acquired by a title." It does not appear that so singular a ruling should be admitted with any degree of preference at common law, much less if it is remarked that if the important requisites of just title and good faith are ignored in it, "uninterrupted possession" is directly exacted, and tacitly in a manner that such possession be "by virtue of ownership, public and pacific."

On enquiring what formalities of national law are required at common law regarding prescription, it becomes evident at once that in the latter less latitude is given to it than in the former. Thus it is seen that in the Civil Code of Spain, article 1930, it is first of all declared that prescription gives the right to acquire dominion and all other royal privileges, and that it also extinguishes all rights and actions of whatever nature. This tallies with the French law, which describes prescription as a means of acquiring or of freeing oneself during a given time and under the conditions determined by law. Such are also the terms of the Italian and Venezuelan laws. It has been shown likewise that in civil law prescription applies as much to real as to personal estate.

By reference to the various treatises on common law, it is found, particularly, in Ortolan's "Means of Acquiring International Dominion," that where that by prescription is reached, it speaks only of the acquisitive, and it heads thus, article 4th devoted to it. On the other hand, in the course of his remarks, he limits himself by restriction to the soil; to territorial property, not to personal estate.

Pradier-Fodéré, also, in his "Treatise on Public International Law, European and American," when expounding, in Vol. II, chap. 5, his doctrine upon prescription, paragraph 890, and after explaining the term as meaning that, in its broad acceptation, "prescription comprises at one and the same time acquisitive prescription or usucaption and destroying prescription, properly speaking," he writes that the first is the only one he has to deal with, and, in fact, upon that one only does he descant in the course of his explanations. Without expressing his thoughts about personal property, as

Ortolan does, he omits all reference thereto, and devotes himself exclusively to his principles on real estate.

It seems, therefore, to be the opinion of both authors that acquisitive prescription of real estate is the one that can come under the heading of international law.

Among the ways in which obligations under public treaties cease to exist is, complete execution, the accomplishment of a decisive condition, the end of the term agreed upon, the direct renunciation of the interested party, the mutual rescission of a bilateral agreement, the complete annihilation of the thing to which it refers, the demise of the party interested without successor to his rights or obligations, a general war with certain restrictions; but there is no record that public contracts become extinguished by any lapse of time, as happens with obligations between private individuals.

The United States of America have positively declared it so. Section 239 of Wharton's International Law Digest says:

> "There is no statute of limitation as to international claims, nor is there any presumption of payment or settlement from the lapse of twenty years. Governments are presumed to be always ready to do justice, and whether a claim be a day or a century old, so that it is well founded, every principle of natural equity, of sound morals, requires it to be paid." [M. Crallé, Acting Secretary of State, to Mr. Crump, October 30, 1844, M. S. S., Inst., Chili.]

A proof that it is not possible always to apply, in their entirety, the maxims of civil law to nations independent of one another, and which have to be guided by the principles of reason and justice that constitute the law of nature.

It is not conceivable why international law should be brought under the most odious form of prescription, which, alleging the convenience to civil society and oblivious of morality, ignores just title and good faith, though not the other requisites to possession, whereas with them it exacts in a cumulative form those two conditions which render it less repugnant and quiet the conscience.

However, this point will be decided by the Arbitrators according to the dictates of their enlightened consciences and impartial reason, and Venezuela so trusts. She believes that prescription being subject to certain formalities, and that only one of these—namely, that of time—having been agreed upon between the parties, the Arbitrators will decide that for the rest the usual rules in cases like the present shall be applied. This was doubtless foreseen when drawing up the Treaty of February 2d, 1897, since it authorizes the Judges to acknowledge and to give effect to rights and renewed claims based upon any other valid ground in accordance with international law, and upon any principles of international law that they may consider applicable to the case and that do not clash against the preceding rule—that is to say, to the efficacy of an adverse possession of fifty years.

CHAPTER XIII.

ANTECEDENTS OF THE TREATY.

The fact that the legislation of a country may have precluded some of the formalities that are essential to prescription, which relate to a lapse of many years, establishing it thus in a positive and definite manner, does not imply that the same is to be applied to international law, about which no rules exist on this subject till now. They would be decisive only in diplomatic conventions on account of the independence of States and the impossibility resulting therefrom that some should be subjected to the law of others. And such acts establish obligations only between those who institute them by their free will and sign them for a specified time or occasion.

It is now for the first time that Venezuela has signed such a compact. It does not constitute a full chapter of prescription, but merely a rule establishing a most essential point of it, namely, the period of possession sufficient to make a valid title; and also two facts considered as equally strong, namely, exclusive dominion of a district or its effective political control. On all other points, it is necessary to apply the rules generally accepted by the expounders of Public International Law. This is what the Government of the Republic has understood—what is in accordance with the antecedents of the question, and what has been explained by the functionaries who have been taking part in it, as will be seen by the following synoptic account.

His Excellency the Secretary of State of the Great Republic, Mr. Richard Olney, said to the United States

Minister in London, in order that he should communicate it to Lord Salisbury, Her Britannic Majesty's Minister for Foreign Affairs, on the 20th of July, 1895, what follows:

"It is, indeed, intimated that the British claim to this particular territory rests on occupation, which, whether acquired or not, has ripened into a perfect title by long continuance. But, what prescription affecting territorial rights can be said to exist as between Sovereign States? Or, if there is any, what is the legitimate consequence? It is not that all arbitration should be denied, but only that the submission should embrace an additional topic, namely, the validity of the asserted prescription title either in point of right or in point of fact."

Here is denied, in most emphatic, though interrogative form, that there is prescription between Sovereign States; and when, through a generous concession, it is admitted, enforces the necessity of *presenting to the Arbitrators the question of the validity of that title, either in point of right or in point of fact.* There are, therefore, in matters of prescription formalities of right and formalities of fact, which the Arbitrators have to examine as a basis for the appreciation of the validity of the title, according to its being or not being attained.

The Secretary is even more explicit in his later correspondence with the British Government, from February 27 to June 22, 1896, in regard to the appeal to arbitration of the Venezuelan-British boundary dispute, and generally of disputes between the United States and Great Britain.

He meets the opposition to arbitration on the part of Great Britain in territorial controversies in the following terms:

It is said, in the next place, that the rules of international law applicable to territorial controversies are not ascertained; that it is uncertain both what sort of occupation or control of territory is legally necessary to give a good title, and how long such title or control must continue; the 'projected procedure' will be full of 'surprises;' and that the modern doctrine of 'Hinterland' is illustrative of the unsatisfactory condition of international law upon the subject under discussion. But it can not be irrelevant to remark that the 'spheres of influence' and the theory or practice of the 'Hinterland' idea are things unknown to international law and do not as yet rest upon any recognized principles of either international or municipal law. They are new departures, which certain European powers have found necessary and convenient in the course of their division among themselves of great tracts of the continent of Africa, and which find their sanction solely in their reciprocal stipulations. 'Such agreements' declares a modern English writer on international law, 'remove the causes of present disputes;' but, if they are to stand the test of time, by what right will they stand? We hear much of a certain 'Hinterland' doctrine. The accepted rule as to the area of territory affected by an act of occupation in a land of large extent has been that the crest of the watershed is the presumptive interior limit, while river banks become the boundaries of lands which they water, the coast being occupied at the river's mouth. The extent of territory claimed by right of an occupation on the coast has hitherto borne some reasonable ratio to the character of the occupation. But where is the limit to the 'Hinterland doctrine?' Either of these international arrangements can avail only as between the parties and constitute no bar against the action of any intruding stranger, or might, indeed, is right. Without adopting this criticism, and whether the 'spheres of influence' and the 'Hinterland' doctrines be or be not intrinsically sound and just, *there can be no pretense that they apply to the American Continents or to any boundary disputes that now exist there, or that may hereafter arise.* Nor is to be admitted that, so far as territorial disputes are likely to arise between Great Britain and the United States, the accepted principles of international law are not adequate to their intelligent and just consideration and decision. For example, unless the treaties looking to the harmonious partition of Africa had worked some change, *the occupation, which is sufficient to give a state title to territory can not be considered as undetermined. It must be open, exclusive, adverse, continuous, and under claim of right. It need not be actual in the sense of involving the* POSSESSIO PEDIS *over the whole area claimed.* The only possession required is such as is reasonable under all the circumstances—in view of the extent of territory claimed, its nature, and the uses to which it is adapted and is put—while mere constructive occupation is kept within bounds by the doctrine of contiguity. It seems to be thought that the international law governing territorial acquisition by a State through occupation is fatally defective, because there is no fixed time during which occupation must continue. But it is obvious that there can be no such arbitrary time-limit, except through the consensus agreement or uniform usage of civilized States.

"It is equally obvious and much more important to note that, even if it were feasible to establish such arbitrary period of prescription by international agreement, it would not be wise or expedient. Each case should be left to depend upon its own facts. *A State which, in good faith, colonizes as well as occupies,* brings about large investments of capital, and founds populous settlements would justly be credited with a sufficient title in a much shorter space than a State whose possession was not marked by any such changes of *status.* Considerations of this nature induce the leading English authority on international law to declare that, on the one hand, it is 'in the highest degree irrational to deny that prescription is a legitimate means of international acquisition,' and that, on the other hand, *it will 'be found neither expedient nor practicable to attempt to define the exact period within which it can be said to have become established, or, in other words, to settle the precise limitation of time which gives validity to the title of national possessions. Again, the proofs of prescriptive possession are simple and few. They are, principally, publicity, confirmed occupation, absence of interruption* (USURPATIO), aided, in general, doubtless, both morally and legally speaking, by the employment of labor and capital upon the territory by the new possessor, while the former possessor remains silent, passive, without making any attempt to exercise proprietary rights. The period of time, as has been repeatedly said, can not be fixed by international law between nations, as it may be by private law between individuals; it must depend upon variable and varying circumstances, but in all cases these proofs would be required.' The inherent justness of these observations, as well as Sir Robert Phillimore's great weight as authority, seems to show satisfactorily that the condition of international law fails to furnish any imperative reasons for excluding boundary controversies from the scope of general treaties of arbitration. If that be true of civilized States generally, *a fortiori* must it be true of the English-speaking nations. As they have not merely political institutions, but systems of jurisprudence, identical in their origin and in their fundamental ideas, as the law of real property in each is but a growth from the same parent stem, it is not easy to believe that a tribunal composed of judges of the supreme court of each, even if a foreign jurist were to act as umpire, could produce any flagrant miscarriage of justice."

Now, since Mr. Olney professes such principles, and has alleged them in his argument against Great Britain in contradiction of her reluctance to adopt arbitration in her boundary dispute with this Republic, it is manifest that he had the intention that they should be applied to it when he proposed to Lord Salisbury the four articles in which they undertook to decide it, and which he submitted afterwards for the acceptance of Venezuela. In his speech at the banquet given by the Lord Mayor of London, on the occasion of his inauguration, the 11th of November, 1896, Her Britannic Majesty's Minister for Foreign Affairs, said:

"But, as you are aware, in the discussion we have had with the United States, their friends, the Venezuelans, the question has been, not whether there should be arbitration, but whether the arbitration should have unrestricted application, and we have always claimed that those who, apart from historic right, had the right which attaches to established settlements—the settled districts—that they should be excluded from the arbitration. Our difficulty for many months has been to find how to define the settled districts, and a solution has been found—*I think it has come from the Government which His Excellency represents* (addressing himself to the United States Minister)—that we should treat the Colonial Empire just as we treat individuals, the same lapse of time which protects individuals in civic life from having their title questioned should also protect the English Colony from having its title questioned. And, furthermore, that where that lapse of time could not be claimed, though there should be an examination of title, yet all that equity demanded in consideration of such inchoate title should be granted. It is a very simple solution. I believe I am not using unduly sanguine words when I say that I believe that it has brought this controversy to an end."

The London Times of November 11, 1896, commenting on Lord Salisbury's speech, said:

"There was never, as our readers are aware, though the fact has sometimes been ignored, any difficulty about the principle of arbitration. As a matter of fact, Great Britain has been ready to arbitrate for a very long time past upon everything that could reasonably be regarded as within the domain of controversy. The only difficulty with the United States was as to the scope of the proposed arbitration, and this has been settled by conjoining with the rules of international law the principles governing the possession of property which are recognized by all nations. *International law does not know anything of right founded upon prescription, while in municipal law it is one of the least disputable claims to possession.* The settlement now happily arrived at is founded upon the indefeasibility of title furnished by a prescription of fifty years. While this term of possession confers an unquestionable right and takes the subjects out of the sphere of arbitration, possession for shorter periods is held to confer an inchoate right, the exact value of which is a matter of impartial appraisement. This principle, as we gather from Lord Salisbury's speech, runs concurrently with the usually accepted canons of international law. At all events, it is the original contention of this country in a slightly altered form. We have proposed, at different times, different boundary lines as defining with substantial accuracy the regions in which settlement has acquired the sanction of prescription. We now agree that the areas in which title is secured by prescription shall define the boundary. Formerly, we offered to arbitrate upon doubtful areas outside the boundary; now we agree to refer to arbitration all the areas in which the prescriptive title remains incomplete."

As will be seen, it was on the part of Mr. Olney that the means of solution, accepted by the British Government, was proposed. Consequently it must be understood in conformity with the ideas which he entertained on the matter, as put forth in his correspondence with Lord Salisbury, already referred to.

What they tried to settle in the boundary question between Venezuela and British Guiana was that which relates to the time of prescription, fixing it, by mutual consent, in fifty years; because it was impossible to settle it otherwise as between nations. All the rest, reputed as essential to this manner of acquisition, that is to say, what is requisite for it, as mentioned by Mr. Olney in support of Phillimore, remains without alteration, viz.: that of publicity of possession; that of its character of adverse, continuous holding; and that of its being exercised with pretension of right, to which the British author adds the employment of capital and labor by the new possessor during the period of silence or inactivity on the part of a previous owner. He spoke of the principal requisites without mentioning others, which no doubt are a just title, good faith in its possession, and peaceful nature.

Another proof of the foregoing assertions will be found in the answer given by Mr. Olney on the 12th of June, 1896, to Lord Salisbury's proposition for the settlement of the controversy then pending between Great Britain and the United States of Venezuela.

Great Britain proposed what follows:

"By covenant between Great Britain and the United States a Commission is to be appointed by agreement between Great Britain and the United States, consisting of four members, namely, two British subjects and two citizens of the United States. The above Commission to investigate and report upon the facts in regard to the rights of the United Netherlands and Spain, respectively, at the date of the acquisition of British Guiana by Great Britain.

"This Commission will only examine into questions of facts without reference to the inferences that may be founded on them; but the finding of a majority of the Commission upon those questions shall be binding upon both Governments.

"Upon the report of that Commission being made the two Governments of Great Britain and Venezuela, respectively, shall endeavor to agree to a boundary line upon the basis of such report. Failing of agreement, the report and every other matter concerning this controversy on which either Government desire to insist, shall be submitted to a Tribunal of three—one nominated by Great Britain, the other by Venezuela, and the third by the two so nominated, which Tribunal shall fix the boundary line upon the basis of such report, and the line so fixed shall be binding upon Great Britain and Venezuela. Provided, always, that in fixing such a line the Tribunal shall not have power to include as the territory of Venezuela any territory which was *bona fide* occupied by subjects of Great Britain on the 1st of January, 1887, or as the territory of Great Britain any territory *bona fide* occupied by Venezuelans at the same date.

"In respect to any territory with which by this provision the Tribunal is precluded from dealing, the Tribunal may submit to the two powers any recommendations which seem to it calculated to satisfy the equitable rights of the parties, and the two powers will take such recommendations into their consideration."

"It will be evident from this proposal," Lord Salisbury continued, "that we are prepared to accept the finding of a Commission voting as three to one upon all the facts which are involved in the question of Dutch and Spanish rights at the time of the cession of Guiana to Great Britain. We are also prepared to accept the decision of an Arbitral Tribunal in regard to the ownership of all portions of the disputed territory *which are not under settlement by British subjects or Venezuelan citizens.* If the declaration of the Commission shall affect any territory which is so settled it will be in the power of either Government to decline to accept the decision thus arrived at, so far as it affects the territory alleged to be settled. But I need not point out to you that even upon that question, although the decision of the Arbitral Tribunal will not have a final effect, it will, unless it be manifestly unfair, offer a presumption against which the protesting Government will practically find it difficult to contend."

It was impossible that a statesman like Mr. Olney should fail to perceive the objections to which Lord Salisbury's proposition was open. It began with the first Commission of four members, which would be useless if less than three of them should be in accord. It omitted to provide some standard by which to determine the good or bad faith of occupations existing on the 1st of January, 1887. And it ended by excluding from arbitration any and all territory *then* occupied by British subjects or by Venezuelan citizens. Such a proposal seemed a repetition of that of 1893, made to the Venezuelan agent, Mr. Tomas Michelena, by Lord Rosebery; namely, that in the arbitration convention it should be declared that the territory in dispute lies to the west of the line marked down on the map sent to the Government of Venezuela on March 12, 1890, and to the east of a line that was to be marked down on the same map and should run from the source of the River Cumano downwards, and upwards of the Aima, and thus along the length of the Usupamo ridge. It constituted a new insistence on the negative resolution of arbitration with which Lord Salisbury ended his note of 26th November, 1895, in answer to that of Mr. Olney, dated the 20th of July previous, that he rejects, on the 12th of June, 1896, with such conclusive arguments that not even one word of it should be lost. It is addressed to Sir Julian Pauncefote, British Ambassador in Washington, and is of the following tenor:

"I have the honor to acknowledge your favor of the 3d instant, to which is attached a despatch to yourself from Lord Salisbury, of the 23d ultimo, embodying proposals for the settlement of the Venezuelan dispute, which you are requested to submit to the Government of the United States. These proposals have been considered with care and with the strongest disposition to find in them a practical, as well as just, solution of the controversy to which they relate.

"It is with regret, therefore, that this Government deems itself unable to treat the proposals either as well adapted to bring the Venezuelan boundary dispute to a speedy conclusion or as giving due recognition to the just rights of the parties concerned.

"It is suggested, for example, that a Commission of four persons, two of them British subjects and two of them citizens of the United States, shall investigate and determine certain facts. But, unless this Commission chances to reach its results unanimously or by a vote of three to one it would as well be that the Commission had not been created. In the not improbable event of its standing two to two, nothing could come of it in the way of ascertained facts, while, by strengthening each party in the conviction of the truth of its own contention, its tendency would be to make any peaceful settlement remote or even impossible.

"Further, this Commission, so constituted as not to be certain of reaching a result as to the subjects which are submitted to it, seems also unfortunately limited as respects such subjects. It is to report the facts affecting rights of the United Netherlands and of Spain, respectively, at the date of the acquisition of British Guiana by Great Britain. Upon the basis of such report a boundary line is to be drawn which, however, is in no case to encroach upon the *bona fide* settlements of either party. But how are the facts showing the existence and *bona fides* of such settlements to be ascertained? As this Commission is carefully disqualified from investigating and reporting them, the first and, perhaps the best, impression is that they are left to be determined by further negotiations, involving another convention and not impossibly still another Commission. If this slow and dilatory procedure is not contemplated, it must be because the Arbitral Tribunal, which is to consider not only the report but 'every other matter concerning this controversy on which either Government desires to insist,' will be bound to receive, and will undoubtedly have laid before it, all matters pertaining to *bona fide* occupation by settlers. Such may be the fair implication from the power given to the Tribunal to make recommendations respecting the equities growing out of such occupation. But if it is intended that the Arbitral Tribunal shall hear the evidence and find the facts on the subject of the *bona fide* occupation, there is certainly no reason why the power should not be given in explicit terms. Even then it is apparent why one and the same Commission should not be charged with determining all the facts which the controversy involves.

"These considerations seem to show that His Lordship's proposals, looked at as embodying a practical scheme for a speedy and final settlement of the boundary dispute, can not be regarded as satisfactory. Another and even graver objection to them remains to be stated. An Arbitral Tribunal is provided, which is to fix the true original boundary line. *If, however, this line sets off to one party territory* BONA FIDE *occupied by a citizen or subject of the other on January 1st, 1887, it is not to be binding as to such occupied territory.* The decision as to this part of the line, it is intimated, will have great weight, and the Tribunal is authorized to make recommendations to the equitable rights of the parties, which they are expected to duly consider. *But the absolute result is that though the Arbitral Tribunal may find certain territory to belong to Venezuela, and may even find that there are no equities which prevent her having it, whether she gets it or not, is to depend upon the good pleasure of Great Britain—upon her generosity, her sense of justice, her caprice, or her views of expediency generally.* It is to be noted, too, that neither in this dispatch nor in any other way, though the attention of the British Government has been often called to the point, is any clew afforded to what sort of occupation it is that is characterized as *bona fide. Would an occupation under temporary and revocable mining license, beginning December 31, 1886, be of that character? While the claims of Venezuela have always been a matter of public notoriety,* could a British subject establish his *bona fide* claim as against Venezuela by showing that, in point of fact, he had never heard of it? (This, however, has reference to minor criticisms.) The decisive objection to the proposals is that it appears to be a fundamental condition that the boundary line decided to be the true one by the Arbitrators shall not operate upon territory *bona fide* occupied by a British subject January 1, 1887; shall be *deflected* in every such case so as to make such territory part of British Guiana. It is true that the same rule is to apply in case of territory *bona fide* occupied by a Venezuelan January 1, 1887. *But as Great Britain asks for the rule and Venezuela opposes it, the inevitable deduction coincides with the undisputed fact, namely, that the former's interest is believed to be promoted by the rule, while the latter's will be prejudiced.* The true question is, therefore, whether the rule is just in itself without reference to its effective application, *so that Great Britain has a right to impose her will upon Venezuela in the matter.* How this question can be answered in the affirmative it is most difficult to perceive, and is not even attempted to be shown by the despatch itself. *It is a rule which is certainly without support in any principle of international law, or in any recognized international usage. It is a rule which would hardly be insisted upon unless its practical application was supposed to extend to many persons and to cover large interests. Yet, if the facts are not to be ignored, nor the ordinary rules of law set aside, its scope would seem to be quite limited, since the Schomburgk line was proclaimed, for the first time, in October, 1886, while in June, 1887, the Governor of British Guiana, by express instructions from the home Government, addressed the Court of Policy of the Colony in the following terms:*

" '*Before we proceed to the order of the day I am anxious to make a statement with reference to the question of the boundary between this Colony and the Republic of Venezuela. Among the applications which have been received for mining licenses and concessions, under the mining regulations passed by the ordinance 16 of 1880, 16 of 1886, and 4 of 1887, there are many which apply to lands which are within the territory in dispute between Her Majesty's Government and the Venezuelan Republic. I have received instructions from the Secretary of State to caution expressly all persons interested in such licenses or concessions, or otherwise acquiring an interest in the disputed territory, that all licenses, concessions, or grants applying to any portion of such disputed territory will be issued, and must be accepted, subject to the possibilities that, in the event of a settlement of the present disputed boundary line, the land to which such licenses, concessions, or grants apply may become a part of the Venezuelan territory, in which case no claim to compensation from the Colony or from Her Majesty's Government can be recognized, but Her Majesty's Government would, of course, do whatever may be right and practicable to secure from the Government of Venezuela a recognition and confirmation of licenses, etc., now issued.'*

"Any equities of a British subject making the bona fides of his occupation of Venezuelan soil January 1, 1887, at all material must apparently have accrued therefor during the seven or eight months between October, 1886, and June, 1887. In the opinion of this Government, however, such bona fides on the part of the British settler is quite immaterial. So far as bona fides are put in issue, they are the bona fides of either Government that is important, and not that of private individuals. Suppose it to be true that there are British subjects who, to quote the despatch, ' have settled in territory which they had every ground for believing to be British,' the grounds for such belief were not derived from Venezuela. They emanated solely from the British Government; and if British subjects have been deceived by the assurances of their Government, it is a matter wholly between them and their own Government, and in no way concerns Venezuela. Venezuela is not to be stripped of her rightful possessions because the British Government has erroneously encouraged its subjects to believe that such possessions were British. But in one possible contingency could any claim of that sort by Great Britain have even a semblance of plausibility. If Great Britain's assertion of jurisdiction, on the faith of which her subjects made settlements in territory subsequently ascertained to be Venezuelan, could be shown to have been in any way assented to or acquiesced in by Venezuela, the latter power might be held to be concluded, and to be stopped from setting up any title to such settlements. But the notorious facts of the case are all the other way. Venezuela's claims and her protests against alleged British usurpation have been constant and emphatic,

and have been enforced by all the means practicable for a weak power to employ in its dealings with a strong one, even to the rupture of diplomatic relations. It would seem to be quite impossible, therefore, that Great Britain should justify her asserted jurisdiction over Venezuelan territory upon which British subjects have settled in reliance upon such assertion by pleading that the assertion was bona fide, without full notice of whatever rights Venezuela may prove to have.

"In the opinion of this Government, the proposals of Lord Salisbury's despatch can be made to meet the requirements and the justice of the case only, if amended in various particulars.

"The Commission that has to decide upon facts should be so constituted, by adding one or more members, that it may reach a result, and not be abortive and possibly mischievous.

"The Commission should have power to report upon all facts necessary to the decision of the boundary controversy, including the facts pertaining to the occupation of the disputed territory by British subjects.

"The proviso by which the boundary line as drawn by the Arbitral Tribunal of three, is not to include territory *bona fide* occupied by British subjects or Venezuelan citizens on the 1st of January, 1887, should be stricken out all together, or there might be substituted for it the following:

"Provided, however, that if in fixing such line, territory of one party be found in the occupation of the subjects or citizens of the other party, such weight and effect shall be given to such occupation as reason, justice, the rules of international law, and the equities of the particular case may appear to require."

From the correspondence just copied the following conclusions are evident:

1. That Great Britain, in proposing a Tribunal of Arbitrators, established with the view of deciding the boundary controversy with Venezuela, excludes the territories occupied *bona fide* on January 1, 1887, by British subjects or Venezuelan citizens, has acknowledged that the *bona fide* is an essential element for this mode of acquisition between States.

2. That Great Britain, in presenting this basis of settlement, completely abandoned the question of time, and virtually affirmed that any period of occupation was sufficient to produce the acquisition of territory.

3. That she unduly put aside the obligations of the Agreement, which by diplomatic notes she had submitted for acceptance by Venezuela in 1850, as to not occupying or encroaching upon any part of the territory in dispute.

4. That the British subjects occupying territory to which the proposition refers had acted without their Government's leave or sanction.

5. That Great Britain was desirous that only such facts should be examined as might influence the rights of the Netherlands and Spain, respectively, at the date of the acquisition of Guiana by Great Britain, so that by virtue of their report and in case the parties should not agree to a boundary line based on it, a Tribunal composed of three members should lay it down.

6. That the United States did not deem acceptable the means of settlement proposed by Lord Salisbury, not only on account of the impossibility of determining the probatory facts of the existence as *bona fide* the establishments exempted from abitration; but above all, on account of the limitation imposed on the Judges not to extend their judgment to any part of the territory occupied in good faith by a British subject or by a Venezuelan citizen on the 1st of January, 1887.

7. That the application of the same rule to Venezuelan citizens did not matter, since it was proposed by Great Britain and opposed by the Republic, which seems to imply that its adoption would be prejudicial to the last and favorable to the first.

8. That Great Britain can not impose the rule on Venezuela, because in itself it is not just, nor is it based upon any principle of the law of nations nor on any recognized international usage.

9. That the reach of the rule was completely limited, for it was in 1886 when, for the first time, the Schomburgk line was proclaimed in the month of October, and in June, 1887, the Governor of Demarara was notified that all persons interested in licenses or concessions of mines within the territory in dispute were to accept them with the understanding that, should they be found a part of the Venezuelan territory, they would have no right to claim any compensation from the Colony or from Her Britannic Majesty's Government.

10. That it could not be admitted that in seven months, from October, 1886, to June, 1887, equitable rights may have been acquired by the *bona fide* occupation of Venezuelan territory.

11. That the *bona fide* worthy of being taken into consideration in such cases is not that of private persons, but that of one or the other Governments.

12. That in case such *bona fide* should exist, if British subjects had settled in a territory they had good reason to believe to be British, the foundation for that belief did not proceed from Venezuela, but from the British Government, which induced them into the error by its assurances, and, consequently, it is a matter between them and no way concerns the Republic, which may not be dispossessed of its legitimate possessions in consequence of the error incurred by the British Government.

13. That such a pretension would only be plausible could it be proved that the alleged jurisdiction of Great Britain, by virtue of which its subjects established settlements in territory afterwards found to have belonged to Venezuela, had obtained, in any manner, the acquiescence of Venezuela, but that far therefrom her claims and protests had been constant and emphatic, and were enforced by all the means a feeble power could dispose of in its dealings with a strong one, even to the rupture of diplomatic relations.

14. That it would, therefore, be quite impossible for Great Britain to justify her alleged jurisdiction in Venezuelan territory, in which, believing in such alleged right, British subjects should have settled down, arguing that it was *bona fide* without perfect knowledge of whatever rights Venezuela might prove to have.

CHAPTER XIV.

International Law Doctrine of Prescription.

Grocius, the Dutch publicist, in his "Rights of War and Peace," published in 1625, begins his Book 2, Chapter IV, by stating that the right of usucaption had been introduced by civil law because time in itself has no productive virtue, nor is anything made by time, although everything is made in time, and that, according to Vasquez's opinion, it can not take place between free States, nor between two kings, nor a free country and a king, nor even between a king and a private person, who is not his subject, nor between two persons who are subjects of two kings or two different countries.

Notwithstanding that he is opposed to this theory, and adduces historical instances of prescription, beginning with that presented in the Holy Scriptures in a specified instance, he proceeds to examine the causes, furnishing reasons for the presumptive abandonment of property and the means whereby this presumption is raised.

In regard to silence, he thinks that it may lead to the presumption of abandonment, *when it is kept with a knowledge of the cause, and he who keeps it does so of his own free will, and that time is a strong element of proof in both these conditions.* If silence has been kept for an immemorial time, that may seem to be sufficient, unless powerful reasons are to be adduced to show that there has been no abandonment. *It is understood that such possession must be uninterrupted; that is to say, in a single, continuous* series of time during which occupation has been enjoyed, always without any interruption, since if a possession be enjoyed only at intervals it produces no effect.

In section 9, he writes: "But perhaps it may be said, not without some plausibility, that this is not a simple presumption, but that the voluntary right has introduced the rule that an immemorial uninterrupted possession, if disturbed by an appeal to arbitrators, effected the full and complete transfer of the property. We have good reasons to believe that nations are all in accord on this point, as it was something in the highest degree necessary to universal peace."

On this passage, Bearbeirac makes the following remark:

> "This rule of arbitrary international law is as little necessary as it is difficult to prove. All there is to be said in regard to prescription is that it is authorized by the opinion and usage of the majority of countries, and is a favorable presumption, leading to the belief that this right evidently has its foundation in some principle of natural law."

The rest of the chapter is devoted by Grocius to the investigation of the law of usucaption and prescription, established by the possessor of the sovereign power and applied only to sovereignty itself. But to questions of this character no prescription is applied, inasmuch as sovereignty remains with the people and is inalienable. Express or tacit consent decides in cases which may happen. On this subject, Eugene Ortolan writes:

> "Grocius' doctrine shows that prescription of immovable things may be applied to nations when it is founded on possession from immemorial time, public, continued, and uninterrupted, and the previous owner having the power to dispose freely of his things. But he is of opinion that immemorial prescription may be objected to with powerful reasons, calculated to show the absence of the abandonment."

He says nothing of good faith, fair title, nor the requisite of peaceful possession necessary to prescription; but as he refers only to civil laws, by which it has been established, and they require these conditions, besides publicity and continued and uninterrupted possession, free from violence, fair title, and good faith, etc., it is evident that he finds acceptable all those points, since he does not reject them.

On the other hand, when possession is looked upon as an origin of dominion, it is necessary to understand that this is the possession to be held by the possessor in the character of proprietor. Ortolan, in other passages, writes on the subject of possessors in good faith and the advantages secured by possession.

The "Lectures on International and Natural Law," by the Italian Professor de Felice, were published in 1769. In Lecture 26, on natural law, he accepts and justifies prescription, saying that it is "an act by which full property of a thing belonging to another is acquired; because having possessed and enjoyed it for a long time without opposition or interruption, in good faith, and with a fair title, so that the old owner loses his right to the thing and can not claim it."

As to good faith, he is of the opinion that it is necessary at the beginning, according to the old Roman law: "It is contrary to natural equity, because, having imposed the establishment of property in favor of whomsoever is in possession of a thing that belongs to another without his consent, the possessor is bound to do the utmost to restore the thing to its true owner, and it follows that since we know that what we possess belongs to somebody else, we must return it to him."

In Lecture 19, while dealing with the law of nations, he asserts that prescription must find its way among nations, as well as among individuals, using the same argument employed by Vattel; but he acknowledges the difficulty of its application to States, even when supported by a long silence, considering the situation of weak parties in connection with powerful nations, and the circumstance that, as a rule, sovereigns have no power to transfer the property of a State.

Martens published, for the first time, in 1788, his

"Summary of the Modern Law of Nations of Europe," of which several editions have appeared. That of Paris, in 1864, is on hand, with notes by Pinhiero-Ferrera, with an introduction and additions by Doctor Ch. Vergé, and enriched with new notes, placing it on a level with contemporaneous events.

In chapter 4, of book 2, he writes on prescription, according to Universal International Law:

"One of the most important questions of the law of nations is to know whether prescription should be considered as one of the sources of the law of nations; if, according to it, property can be acquired and lost; if the Universal Law of Nations acknowledges it; and if it has been introduced by the positive law of nature of Europe."

"No doubt that in the same way that property may be expressly renounced, as well as other rights, it may be likewise tacitly renounced by means of acts showing the renouncement, and thus authorizing others to acquire the things so renounced, whether rights or immunities. But when it is asked, whether prescription has any place among nations, then, what we want to know is, whether the simple use of property or any other right, the silence voluntarily kept, and with a knowledge of the cause, when another person possesses our property, or when it disposes of our rights, whether this use and this silence, continued for a long time, are sufficient to cause us to lose our property or our rights, so that the actual possessor may irrevocably acquire them.

"Now, the simple fact of non-use, the simple fact of silence, considered in themselves, have not the force of abandonment or consent, inasmuch as we are not bound to make use of our property or to protest. Moreover, such an obligation does not exist by strict natural law. The simple interruption of the acts of possession does not extinguish our rights nor subject us to censure on the ground of a culpable negligence, and that silence or simple non-use may induce the presumption of abandonment, this presumption is not sufficient to cause us lose our rights, so that prescription can not be founded upon strict natural law. Indeed, it seems that only the mutual welfare of nations requires that it should be acknowledged, so that it may be converted into a natural social law in regard to nations living in general society; nevertheless nothing has been gained until a lapse of time, necessary for the acquisition of property or the extinction of rights by prescription, shall be fixed, and it is evident that the law of nations can not fix this length of time with the necessary precision.

"The possessor of a thing is indeed authorized to continue in possession so long as no one else can show a better right, founded on safer grounds. Now, by imagining a possession as immemorial; that it can not be proved that before him and his predecessors somebody else had possessed, it would be naturally shown that he would not have to yield to any one else's pretensions. But this natural advantage of possession—*favor possessionis*—can not be but very improperly called immemorial prescription." (571. "Of prescription according to the positive law of nations.")

"In the practice of the European countries the powers, indeed, very often invoke prescription. It appears, likewise, that they have a recourse to protests, so as to preserve those rights, and while they themselves hope to prevent expropriations that may be made in time, so that the presumption which they have caused may induce other nations to a prejudicial error, it seems that they acknowledge in that form their obligations to interrupt their silence in regard to rights they do not want to abandon."

"Notwithstanding the way in which European powers explain, in their writings, what concerns prescription, their assertions are so different and sometimes so contradictory, under different circumstances, that no fixed opinion is possible. In public acts the term prescription is improperly used as designating *the loss of rights that have been renounced by positive acts, showing a proof of consent.* Sometimes protests are necessary to prevent silence being mistaken for consent on account of acts where it is foreseen that can not be avoided. In other cases even the choice of the surest way of protest does not show that the powers should believe their rights to be lost for want of protest. Finally, the duty of breaking silence, so as not to induce others into error in regard to a presumption that has been raised, although acknowledged in Europe, it is not a perfect obligation.

"And while, on the other hand, no convention, general

or special, nor usage, has ever fixed the length of time required among nations, prescription, properly speaking, can not be considered as being introduced among the sovereign powers of Europe, nor will it be of any use to oppose it."

"The same thing does not happen in those States not fully sovereign, which still recognize over them a common legislator, that may have introduced prescription, regulating it by law. In the mutual relations of these States prescription may produce its effects; but in their relations with foreign powers, it can not be invoked except only in those cases of the competence of the tribunals of the sovereign of the former States, to be tried by the laws of the country."

It seems that de Martens' theory is the true one, notwithstanding his commentator, Vergé, holds the opposite opinion, and fails to make any mention of the affirmation of the author about prescription not being in use among the nations of Europe.

"Institutions of Natural Law" is the title of an English work on hand, third edition, published in Philadelphia in 1799, by F. Rutherforth, Archdeacon of Essex. Here is his doctrine on prescription, the subject of Chapter VIII; it is a sound theory of the case:

"Prescription is the right to a thing acquired by a long possession, honest and uninterrupted, although before that possession the owner were another person and not the possessor."

"This right of the possessor is founded on the presumption of *dereliction* by the owner. It is not indeed in conformity with the law of nature that a moral defect, for instance, the laws of acquisition of a right, may follow the mere intention of the mind; but when the intention of prescinding a right or acquisition is sufficiently shown it is natural that such an intention may produce its effects."

After explaining the several ways of making known our intentions by word of mouth or acts, he adds:

"Notwithstanding, it is necessary to bear in mind that in this case, as in all others, when we estimate the negligence of a man in claiming a thing as a sign of his intention to relinquish the same, it is necessary that his silence be not the result of ignorance or fear. If he does not claim it, it is because he does not know where it is nor who possesses it, or because he is restrained by fear to claim it. Under such circumstances his silence may not signify an intention to relinquish it; such a silence is decidedly the result of another cause, and therefore requires another intelligence."

He dwells, afterwards, on the necessity of a long possession, not because time works as an efficient cause to produce a right in favor of the possessor, but as an indispensable condition to construe the silence of the owner as a reasonable foundation of the presumption of abandonment.

He likewise considers it necessary that possession be uninterrupted, for otherwise, it is not possible to presume any abandonment. The text of what he writes about prescription is worthy of repetition:

"It must be observed that prescription can not go on without an honest possession. If the possessor took things dishonestly, no matter how long and tranquil his possession may be, he does not acquire any right to them. We may, in various ways, become honest possessors of what belongs to another man, without having any right to it at the beginning of the possession. Let us suppose, for instance, that a thing has been given to us by anybody who was not its true owner, although we thought that he was; let us suppose that we have purchased it from a person who had obtained it by force or fraud, without our knowledge of how he obtained it; or let us suppose that we have found it and endeavored unsuccessfully to discover the true owner; in each of these instances our possession is honest, although the thing possessed be not yet ours. When the possession of a thing begins in a manner such as has just been mentioned, without dishonesty on the part of the possessor, and he has it, and has continued to have it without any interruption for a considerable length of time, it will give hom a right to the thing. But if possession was dishonest from the beginning, no right can be acquired

A dishonest possession implies fraud or violence in the person who obtained it. When fraud is employed the owner certainly is unaware of something that he ought to know; and if violence is employed the owner is certainly under some kind of a fear. Now, then, a long time only induces the presumption of the removal of that ignorance or fear of the owner; and, consequently, as no presumption may prevail against a certainty, no time, no matter how long, may remove the ignorance or fear of the owner, in case of a dishonest possession, going as far as to convert his silence as a sufficient sign of his intention to relinquish his right. As his ignorance or fear were certainly at the beginning, it must be supposed that the same ignorance or fear continues as long as they are certainly removed. A long time only induces the presumption that it is so. Therefore a long time does not remove said vices sufficiently. But, as long as his silence is understood to be the effect of ignorance or fear, it can not be reasonably considered as a sign of an intention of abandonment of his right, and therefore it can not give way to the right of possession. It is evident as a sequence, that no possession, although kept for a long time, and without any interruption, may give the rights of prescription when dishonestly begun."

He afterwards makes his remarks on the case of immemorial prescription in the strict sense of the term, where it is impossible to trace its origin, and considers, as it is admitted, that the possessor is undoubtedly the owner of the thing, but not by any right of prescription, but by that of first occupant, from which, then, no distinction is made.

Kluber, in his "Modern Law of Nations in Europe," follows de Martens, as may be seen in the new revised edition, with comments by M. A. Ott, in 1861, the work having been published for the first time in 1819. In Chapter I, title 2, on the nation's rights of property, he writes: "A State may acquire things that do not belong to anybody (*res nullius*) by means of occupation (*originally*), and things belonging to another person, by means of *conventions* (*occupatio derivativa*); *but it can not acquire anything by means of prescription against those that are not bound in virtue of positive regulation to acknowledge this means of acquisition.* In order to make occupation lawful, the thing must be susceptible of exclusive property and ought not to belong to anybody; the State must have the intention to acquire its property and take it in its possession; that is to say, place it entirely at its own disposal and within its physical power. This last condition is fulfilled when its action has been exercised on the thing in such a manner that it can not be taken out from it without carrying away, at the same time, the fruits of the lawful change effected in it."

The author does not admit prescription, except among nations having agreed to accept it.

He does not consider immemorial possession as the origin of property, nor in the sense that there may not be any notice of its beginning.

The work, "Elements of the International Law," by Henry Wheaton, considered the leading authority in the United States of America, the earliest edition being that of 1836, deals, in chapter 4, part 2, section 164, with the rights of property in these terms:

"The writers on international law have mentioned how far the peculiar kind of presumption, emanating from the lapse of time, that is called prescription is justly applicable between nation and nation; *but the constant and approved practice of nations shows that, whatever it may be called, an uninterrupted possession of territory or other property during a certain length of time by a State excludes the pretensions of any other State,* in the same manner that, by the law of nature and the national code of every civilized country, similar possession by an individual excludes the pretension of any other person from the article of property alluded to. This rule is founded on the supposition, confirmed by constant experience, that every person looks naturally for the enjoyment of what he owns, and the inference that may be drawn from this silence or neglect, as to the original defect of his title or his intention to abandon it."

And again, in section 165:

"The title of almost every nation of Europe to the territory they possess to-day in that part of the world was derived at the beginning from conquest, that has been subsequently confirmed by long possession and international compacts, to which all the European States have successively become parties. Their pretension to those possessions which they hold in the New World, discovered by Columbus and other adventurers, and to the territories they have acquired in the continents of Africa and Asia, was originally derived from discovery or conquest and colonization, and has been, since then, confirmed in the same manner by positive compacts. *Independently of these sources of title, the general consent of the human race has established the principle that a long and uninterrupted possession by a nation excludes the pretension of any other.* Whether this general consent has to be considered as a tacit contract or as a positive right for all nations, it is equally binding, since they are all parties to it, and none can surely disregard it without impugning its own title to its possessions, and therefore it is founded on mutual utility and tends to promote the general welfare of the human race."

Paragraph 164, already quoted, establishes that an uninterrupted possession of territory or any other property during a certain period of time by a State excludes the pretension of any other State in the same way as, by the law of nature or the national codes of all civilized nations, such possession by an individual excludes the pretension of any other person to the article of property in question. But no code has ever established that rule. They all require an uninterrupted possession for some time, and other concomitant conditions; that is to say, an unequivocal possession, and the belief of ownership by the holder, besides the qualifications of public and peaceful possession, chiefly that of good faith, consisting in the belief that the thing was owned by the conveyor who had capacity to convey, and that the title was not tainted with any vice. Good faith and fair title are indispensable according to present French legislation, even for the acquisition of movable things, and, according to the same legislation, is instantaneous, while by the Roman laws, as well as by those of Spain and Venezuela, three years are wanted.

In what Wheaton adds with regard to the general consent of the nation, in the consideration of the exclusive right derived from a long and uninterrupted possession, he undoubtedly refers to an immemorial possession, which can not be traced to any well-known origin, and that, therefore, has to produce that consequence. As Martens observes, that is no prescription.

The course of natural law and philosophy of jurisprudence by E. Ahrens, published for the first time in 1840, has had many editions since that time, and is translated into Spanish. That of Don Pedro Rodríguez Ortolano, of the College of Jurists, Madrid, and Don Mariano Ricardo de Asensi, says, that

"Possession, pending the change of property by usucaption (*possessio ad usucapionem*), is accompanied with most important positive conditions. It must be in good faith (*bona fide*); (which by the Roman law is not required, but only at the beginning of the possession); to have a certain time duration, and to be founded on a just title (*justus titulus*). In the extraordinary usucaption a fair title is not required, but only in a longer time.

* * * * * * *

"These three kinds of possessions are equally enumerated among the real rights (*jura in re aliena*), only usucaption in personal rights is excluded, on the ground of the intimate connection of right in every moral person, and in obligations, prescription, which does not require even possession, is founded on other principles. *In public law (publicum just) there is no usucaption nor prescription.*" (Chapter I, on the property and rights of property, § LIX.)

In Chapter IV, on the diversity and conflict of laws, the author favors prescription by private law (*jure privato*), because he thinks it is necessary to the general safety and convenience by putting a limit to the power of exercising or not our rights in time, and in a useful time, by the one to whom they belong, in view of the imperfections of human society, of which it is impossible to prescind. Then he adds:

" *In the public law, on the contrary, where laws and instructions must have their reason, in the wants and interests of the moment, and where the long life of an institution is no reason for its maintenance, there is no room for prescription.*

" The International Law of Europe," by A. G. Hoffter, published in 1848, and reprinted several years afterwards with considerable changes and additions, has been consulted, eighth German edition of 1888, with notes by F. Heinrich Geffcken, and the French, fourth edition of 1883, translated by Jules Bergson.

At the introduction, No. III, on " Reciprocal Special Law of Nations," § 12—about the " Ways of Acquisition," there is a passage as follows:

"The particular foundation on which private rights of the State rest are * * * (3d) *immemorial possession.*" Prescription, although forming a necessary and integral part of the whole complete system of legislation, the "*international law can not indistinctly admit the authority of prescription.*

"It is therefore plain that rights once acquired, to which special clauses, or the object of them, do not assign any limited time, must subsist indefinitely, and for such a length of time as it is not renounced by the interested parties or until they do not find themselves in the impossibility of carrying them out. Renunciation may form the subject of a convention or lead to a voluntary abandonment, placing the possessor safely against any contest. At the same time, *it is incontestable that the the abandonment may be presumed, in case of a very long possession not contested or interrupted. In similar questions it is always necessary to resort to principles. Prescription is purely a question of fact.*

"The same thing happens in regard to the immemorial prescription (*antiquitas, vetustas cujus contraria non existit*), that is to say, possession, the origin of which is unknown, and which contains a presumption of ownership. Immemorial possession is an approbatory title of an accomplished fact, a title before which the authority of history must keep silent. To how many objections these territorial limits might not be open, and the rights of States, if there were any pretensions to ask them for their legitimate titles, if their existence were not derived from the strength of accomplished facts? *Nothwithstanding, it is necessary to admit, at the same time, that a century of an unjust possession is not sufficient in itself to clear the vices of its origin.*"

Heffter, therefore, opposes prescription, except in cases of presumptive abandonment, founded on a very long protracted possession not contested nor interrupted, and public, so as to be able to reach the knowledge of the former owner. *He agrees as to the necessity of a long possession—continuous, uninterrupted and peaceful.* It is understood that it must be held under the belief of ownership by the holder, as he will himself take the place of the first owner. The vices of possession can not be wiped out even by the lapse of a hundred years.

Heffter attributes to possession truly immemorial effects that can not be left unnoticed. In § 43, in dealing with the subject of servitude, he holds that "among sovereign or independent States mere possession can not be sufficient to establish any permanent right."

Theodore D. Woolsey, another author of the United States, in his "Introduction to the Study of International Law," first edition of 1860, in § 54, says:

"Here it may be asked if in public law (*jure publico*) is there any right of prescription corresponding to the rights admitted by the private law? (*jure privato*). This law, as it is commonly understood, may be defended by showing the practical evil consequent upon the disturbance of old titles and the ordinary insufficiency of evidence after a long possession; and, on the other hand, by economical reasons, such as that of the labor invested in the soil which, after sixty years, for instance, constitutes a principal value, or else on the ground that having been abandoned and become *res nullius* it becomes the property of another by occupation, although none of these reasons are applicable to the international law, except perhaps the first one. But the title to a territory rests on more solid foundations to a greater extent, the express consentment of the other parties in the international law, or at least the tacit acknowledgment by a lapse years of the right of one State; that is to say, of an organized community of certain limits existing as such. To trace ancient pretensions, based upon a forgotten state of things, after having been buried in oblivion by treaties or long use, is a perversion of things. Louis XIV. may have committed a great crime by seizing Strasburg, but after his possession was sanctioned by the German Empire at the time of the peace of Ryswick, there is no room for any claim derived from the past. Prussia may have acted very scandalously with the conquest of Silicia or in the matter of Schleswig-Holstein, but after all disputes were settled by *treaty*, further disputes on the subject resuscitating an old state of things; that is to say, upon ancient reasons are unjust, although new wars based upon new foundations may involve the resurrection of conditions for a long time antiquated.

§ 55. "The territory of a nation or that portion of the land upon which sovereign rights are exercised may have commenced to belong to it in various ways. It may have derived its title—

1. By the occupation of the land which was vacant before and by *prescription, public and not interrupted.*

2. By occupation by colonists or another incorporation of land occupied before.

3. *By conquest accepted as a fact, and that finally ends by a prescriptive right.*

4. By purchase or donation.

He adds, besides, two ways more or less in doubt, but generally acknowledged; that is to say—

1. The bull of Nicholas V. in favor of Alfonso V., King o Portugal, and those of Alexander VI. for the Kings of

Spain after the first voyage of Columbus to the New World; and 2, the title founded on discovery.

The author does not consider applicable to political relations the foundation of the ordinary insufficiency of proofs after a long possession by another party, nor the economical reason that the labor expended on the soil constitutes a principal value, nor the abandonment of the thing and its change into *res nullius;* but he admits the first, or the injury consequent upon a disturbance of old titles. He finds that the most powerful title is consent, formally expressed by all the parties in regard to international law, or at least the tacit acknowledgment during a lapse of years of such a right of a State, or a community organized within certain limits in order to exist as such a State. The instances he cites from treaties in which the change of things have been renounced show acquisitions confirmed by conventions on the basis of formal consent, so that in those cases nothing can be said about prescription under any hypothesis. He presents no case of a long use, and being immemorial it does not constitute prescription, as has already been remarked.

Finally, he considers as a title the acquisition by prescription whenever it is public and uninterrupted. It is well known that these are two requisites of prescription, but it remains to consider all those not mentioned by the author who overlooks the subject and only pays a slight attention to it without the necessary care demanded by the gravity and importance of the subject.

The professor of the University of St. Petersburg, member of the Institute of International Law, Mr. F. de Maertens, in his recent "Treaty of International Law," while examining (in § 87) the means of acquiring territory, classifies among the original ways, accession, prescription, and occupation and explains in the following manner the second:

"Prescription (*usucapio*). In a different way from the private law the international relations only admit prescription within very restricted limits. The importance of this means of acquisition may be resumed in the following propositions:

1. "International law does not acknowledge any time for prescription, as a State is master of its territory as long as desired, and its authority is maintained.

2. "In the sphere of international relations nobody can interrupt the continuity of an old right.

3. "In international relations importance is given only to *immemorial antiquity* (*antiquitas, vetustas, cujus contraria memoria non existit*); that serves as a basis to the whole political map, and to the existence of the civilized and barbarous States. The lapse of time and the sanction of history imposes silence to all recoveries and accusations that might be justified at the beginning by violence or injustice done in the way of aggrandizement of territory. In this sense it may be said chiefly to States *beati possidentes*. The accomplished fact that immemorial antiquity protects all rights is converted into a lawful one before international law."

The author's doctrine is that international law admits prescription only in very few cases; that the period of time can not be fixed; that it is not possible to interrupt an old right; and that only immemorial antiquity, the origin of which can not be known, places the possession by States in safety.

That is what we have held to show the sacrifice made by Venezuela in admitting prescription, and in fixing the term at only fifty years, and in consenting to raise prescription for this particular case to the level of an exclusive dominion or the colonization of a district.

PRESCRIPTION.

Mr. Richard Wild, an English lawyer, in his work entitled "Institutions of International Law," printed in 1850, in Volume I, § 74, writes as follows:

"In the third place prescription, in the strict sense of the word, as it implies a definite period of time, is a creature of civil law, but the principle of prescription is applied with no less force to national than to private possessions, as the security of title is never more important than in dealings with sovereigns. The principle is, indeed, true that '*quod non valet abinitio tractu temporis non convelescit*,' but in practice the observance is somewhat different. A title that may have been defective in its origin necessarily becomes indefeasible by the long lapse of time. *On that ground the highest authorities on international law hold that national possession may prescribe, when a long possession has been attended by circumstances originating a presumption of right.* Title by occupation, as it has been explained before, ends with possession, and a new occupant acquires it. A long possession creates the presumption of title, as it is not to be supposed that the previons master would have allowed any one else to take possession had he not abandoned or ceded his right. When a loss has to fall on one of two innocent parties it is right that it should fall on the one neglecting its right. Among sovereigns it can not be pleaded any ignorance of the fact, as national possessions are too notorious. *Immemorial possession creates a conclusive presumption of title; a presumption 'juris et de jure' which does not admit of any proof to the contrary, since the right of possession has to prevail as long as no better title can be shown, and it is legally presumed that immemorial possession has survived every proof of title on either side; but the conclusive effect of immemorial possession is not to be considered as based on mere presumption of fact, but on a pre-emptory rule of the law of nations established by general use as essential to universal peace.* Thus a claimant of territory who makes a contract with the sovereign in possession of the same as the owner of it, is understood to have abandoned his rights. A party to an act authorizing or requiring its sovereignty or to a treaty reviving it, is understood to admit everything necessary to its validity. The adjustment of a treaty is an acknowledgment of sovereignty on the part of the person that makès it, as a treaty is an act of sovereignty. The reception of an Ambassador is a similar case. That was the reason why the Minister of Spain, in the passport given to the deputies of the United Provinces to the Congress of Munster, refused to call them Ambassadors, since that fact would have been equivalent to an acknowledgment of the independence and sovereignty, which was intended to be one of the subjects of negotiation in that Congress.

"The proof required in support of a title by prescription varies with the nature of the thing prescribed. In matters in which a general and common use is to be presumed the pretension of private or exclusive property is against the general run of the law. In regard to rivers or the sea, such a pretension may originate only in portions of the same or on rivers running across different States. It is perfectly clear in regard to the right on those rivers, the whole course of which is through only one State."

It is important to observe, in the above passage, that the author asserts that " national possession may be prescribed, according to acts of the highest authority, when attended by circumstances creating a presumption of right." These circumstances are the requisites so often enumerated here, and so often referred to by the authors quoted herein.

What the author establishes in regard to immemorial prescription is admitted; but the instances that he refers to of a claimant, who makes a contract with the sovereign acting as possessor and owner, or makes himself a party to an act or authorizes it, or requires or concludes a treaty, and thus acknowledges the sovereignty of the other contracting party, do not belong to immemorial prescription. They are a voluntary transfer expressive of consent and abandonment of the rights which, being his own, he nevertheless cedes to another.

In 1861 "The Law of Nations Considered as Political

Independent Societies," was published by Travers Twiss, royal professor of civil law in the University of Oxford, and member of Her Majesty's Counsel. In chapter 7 of Vol. I, in dealing with the right of acquisition, he writes:

"The title by settlement, therefore, in so far as it is distinguished from title by discovery, is resolved into a title by usucaption or prescription. Wolf defines usucaption saying, that it is an acquisition of dominion founded upon a presumptive abandonment. Vattel says that it is the acquisition of dominion founded on a long possession, uninterrupted and undisturbed, that is to say, acquisition only proved by this possession. *Prescription*, on the other hand, according to the same author, is the exclusion of any pretension to a right; exclusion founded upon a long period of time in which that right has been neglected; or, according to Wolf's definition, is the loss of an inherent right by virtue of a presumptive consent. Vattel, writing in French, and observing that the word *usucaption* had very little use in that language, made use of the word 'prescription,' when there was no particular reason to employ another. The same observation may apply to our own language, and thus, generally speaking, we call this part a *title by prescription*. No definite lapse of time has been fixed to make a valid title by prescription. The law of nature does not set any rule. *Notwithstanding, when the claimant can not allege indubitable ignorance on his part, or on the part of those from whom he derives his rights, or can not justify his silence by solid and legitimate reasons, or has neglected his right for such a number of years that he allows the respective rights of the two parties to be doubtful a presumption of abandonment will be established, and he will be excluded by ordinary prescription.* The lapse of time with nations as well as with individuals deprives the parties from the means of proof; *so that if no questions were to be raised as to a good faith possession* by those who have for a long time assented to the enjoyment of a thing by its possessor, long possession, instead of strengthening should weaken the possessor's title. The result of such an inconvenience is so obvious that in the practice of nations as well as individuals, it has been equally repudiated."

These words express unequivocally that prescription requires a knowledge by the former owner of the possession of a third party, a long lapse of time, silence not justified, and good faith. It consists, as it has been repeatedly explained, 1. In the belief that the conveyor of the property was its owner; 2, that he was capable of making the conveyance; and 3, that the title of transmission has no vice. Therefore, good faith involves the idea of a peaceful possession in the opinion of the owner.

This theory agrees with that of Twiss himself, and is confirmed in the following Chapter VIII, about the rights of possession, which begins thus:

"Having considered in the previous chapter the conditions by which a nation may legitimately acquire possession of a country, we may proceed to consider the rights that a nation may exercise in virtue of that possession; in other words, *jura possessionis* (the rights of possession), so far as distinguished from the *jus possidendi* (right to possess)."

When a nation, Vattel writes, "takes possession of a country, it is considered as acquiring an empire or sovereignty on it, at the same time that of a dominion. For, as the nation is independent and free, it is not to be presumed that when it settles a new country it may have in mind any intention to allow others the right to rule it or exercise any of the rights constituting sovereignty. All the space upon which a nation extends its dominion is converted into the seat of its jurisdiction, and called *its territory.*" De Wolf writes to the same purpose, "*si gens quaedam regionem vacuam occupat, imperium in ea simul occupat.*"

It is well known that true possession is a detention exercised *animo domini*, in the opinion of ownership, by ourselves, or by means of any one representing us, as held and proved by Marcadé against Troplong, in his commentaries on article 2228 of the French Civil Code, title 20, on prescription.

Now, the highest British authority on the subject of international law, Sir Robert Phillimore, Member of Parliament and of the Private Council of Her Britannic Majesty, in his "Commentaries on the International Law" (first edition, 1854, second, 1871, in four volumes), says, in Chapter XIII of the first volume, that "the second way of original acquisition is by the operation of time, by what the French and English jurists call *prescription.*"

The French Civil Code, he says, defines it, "a means of acquiring or of liberation, through a certain lapse of time and *under conditions defined by law.*" It is, nevertheless, censured by Troplong, who observes that time in itself or by itself can not be a cause of acquisition or of liberation; that prescription is realized not only by the operation of time, but likewise and chiefly by that of possession of things or by the inaction of a creditor. Marcadé thinks that the charge of inaccuracy made on the definition of the code would be right if the law should only state that the right *is the work of a certain lapse of time*, without anything else, thus presenting time as the only condition; but from the moment the definition had been so completed, by this reference to other articles of title, it is not accurate to claim that the code presents time as if it were by itself a means of acquiring property or of being liberated from obligation. Now, then, as the definition of Phillimore is limited to the present time as the only element of prescription, it is clear that the censures of both French jurists are well founded.

The English author proceeds to give as an introduction to his international doctrine on the subject, a few pertinent considerations on the private and public law.

In regard to the former, he affirms that in every system of jurisprudence the lapse of time is of great influence on questions of ownership, and that there is a period in which a possession *de facto* is converted into *de jure*, and in which possession is changed into dominion; that such is the exigency of the nature of man, the reason of the thing, the existence of society itself. He recalls the doctrine of the usucaption of the Roman law, by which the possessor *justo titulo et bona fide* of lands for two years, and for a year of movable things that had not before belonged to him, property was required over both; that that institution, formerly reduced to *prædia italica,* was further extended by the Prætor to *fundi provinciales,* and to *peregrinos,* under the denomination of *præscriptio longi temporis;* that Justinian, who abolished the difference between civil and natural property, did away also with the distinction between *fundi italici* and *provinciales,* and made *usucapio* and *præscriptio* to mean the same thing; and gave not only a right of possession, but that of ownership, to the person who had possessed movable things for three years or immovable for ten years, *inter presentes,* or twenty years *inter absentes,* provided the thing was susceptible of *usucapio* and *præscriptio,* and had been held with fair title, *justus titulus,* and in good faith, *bona fides;* that he added another kind of prescriptive acquisition, *præscriptio triginta vel quadraginta annorum* and that this *longissimi temporis possessio,* possession for such a long time, did not convey property to a possessor nor take it away from its owner; that only gave the former a defense against every other claimant, and that even when there would not have been any fair title, *justus titulus,* and that beyond these two classes there was besides the immemorial prescription, *inmemorial tempus possessio vel præscriptio inmemorialis,* which was called *adminiculum juris quo quis tuetur possessionem quæ memorien haminum excedit.*

According to the quotations from the Roman laws, a simple lapse of time is not enough for the purpose of prescription, but it was required in the first case *justo titulo,* and good faith; and in the second case, besides the lapse of three, ten, and twenty years, that the things were susceptible of prescription, which we may call *prescrip-*

tibility of the thing, and fair title and good faith, so that the resort to that antecedent does not serve the purpose of the author in making time as the only source of right.

He says that immemorial prescription is only available when the origin of the possession is not capable of proof when nobody may recall that it had belonged to another, and that it is only applicable in three cases of what may be called public law, *jus publicum*, that is to say (1), the public or neighboring roads; (2) the right not to receive the rain water; and (3) in relation to aqueducts. He suggests that it is not strange, for that reason, that it should have hardly taken a secondary rank in the Roman jurisprudence, nor that considering the reason of the thing itself, should have been raised during the mediæval era to the level of an institution of constant use and of the greatest importance. He brings two instances, taken from the common law, in which immemorial prescription was recognized (1), in 1209 in favor of the Count Tolosa, who was allowed to continue laying contributions, supported by an old custom from a time of which there is no memory; (2) besides that of a Bishop, who claimed by prescription the tithes and churches situated within the diocese of another Bishop. He recalls that, according to the Roman law, the possession for three, ten, and twenty years with title and thirty years without title gives the possessor a good defense, founded upon prescription, against every other individual claimant; that the churches have the privilege of being protected against prescription of less than forty years, and that did not require a title, provided there was good faith; and it was of no avail in the case of the Bishop, as it was contrary to the common law (*jus non scriptum*), "*ubi tammen est ei jus commune contrarium vel habetur præsumptio contra ipsum bona fides non sufficit; sed est necessarius titulus, qui possessori causam tribuat præscribendi; nisi anti temporis allegetur præscriptio, cujus contraria memoriam non existat;*" (but when it is contrary to common law, or there is a presumption against it, good faith is not enough; a title is necessary to afford the possessor a cause for prescribing, not a mere allegation of prescription of such a long time that any memory against it does not exist.)

He contends afterwards that the tendency and spirit of modern legislation and jurisprudence has been to substitute *to private law, jus privatum*, a short and definite period of time, instead of immemorial prescription, and thus, in England, time is referred to the reign of a particular monarch, and was fixed in the prevailing custom before the reign of Richard I.; more recently a prescription has been introduced of a shorter number of years instead of the doctrine of immemorial use, as well as in France, Austria, and Prussia.

In regard to the public law, Phillimore thinks the doctrine of immemorial prescription indispensable, and therefore it is mentioned more than once in the constitutions of the old German Empire as a means of acquiring public right. He quotes Savigny, who speaks of the State of England since the revolution of 1688, until the death of the last of the male Stuarts, the Cardinal of York, in 1806.

He then investigates the subject of international prescription, which he considers as rather arduous, following Grotius' authority, and asks, Is it produced among nations just as among individuals, and between State and individuals? Is there a *presumption*, founded on a long possession of a territory or of a right, that has to be considered as a lawful source of international acquisition? He answers by setting aside all subtleties, such as that prescription is an offspring of the natural law or the creation of the civil law, whether founded on the abandonment by the owner, and fixes his consideration only on time, and says that, on one hand, it is irrational in the highest degree to deny that prescription is a lawful way of international acquisition, and on the other, that it is inconvenient and impracticable to endeavor to fix the exact limit of time necessary to the validity of a title. And as to the question, What length of time? he answers:

"First, that the title of nations, *in the full enjoyment and pacific possession of their territory*, whatever may have been the original means of obtaining it, can not be questioned or disputed at any time. Second, that the unjust and violent capture of a country, where the inhabitants have been so overcome by a superior force that they could not successfully resist, is a possession devoid of fair title in its origin, and requires the help of time to wipe out the original defect; and if the nation thus subjugated, before the vice is removed, succeeds in shaking the yoke, it has a legal and moral title to resume its former position in the society of nations."

Here the author deals with two cases—that of prescription of territory and that of prescription of sovereignty. For the first he asks only peaceful possession and effective enjoyment, without paying any attention to its origin or to the time of its duration. For the second he requires fair title and the lapse of time to cure the vice of a violent and unjust capture. He does not explain or discuss the causes of the several rules he sets in both hypotheses. But as to the one in question, he admits the necessity of the *effective enjoyment* and *peaceful possession*. After having asserted that it is impracticable and inconvenient to fix the time for prescription, he advances the idea that at no time the title of possession of a nation may be questioned or disputed.

So that violence and injustice of a capture need, in point of sovereignty, the remedy of time, and the vice of an original, unjust and violent usurpation of a territory is at once removed.

But we must bear in mind that the acquisition of territory among nations involves the question of sovereignty contrary to what the case is among individuals. Indeed, "international dominion or property of a State among nations is," according to Eugene Ortolan, "a right that belongs to a nation of using and taking the products and disposing of a territory, and *to rule there as a sovereign power, independent of any exterior power, a right carrying with it the correlative obligation of the other States not to place any obstacle to the use made of said territory by the proprietary nation and not to arrogate to themselves any right to rule in that same territory.*" * * * "In conclusion, we find that the words international dominion, property of State, exterior territorial sovereignty, and even independence of nations, when this independence is considered in regard to territory, concur to express the same complex idea—that kind of international law with which we are dealing. Sovereignty and independence of nations embrace other objects, and are extended, sometimes, beyond their territory. Thus, a people exercise their sovereignty by concluding alliances and contracting obligations with other countries corresponding in the private law to the ideas of debt and credit. Its interior sovereignty rules the individuals of the nation even beyond its frontier. It rules in capacity of sovereign; can make them responsible and call them to account for their conduct abroad within certain juridical limits. In the same manner the countries are independent from each other everywhere. In the ideas of international dominion, of property of State, it is not, therefore, the exterior sovereignty, the independence of nations in all its spheres, that is understood, but only this sovereignty, this independence, considered in all that concerns the territory."

Phillimore reviews the opinions of several jurists who have denied the doctrine that prescription may have any place within the scope of international law. But he does not refute them; he states only that their opinion is at variance with practice, with use and reason of the thing itself, and is overwhelmed by the preponderance of the authorities of Grocius, Heineccius, Wolf, Mably, Vattel, Rutherford, Wheaton, and Burke.

He thinks that the same notice, by which prescription was introduced among individuals, bears out its use among States chiefly on the ground that their legal contentions bring about wars. But it is not intended to justify immemorial prescription, which, according to Martens, does not exist among the nations of Europe, but to examine whether it is enough for a mere lapse of time, as the author pretends.

He argues that immemorial prescription is admitted, but he thinks that it does not mean anything if it is not to be understood as meaning that a State which primitively acquires anything with bad title does not maintain its possession against another State having no better title.

He holds, indeed, that immemorial prescription, meaning that its origin is unknown, has to prevail as an advantage of possession, but in no other case. In this passage there is a note, quoting Puffendorf, about the application of prescription to nations, and his remarks are considered to be perspicuous and wise. They are of no use to him, as they are intended to protect possessors in good faith, but not anybody else who may have originally acquired possession and concludes by rejecting *precarious, clandestine, and violent possession.* "Therefore, when separate dominions were introduced, it was likewise established on the score of peace, that whoever should possess an immovable thing, *not by force nor clandestinely or precariously,* should be consequently presumed to be its owner until the contrary was proved by any one else; but he would have possessed in good faith for a very long time, during which, it is not thought that a moderately diligent man would have neglected his right, could very well reject a slow claimant, who had not sooner asserted his rights." He quotes Vattel in his support, and contends that prescription is a presumptive abandonment, against which there may be a claim; and, moreover, he approves of requiring conscientious good faith to the last.

The opinion of Wheaton, to which he appeals, has already been explained.

He at last invokes Burke, who makes the highest encomium on prescription, and states that in England they always had prescription or limitation *just as well as all nations* have them among themselves.

Returning to that matter he repeats, that in his opinion prescription does not consist necessarily in the abandonment or *dereliction* by the State in possession before, but in the long time of the possession held by the prescribing State, and that such an abandonment among nations does not necessarily precede the acquisitive prescription.

Then he writes: "*The dereliction or voluntary abandonment* by the original possessor may be often incapable of proof among nations after the lapse of centuries of adverse possession, inasmuch as the proofs of *prescriptive possession* are few and simple. In the first place, they are *publicity, continued occupation, want of interruption* (*usurpatio*), attended in general, undoubtedly, morally and legally speaking, with the outlay of labor and capital in possession of the new possessor, pending the period of silence, or inertness, or absence of any attempt to exercise any rights of property by the preceding possessor. *The period of time*, as it has been repeatedly asserted, *can not be defined by international law*, as it is by private law among individuals. It has to depend on variable and varying circumstances, but in every case proofs are required."

He spoke before of the necessity of an *effective enjoyment of the peaceful possession* in regard to territory, and *fair title* in regard to sovereignty. Now he wants additional requisites—*publicity, continued occupation, non-interruption, investment of capital and labor* by the new possessor, and *lapse of a time* that can not be fixed by international law, as it depends on variable and varying circumstances. That fact contradicts the assertion of paragraph CCLVI, that the "nation's title, in the *effective enjoyment and peaceful possession* of its territory, *no matter how it may have been originally acquired*, can not *at any time* be questioned or disputed." If that is so, from the moment in which a nation may have entered into the effective enjoyment and peaceful possession of any territory of another, its title could not be questioned or disputed.

In Chapter XVI, on the extinction of dominion, he holds that, as dominion is acquired by the combination of two elements, it may be extinguished in fact or lost by showing a contrary fact and intention; that in such a case the dominion is lost actually or presumptively with the consent of the State losing it; that the title of prescription in another State is founded frequently, although not necessarily, on a presumptive *dereliction* of possession by the original owner; that this presumption, as every other of the kind, may be rejected by an adequate proof of sufficient strength, that is to say, by showing a state of things entirely incompatible with it; that, on the other hand, it must be observed that there are acts on the part of a State which need to be construed as an abandonment of its previous rights, as, for instance, when it becomes a party to an agreement on another subject, but in which, indirectly, although necessarily a possession or right originally belonging to him, is mentioned as belonging to the claimant by prescription, without making any reserve as the owner-nation before; and that if a nation suffer in its dealings with other nations, the right of the possession in question is to be considered as belonging to one of them, and if no protest is made by the adverse claimant, he may be held as assenting *de facto*.

The most popular of authors on *International Law*, Vattel, in the work that he calls by that name, or "Principles of the Natural Law, as applied to the conduct and affairs of Nations and Sovereigns," in Chapter XI of Vol. 2, deals with usucaption and prescription among nations.

After having defined them and proved that they are parts of the natural law, he contends in § 141 that the possessor in good faith, supported by the presumption of abandonment, has the right to keep the thing, after a long and peaceful possession; *but insists that if at any time he discovers with certainty that the claimant is the true owner and had never abandoned his rights, the possessor must in conscience make a restitution of all by which he has been enriched out of the things of the claimant.* In § 151 he returns to the same subject and says that "prescription is not legitimate before the tribunal of conscience except for the possessor in good faith."

He does not consider it as such when the owner has truly neglected his rights, a condition involving three cases: 1. "That the owner may not plead unavoidable ignorance, either on his part or on the part of his conveyors; 2, that his silence could not be justified by solid and legitimate reasons; 3, that he may have neglected his rights or kept silence for a considerable number of years, for a negligence of a few years only, is not sufficient to produce or authorize a presumption of abandonment. It is impossible, he thinks, to determine by natural law the number of years required to establish prescription. That depends on the nature of the thing, the ownership of which is in dispute and its circumstances.

As to immemorial possession, the origin of which is, of course, unknown, he is of opinion that it protects the rights of the possessor against eviction as long as there is no solid reason to oppose him, and these can not exist, since time has destroyed the means of proof; so that it forms an incontestable title.

Returning to ordinary prescription, he thinks it can not be opposed against any one alleging good reasons for his silence, such as the impossibility of speaking a well-founded fear, etc., for in that case there is no room for any presumption of abandonment of his rights. And he affirms that this means of defense has been many times used against princes whose formidable force had reduced, for a long time, to silence the weak victims of their usurpations. He contends that prescription can not be opposed against anyone who, being unable to institute a claim, limits his action to signifying in a substantial manner, by means of any signal, that he does not want to relinquish his possession, and that such is the use cf protests. The author reasserts the necessity of a quiet and peaceful possession.

He then goes on to contend that usucaption and prescription must apply to nations governed by the law of nature in a manner befitting the case, chiefly because litigation is apt to terminate in bloody wars, and thus, for the sake and welfare of the human kind, the possessions of sovereigns must not be easily disturbed, and when not disputed they must be held after a considerable number of years as just and indisputable.

He, nevertheless, acknowledges how difficult it is to found prescription among nations only on a presumptive abandonment derived from a long silence on account of the danger attending a weak State in allowing to transpire the least pretension to recover its possessions from a powerful monarch.

But nevertheless prescription has to prevail *in case of a very long possession, uninterrupted and not contested.* As to the immemorial prescription it must exist among States. He deems that only long time usucaption and prescription are admitted by the law of nations. He observes that prescription must have its effect among nations, since it is founded on a long, undisputed possession. It is not permitted, unless on substantial evidence, to oppose the plea of bad faith, because, except in that case, every nation is held to possess in good faith.

Finally, after reviewing the many difficulties of prescription, he advises that the neighboring nations try to settle this point by treaties, especially the question of the number of years required to make prescription legitimate.

From all which it is found that Vattel considers prescription applicable to nations only when founded on *possession in good faith, continued for a long time uninterrupted, and when the silence of the owner has not been imposed by fear or force. He insists sufficiently upon good faith to the end, so as to be able to justify it in conscience.*

Only about the immemorial prescription does he speak without doubt or vacilations, in private as well as in public.

The well known Argentine author, Dr. Carlos Calvo, in his extensive work, in five volumes (to which he added one more in 1896), entitled "Theoretical and Practical International Law," fourth edition, in §§ 664 and 665, adheres to Vattel's ideas, and considers usucaption and prescription admissible for States and countries. He refuses to share in the theoretical scruples of certain jurists, and classifies usucaption and prescription as entirely legitimate titles for acquisition among nations.

In § 285 he sets forth as a source of the right of property among nations "the exclusive possession, not contested and sufficiently prolonged, of any territory." "This principle," he continues, "founded on the tacit consent of men, is obligatory upon all States, and by the sanction of time acquires the same force as a formal contract or as a rule of the positive international law."

These words contain requisites of prescription so repeatedly explained before. To exact for any possession the character of exclusiveness is tantamount to requiring that it should be in the character of property, excluding everything adverse to claimant. To add "*not contested*," means that without violence it has been acquired and without violence kept. And to be "*sufficiently prolonged*" is to ask a long possession, and besides being long, never to have been interrupted. It is true that the author does not fix the time; but, as before remarked, he agrees with Vattel that good faith must last during the whole of the time, and that in regard to the length of time nations should agree by treaty.

In regard to the American countries, the author holds that they occupy a peculiar situation, brought about by the dominant principles in the world at the time the Continent was discovered, near the close of the fifteenth century. At that time the public law of Europe was controlled completely by the Church, and the Pope was considered the supreme authority, capable of deciding all international questions. It has been admitted besides, so as to better justify the *appropriation* by way of conquest, that Christians had an implicit and absolute right of domain over all pagan countries. From the continuation of these two principles came the situation created for the American countries in regard to the nations of Europe by the Bull of Pope Alexander VI., who mapped out by a line traced from pole to pole the limits between the acquisitions of Spain and Portugal, and that were modified afterwards by the Treaty of Tordesillas. Calvo concludes by asserting that the domination of Europe over the land and islands of the New World did not consist exclusively in any division by the Holy See or the precepts of the canon laws, but was founded, besides, on the title of discovery, which Spain itself invokes several times in support of its rights over territories of which its bold navigators had taken possession.

The author admits that the general doctrine he sets forth in regard to possession is not applicable to Spanish-American countries, but that they must be ruled by the preponderant maxims of the fifteenth century, when the New Continent was discovered.

Pradier-Fodéré, in his work already mentioned, explains, in his Chapter V, the subject of property, and includes prescription among the means of acquiring property among nations, and writes, in § 820:

> "Acquisitive prescription, or usucaption, the only one of which we speak as in accord with the civil legislation, is a means of acquiring, or more properly of confirming, with the help of an acknowledged possession, under certain conditions (*that is to say, exempt from precariousness, clandestinity, and violence*), and continued for a fixed length of time, an acquisition subject to eviction, and even merely presumptive."

Farther on, in § 825, he contends that "prescription is of necessary application, indispensable to international law, if we wish to avoid interminable disputes about the formation and existence of all States." He adds that, "without going so far as Bluntschli (who seems to be too accommodating in his theory of taking primitive possession accompanied by violence), it is necessary to admit with this author that, allowing to time the power to make law, is the only means of perpetuating among States a feeling of safety and of general peace; but we can not fail to admit that by taking a view, not from the point of an acquisition of property, but of morals and history, under a due appreciation of human events, *a century of unjust possession is not enough to wipe out the vices of its origin.*"

The author examines the thesis that he classifies as useless, whether prescription is an offspring of the natural law (and he believes it to be so) or of the civil law. From thence he goes on to inquire whether prescription may exist and be invoked as an international law, a point, he says, very much discussed and upon which authors have thrown little light.

He advocates the affirmative side, impugning the adverse opinions of G. F. de Martens and Heffter. He adopts, as his own, Vattel's teachings, already mentioned, to strengthen his own, and, as in common with that author, advises nations to settle this point by treaties, especially in regard to the precise limits of time. He concludes by observing that authors adverse to enlist prescription as deriving its origin from international law do not fail to acknowledge the principle of possession—*uti possidetis jus et favor possessionis*—must be respected before resorting to arms, and have their disputes settled according to the international law.

Pasquale Fiore, in his "Public International Law, according to the wants of modern civilization" (second edition, translated from Italian into French by Charles Antoine, and published in Paris in 1885), speaking of the non-use of a territory by a State and its acquisition by another, § 850, Chapter V, writes "of the means of acquisition and loss of legitimate possession of things by a State," as follows:

"Now let us examine if, in certain cases, even among civilized States, the right may exist of taking legitimate possession of a territory of which the government possessing it does not make any use.

"We must lay down the general rules that it must not be confined to the *non-use* of a thing with *abandonment* of the possession of the same thing. Every State continues in possession of everything that has been submitted to its power and acquired for the purpose of using it. Possession does not imply, as a necessary thing, its practical use, but the power to use the thing possessed at pleasure.

"Nevertheless, there may be cases in which the non-use by a State may be equivalent to a true abandonment of the possession, and produce on the part of another State, having it in its power, a legitimate right to possess it and defend its possession. That is the case when the State that has no right to possess, without the consentment of the other State, to which the thing belongs, has taken possession of it, with exterior unequivocal signs, and such a situation of fact is known to the other State and perfectly well tolerated. Under those conditions, a true abandonment is to be presumed on the part of the State to which the possession of the thing originally belonged. Thus, the fact of another State holding the thing may prescind of every right on his part, and produce in time the legal consequence of legitimating the possession.

"*It seems that on the ground of such an idea we may draw in conclusion the legitimacy of the acquisition among States by prescription. Occupation as a bare fact may lead to legitimate possession on part of a territory when the following conditions are fulfilled: Notoriety, non-interruption, and the length of time sufficient to support the presumption of the abandonment of possession on behalf of a party and the acquisition on behalf of the other.*

851. "But how long has to be the time of the occupation to furnish the necessary ground for the legal presumption of the acquisition of the right on the part of one State in virtue of the tacit renouncement of the other?

"There is the difficulty, and we have no true principles in the international law to prevent controversies. It is not easy to lay down precise rules, applicable to every case.

"We can not propose any better solution than to submit to an Arbitral Tribunal the point of deciding how long time is necessary to make a possession *de facto*, accompanied by special conditions, a sufficient basis of the *jus possidendi*. It ought to be taken in consideration, the more or less importance of the territory possessed, the manner of the exterior and unequivocal acts of carrying out the possession, the circumstances in which they have been shown, and the position in which the claimants are found. In regard to a large extension of territory, the necessary time to found the *jus possidendi* ought to be less, when possession should have been apparent, continuous, and unequivocal, making much easier the admission of the presumption of abandonment.

"If, on the contrary, in a very extensive tract of territory, possession being comparatively less apparent and the vigilance involved less, the length of time ought to be greater. It should be of the utmost importance that the territory occupied were contiguous to that of the State, or else if it should form a part of possessions situated in far distant regions."

The author assigns as the chief foundation for prescription the *non-use* or the abandonment of the thing on the part of the owner, *and the possession of some other person, when it is notorious, uninterrupted, and durable.* It requires then the condition of *publicity, uninterrupted continuance, and sufficient time.* He says nothing of *good faith* nor *fair title.* But, in the absence of those things, the occupant is nothing but an usurper, and if the former owner has not abandoned his title and it comes to his notice that some one else is possessing his property, it is plain that he will claim it and put an end to the spoliation in case of a true relinquishment, (*derelictio*).

If he has left the property with the purpose not to keep it any longer, then it has entered into the class of *res nullius*, and therefore whoever occupies it makes it his own, and there is nothing that he may prescribe. The acquisition, then, is accomplished likewise, as if the thing never had been occupied before. We see very plainly that by alleging the presumption of abandonment so as to justify the prescription, we run the risk of confounding it with the occupation, while both are means of acquisition widely different. The only thing that may then bear out prescription is the coexistence of good faith and fair title kept to the end.

In the treaty by Venezuela and Great Britain, what is given as the origin of valid title is "adverse holding," or possession of the territory for "fifty years." In order that possession may deserve that qualification it must be adverse to the possession of any other State or to the primitive owner, whose rights are to be impaired, when prolonged for fifty years, under the circumstances and conditions so often specified.

It will be noticed, as de Fiore does, when giving his advice to submit the question of time to the decision of a Tribunal, that it is of the greatest importance, the fact of the territory occupied being contiguous to the territory of the State, or would form a part of the possessions situated in distant places.

Here the rivers and territories disputed by England

constitute a portion of the Venezuelan domain. The rivers constitute a natural highway for the satisfaction of its wants of every kind; are indispensable to its preservation, safety and aggrandizement; while British Guiana is an isolated possession, far distant from the territory of the metropolis, and therefore can not command the same importance and value to it as to Venezuela. The Guayana region, watered by immense rivers, brings it in contact with the world, and particularly with the other sister Republics of South America. Its loss to Venezuela would therefore bring her down under the foot of a formidable rival and possible enemy.

Don Antonio Riquelme, chief clerk of the Department of State in Spain, is the author of a book entitled "Elements of the International Public Law," printed in Madrid in 1849. In chapter 2, while writing on the subject of the property of nations, sets down the follow- doctrine:

"Finally, the dominion of States is acquired and lost by prescription. On this point many questions are brought about among jurists, some of them contending that prescription can not exist among nations, since the right of property from which it comes does not essentially emmanate from nature, because in a state of nature all things are held in common. But, society being the first condition of man, it is plain that man, once constituted in society, needs to have a division of things and properties. So that society, as well as property, are natural to man; they are in accord with his condition, being two indispensable elements of the peace and welfare of the human race, such as constituted by his nature. Upon this principle of the convenience of nations, not allowing property to remain uncertain, and *that peaceful and quiet possession in good faith is in itself a respectable means of acquisition of the dominion* of things (as the consent of all those who might allege a better right is presumed), we hold that prescription among nations is legitimate."

"*In order that prescription may bear its effects, it is necessary that possession be held in good faith and the possessor be conscious of the legitimacy of his title, else there is no pre-*

scription but usurpation; that possession must be uninterrupted, for if it is shown that there have been any claims or protests against the possession, the tacit presumption of consentment of the aggrieved party ceases to exist, and that is an indispensable condition of prescription; and, finally, that possession must be for a long time. Upon this point it is not an easy matter to determine a fixed number of years; the most natural rule is that the time during which the thing has been abandoned should be sufficient to produce confusion and uncertainty in the respective rights; conditions, depending upon the nature of things and other circumstances."

"Immemorial prescription, therefore, is a true title of property, as firm and valid as the best, for, if *possession, the origin of which is lost in the past,* is not to be respected as a genuine title, *no nation could be safe in the possession of its domain.* The work of time is always respected, particularly in dealing with the interests of nations, involving the existence and future of so many families."

"Acts meaning relinquishment of a right, such as failing to perform those which constitute its preservation, give a title of prescription, even of the kind called passive. According to this rule, the State that does not wish or *can not utilize* a territory is understood to renounce its rights to it when the contrary is not fully shown."

According to these passages, prescription requires *good faith or ligitimacy of title of the possessor; possession uninterrupted, quiet and peaceful, and one that has been carried out for a long time.* Claims and protests destroy the presumption of consent on the part of the aggrieved parties, which is an indispensable condition. Immemorial possession gives good and valid title. Undoubtedly this one is understood and advocated by Martens and those who look upon possession as a source of property among nations.

What the author adds about passive prescription makes only a new kind; that is to say, as he understands it, prescription is a means of acquisition for the actual possessor, and of a loss for the primitive owner, whom the possessor has substituted.

He does not seem to be just in his observation that a State is understood to have renounced the right to a territory when it can not utilize the same. If it were applied to an owner that would not wish to avail himself of that territory, we could understand the case, and it seems to be admissible, because all proprietors are at liberty on account of their dominion to give up or keep their advantages; but the one who does *not* do a thing because he *can not* must be looked upon in a very different light. Here we have to invoke the rule of law: "*ad impossibilia nomo tenetur.*" A State owes protection to foreigners received in its territory, for instance, against the internal factions, or foreign invasions, notwithstanding he is under no liabilty, after having even unsuccessfully employed the means in his power to meet similar obligations. A State must prevent the acts of hostility among belligerents within its territory, and in case of omission he is found derelict, and must pay the damages incurred through its negligence. Nevertheless he will be exonerated, if he shows that he was in actual want of and did not possess the necessary means to stop the trespassers of powerful belligerents.

There was submitted to the President of the French Republic a demand by the United States against Portugal for the destruction of the American privateer, "General Armstrong," by a British man-of-war in the port of Fayal, in the year 1814. The defendant was absolved because "the weakness of the garrison of the Island and the constant dismantlement of the fort, with the removal of the cannons for their defense, made it impossible for any armed intervention on the part of the Governor of Fayal."

The distinguished Venezuelan, Andrés Bello, author of the oldest work on international law, published in America ("Principles of the Law of Nations," printed for the first time in 1832), in chapter 2, § VI, writes about prescription. He condenses Vattel's doctrine and more methodically he expounds the same principles of his model. He contends that the ordinary prescription requires three conditions: *Uninterrupted possession for a number of years; the possessor's good faith, and that the owner has neglected the use of his right.*

In regard to the neglect of the owner he considers three conditions to be necessary: *1, that no insurmountable ignorance may have occurred on his part or that of those from whom he derives his rights; 2, that he had kept silence; and 3, that his silence could not be justified with plausible reasons, such as oppression or well-grounded fear of a serious evil.* He contends that immemorial prescription gives an incontrovertible title to the possessor.

He repeats that in conscience, if the possessor discovers that the true owner is not himself but somebody else, he is bound to make the restitution of everything by which said possession has made him richer; that he can not oppose the exception of bad faith, but only in cases where his evidence is incontrovertible; that in other cases it is always supposed that a nation has possessed in good faith.

He notices that international and civil prescription must not be confounded, as the civil one may be alleged in favor or against individuals.

In 1874 a "treatise on international, diplomatic and consular law," in accordance with the principles and modern practice in Europe and America, was published in Bogotá by Dr. Manuel María Madiedo, professor of jurisprudence. In chapter 4, on territory, speaking of prescription, he writes: "Before discussing certain unavoidable fictions of international law we want to explain the manner of territorial acquisition among nations, heretofore relegated to the empiricism of opinions, more or less arbitrary. We want to speak of the acquisition of the territorial dominion among nations by the *prescription* of a first owner, and the *usucaptio* of a second one. By the civil law of States the prescription of the action to recover dominion and the usucaption to acquire said dominion are given in detail, and regulated in a precise manner from the time of the Romans down to the present day. But among nations nobody can tell, that we know, which rule may serve as a sure basis to consider a right as prescribed and a territorial dominion as acquired."

151. "As is well known the acquisition of dominion through a length of time is founded on a presumption of voluntary abandonment on the part of the first owner of the thing in favor of a successive acquirer. But what time is necessary, according to international law, to consider the first owner as having abandoned his right of ownership? We think the time may be very long or very short according to the circumstances.

152. "As by international law it is not easy so far to fix the necessary time so as to presume the abandonment of a territorial right, we shall have to rely on a fact that seems to be fully conclusive on the subject.

153. "There is an evident proof of presumptive abandonment of a territorial right on the part of the nation when its agents or subjects, with the approval of their Government, enter into any official relations or make any contracts, in a manner that takes for granted the acknowledgment of the right of the new possessor of the territory that did not belong to him before. It does not matter if the seizure of territory by its last possessor is of a very recent date. The fact of dealing with it as having full authority to do so, of allowing subjects of the first owner to be submitted to the new domination going to that territory, and obeying and respecting the laws and regulations of the second owner without any prohibition or protest whatever from the first owner, is enough to form a presumptive abandonment of any pretension of ownership.

154. "Beyond this case, that seems to be decisive, there is another one which may be resorted to, in order to allege prescription in our favor; that is, the absence of any protest whatsoever against the new owner intended to protect the owner's rights.

155. "To allege in similar cases the simple lapse of time as the reason for an acquisitive title of territorial

dominion does not seem to be sufficient, as the primitive owner may have found himself unable to recover or even affirm his rights. For instance, a long war, followed by embarrassments and complications, the fear of a formidable coalition, etc., may be reasons for the despoiled person not to have done anything to secure his rights. But could he not have made a protest for the safety of his rights? For doing that there is no need of armies or navies, but only to open his mouth, and that can be done by even dying persons. He who does not do it, it is not because he can not but because he does not wish to; and if he does not wish to he can not excuse the silence which he could have very easily broken, and when it is not broken it is equivalent to consent."

The author does not admit prescription, although admitting that among nations it seems to be relegated to the empiricism of opinions more or less arbitrary; that until now nobody has said what rule, really certain, may serve as a basis of it; that it can not be determined what time is necessary to produce it; and that it is founded on the presumption of abandonment by the primitive owner. He says that the time may be short, when there is proof of an *acknowledgment* of the right of the new possessor. Then there is not properly any prescription, but a clear renouncement of the right of the previous owner; he abandons his right in favor of the actual occupant. *The author does not agree in the allegation of the lapse of time only as a foundation of the acquisitive title on a territorial dominion.*

In regard to the American nations, he thinks, as many others do, that they have the ownership of the territories which they really occupy, and of those not yet occupied, but which are a continuation of the former, according to the limits marked out by the *uti possidetis juris* of their predecessors. He says that the European nations that gave authority to all adventurers wanting to go in quest of discoveries of countries for themselves in the New World, founded their right, not on a real occupation, but in a kind of possession *longa manu*, each one admitting such an equivocal title of dominion in others, so as to establish an authoritative precedent in support of the acquisitions made by themselves on like terms. Therefore, in the American Republics (once European Colonies) there are not, nor have been so far, any lands subject to the occupation of any other State, or that can be prescribed by possession of such and such a number of years. The same principle is understood theoretically and practically in the United States of America.

There is a work entitled "Elements of Public International Law," by Dr. Manuel Torres Campos, professor of the University of Granada and associate to the Institute of International Law, printed in Madrid in 1890. In lecture 22 he writes on acquisition and loss of property among nations. In section 5, he writes:

"The international relations, unlike the private law, only admit prescription within very restricted limits. There is no term for prescription, as a State is the ruler of its territory, as far as it can and wishes to maintain its authority therein; nothing can interrupt the continuity of an ancient right. A government may, in fact, lose possession, but it generally will be able to recover it in one way or the other. Only to an immemorial antiquity is given any importance to make it the basis of a political charter and of the existence of civilized and barbarous States. The fact already accomplished, supported by an immemorial antiquity, becomes legitimate before the international law."

Accordingly, the Spanish author does not accept any other prescription than the immemorial, which is not susceptible of arguments, since its origin is lost in the obscurity of time.

That the practice of nations confirms this theory, because they often raise protests in favor of their alleged rights, when treaties are concluded which explicitly or implicitly deny them, and that it is hardly necessary to say that the nation which is itself a party to such a treaty without protesting has unquestionably abandoned its rights.

Speaking afterwards of the right of *postlimininium* he says that it is the right to be reinstated in the property and rights that have accidentally been lost or unlawfully taken away, and that the best opinion of jurists is that even the *possessor in good faith* and purchaser must restore them to the lawful owner and, besides, without compensation for the expenses which the purchase thereof may have occasioned him.

From such doctrines it results that the presumption of abandonment arising from the silence of the former owner may be contradicted and destroyed with evidence of sufficient force, by which circumstance prescriptive possession would fall to the ground in opposition to the assertion made by the author, when saying that "the title of nations which are in the actual enjoyment and peaceable possession of their territory can not at any time be questioned or disputed, whatever the manner may be in which they have originally obtained it."

When any right is more or less explicitly recognized to the new claimant there is, it need not be said, no prescription, but abandonment of his property by him who was the owner.

The passages of the several authors cited by Phillimore in support of his doctrines have been examined, and it has not been found that they support him. It remains to consult Eugene Ortolan, who also is invoked by him and who is far from his ideas.

He also recalls some English laws, the statute of 2 and 3, William IV., Chapter LXXI, an act "for shortening the time of prescription in certain cases," and says that its purpose was to fix practically and generally a prescription of thirty years, and certainly and universally one of sixty years.

He finally brings an instance which occurred between France and England in 1754 respecting Saint Lucia, one of the West Indies, to which both nations laid claim. Commissioners were appointed to determine the controversy. The French negotiators alleged that, although the English had settled there in 1630, they had been ejected or killed by the Caribbeans, in 1640, and had abandoned the island without any intention to return, and that it being thus vacant was retaken by the French in 1650, who immediately acquired it without necessity of prescription. The English negotiators maintained that its *derelictio* had been the result of violence; that they had not abandoned the island without hope of returning, and that France had no right to avail herself of that act of violence and surreptitiously to obtain the territory of another State by which conduct the French could not acquire any dominion. Great Britain, therefore, believes that violence confers no right.

Eugene Ortolan, doctor of law and member of the Ministry of Foreign Affairs of France, published, in 1851, a treatise entitled "On the means of acquiring international dominion or State ownership between nations, according to the public law of nations, compared with the means of acquiring ownership between private persons according to private law, and followed by the principles of political equilibrium."

Article IV thereof treats of the acquisition of international dominion by possession during a certain lapse of time and discusses the subject under three divisions—rational ground of this mode of acquisition; how and under what conditions acquisitive prescription takes place in international law; it does not apply to the right of sovereignty, whether interior or exterior, or to nationality.

Prescription being admitted, as it is, in the treaty of the 2d of February last, the point which it is interesting to study is the second of the three above enumerated.

The author requires in the first place that the possession should be the one announced by the claim of a nation that is the owner and sovereign of the territory, "Therefore," adds he, "it would not be sufficient, for instance, that some private persons pertaining to the nation had exercised in their own name acts of private ownership in that territory; the possessiom must be held, in the name of the State, with those acts of enjoyment, disposition, and control which constitute the exercise of international dominion."

It will seldom happen between nations that a territory be lent, rent, or leased by a State to another, but it is not impossible. In other times Governments were seen to borrow from another sums of money, more or less considerable, by mortgaging some parts of their territory, and even giving the lender the possession thereof by way of pledge."

After citing several instances, Ortolan says: "It happens more frequently, even nowadays, that a power occupies certain points in the territory of another by reason of alliance, common defense, or protection, assistance against a danger, interior or exterior. Such kinds of occupation, which only take place by way of lease, pledge, common defense, protection, or tolerance, can not furnish ground, however long they may have lasted, for an acquisition of international dominion by prescription. They do not begin to be capable of producing that effect till the moment when the occupying nation changes the nature of its possession by denying the rights of the other State and pretending to possess thenceforth as owner and sovereign."

Another of the requisites demanded by Ortolan is that of publicity. "It is also said," says he, "that the possession held in the belief of being the owner, of which we have just spoken, must be *public*—that is to say, manifested by exterior acts ostensible to all. In effect, furtive, clandestine acts which the true owner has not been able to observe, do not constitute that fundamental act of prescription—the part of owner taken by the one and abandoned by the other."

In the third place he speaks of the continuity of these terms. "It is said that possession must be continual. Such is to-day, in effect, the spirit, the character of the part of owner. Transient, transitory, intermittent acts do not constitute this part."

"Or else, if being held at the beginning with a spirit of continuity, possession has afterwards been abandoned and again retaken, each interruption has irrevocably destroyed the effect of the former possession, as far as the unaccomplished course of prescription is concerned. The several fragments of those several possessions can not unite into one body; but every new taking of possession constitutes a new starting point, and the time shall only be computed from this new starting point. In effect, is it not the permanency, the persistency, sufficiently prolonged in the performance of the part of owner, that at length destroys the consideration of the primitive work of appropriation and transfers the right of property to the person of the possessor?

"These three conditions of publicity, continuity, and uninterruption, necessary in private law for acquisitive prescription, are equally necessary in international law. Indeed, a clandestine territorial possession can hardly be conceived between nation and nation; but the cases in which this possession should not have been continual (as, for instance, when consisting only in the reiterated landings in an island for the purpose to hunt, fell wood, take some products, and then retire;) or the cases in which it should have been interrupted, may occur and ought to be regulated in accordance with the principles which we have just set forth."

That clandestine possession may occur between nation and nation is by no means difficult in some American territories—vast, deserted, distant from the centers of population, and therefore seldom or never visited. In this same question Lord Salisbury revealed, in a note dated November 26, 1895, that from 1844, when the proposal of Lord Aberdeen was made to Doctor Fortique, up to 1881, "natives and others had settled in the territory under the belief that they would enjoy the benefits of British rule, and that it was impossible to assent to such concessions as Señor Rojas' line would involve."

This the English Government did not know till the year 1881, when they consulted, concerning Señor Rojas' proposal, with the Lieutenant-Governor and the Attorney-General of British Guiana, who were then in England, and who presented an elaborate report in which they declared the fact.

Passing to the requisite of peaceableness, M. Ortolan expresses himself as follows: "More serious, more delicate difficulties occur concerning the circumstances more or less irregular, more or less unlawful, which may have given rise to possession, or respecting the means, by the help of which this possession may have been maintained.'

" It is of itself understood that violence, however long it may last, can not by its duration become lawful and transform to right. On the contrary, the longer it lasts the graver the culpability becomes, the more harm is done to right. It can not be said, especially in point of prescription, that he who is ejected and by force kept apart, abandons the part of owner. A possession, therefore, that is maintained only by violent means can not be considered as useful. This is what is expressed in private law by saying that possession, in order to be useful to the purpose of prescription, must be peaceable. It is true that between private parties, and in a civilized State, in which the person ousted may resort to the cousrt of justice and invoke the help of public power, there can hardly be a possession of immovables kept by violence, but is also true that the case may occur between nation and nation. The same preponderant force, the same means of compulsion by the help of which a State shall have taken possession of a territory, may enable it to maintain itself in that possession and to suppress the claims of the State dispossessed. Such a possession, not only violent in its origin, but also violent in its duration, can not lead to the acquisition of international dominion. So long as violence exists prescription can not begin."

The author then explains that the Roman law had gone farther, for the ownership of an immovable of which possession had been violently taken was voidable through a radical and permanent vice, which always was an obstacle to prescription, even after violence had ceased, whatever the good faith of the new possessors might be and whatsoever period might have elapsed. The vice was only removed by the return of the immovable property to the hands of the owner. Ortolan sees in this a perpetual reprobation of violence that survives events and persons, and considers it as an exaggeration which modern jurisprudence has abandoned. "From the moment that violence ceases," says he, "and a public possession exists, and the ousted owner is at liberty to reclaim his property, the normal conditions of prescription are re-established."

He also observes that the severity of the Romans had not stopped there, for, even in case of a vicious possession, less grave than theft and violence, their civil law did not admit usucaption, except to the benefit of possessors in good faith. This he also condemns as prejudicial and affirms it abolished by those legislations which recognize in the possessor bad faith, during a long period, a true acquisitive prescription.

This may be a sign of progress, although at variance with morality, and has been adopted by the internal laws of some countries; but, to say the least, it is doubtful whether it should be applied to nations.

Article 199 is of the following tenor:

"The foregoing solutions, just in private law, are equally just in international law. The circumstances which constitute the possession in good faith between private parties (for instance, the fact of having received an immovable property by sale, barter, payment, donation, or any other similar cause, from somebody who believed himself to be the owner thereof, but who was not) can hardly occur between nation and nation respecting their territory. Most often the territorial occupation will be the result of aggressions, encroachments in fact, or violent invasions, and most times also it will be the invading nation that will remain in possession. Even in this last case, and excepting the prolongation then of the time required for prescription, we are bound logically to recognize that from the moment that violence shall have ceased and the State dispossessed shall have been at liberty to reclaim his property, if it has not done so and has remained inert in this respect, a prescription shall have begun to the profit of the State possessing the territory, by means of which this possession will at length transform to international dominion."

"We have already said (No. 166) how the military occupation of a territory in consequence of a regular war, insufficient to give the ownership of this territory, confers, however, a possession which international usages assimilate to the possession *held in good faith.* Good faith does not consist here on the part of the occupying State in believing itself to be the owner of the occupied territory; it does consist in believing itself to have a lawful motive for occupying the same as a means of compelling its enemy to just compensations and to the treaty of peace which will put an end to the war. If this treaty of peace or any act of cession has not intervened, occupation prolonged without any claim on the part of the State dispossessed will lead to the acquisition of dominion by prescription, *as would a true possession in good faith.* It would not be difficult for us to show an analogous situation and analogous effects between private parties if we were willing to continue to compare private law with international law, even in those details and little things with great ones."

The requisite of time now remains, of which the author says:

"On all hypotheses, acquisitive prescription is founded on a sort of compensation of the primitive work, the origin of the right of ownership by the new work of the possessor during the inaction of the owner. After what duration will this new work be sufficient for effecting that compensation? This question has no absolute answer. Variable terms are the question; the primitive and the inaction of the owner; the new work and the purpose which has prevailed on the part of the possessor; the circumstances under which the one and the other have taken place—all that is liable to several modifications. The compensation is not a numerical compensation between quantities expressed in ciphers; it is a moral compensation between elements which ought to be appreciated mentally. It is evident that, rational law being observed, the appreciation ought to be effected in a special manner for each case."

"Positive law respecting private parties is applicable here as in numberless other like circumstances. In order to give a permanent and common rule it only distinguishes some great categories; the cases of movables or immovables, of presence or absence, and of good or bad faith; and taking, in every category an average, it establishes determined ciphers."

"The same can not occur, however, in international law. Nations, in the absence of a common legislator, remain subject to the purely rational rule, and only by means of diplomatic negotiations and taking into consideration the especial circumstances of every transaction can we show that the duration of possession has been sufficiently long to produce international acquisition, and convince the State which was the former owner of the loss of its rights. This duration is nothing precise, and m change from one case to another. It can not be concealed that this want of precision deprives acquisitive prescription between nations of one of the great advantages which it possesses, between private parties, by virtue of positive law, the advantage of putting a prefixed end to litigations."

"There is also a consideration important to the purpose. The life of nations is of a duration very different from that of the life of private individuals; and a people require, before taking a course and acting in its relations in its international negotiations and claims, a much longer time than individuals require before taking a course and acting in their private relations. On the other hand, the scope and the series of its works are very different in the establishment and the action of a people in a territory and in the establishment and the action of an indvidual in a portion of land. The duration of the possession necessary for acquiring ownership by prescription between State and State can not be measured after the duration required for the acquisition of private property. The usual terms of ten, twenty, or thirty years, proportioned to the life and action of individuals, are not proportioned to those of nations. Without the possibility of determining precise ciphers and leaving to the circumstances of each transaction the influence which they must have, *it is conceived that, in order to transfer the right of dominion and territorial sovereignty over a country from a nation to another, long series of years are necessary.*"

In the treaty of the 2d of February, 1897, a term of only *fifty years* was fixed. For prescriptions between private individuals it has been seen that up to sixty years have been fixed. In those relating to estates of the Church the term of a hundred years has been established.

As prescriptive possession must not be interrupted, Ortolan undertakes to examine the means of producing that effect, and writes:

"Since the inaction of the owner, the want of exercise, on his part, of the rights and functions of ownership, constitute an essential element of the justifying causes of prescription, *the means he has of stopping the course of a begun prescription is to break that inaction, to reassume, or at least claim, the performance of his part of owner before such course has been completed and the acquisition accomplished by the possessor.* In private law he must not do justice to himself by violent means, but must resort to the judicial authority. This recourse, this judicial prosecution before the expiration of the term interrupt prescription. Thenceforth, the time of the possession prior to said prosecution remains useless and can no longer be computed. But, in order to produce that effect, neither claims nor protests, nor even extra judicial intimations would be sufficient, the judicial action would be necessary, because, since the date thereof, but only since that date, the owner would find himself as actually reinstated in the possession of his property, the delay in ascertaining the existence of his right depending only on the imperfections and slowness of human justice."

"The same rule can not be applied in international law, as there is no jurisdiction. Nations find themselves confined to claim their rights, one from another, by means of diplomatic negotiations, and, if necessary, to do justice to themselves by their own forces. That prescription should be interrupted it is not necessary to employ that last means, or that the State claiming international dominion over territory should have begun war for recovering possession of the same. A war is not understood unless it is prompted by grave motives and made with probabilities of success. A people weak or temporarily placed in a difficult situation may find itself forced to wait for other succors or other times to act by the force of arms, and meanwhile to confine itself to diplomatic claims. Such claims interrupt prescription, because from the moment they are entered it is the duty of the State in possession of its property to satisfy them, if they are just, and immediately to deliver its possession to the State which is the owner thereof."

Ortolan examines afterwards several methods of mere form, by which, in the middle ages, reciprocal pretensions were manifested, as the use of titles, shields, protests, public and solemn notifications. Respecting protests and notifications, he writes that, "taking into consideration the difficult situations and the impossibility to act in an effectual manner in which a power may find itself, it may generally be said that they will only produce an interruptive effect when assuming the character of a true diplomatic claim addressed to the adverse power, and placing this in the obligation of restituting the territory by it unduly occupied. The notifications to the other States are but means of a greater publicity, which allow to call those States to witness the violation of its rights and the claim entered against it."

The attempts made to actually recover the possession of the territory in dispute would be, with still greater reason, a cause interruptive of prescription, even if they were not followed by success; but it is necessary that they should be made in the name ot the State as a public enterprise, approved by it, and not by simple individuals acting without authority and in a private capacity. The acknowledgment of the State possessing the territory of the adverse power, or even the mere endeavor to submit the difference to an examination or to diplomatic discussion, would likewise interrupt the course of an unaccomplished prescription. Negotiators usually, for this reason, carefully avoid that such acknowledgments or endeavors may, even apparently, result from treaties on other matters or be inferred therefrom in an indirect manner, notwithstanding their not having really entered into the scope of their purposes. In the memorials exchanged between the English and the French Commissioners concerning the question of Saint Lucia, of which we have already spoken, it may be seen how the different enterprises are discussed which the English claim to have undertaken for the recovery of the island, but in which the French Commissioners see but private attempts, deprived of any public character, and how the one and the other invoke, in an opposite sense, in support of their claims, the treaties of Breda concluded in 1667, of Ryswick, dated 1697, and that of Utrecht.

From the foregoing ample doctrine of international prescription, it is evident that it requires the following formalities: *A public, continual, uninterrupted, peaceable possession, held by a sovereign State in the belief of being the owner, and strengthened by a long period of time.* This must not be of ten, twenty or thirty years, as fixed for prescription in private law, although it has been seen that in Great Britain there are also prescriptions of forty and sixty, and in canonical laws one of a hundred years, applicable to the estates of the Church. In international law, for the reasons indicated by Ortolan, *series of years* are required, *proportioned to the difference existing between the life of individuals and the life of nations.*

Others are of opinion that from among them the only one admissible is the immemorial prescription, if taken in the sense of the possession the origin of which can not absolutely be traced.

It has been noticed already that Phillimore requires the actual enjoyment and the peaceable possession, as well as publicity, continual occupancy, uninterruption, with the help of the investment of capital and labor in the occupancy by the new possessor during the period of silence or inaction, or total absence of attempt on the part of the former possessor to exercise rights of ownership. He says that the proofs of prescriptive possession are principally those above cited, and therefore omits the specification of those he considers as subaltern. It is presumable that he alludes to the effective and peaceable character of possession, of which he had previously spoken.

Ortolan also explains the modes in which prescription is interrupted in international law, which consists in protests, claims, attempts to actually recover possession, and wars. There is no necessity of this last extreme when there is no probability of obtaining the victory; the other means produce the effect of paralyzing the pretension of the new possessor who claims the dominion. But it is not to be forgotten that all these remedies are to be applied by the nation, the rights of which are those of the State; and not by private individuals pertaining to it, acting without the necessary authority. It matters not that the negotiations or the demands for the restitution of the territory unduly occupied are unsuccessful; for they show in an unequivocal manner the determination to maintain it, not to abandon it, thus destroying the presumption arising from the tolerance or inaction of the true owner, which is least objectionable of the grounds invoked for justifying such acquisitions.

Among the conditions of acquisition the author does not mention good faith; but it seems to be implied in the condition that the possessor should act as owner. For how could any one believe himself to be such, possessing the thing without a just title translative of dominion, proceeding from its lawful owner, capable of alienating and furnished with the formalities prescribed by law for the particular case of the transfer made?

In the "General Review of International Public Law," a bi-monthly scientific paper edited at Paris since 1894, by Drs. Antoine Pillat and Paul Fauchille, No. 3, dated May and June, 1896, a writing was inserted under the title: "On Acquisitive Prescription in International Public Law—the Part It Performs, Its Object, and Its Conditions of Existence."

It begins by asking whether, when a State occupies, without having regularly acquired, a territory belonging to another, or has taken possession of it fraudulently or violently, such possession, deprived of a just title or even vitiated from its beginning, will transform, after a certain time, into a lawful right of ownership or sovereignty? In answer, it says that the question has been discussed several times, and that there are scarcely any authors who have not treated the same, most of them deciding it in the affirmative; that, while the principle is admitted, its application is, as yet, undecided; that the object of prescription and the part it performs in the claims between State and State, as well as the conditions to which it is subjected, have not been sufficiently determined, and its author proposes to try a better specification of the latter.

He considers the question the more important, as the acquisitions by which States have transformed and aggrandized show some vice in their origin, which vice could not resist rigorous examination; and the question ought to be studied at the close of a century which has seen the map of Europe so often altered, new States formed in the Old and the New World, and the old ones enriched with new possession, now at the expense of their neighbors, now in the distant colonies.

He states that most authors admit that prescription is a mode of acquisition as well between State and State as between individual and individual, although some deny it, on the ground that time does not confer, by itself alone, any right whatever; that prescription is in every State a creature of positive law; and that, as this does not exist between nation and nation, no prescription can be given between them unless it has been expressly admitted by treaties, of which till then there had not been any instance. Besides that, even if the principle of prescription were admitted, no improvement would have been obtained, on account of the impossibility of fixing the term of that mode of acquisition.

He says, and with reason, that when the origin of possession is so remote that nobody can be sure when it began, nobody can either prove that it is not grounded on a lawful title; but that this is not prescription, the object and effect of which is to paralyze the action of an owner whose title, on the other hand, would be known and certain.

He says that such a doctrine confounds the right of prescription with the law of prescription; that the principle of it is found at all times and in all countries; is inherent in the nature of things; is essential to the existence of society; and rests on reasons as valuable, if not more, in the society of States as in that of individuals.

He then invokes the abandonment of the owner, the labor and capital of the possessor (especially if he possesses in good faith), the results of good government, which conciliates the affections of the people, and the necessity of preventing litigations and preserving the peace of society, stopping the source of disputes arising from antiquated titles.

He believes that prescription is applicable without difficulty *when a State has acquired a territory peaceably and without violence, but without a regular title, or when the title is one unknown or forgotten, the defect of which it supplies.* For instance, two neighboring States lay claim to a territory on their boundary; that which has possessed it during a sufficient time ought to be considered as its lawful owner; or a State, after having occupied a territory without owner, has abandoned it, and another State has occupied it in its turn; the latter may acquire by prescription a right opposed to that of the former occupant.

The article proceeds to examine whether prescription is applicable when a State has annexed another State in its entirety, or at least a province of it, by an unlawful act, especially by an unjustifiable conquest. It determines the question in the affirmative after presenting several considerations on the nature of the sovereignty.

Finally, it asserts that "*the possession of the State, in order to produce prescription, ought to be public, peaceable, continual, uninterrupted, held in the belief of being the owner, and of a sufficient duration to induce the presumption of the tacit consent of the State dispossessed of a part of its territory and by the people subjected to its new domination.*"

Public, because otherwise it could neither be known nor claimed against by the State deterrated by it. The writer finds it incomprehensible that a State which has dispossessed another of a province should not possess the same publicly; but he understands that the taking of possession may remain unknown when it has been violent, or on account of the remoteness of the territory, as when situated in the colonies, or by reason of its little importance, as in case of a land disputed on the boundaries.

In the present case the possession has been clandestine on account of remoteness from the centers of population, deserted or even little explored.

Peaceable, without the necessity of having been so from the beginning. He considers it as possible even when taken by conquest, but believes it will only produce effect from the moment that violence ceases; and he requires, above all, that the Government should neither resort to force in order to keep under its obedience the people it has annexed, or to prevent them from making known their true sentiments, nor employ punishment or exceptional measures causing complaints or protests.

Continual and uninterrupted. Intermittent possession is of no avail. It is necessary to recognize in the States and peoples the right to interrupt the prescription begun against them, which recognition is in such case more difficult, vague, and uncertain than between individual and individual, on account of the non-existence of tribunals before which nations may enter their actions. States interrupt prescription by their protests against the conquests which dispossess them, although *it is not always possible for them to make* such protests on account of their weakness or of their not being in a position to maintain their claims by the force of arms.

The State must possess in the belief of being the owner, or rather the sovereign. It is not impossible that it may retain and rule over a country or province, while it recognizes that the sovereignty pertains, according to law, to another State, as the effect of a political combination. Thus, Austria, by the Treaty of Berlin, dated 1878, occupies and rules over Bosnia and Herzegovia, of which the Sultan continues to be the sovereign, and England does the same in other countries. A protectorate State that should absorb the government and administration of the State which it protects, going as far as to leave it an independence merely nominal, could never acquire sovereignty over that State, however long such a possession might last. Neither a State nor an individual is permitted to prescribe against its or his own title.

If, as Ortolan has written, international dominion is "*the right of a nation to take the products of a territory, disposing of it to the exclusion of all other nations, and to rule over it as sovereign power, independently from any exterior power,*" it is evident that the idea of international ownership can not by any means be withdrawn from that of sovereignty. The writer of the article is, therefore, in the right when requiring that the possession should be held in the belief of being the owner or sovereign.

" When the possession presents the conditions above enumerated," he asks, " how long shall its term be?" He answers that, this term cannot be fixed *a priori;* that Vattel advises neighboring nations to settle their differences in this respect by means of treaties, which, to all appearances, is not likely ever to take place; that, in the absence of an agreement, Phillimore proposes to fix such a term at 50 years or even at 30, in case of a considerable extent of territory; and that international usage has not sanctioned those figures, while, from a legal point of view, there is no reason for preferring them to others.

He adds that all that can be said is that the term must be sufficient to induce the presumption of the implicit consent of the State dispossessed of a part of its territory, and of the people submitted to a new domination; that, generally, it will be longer than the term for prescription in private law, because States have a longer life than individuals and their rights are also of a greater importance; and that, for the rest, the length of the term will vary according to the circumstances.

Audinet is therefore of the same opinion as Ortolan respecting the conditions of prescriptive possession.

So it seems, there are two kinds of doctrine. Accord-cording to the one, good faith, continued to the last, and the just title involved in it, are considered as indispensible to render prescription lawful and honest. According to the other, such commendable conditions are laid aside, and although no little value is ascribed to time, other requisites are added to it, without which it will not produce any effect.

Just as in other times the Roman legislation served as an almost universal pattern, so in the present century the codes of several other nations have been patterned after those of France.

It has been seen that in the Civil Code of the Great Empire three kinds of prescription were created, some of a short, others of a long time, and the last of a still longer period.

It is not known that in international law the first has ever been adopted, and for this reason there is no necessity to speak of it.

For the second, the French law fixes the term of ten years between present parties and of twenty between absent parties; provided, however, that possession be continuous and uninterrupted, peaceable, public, unequivocal, and had in the belief of being the owner, and on condition, moreover, that the immovables in question shall have been acquired in good faith and with a just title.

Respecting movables, prescription is only instantaneous when the third party has acquired them in good faith and through a cause translative of dominion, and provided that the movable shall not have been either lost or stolen, for, in this last case, three years are required.

The longest prescription is of thirty years, and refers to all actions, whether real or personal, without any obligation on the part of him who alleges it to produce any title, and without the possibility of his being opposed—the exception arising from bad faith.

It is understood, commentors say, that the law supposes the prescriptibility of the thing and the absence of interruption or suspension to be accompanied by the other conditions which it requires; and that, while the inaction of the person having right, for a period of thirty years, will be sufficient in case of personal actions, it is understood that in case of an action for the recovery of immovable estates, it will not be prescribed unless the defendant has had, during all that time, a possession furnished with all those characteristics that are necessary for acquiring by prescription. In other words, possession must have been continual and uninterrupted, peaceable, public, and had in the belief of being the owner.

If, therefore, the purpose has existed to transfer the doctrine of prescription from the civil to international law, a prescription ought to have been adopted with all such requisites as are provided in the former for that of ten or twenty years, but raising these terms to, say, fifty, and another corresponding to that of thirty years, but prolonging its duration to at least a hundred years.

It is not understood why some writers have not adopted the first system, the least repugnant to morality, and have exclusively adhered to the second.

But, even following them in this direction, it will be seen that the mere lapse of a certain time is never sufficient to produce prescription; but that, on the contrary, the compliance with the other formalities aforesaid is also required.

Article IV of the Treaty concluded at Washington on the 2d of February, 1897, between the United States of Venezuela and Her Britannic Majesty, contains this clause:

"In deciding the matters submitted, the Arbitrators shall ascertain all facts which they deem necessary to a decision of the controversy, and shall be governed by the following rules, which are agreed upon by the high contracting parties as rules to be taken as applicable."

The short review which we have made of the doctrines of publicists shows that none of them regards the mere possession of a territory belonging to another as a sufficient title to dominion; and that even the English, in whose opinion support is sought for such an assertion, require a possession long, public, peaceable, uninterrupted, and had in the belief of being the owner, together with the investment of labor and capital in the places possessed, and consider that the protests of him who believes himself to be the owner are equivalent to claims in civil matters and produce between nations the same effect as those do between individuals.

It has at the same time been made evident that for the acquisition of sovereignty just title is required, according to Phillimore, and that, consequently, it is impossible to prescind it in the acquisition of international ownership, which is not confined to the scope of private ownership, but implies, besides, sovereign attributes.

The very actor in the case at bar has insisted, again and again, on the good faith in which "natives and others" settled in territory disputed between Venezuela and Great Britain; and this shows that Lord Salisbury himself considers it as an essential element in questions of territory.

The principles concerning prescription already enumerated, are undoubtedly those which the Arbitrators are, by rule "*b*," authorized to apply, inasmuch as they do not contradict the rule "*a*," the only object of which is to fix the period capable of rendering valid the adverse holding.

CHAPTER XV.

Prescription not Applicable in this Case.

In the Treaty of February 2, 1897, for the settlement, by Arbitration, of the boundary dispute between Venezuela and Great Britain, the doctrine of prescription is admitted; but all the requisites of such mode of acquisition are not specified, only the one which presents the greatest difficulty—namely, the requisite time of possession, which is fixed at fifty years.

Far from excluding the other conditions, they are tacitly admitted where it is stated that "adverse holding or prescription during a period of fifty years shall make a good title." Because "adverse holding" can not exist unless a new possessor should contest the rights of a former possessor; should pretend to substitute him, or oppose him in his efforts to recover; or pretend to eject the former possessor by all possible means, or to make the present state of affairs prevail against the old.

Since "prescription is a mode of acquisition or of deliverance during a certain lapse of time, in accordance with the conditions determined by law," it is evident that there exists a presupposition of rights belonging to another against whom an effort of disseizen is being made.

Prescription is founded mainly on passivity or negligence on the part of a former owner, who allows the years to pass without making use of his rights of ownership, when he knows, or may know, that another has taken possession of his property, and is deriving therefrom all possible advantages. The convenience of maintaining society on a more secure basis is also one of its foundations.

This constitutes the difference between prescription and usucaption, which is the original mode of acquisition, applicable only to property without an owner, either because no one has appropriated it so far, or because the former occupant abandoned it with the intention of relinquishing his rights of domain.

It must be borne in mind, also, that this right pertains exclusively to nations. It is not to be extended to private individuals, acting on their own responsibility and not in the name or by the authority of the nation, and that on this account can not be said to apply to territory lying in the remote interior of a country. Such is the purport of the laws of various nations.

This is the principle of the law of nations, which Vattel explains as follows, in § 205, Book 1, Chapter XVIII:

> "When a nation takes possession of a country which does not belong to any one, it is supposed that she exercises over it the rights of sovereignty at the same time as those of dominion; because, being free and independent, there can be no intention in settling in a country to leave to others the rights of domain over it, nor any other rights constituting sovereignty. All the territory over which a nation extends its domain forms the district of its jurisdiction, which is called dominion."

Paragraph 235, Book 1, Chapter XX, states: "All that is susceptible of being possessed is supposed to belong to the nation occupying the territory, and forms part of the whole of its property. But nations do not possess all these properties in the same manner. Properties not divided among private communities or individuals of the nation are called *public property*. Some properties are reserved for the necessities of the State, and constitute the dominion of the Crown or of the Republic, as the case may be. The others are common to all citizens, who make use of them according to their needs, or in accordance with the laws regulating their use. These are called *common property*."

In § 235, Book 1, Chapter XX, the same author states that "All things that are included in a country belong to a nation, and no one but the nation, or the person in whom the nation's rights are delegated, is authorized to dispose of them. If there should be in the country uncultivated and desert lands, no one has a right to take possession of them without the authority of the nation. Though the nation makes no actual use of these lands, they are, nevertheless, her property; she has an interest in preserving them for her future use, and is responsible to no one for the manner in which she makes use of her property."

From the foregoing, it is inferred that even in conformity with the amplest doctrine, Great Britain must prove that *she herself, and not individuals devoid of authority, has been enjoying the adverse holding of a territory which formerly belonged to Spain, and that this possession has not only lasted for fifty years, but also has been public, pacific, continued and uninterrupted, and in the capacity of owner.* Phillimore considers a lawful title indispensable in the case of sovereignty and as regards *good* faith. Lord Salisbury is of the same opinion, as he asserts it repeatedly; as, for instance, in his note of May 22, 1896, making proposals for the settling of the boundary question between Venezuela and Great Britain, he says that the Tribunal of Arbitrators appointed to decide the question "shall not have power to include as territory of Venezuela any territory which was *bona fide* occupied by subjects of Great Britain on the 1st of January, 1887, or as territory of Great Britain any territory *bona fide* occupied by Venezuelans on the same date."

Be it remarked once more that good faith consists in—1st, the belief of the alienor that he is the proprietor; 2d, that he may make transfer of the property; 3d, that the title of transfer be devoid of all imperfection or error.

We have already pointed out that all questions of international property embody the requisite of sovereignty.

Venezuela, in consequence, maintains to-day, after the Treaty of Arbitration of the 2d of February, 1897, what she had previously maintained, especially in the Memorandum of March 24, 1896, viz.: That in the Dutch or British occupations the circumstances capable of conferring title among nations have not existed; that Great Britain did most solemnly recognize the sovereignty of Spain over America as Holland did regardless of the rights claimed by the Catholic Kings.

These remarks are intended to show that the Arbitrators, as judges, must apply the principle which Venezuela formerly invoked and still invokes in opposition to the species of prescription to which Great Britain now appeals in order to retain territories of which she has taken undue possession, particularly since 1864.

Notwithstanding the changes in the situation, the arguments presented in the Memorandum of 1896, already referred to, are considered applicable and sufficiently forcible to destroy the effects of the doctrines of prescription. It is true that the Republic has, in good faith, accepted a fifty-years' prescription; but Venezuela has not understood, nor could she have undrstood, that the mere lapse of this period is sufficient of itself, unattended by the requisites universally accepted as indispensable, to give appearance of equity to a mode of acquisition which, notwithstanding all that may be said, presents in certain cases characteristics incompatible with the eternal laws of justice.

It is plain that the acts of usurpation performed on the Amacuro, Barima, Guarima, Morajuana, and other places—acts which have given rise to energetic and incessant protests on the part of Venezuela, and in 1887 the suspension of the diplomatic relations between the two countries, have no value whatever in themselves, though the condition produced by the use of force still continues and constitutes an unjustifiable infraction of the Agreement of 1850. Without entering into a minute examination of such acts, the sole reason that, up to the 2d of February, 1897, the time agreed upon, had not elapsed, excludes the possibility of the pretension to apply said provision to this case. From October, 1884, when the series of acts of trespass against Venezuela began to take place, up to the date of the Agreement, only twelve years and four months had elapsed, whereas fifty years is the full period named in the Treaty.

It has been suggested that the time began to run from the year 1841, when the German engineer, Robert Herman Schomburgk, was on the Amacuro, the Barima, and other points planting posts or fixing marks which appeared to be indicative of English sovereignty. It is well known, as has been already pointed out in this brief, that such posts and signals placed by Schomburgk were not an indication of what he pretended, but of what Lord Aberdeen informed Mr. Fortique in his communication of October 21 and December 11, 1841, and of January 31, 1842, when he stated that Mr. Schomburgk planted boundary posts at certain points of the country which he had surveyed, and that he was fully aware that the demarcation so made was merely a preliminary measure open to future discussion between the Government of Great Britain and Venezuela; that much unnecessary inconvenience would result from the removal of the posts fixed by Mr. Schomburgk, as they would afford the only tangible means by which Her Majesty's Government could be prepared to discuss the question of the boundaries with the Government of Venezuela; that those posts were erected for that express purpose, and not, as the Venezuelan Government appeared to apprehend, as indications of dominion and empire on the part of Great Britain; that he was glad to learn from Mr. Fortique's note of the 8th December, 1841, that the two Venezuelan gentlemen sent by their Government to British Guiana had had the means of ascertaining from the Governor of that Colony that the *British authorities* had not occupied Punta Barima; that in order to meet the wishes of the Government of Venezuela, who had represented the alarm and excitement created here on account of the marks fixed by Mr. Schomburgk at different points surveyed near the mouth of the Orinoco and insisting upon their removal, instructions would be sent and were sent to the Governor of British Guiana directing him to move the posts.

Mr. Daniel O'Leary, British Consul at Caracas, while informing the Minister, Mr. Aranda, that the above-mentioned instructions had been given and transmitted to him by the Governor of British Guiana, expressed, in the name of the Governor, the hope that the Government of Venezuela would consider all the grounds of remonstrance removed by the concession thus made by Her Majesty's Government. This took place on the 8th of April, 1842.

So, then, even the shadow of the occupation initiated by Schomburgk in 1841 was removed.

Moreover, Mr. Belford Hinton Wilson, Chargé d'Affaires of Great Britain in Caracas, in the name and by the order of his Government, declared to the Venezuelan Government, in a communication dated November 18, 1850, that the British Government had no intention to occupy or to encroach upon the territory in dispute between the two nations; that it would neither order nor sanction such occupations on the part of the British authorities; that if, at any time, there should be any error about the British Government in this respect they would willingly renew their orders on the subject; and that the right of possession of *Punta Barima* was in dispute between Great Britain and Venezuela.

In view of such positive promises and statements identical assurance was asked from Venezuela and were obtained.

The new occupation began on the 11th of October, 1884. Aside from this, that occupation has never been pacific; for ever since then Venezuela has shown herself untiring in asserting her rights by remonstrances, protests, removal of other signals, appointment of officials, notices to the inhabitants of the districts encroached upon, and by demands for the restitution of the territory thus forcibly taken from her. The occupation, therefore, has not been of the fifty-years' duration agreed upon.

If, in some cases acts have been consummated by the agents of the British Government, that Government doubtless being the author of them, the same can not be said of other invasions, the work of private individuals without any official authority to encroach upon a territory where they have gone on their own account and for their own benefit.

Lord Salisbury, in his note of 26th November, 1895, addressed to Sir Julian Pauncefote, says *that "in the thirty-five years which had elapsed since Lord Aberdeen's proposed concession natives and others had settled in the territory under the belief that they would enjoy the benefits of English rule, and that it was impossible to consent to any such concessions as Señor Rojas' line would involve."*

This seems to imply that the British Government, not only did not authorize the settlements referred to, but that Lord Salisbury himself was not aware that such was the fact, and would have remained in ignorance of it but for the report of the Governor and the Attorney-General of British Guiana, who, being in London, were consulted in reference to the proposition made by Doctor Rojas; and, what is more, the foregoing quotation asserts that the settlers are natives and others, that is, foreigners, who, under the belief that they would enjoy the benefits of a government of which they were not subjects, pretended, nevertheless, to enjoy the benefits of its protection, even if, by so doing, Venezuela should suffer loss of her territory.

But, as the natives did not act in representation of a nation, but simply as private individuals, the inference is obvious that they acquired no rights, either for themselves or for the nation, the possession not being public, so that it could come to the notice of Venezuela, much less was it a possession in good faith.

The labors of the Washington Commission, appointed towards the end of December, 1895, by the President of the United States of America, with the concurrence of Congress, " to investigate and report upon the true boundary line between Venezuela and Great Britain," have clearly shown that the " most westerly Dutch possession in Guiana in 1648 " was Fort of Kykoveral, near the confluence of the rivers of Cuyuni, Mazaruni, and Essequibo; that it is improbable that the idea of those who drafted and those who ratified the treaty of Munster was to grant to the Dutch the rights to acquire from the natives lands claimed by Spain ; and that it does not appear that either Spain or Holland ever so interpreted it. This is tantamount to denying that Articles 5 and 6 of said Treaty should give authority to make new acquisitions in Guayana which Spain claimed in its entirety as her own.

It also appears from the work of the same Commission that the Dutch Government unquestionably assumed the right to establish colonies, either directly or through the West India Company, on what was known as the " Wild Coast ; " but that in none of the grants there does it appear that this was assumed as an exclusive right of the Dutch or as an indication of pretension of dominion over that entire coast. The Dutch occupation of portions of the coast was not, therefore, adverse to the Spanish possession ; did not destroy nor substitute it ; nor could the Dutch or the British possession of Guayana have been continued uninterrupted, because, as regards the latter, since 1841, and, notably, since 1884, the protests of the Government of Venezuela have been repeated, and these protests have the same effect on international prescription as suits at law in civil prescription, as may be seen in the chapter of the brief submitted to the Boundary

Commission, wherein, under the heading, "What Venezuela has done in her defense," the point is fully discussed.

As regards the Dutch possessions, beside incessant protests, certain highly significant facts took place tending to the same ends.

Being once known, the principle deemed in international law applicable to prescription and rule "*a*" of the Treaty of February 2d, let us consider whether the pretensions of Great Britain, as put forth in the Blue Books Nos. 1 and 3, and the maps annexed thereto can be accepted.

The second map annexed to the first Blue Book shows three lines:

1st. A line that is called "extreme claim" of Her Majesty's Government, as stated in a letter to the Venezuelan Minister, of January 0, 1880.

2d. Provisional line within which no question of title can be admitted, and proclaimed by Gazette notice of October 21, 1886.

3d. Line of territory, respecting which it is thought fair to propose arbitration, April, 1886.

Professor Marcus Baker remarks, page 365, Vol. III, of the Washington Commission, that, according to the first line of Lord Salisbury, shown in the Blue Book No. 1, the disputed area is of 53,248 square miles, and, according to the map inserted on page 413 of the same book, the area is of 55,563, or 2,315 miles more.

The British Government having stated that they will not insist on the extreme line, the one presented as unquestionable will be mainly discussed.

On the coast, that line starts at the Amacuro river, thus embracing, outside of the Essequibo, the rivers Pomerón, Moroca, Guaima, Barima, and Amacuro.

Now, Mr. Michael McTurk, special magistrate *ad interim*, and superintendent of the lands and forests of the Colony in the district of the Pomarón river, in a communication bearing date of November 22, 1884, addressed to Mr. Thomas A. Kelly, president of the Manoa Company, notified him, for the first time, that the Barima river was in the county of Essequibo and Colony of British Guiana, forming part of the judicial district over which he presided. In the same year he began to visit the rivers Amacuro, Morajuana, Guaima, and other localities, and to post thereon notices that they belonged to the Colony. Leaving aside other arguments, the Arbitrators will see that these occupations, contrary to the Agreement of 1850, can not have any effect, as they took place at a date (October, 1884) not fifty years back, but only twelve years and three months prior to the 2d of February, 1897, when the Arbitration Treaty was signed.

But even in case the fifty years had elapsed, no prescription could be effected, as such was interrupted by proper means according to international law; that is, by protests on the part of Venezuela against such acts, and also those following on July 28, 1886, February 20, 1887, June 15 and October 29, 1888, December 16, 1889, May 2 and September 1 and 30, 1890, December 30, 1891, October 6, 1893, November 19, 1894, and January 3, 1896. These remarks apply also to the British occupation effected in a similar manner on the Cuyuni, a territory which the English Government itself declared was included in the Agreement of 1850, when, in June, 1887, it ordered that the Court of Policy of British Guiana should be notified that they could not recognize any claims for compensation on the part of the Colony nor of Her Majesty's Government, growing out of mining concessions granted in conformity with ordinances of 1880, 1886, and 1887, that should be found to be located within the territory in dispute with Venezuela, in the event that they should become a part of the Colony by virtue of settlement of the frontier line.

Such British possession was not only effected by force, but was forcibly maintained, and against which Venezuela has unceasingly protested (not to mention the suspension of diplomatic intercourse with Great Britain, on February 20, 1887, and the appeal madė by Venezuela to all the American Republics, particularly to the United States); it has not been attended by that pacific possession which even Phillimore himself, in common with all other authors, declares to be essential to prescription, and which all the laws of other nations adopting it deem necessary. And the same reasons apply also to the intention of claiming a possession continued and uninterrupted, as the energetic and frequent protests of Venezuela have interrupted the course of prescription, thereby depriving it of another of the requisites for its validity and effectiveness.

Nor could any reliance be placed on a possession which has lacked the requisite of publicity, as Lord Salisbury himself, in a note already referred to, addressed to Mr. Olney, November 26, 1895. He therein affirmed that it was not possible for Lord Aberdeen to accept the line proposed by Doctor Rojas, as the Minister of Venezuela in 1880, because of a report of the Lieutenant Governor and the Attorney-General of British Guiana, then in London, who, after being consulted, presented an elaborate report showing that in the thirty-five years elapsed since the concession proposed by Lord Aberdeen in 1884, natives and others had settled in the territory in the belief that they would enjoy the benefits of British rule. If such settlement did not come to the notice of the British Government except through the medium of the Colonial officers, why should not Venezuela be unaware of it? How could she have protested against such settlement unless aware of it? How could she assume that such settlement would be attempted in the face of the solemn and formal Agreement of 1850; an agreement which the British Chargé d'Affaires in Caracas, acting under instructions from his Government, recommended with great earnestness, and which was finally signed in deference to his zealous representations, namely, that Great Britain had no intention to encroach upon the disputed territory. Surely we are not justified in assuming that while this pledge was being given by Her Majesty's Government, the settlements to which the Governor and the Attorney-General for the British Colony referred were already under way, regardless of that pledge given by and in the name of Her Britannic Majesty.

It is to be particularly borne in mind that the British Government never charged Venezuela with infraction of that Agreement till it was done through Lord Rosebery in 1893, and that in January, 1887, after the acts qualified as infractions took place, Lord Salisbury made use of them to oppose the erection of a light house at Punta Barima without his consent. Are we to assume, then, that this Agreement of 1850 was still binding on Venezuela, but *not* on the other contracting party?

When the violation of a treaty is detrimental to one of the contracting parties, the injured party has a right to demand, by all possible means, compliance with the agreement; and should these fail to obtain redress from the violator, there is a way open, otherwise than war, namely, not to consider itself bound by the compact, giving, of course, due notice to the other party. But never to utter a word of complaint against the infraction, nor, at the same, demand from the other party the fulfillment of the obligation contracted by both, is, to say the least, to ignore the violation and let events take their course as though nothing had happened.

Prescriptive possession must be effected in the capacity of owner, particularly when, as in rule "*a*," it is called "adverse." The authorities are agreed that the only possession which can serve as a foundation for prescription is that wherein the possessor claims the property as though such were his right. Ortolan states that in this case the possession denies the right of some one else; places the lawful owner in a position to make a claim; it is in this case of prescription that if the lawful owner be silent and remains passive, it may be said that he has relinquished his proprietary rights, while the other enjoys them in his stead. But whoever does not occupy the thing, nor acts toward it except as a borrower, a tenant or a lessee, far from denying the rights of the proprietor, acknowledges them, and abides by them, acts in behalf and stead of the proprietor, and in accordance with their agreements. The principle justifying prescription can not find its explanation in this.

"For the identical reasons, in international law, possession must be that which announces the pretensions of a nation to sovereignty and dominion over the territory in question. It would not suffice, for instance, that some private *individuals* belonging to a nation should have performed in their own name acts of private ownership in that territory; possession must be effected *in the name of the nation*, through the acts of enjoyment, dominion and jurisdiction. This alone constitutes the exercise of international dominion and sovereignty.

"It rarely occurs between nations that a State should loan, rent, or lease a territory to another State; this, however, is not impossible. In other times, Governments have been known to take from other Governments more or less considerable sums as a loan, mortgaging some portions of their territory, and even delivering their possession to the lender as collateral."

The author quotes, in this connection, examples from the Venetians in the Middle Ages, and from Charles the Bold, Duke of Burgundy, in the seventeenth century. He also states that it more frequently happens, and even in our days, that a power occupies certain portions of the territory of another power by reason of an alliance, common defense, protection, assistance against perils, either domestic or foreign. He also affirms that such occupations as are effected by virtue of a security, common defense, protection or tolerance, can not be taken as grounds for acquisition of international domain, and that these acts would not begin to have such effect except from the moment that the occupant-nation changes the character of its possession, denying the rights of the other State, and pretending to possess thereafter with title of dominion and jurisdiction; as was the case of the Venetians in the question of Frioul, when, on account of failure to reimburse the amounts loaned by them, they pretended to have the right to take in payment of the debt the property of the mortgaged lands—thus changing the whole character of their possession, and acting thenceforth in the capacity of proprietor and sovereign.

It is understood that the *animus domini* exists only in whoever possesses property by virtue of transferred title, such as by sale, exchange, or donation. Some are of the opinion that it is also found in the usurper, who, although knowing that the title to the thing does not belong to him, but to another, and for this reason acts in bad faith—that in such case he may have the *animus domini*, since he calls himself a proprietor, and acts as such. This may be so in civil law, although it is not clear why one who has deprived another of his property, with the intention of appropriating it to himself, should be considered as the owner. This principle once admitted, there is no reason to condemn as thieves and robbers those who, notwithstanding, are considered by general consent of men and nations as guilty of enormous crimes, punishable not only by those in whose territory the crimes were committed, but by others.

Be it as it may, that doctrine does not seem admissible in international prescription which deals with ownership apart from sovereignty. We understand that to own in the capacity of proprietor is paramount to possessing with a just title and in good faith. We have already pointed out that both of these requisites are demanded by the legislation of nations for the ten to twenty years' prescription; and we fail to see why it should not apply to them, and why it should apply to the thirty years' prescription which prescinds these saving requisites. We have already seen that Rutherford, Felice, Vattel, Bello, Riquelane, Bentham, and Torres Campos all insist on the requisite of good faith, as well at the beginning as during the term of prescription.

That *bona fide* prescription is requisite, according to the English Government, is shown by their argument in favor of the "natives and others;" that is, foreigners, who have settled in the disputed territory "in the belief that they should enjoy the benefits of British rule."

We have already referred to the protests of Venezuela. We must also mention the acts of Spain to prevent the usurpations by the Dutch from becoming prescription by interrupting its course.

In the brief for Veneznela for 1896 (Docs. Wash. Com., Vol. IX), reference is made to the Spanish expedition which, in 1595, ejected the Dutch from the Pomarón; to the one which, in 1597, captured five Flemish men, who were trading with the Barima Indians; the one which, starting from Trinidad in 1613, went as far as the Corentin and burned the building erected on that territory by the Dutch, destroying also their tobacco plantations and carrying away with them knives, swords, axes, guns, and other articles found in that territory by the Spaniards; to the alliance between Spain and Portugal, in 1750, to expel the Dutch and French from the territory on the rivers Orinoco and Amazon, which unquestionably belonged to both Crowns, and where any settlement whatsoever ought to have been regarded as an act of usurpation; to the secret expedition sent on the 21st of July, 1758, against the Dutch post in the Cuyuni, which was burned and the persons found in the locality arrested; to the expedition ordered by Centurión, in 1768, against the Dutch who had gone to Barima; to the foray made later by the Spaniards in the Guaima and the Moroco; to the orders given, in 1779, by His Catholic

Majesty to hostilize the British subjects by reason of the usurpation of His Majesty's dominions in America by the court of London; to the war declared by the Spanish Crown against the English in 1779 because of the sending of English ships to the coasts of Peru and Chili to carry on contraband and to survey the coasts; to the sending of large expeditions and arms to the West Indies, and on account of the establishment of trading companies in North America, and on account of the conquest in South America of the Colony and river Demarara belonging to the Dutch, whose advantageous position placed England on the way to occupy other more important territories; to the attack on the Dutch post on the Moroco in 1797; to the capture and confiscation of vessels, the greater part of which were Dutch, English, and French, which vessels were carrying on contraband, and had sailed into the Orinoco; to the authorization given in 1780 to Commissioner Don José Felipe de Inciarte to build forts, settle districts, suppress the Dutch post on the Moroco, and take measures to compel them to retire to the Essequibo; and, finally, to the continued hostilities of the Spanish corsairs on the Essequibo during the new war declared by Spain against England in 1804.

It may be added that the Dutch documents, published in the British Blue Book No. 3, furnish further proofs of the uneasiness constantly felt in the Colony of the Essequibo for fear of the Spanish invasions—invasions in addition to those already mentioned; and so we see (page 74) that on the 7th of January, 1713, the Dutch "post-holder" of Wacupo gives an account of how the post was attacked on the 12th of December previous, by twenty-five of the enemy—French, Spanish, mulattoes and others—who, as he affirms, were routed three times and had a bark at the mouth of the river Pomarón—doing no other damage than burning some Indian huts and destroying or taking away some canoes. The Commandeur of the Essequibo writes that this was the second time that the post-holder gave splendid proof of his courage.

On page 80 it is found that Pieter la Rivière, at the end of August, 1727, went to the Orinoco to claim twenty-three "red slaves," which had run away, and that, upon arriving at the usual landing place he was attacked and killed by a vessel carrying the Spanish flag, and the crew of which took all the merchandise and said that they had orders from the Governor of Trinidad to stop trade on the river.

On page 81 we find that the Spaniards of the Orinoco, with armed force in the neighborhood of the river, had taken possession of a Surinam vessel fishing in those waters.

On page 88 we read that, in 1747, the Spaniards had made a journey in a southwestern direction and had discovered the source of the rivers Cuyuni and Mazaruni, with the intention of establishing themselves permanently near the sources of said rivers, to serve as a cordon, etc.

On page 93 it appears that Jan Dudonjon, having sent a canoe to Barima in charge of Adrian Christiansen, had the "misfortune" to have it captured on the return trip by the Spaniards, who took him to the castle of Guayana, on the Orinoco, June 8, 1790.

On page 99 we find that a large number of vessels, with five hundred men, arrived at Trinidad from Cumaná, their destination being the Upper Orinoco through the estuary running to the *southeast*, to take possession of some mines situated near the head of the Orinoco, which "might" have been on Dutch territory, August 8, 1754.

On page 105 we find that a missionary father had requested the post-holder to deliver and send to him some Indians of the Chiama nation that had been dwelling at the "post"—threatening the post-holder to come with force and take them away in chains in case of refusal.

On page 109 we find that the Spaniards made an attack upon Ignatius Courthial on his return trip from a trading expedition in the Orinoco, which was a profitable one, depriving him of all he had, March 6, 1758.

On page 115 we find that the Spaniards were beginning to "show their horns again," as, besides taking a fine boat belonging to Mr. Persik, and used only for trade, they had also taken five canoes of the Colony, which were engaged in salting, and also some other canoes on the other side of the Barima, and thus, within the territory of the Dutch Company, as claimed by the Director-General Gravesande, October 24, 1760.

We find, on page 117, that a party of Spaniards and Spanish Indians had been down the Cuyuni to the lowest fall, where the indigo plantation of the Company was situated, driving all the Indians thence and even killing some of them. The Director of Essequibo feared that a conflict would take place should the Spaniards go *below* the fall, because the inhabitants would fire upon them to prevent them from coming nearer, and the Director complained that he could not live in peace, when he directed all his efforts to prevent the Indians from doing harm to the Spaniards, August 28, 1761.

On page 120 we see that the Spanish Indians of the Missions continued to send out daily patrols as far as the great fall, below which the creoles of the Company lived, and that all the Caribs had likewise left the river (the Cuyuni) and had gone to live above, in Essequibo, May 17, 1762.

On the same page we read that the Spaniards had captured a salters' canoe, near the river Guiama [Waini], with eight and a half hogsheads of salt-water fish, August 25, 1762.

On page 21, that the post-holder of Moroco had reported having been warned three times that the Spaniards intended to make a raid on the place; that he was staying in the bush for fear of the Spaniards, and did not want to return to his "post."—*August 28–November 6, 1762.*

On the same page we find that the Spaniards were up the Cuyuni engaged in "building boats." The Director did not understand the meaning of this, and feared it might lead to the entire "ruin of the Colony" unless vigorous measures were taken. He again states that forbearance made them (the Spaniards) bolder and bolder, and mentioned the absence of the Caribs.—August 29, 1762.

On page 136, that the Spaniards were at Pomarón in some canoes filled with people, and that among the murdered Itabos some Indians were found.

On page 141, that the Spaniards had captured and carried off "Tampoko," a creole of the Company, together with an Indian slave belonging to the daughter of Gravesande, who had gone with the creole to buy birds and other things from the Indians of the upper Cuyuni, and even some of the Caribs asserted that the slave had been killed.

On page 144 we find that, according to a report from the post-holder in Cuyuni, the Indians had been bribed and incited to such a degree that they were unwilling to do the least thing for him (the Commandeur), and that when they were ordered to go alongside the passing boats to see whether there were any runaways on them they obstinately refused to do so, and that when they were threatened with being shot, they replied that they had bows and arrows with which to answer.

On page 156 it is stated that a Spanish privateer from Orinoco, cruising along the coast of the Dutch Colony, made an attempt to capture the Company's salter before the (mouth of the) river Guaima (Waini), which the Director-General "believed to be indisputably the Company's territory," and fired very strongly upon him, but he ran his boat high and dry upon the bank so that he could not be reached by the privateer, which still continued to fire upon him for some time, but seeing that he could do nothing finally departed. That some Caribs from Barima had gone to Director Gravesande and complained that some deserters, with a party of Spaniards, were continually molesting them in Barima and robbing them of everything.

On page 158, that the assistant post-holder of the Cuyuni, Gerrit van Leuwen, reported having heard from the fugitive Indians, February 9, 1769, that a detachment of Spaniards had come to just above the "post" and had captured and taken away a whole party of Indians, threatening to return the next dry season and proceed as far as the Mazaruni to capture a party of Caribs; that they would then sail down the Mazaruni and again up the Cuyuni and visit the "post" on their way.

On page 159 (February 21, 1796,) we find that the Caribs had reported that the Spaniards had established a mission not far from the "post" on the Cuyuni, and another on a creek a little higher up, both of which had been strongly manned; this makes Gravesande exclaim that "all is finished;" that neither post-holders nor posts were of any use; that the slaves may now proceed to the Missions without fear of being pursued; and that in a short time the possession of the Cuyuni would be entirely lost.

On page 161, of March 15, 1769, we read that an Indian named Adahouva, reported that the Spaniards, with two Capuchin fathers, a detachment of soldiers, and a large party of armed Weykiers, were capturing and taking away as prisoners all the free Indians between Barima and Pomarón, and that they had actually overpowered the Company's trading place, and that they were then, as confirmed subsequently by the report of the post-holder, giving an account of the invasion by two fathers, twelve soldiers, a party of Weykiers (Guaqueries), and small canoes and a vessel provided with eight swivel guns, and in the forecastle a four-pounder piece; that in the Guaima and Moroco they had captured a whole party of Indians, the others fleeing inland; they also carried off two female slaves, with their children, belonging to the post-holder, and when he told the fathers that such acts were not permissible on Dutch territory they answered that they had orders from their Governor.

On page 163 (April 4, 1769,) we read that two canoes were seen off Oene full of Spaniards; that the latter, unable to come off on account of the tide, pushed off into deep water again, and that another Spanish crew was on the plantation of Mr. Buisson, who, firing upon them, caused them to withdraw.

On page 175 (December 21, 1769,) we find that two privateers were again fitted out with a much stronger crew than the former one, and that with them the Spaniards, in about five or six weeks, would go to Moroco and Pomarón to carry off all the Indians whom they could get and would probably go as far as the mouth of the Essequibo.

On page 186 (September 3, 1774,) we see that the Spaniards, constantly annoying the Dutch, had recently gone down, forty strong, as far as the post of Moroco, carrying off or killing all the free Indians in those parts; by which acts the people, who were of such advantage to the Dutch Colony, were driven out of the land, fleeing in whole troops to the river Corentyn.

On page 190 (October 22, 1775,) we see that on the 11th of said month the Spanish Captain Mateo, with fifty men, was in Moroco and took away all the Indians and boats, although the post-holder who sent the report told them that the Indians were in his employ; that no longer was an Indian to be found in those parts; that the Spanish captain said they had come to look for the Indians who had killed the Spaniards from two large vessels laying at Biyarra; that he had been sent from those vessels; that his lord and master would shortly set a guard on the arm of the Guaima, called Barmani, and that the whole of Moroco belonged to the Spaniards.

Three events of the greatest importance and elsewhere mentioned, are not included. We now group them together, as they are pertinent to the case, viz.:

First. The ejection in 1758 of two Hollanders, a negro, and a female creole occupying the "post" of the Cuiba; the capture and burning of the hut where they staid; imprisonment of them all for carrying on an illicit commerce on an island in the river Cuyuni, which, with its dependencies, belonged to the domains of His Catholic Majesty. Not only did the Governor of Cumaná, Don Nicolas de Castro, refuse the demand made by Governor Gravesande for restitution of the prisoners, but the Spanish court declined for fifteen years to even consider the claims presented by the Dutch Court, who, in truth, showed little interest in the matter, since the question was not agitated during all that time, and was finally abandoned.

Second. The capture by the Spaniards, in 1760, of a schooner, two launches and two canoes of Essequibo, which were said to be, according to Don Juan de Dios Flores, in the mouth of the river Barima by order of the Commandeur of Esequibo. Holland never made a claim for or complaint against this.

Third. The expulsion, ordered in April, 1768, by Don Manuel Centurion, Governor of Guayana, of the Dutch families who had gone up the Barima river, close to the great mouth of the Orinoco and one of its affluents (within jurisdiction of the province of Guayana), and built thereon works and houses to engage in the clandestine exportation of timber and other products. Such expulsion was ordered in accordance with several laws and very recent decrees prohibiting foreigners to settle on the Spanish dominions under any pretext whatsoever, or to establish new colonies thereon.

The Dutch fled; their houses and plantations were burned; and the utensils and other property found on deserted places were carried to the city of San Thomé de Guayana to be confiscated for the benefit of the Royal Exchequer. If this act was included in the complaint made by the Dutch in 1769 it did not produce any results. Spain took no notice of it.

CHAPTER XVI.

ARTICLE III OF THE TREATY.

Article III of the Treaty of Arbitration reads as follows:

"The Tribunal shall investigate and ascertain the extent of the territories belonging to or that might lawfully be claimed by the United Netherlands or by the Kingdom of Spain respectively at the time of the acquisition by Great Britain of the Colony of British Guiana —and shall determine the boundary line between the Colony of British Guiana and the United States of Venezuela."

This is what Lord Salisbury had proposed to Mr. Olney, when, in 1896, he suggested the creation of a Commission to investigate and report the facts affecting the rights of the United Netherlands and Spain, respectively, at the date of the acquisition by Great Britain of British Guiana.

According to this, it is necessary to go back to the year 1814, when, by the Treaty of London, August 13, His Britannic Majesty engaged to restore to the Prince Sovereign of the United Netherlands the Colonies, factories, and establishments which were possessed by Holland at the commencement of the late war (on the 1st of January, 1803), in the seas and on the continent of America, Africa, and Asia, "with the exception of the Cape of Good Hope and the settlements of Demerara, Essequibo and Berbice, of which possession the High Contracting Parties reserve to themselves the right to dispose by a Supplementary Convention, hereafter to be negotiated, according to their mutual interests, and especially with reference to the provisions contained in the VIth and IXth Articles of the Treaty of Peace, signed between His Britannic Majesty and His Most Christian Majesty on the 30th of May, 1814."

According to the provisions of the Supplementary Convention, signed on the same day, and "in consideration of the above engagements (payment of certain sums), the Prince Sovereign of the Netherlands agrees to cede in full sovereignty to His Britannic Majesty the Cape of Good Hope and the settlements of Demerara, Essequibo and Berbice upon the condition, nevertheless, that the subjects of the said Sovereign Prince, being proprietors in the said colonies or settlements, shall be at liberty (under such regulations as may hereafter be agreed upon in a Supplementary Convention) to carry on trade between said settlements and the territories in Europe of the said Sovereign Prince."

Both articles were conceived in a general sense, defining only the ceded possessions by their simple names, and without fixing their extent with boundaries of any description. The demarcation was never effected, and some years later Spain ceded to Venezuela her territorial rights to what was called the *Capitania-General de Venezuela,* embracing Guayana within its radius.

It must be borne in mind that Great Britain, by an act of war, had occupied, in 1796, the Dutch settlements in that region, and that by the Treaty of Amiens, in 1802, she engaged to restore them, which she did. But peace being disturbed almost immediately thereafter, England again took possession of them in January, 1803, and when peace was made between the coalition and France, the sovereignty over the establishments of Demerara, Essequibo and Berbice (till then Dutch possessions) were definitely transferred to His Britannic Majesty. From 1803 to August, 1814, the British were mere military occupants of these colonies, not their owners; they could not, for this reason, act as lawful owners do.

Eugene Ortolan, in his work already quoted, states as follows in reference to this case:

"But leaving aside this usual exception, which at the end of a very short time and before any Treaty gave recognition to the right of property, to booty or maritime spoils, we must be certain of the fact acknowledged by the laws of nations ruling to-day in Europe, that war is a method of procedure where there is no definite sentence valid as in law in reference to property, except by virtue of a Treaty ending the war, and from the moment that this has been agreed to."

If this were otherwise, there would be the necessity of legitimizing the most iniquitous acts; one nation might fall upon another and deprive it of its territory. Should it be admitted that conquest could, in itself, give validity to the right of property between two nations, it would not be necessary any longer to establish and determine so carefully the cases in which a first occupation may be just, nor to demand that this should not take effect except in a territory without an owner.

"But if military occupation, if conquest would not suffice to transfer international domain, it must not follow from this that they have no effect prior to the definitive Treaty. If we consider that during war and until its termination the belligerent parties, each and severally, are exercising their rights, it follows that military occupation, the possession of the territory of the enemy by the victor, can not be treated as a forcible occupation; on the contrary, such occupation constitutes a valid possession; the victor may perform in the territory by him occupied the acts of a *bona fide* possessor; may collect taxes, exercise authority, jurisdiction. The foreign nations, if they wish to remain neutral, are under obligation to recognize such possessions, and the belligerent nation itself, upon recovery of the territory, could not derogate such acts that imply not only definitive property but also a passing possession."

"*The victor, however, can not validly perform any of the acts which indicate a right to international domain; can not sell the property, mortgage the country, alienate the territory to a foreign nation, dispose of it in any manner whatever. The power of the victor is transient as the probabilities of the success to which it is due, and this power expires at the same time of the possession and nothing of it remains thereafter.*"

If the military occupant of a territory is not its owner; if he can not perform acts of proprietorship, such as sale or mortgage, nor dispose of the territory in any other way; if his power be ephemeral and ends with possession, leaving no trace behind it; if the owner of the territory of which he is transitorily dispossessed may recover it either by a military victory or by a treaty of peace; if, in the meanwhile, the status of affairs is merely provisional, it seems clear that the military occupant can not act as the indisputable owner of the retained territory, nor perform acts as such.

Not being able to contract obligations affecting the territory, nor to change the state of the property belonging to some one else, the military occupant can not increase it by new acquisitions. His duty is to maintain the state of affairs prevailing in the territory before its acquisition, and nothing contrary that the military occupant may do can have any legal value.

The Blue Book No. 1 says, on page 19, that in 1796 the English again took the Dutch colonies and "marked the boundaries." Such an act is not even within the province of the lawful owner, because in cases of separation of one's property from his neighbor's, the concurrence of all the adjacent owners is necessary to effect the demarcation. Although this is an obvious fact, we do not think it amiss to state that our code of civil procedure, for instance, directs that in cases of demarcation of boundaries before a court of justice the petition must be presented before the justice under whose jurisdiction the territory lies, accompanied with the deed wherein the extent and limits of the property are described, and the justice shall summon all the *adjacent owners* and appoint the day of proceedings. If all are in accord, the demarcation of the limits is performed without any difficulty; but in case there should be any opposition, a suit will follow, and judgment will be passed in conformity with the proofs shown during the trial. This being the case between private individuals, the more reason there is to act in a similar manner between nations; unless, indeed, there is a pretension to let the one pass the law upon the other, detrimental to the independence of the excluded nation.

The same Blue Book asserts, on page 25, that after 1796 Great Britain "extended her settlements and continually exercised over the territory originally held by the Dutch all those rights by which nations indicate their claims to territorial possession."

Great Britain had no right to "extend" her settlements in Guayana, neither from 1796 to 1814, when she effected its military occupation, with the exception of a short period, nor after its definite acquisition by the Treaty of London in the latter year; nor in the first period, because she was not then an owner *deforciant pro tempore;* nor in the second case, because the Treaty of Munster (1648) prohibited to Holland new acquisitions in Guayana, and this prohibition affects Great Britain. She acknowledges it, and because of this Lord Salisbury wrote to Doctor Pulido (Blue Book No. 1, page 422) that "That territory and by far the largest portion of the great tract of land that the Venezuelan Government seeks to put in question accrued to the Netherlands under the Treaty of Munster, in 1648, by right of *previous* occupation."

Whatever acts may have been performed by the English, and whatever other questions may have arisen (including those consummated from 1884 to this day), Article III of the Treaty under discussion does not authorize the Arbitrators to grant them other rights than those which belonged to Holland at the time of the cession in 1814.

It is true that mention is made in it of the rights tha might "lawfully be claimed" by Holland or by Spain; but we have already shown that Holland had no righ whatever to claim jurisdiction over the disputed territory.

We have already called attention to the fact that the Netherlands never did claim any determinate boundaries, and that the only occasion on which they referred to this matter was in their complaint of August 7, 1769, in reference to the proceedings of the Spaniards of the Orinoco against the Colony of the Essequibo. On this occasion they asserted that "from time immemorial they had been in possession, not only of the Essequibo and of the several rivers and creeks that flow into the sea along the coast, but also of all the branches and streams which fall into the same river Essequibo, and more particularly of the most northerly arm of the same river, called river Cajoeny, which is considered as a domain of the State;" that its territory is extended "from the river Marowyne to beyond the river Weyne, very near the mouth of the Orinoco."

The pretended boundaries of the Dutch were not stated with precision, neither as regards the interior nor the coast. But it is clear that, upon treating of the subject, they had no reason for not stating the totality of their claims or for reserving a part of them. There are certain rules of sound interpretation, as stated by Vattel, which we think are applicable here.

One of these rules is that whoever ought to have and could have explained himself clearly and fully but failed to do so, is to blame. It can not be admitted that he subsequently put restrictions on what he did not then express. This is the maxim of Roman law: "*Pactionem obscuram iis nocere in quorum feirt potestate legem apertius conscribue.*" The equity of this rule is plain; nor is its necessity less evident. No agreement would be secure, no concession stable and firm if they could be invalidated by subsequent limitations, which ought to have been stated at the time if they were in the mind of the contracting parties.

The other rule is: "*Whenever some one has been able to make a statement of his intentions, and should have done so, whatever he may have sufficiently declared will be taken against him.*" This is an unquestionable principle which we apply to the treaties, because if they be not mere play, the contracting parties must state in them the truth and follow their intentions. If the intention, sufficiently declared, of the one who acts and places himself under obligations were not accepted in law as the true intention, it would then be useless to make contracts or to conclude treaties.

Therefore, Holland, in the event of having considered herself to have rights to a larger portion of territory than the one mentioned in the aforesaid remonstrance, ought to have stated it plainly, and not have left it for another occasion to give new increase to her claims. In cases of a civil suit, the plaintiff is at liberty to notify his claims, but this only before, never after, the defense has been presented. It is necessary to state in the complaint, besides certain other circumstances, the object of the suit with great precision and the reasons and foundations upon which the charges are based. The same must be done in international questions; and as, in this case, the nations are both judges and clients, the moment one of them has presented her claims before another she must not change or expand it, as this would show either doubt or uncertainty on points that should have been previously considered.

The Arbitrators, therefore, must decide the question of boundary between the Republic of Venezuela and British Guiana according to the state of affairs in 1814, date of the transfer made of the Dutch settlements of Essequibo, Demarara, and Berbice. They can not, consequently, take into consideration either what the English may have done from 1796 to 1802, nor from 1803 to 1814, nor their later acts, as the question has been reduced to an investigation of the rights of the English and the Spaniards in 1814. The increases effected since that time by the English are out of the question, as well as the continued jurisdiction that England claims to have exercised on the territory originally claimed by Holland, to which mention is repeatedly made in the Blue Book No. 1. This must refer to the discoveries so energetically conducted by the committee of the Royal Geographical Society from 1834 to 1839, because at that time the headwaters and tributaries of the Essequibo were entirely unknown; also, to Schomburgk's ascension of the Essequibo far beyond the farthest point ever reached before; to his exploration of the course of the Rupuruni, the Berbice, and the Corentyn to their headwaters in 1836, and the exploration up to the headwaters of the Essequibo in 1837–1838, and also those of the Guaima and Barima. The same must be said of the discoveries of the falls of Koloteur, on the Potaro, made by C. B. Brown; the visit made to the Roraima Mountains by Flint, Wittley, Thurns, etc.

It is also necessary to exclude all the advances made by Great Britain beyond the limits belonging to the Dutch in 1814, when their cultivated area did not go beyond the Pomarón, as shown by map No. 14 of the Boundary Commission of Washington. The same fact is shown by the various documents transmitted by the Venezuelan Government to the said Commission, and which are printed by them and herewith submitted. These documents also show that the acts of jurisdiction exercised by Great Britain prior to 1884 did not go beyond the Pomarón.

In regard to the events which have taken place between that time and the present, we have shown again and again that they have no value whatsoever, as they were performed in flagrant violation of the Agreement of 1850, in the face of repeated protests by the Venezuelan Government, and by an abuse of force—circumstances insufficient to produce legal effects. Such occupation, besides, has not lasted the fifty years required by Article IV of the Treaty of February 2, 1897, under which we are proceeding.

Reference is made in the Blue Book No. 3 to the establishment of Dutch "posts" which had jurisdiction in various parts of the Colony, their duty being to give notice of any interference with Dutch jurisdiction, to control the relations with the native tribes, bringing them into alliance; to promote trade, taking care that this should be in the hands of those entitled to it; to examine passports and other documents permitting persons to travel in various parts of the Colony; and that since 1683 Barima was made a substation under the post-holder at Pamarón, "to whose jurisdiction it appears to have already belonged."

The letter from the Commandeur of Essequibo to the West India Company, shown in support of this assertion, states only that the writer had sent one of the Company's servants to sojourn in Barima, as much annatto and letterwood is found in that place, which shows that Barima is near Pomarón. Approval of this step was asked for, and that the Commandeur wished to see the Company "take possession" of those rivers, as he had done provisionally and subject to the Company's approval, which was never given; and that, in the opinion of the Commandeur, the Company had as good a right to trade there in "open river" as private persons. And that is all.

March 31, 1684, the Commandeur, in another letter, wrote that in order to check the trade carried on by Gabriel Biscop and other interlopers from Surinam, who used to buy much annatto, letterwood, madder oil, and hammocks from Barima, he had caused a "small shelter" (*not* "station") to be built somewhere on the Barima, and that Abraham Caudart, post-holder at Pomarón, should occasionally "visit" those places and encourage the Caribs to trade in annatto and letterwood, which even the French from the islands frequently came with their vessels to fetch away. The letter ends as follows: "I submit, therefore, under correction, *that it would not be a bad idea for the honorable the West India Company to take in possession the river Barima, in order to acquire the trade aforesaid, and erect there a strong little place for a post-holder."*

It is evident, then, that the Company had *not* taken "possession" of the Barima; that the Commandeur of the Essequibo asked the Company to do it, moved by the desire for gain, as he had done provisionally; that he asked the approval of his conduct; that he would submit himself to the superior determination, and urged the construction of a small lodge for a post-holder. The strange part of this is, that under such circumstances he should have undertaken to prohibit trade in Barima; but his prohibition was a mere *brutum fulmen,* meant nothing, and never amounted to anything.

The Company never approved Mr. Beekman's action, and the consequence was the withdrawal of the employé who had been sent without any authority whatever.

In 1744 Gravesande urged the establishment of a post in Barima, and his representations were heeded by the Company, which sent the necessary authority which, however, was never carried into effect. The Spaniards again appear performing acts of jurisdiction in Barima, notably in 1769, when the Governor of Guayana ordered the Dutch who had gone in there to be ejected, their effects to be seized, and their lodges burned. Their effects were confiscated as belonging to persons who, by their trade and their settlement, were committing a violation of the territory of Spain.

What, then, was the value of the Barima "post" which never even existed nor, if it had, could be placed under the jurisdiction of Pomarón?

It is asserted that up to 1703 four post-holders had been established, one of them going to the post of Pomarón and another to Cuyuni and the savanna of Pariagotos, stationed at six weeks' journey from Kykoveral.

This information, however, needs to be completed. In the first place, where the far-distant "post" of Cuyuni was situated no one was able to ascertain. In the second place (this is the more important fact), it did not last long, scarcely four months and seven days, as it does not appear again, either in the list of servants nor on the pay-rolls.

The second Dutch "post," established shortly prior to 1758, was the one then destroyed by the Spaniards, situated in Cuiva, near the Curumo. It is pertinent to remark that there were only two Dutchmen in said post—a negro and a female creole, with her children. They could not offer resistance to the detachment of 100 Spaniards, nor did Gravesande, whose garrison was no more than sixteen men strong, think of doing so. The representation addressed to the Government of Spain, asking for reparation for past wrongs and for orders to be given concerning the future, was never attended to. The post was not re-established for fear of new attacks. It is asserted that it was re-established between 1765 and 1767, in Tokoro, and that in that year, the Director-General asked for a reinforcement to be able to defend it against possible attacks by the Spaniards. But the post-holder, of his own accord, transferred the post a short time after to the Island of Tonaremo, through fear of the Spaniards, etc., and in 1772, when his term expired, he was not replaced by any one. It can not be said, therefore, that it had the character of being permanent.

We are told that about the year 1756 the post of Wacquepo (Wacupo), which had superseded that of Pomarón, was moved forward to Moroco, at which place it became of special importance in connection with the trade relations with the Spaniards, who were well aware of their establishment and object, according to various reports.

It is true that the authorities of Guayana were not ignorant of the removal of the post from Wacupo to the right bank of the Moroco, but they only "tolerated" it, as they themselves said, without taking it into account. They did not believe that they had lost their jurisdiction, for which reason they ordered an investigation to be made to find out whether a "fort" had been established near there, and on several occasions attacked the place and carried away the runaway Indians, or those whom they needed to build towns, and because of this they came and went at pleasure on the territory.

In reference to the Dutch post at Armida, said to be the result of the important explorations effected in 1714 in search of conquest and gain for the Company, and of the repetition of the attempt in 1725, it seems proper to remark that Spain considered the Essequibo the limit between her possessions and those of Holland, and consequently did not object to the establishment of "posts" on Dutch territory. If, in 1764, the post was moved higher up, above the mouth of the river Rupuruni, this may probably be ascribed to the fact that the Spaniards had erected, near that spot, the formidable station of Siparuni, mentioned by Gravesande in his letter of the 17th. We may well recall here what we have stated before in reference to the commerce of the Spaniards on the upper Essequibo.

There is another argument which needs a decisive refutation, namely, that, "in 1744 a suggestion was made by the Commandeur of the Colony of Essequibo to the West India Company as to stationing a post-holder at Barima, *but this was not acted upon, and Barima remained under the post-holder of Moroco.*" In proof thereof the document printed on pages 86 and 131 of the Blue Book No. 3 are presented. The first of these documents is a letter from Gravesande to the Company relative to the permit solicited by Courthial to cut a road through the woods on the river Cuyuni. The last paragraph reads as follows: "I have not yet established my post at Barima, because I have not yet been able to find any competent person to my liking to whom to intrust the same, for I think that a post there might become of great importance." The indication was made beforehand, the permission obtained, and the Commandeur reports not haveing carried it into effect by March 17, 1746, nor did he ever accomplish it.

The second document quoted is another letter from Gravesande to the Company, dated August, 1761, with two enclosures. In the first, which is a brief description of the Company's trading posts (page 131), there is no other reference to Barima than this: "There now remains only the post situated on the seacoast between Essequibo and Orinoque, in the creeks Wacquipo (Wacupo) and Moroco, not far below the river Powaron, which creeks have an inland water communication with Powaron, as also with the river Wayna, *which has one with the river Barima,* which are all navigable in the rainy season, and thus of very great use in furthering commerce, both with the Indians and with the Spaniards, as all who do not sail in very large ships have to pass the post on their journeys from Orinoque. The trade of that post formerly consisted, mostly, in boats and orange dye, of which last it used to yield a very large quantity, though now it sends none."

There is nothing in that reference to the trading posts to warrant the assertion that "Barima remained under the post-holder at Moroco." Perhaps this conclusion has been arrived at by deduction. At certain seasons of flood the Moroco communicates by water with the Pomarón; the Moroco always communicates with the Guaima, and the Guaima with the Barima. But this mode of arguing is novel, to say the least of it. What ought to be proved is that the Company placed Barima under the jurisdiction of the post at Moroco, and this can not be done. Nor could what the Commandeur of Essequibo wrote in 1864 be shown as proof, as he limited himself to stating that, in order to check the trade in annatto and letter wood carried on in the Pomarón and Barima by private parties and other interlopers from Surinam, he would occasionally "visit" those places and encourage the Caribs to trade in said products. He also suggested to the Company that, in order to exclusively acquire said trade, they should " take possession " of the river Barima, which, as has been seen, did not belong to them. The Company did not authorize either the taking " possession," as suggested, or the " visits " to Barima by the post-holder at Pomarón (or at Moroco), and was never given authority to do so.

As regards the physical nature of the country it has been shown that the configuration of the mountains in Guayana; the basins of the rivers; the falls of the larger portion of them; the difficulty to sail up stream; the easy access to all these places by entering through the Orinoco, and the opinion of many who have been on the spot, all demonstrate the advantage of keeping the region of the coast separate from the interior, as it has always been.

The possession of the mouth of the Orinoco is of vital importance to the security of Venezuela. If, for example, the river Barima or the Amacuro should remain in the possession of Great Britain (as from any of these rivers the great artery of the Republic would be under their control), Venezuela would neither be protected against sudden attack, nor would she even have clear traffic on the Orinoco, either going in or out. Schomburgk advised taking possession both of the Barima and the Amacuro, precisely to enjoy the benefits and advantages of the " control " that, by these means, England would be able to exercise over Venezuela, both commercially and militarily. Lord Aberdeen, in 1844, Lord Granville, in 1881, and Lord Rosebery, in 1886, of their own free will acknowledged the importance of Venezuela's possession of the Orinoco to the exclusion of strangers. The large number of rivers that fall into the Orinoco in its great extension, and the trade and the traffic of the countries along its course, will make it, in course of time, the main and general waterway of Venezuela. This is not a matter of interest for Venezuela alone. All the South American States whose waterways connect one with another are also interested in the matter.

Nothing of this could be applicable to British Guiana, which belongs to a great European power that has nothing to fear from her neighbor.

Holland had no control over the indigenous races of Guayana. History shows that Holland not only did not control them, but that she was in fear of them and took advantage of the wild nature of the Caribs to improve her principal aim, encouraging them to make slaves of the more pacific Indians by dint of promises of gain, and to pursue the African fugitive slaves; to capture or kill them, and to present one of the hands of those killed in proof of their death, and as a title by which to receive the promised reward. They also made use of the Caribs to defend themselves against the rebellious slaves in arms; to destroy the Spanish Missions and the Fathers who founded them. Whenever menaced by a danger they called on the Indians to defend them, being more the proteges of the Indians than their protectors. They endeavored to win them over by means of promises and presents when they often, impelled by their ambition, took sides with the enemies of the Dutch, as it happened in 1684, when the Caribs from Barima killed Captain Gabriel Biscop and fifteen of his companions, destroying and foundering their vessel. They also contributed to the capture of the Dutch Colonies in 1676, uniting with the Frenchmen.

The Indians went from one place to another regardless of the Dutch authorities, as, when they were ejected from the Cuyuni in 1758, they, fearing the Spaniards, went to the Mazaruni.

At times the Spaniards entered the Dutch post, for instance, the one at Moroco, and carried away with them the Indians they were in search of, this conduct never having caused the Dutch to protest against it.

The Indians either made alliances or went to war between themselves, and there is nothing to show that the Dutch ever intervened, either to prevent or put an end to their fratricidal wars. If they asked the Indians to render them any service and the Indians refused, the Dutch had no means to compel them. It could not be otherwise when the force in the Dutch posts was insignificant in the extreme, while the Indian tribes were numerous and some of them strong, possessing European arms and being proficient in the use of them.

As regards the exploration of a country, this is not considered as capable of giving title of property to a territory. The mere fact of visiting a country and penetrating to its unkown regions, of making observations, of reporting on the travels, publishing the results of the studies made, does not necessarily imply that the explorers have any rights of jurisdiction over the territories visited. In proof of this we may recall the fact that similar acts are frequently performed in foreign regions with or without the previous consent of the Government to which these regions belong.

In regard to the construction of roads, we find on page 86 of the Blue Book No. 3 the following letter from the Commandeur of Essequibo to the West India Company, under date of March 19, 1746:

"On the 7th of this month one Ignatius Courthial made an application to the Court for permission to cut a road through the wood in the river Cajoeny [Cuayuni] in order to bring mules and cows into the river by that road. It being possible that this may be of great profit and advantage, the permission was granted him on condition that there shall be paid to the Company three guilders, recognition money, for every mule and two guilders for every horse or cow, and in order to prevent any fraud in this matter it is my intention to place the post which lies in Demarary (and now unnecessary there on account of the opening of the river) on this road instead, which post, in addition to the trade which it will be able to carry on for the Honorable Company, will be amply provided for out of the recognition money."

There is no evidence that the intentions of the Commandeur of Essequibo to move the post at Demerara to the said road was ever carried out, nor as to the site whereon the proposed post was to be placed. The " road " must have been a very short one, as, in another letter, dated on the 2d of December, 1748, the same Commandeur ports to the Company that Ignatius Courthial, who had constructed the road up the Cuyuni, and had now gone up the Orinoco for some hundred head of cattle and mules to import for trade, " before his departure showed me a letter which he had written to be sent by this ship to your Honors, wherein are some proposals which are somewhat strange and which proceed from his Gascon ideas."

With this letter was sent an enclosure from the aforesaid Courthial, in which he writes as follows:

> " It is notorious to all this Colony that I was the first who, in 1736, ascended this river, and, having wandered several months from river to river, I discovered the mouths of these different rivers and taught them to the Spaniards, who, till then, were ignorant of them, and from that time the Island of Martinique and even the Colony began to derive some advantage from my discoveries. * * *
>
> This enterprise will scarcely appear to you less bold than that which I have executed, viz.: To open and make at my cost and expense (a work for a Colony) a road across the forests, until then unexplored, of 130 or 140 leagues, to the old fort, and thence to Berbice, by means whereof one can, at a very moderate expense, perfect it, so as to be able to go on horseback, and with consignments from Fort Nassau of Berbice up to Peru."

The Director-General of Essequibo does not make any further reference to Courthial until 1754, when he says that he had not seen him; that one of his men had returned with a lot of tobacco; that he feared Courthial might have changed his mind, due to the long duration of the negotiations, and that upon his arrival he would try to encourage him. The last mention made of him is on March 6th, 1758, when it is reported that, after a very successful voyage, the Spaniards watched for him as he came down the Orinoco and deprived him of all he had, but that he and his crew, with the exception of two, who were made prisoners, managed to escape overland.

According to Courthial, in 1736, neither the mouths of the rivers nor the woods had been explored, nor had roads been constructed, except by himself and at his own expense.

The important points to know are the places through which the road passed and the absence of opposition on the part of the Spaniards, and this is precisely what is lacking in the reports of Gravesande to his superiors.

The expulsion of the Dutch from the post in Cuyuni had already taken place, and it is evident that no thought could have been given then to the construction of roads towards said river, closed as it was to the Colonists, who did not offer any resistance, nor, indeed, could they.

The colonization of a territory is different from its prescription, though the former may have lasted fifty years. States have established colonies in places *nullius*, which they have taken with the intention of appropriating. In this case there is title by occupation, and it is acquired from the moment that this takes place.

In the case of prescription the *nullius* property is acquired by a transferable title of domain, sufficient in itself to produce its effects; it happens, sometimes, however, that the alienor is not the rightful owner. Then the law intervenes and establishes conditions, the fulfillment of which makes the act good. Although both titles are valid, there is no analogy between them; they occupy different places in legislation and are governed by different principles.

In the case of prescription the title of the former owner is recognized, but the aim is to exclude it by imputing to him the abandonment of his rights during all the time prescribed by law to effect its recovery, and upon the expiration of such time the means of recovery are denied to him.

There is nothing similar to this in the case of occupation, which can not apply but to things which belong to no one, either because man has never made them his own or because the former occupant, and as such its owner, did abandon them with the deliberate intention of not holding them any longer as his own.

In the case of prescription, the property is obtained after the legal time has expired; in the case of occupation, property is obtained from the moment that occupation is effected.

Prescription, at times, offends the sacredness of justice, and for this reason it is not generally accepted. Occupation does not present any difficulties against conscience, and therefore no one has ever condemned it, it being considered by some as the legitimate origin of property.

Both are similar in this, international occupation of territory is denied to private individuals, as sovereignty is therein involved. This should also apply to international prescription, since it gives the right of property from one State to another, this being the right of nations.

We know that nations are colonizers. They commence by the occupation of the territory where they will take inhabitants, animals, tools, implements, and seeds, officers to represent the authority, priests for their religious instruction, and there establish rules for the maintenance of peace. The lands are apportioned among the colonists; habitations, churches, and public offices are built; revenues and tribunals are created; the necessary public force is raised; modes of defense are prepared; and by means of proper legislation a regimé is established for the benefit of the Colony.

All this has been done since remotest times by nations, and was done by Spain in the New World upon its discovery, and is still done on the African Continent and other places.

In order to prevent conflicts arising from occupation by colonizing powers in the same territory, and with other objects also, a conference was held in Berlin in 1885 which sets forth several rules governing these cases. We find in Chapter VI a "*declaration relative to the essential conditions required in order to consider as effective the new occupations on the coast of the African Continent, to wit:*"

"Any power that hereafter shall take possession of a territory on the coast of the African Continent, lying without its actual possessions or not having them at that time, should thereafter acquire them; and likewise any power that should assume a protectorate shall accompany the respective act with a notification addressed to the other powers subscribing this present act, so that these may be enabled to present their claims should there be any.

"The powers subscribing to the present act recognize their obligations to insure in the territories occupied by them on the coasts of the African Continent the existence of an authority sufficient to make the acquired rights respected, and, in case of necessity, the freedom of trade and transit under the agreed conditions."

It is well understood that these rules apply to the future only, to the powers which adopted them, and to the African Continent.

We must not forget that on the American Continent there were no territories open to colonization after the Declaration of 1823, and to which England and all Europe assented.

Calvo, having quoted the case of Yucatan, in 1848, when the armed intervention of the United States was solicited, says that the President of the United States, in support of that Declaration, and fearing that Yucatan should fall into the hands of a European State, "*which*" the President said, "*would never be tolerated by the Government of the Union,*" obtained from Congress a resolution ordering the formation, without delay, of an expeditionary army, and the authority to take temporary possession of Yucatan, in order to drive out the Indians. This was never accomplished, because of the treaty of peace signed between Yucatan and the insurgent Indians; but the debates had the great advantage of elucidating the purport of the Declaration of 1823, and of showing more clearly the fundamental thought of those who, like Adams, endeavored to put it in practice. "And thus it is established"—

"1st. That the colonial system of Europe is not applicable to the new situation of America, because all the nations forming the American Continent are civilized nations, having precisely the same rights as the European nations to have their independence and sovereignty respected.

"2d. *That the questions of boundary arising between the old European settlements and the new American States can not be solved only in accordance with the general principles of international law.*

"3d. That the fact of first occupation or first exploration does not create at the present time any rights of sovereignty over American territories, the rightful possession of which can not be acquired in the future, except by either treaties or war. This taken into consideration we may state that American public law is the same as in Europe and is based on the same principles."

How the Monroe Doctrine is understood in the United States may be seen in the correspondence arising from the question of boundary between Venezuela and Great Britain, notably in Mr. Olney's despatch, under date of July 20, 1895.

That Lord Salisbury accepted, in the name of his nation, the Monroe Doctrine, is shown in the bases stipulated to settle the controversy and embodied in the four substantial articles of the Treaty of February 2, 1897—bases agreed upon by the United States and Great Britain on November, 1896.

Doctor Manuel María Madiedo, a Colombian, in his Treatise on the International, Diplomatic, and Consular Laws of Nations, declares himself to be in favor of the *Utis possidetis juris* adopted by the American States, which were European colonies until 1810, on the territories occupied by them by virtue of the doctrine on occupation followed by their former metropolis. In order to give this more force, Doctor Madiedo says:

"140. The principle of actual material occupation as a title to sovereignty over a territory is a common and incontestable title in the case of peoples who do not yet enjoy the rights of citizenship properly, according to international law. These peoples are not ruled by the law as *between nations*, but by the law *of* nations which is the foundation and spirit of the originary superficiary community of human kind, in which the *whole* belongs to *all* for the satisfaction of the necessities of everyone. But in international law every nation has the right to the demarcation of the territory with which she has entered into the great family of the sovereign and independent powers of the globe, as being the frontiers which she assumes as her own, and that no one disputes with better titles.

* * * * * *

"142. As already seen the doctrine of *Jus Gentium* is very different from international law on this point, as we have already remarked in the exposition of our preliminary chapter.

"143. It is impossible to imagine a nation without ascribing determinate limits to the same. What limits this extension of territory? The consent of the other States of the world, inasmuch as by this demarcation they are not deprived of their own territory, which can not but be based on the same principle.

"144. It is undoubted that the lakes and rivers found

in the interior of the territory of a nation belong to her, as also the straits of a lesser width than those marking her domain in the waters adjacent to her coasts, and equally so the navigation to the sea of the boundary rivers which irrigate her territory. There is not nor could there be any doubt in regard to this; were it otherwise, the international spirit of which we have treated in our second chapter, would simply be a mere hypothesis of a very precarious nature, and the whole structure of international law would be overthrown."

The Kings of Spain, by royal decrees issued in 1519, 1520, 1523, 1547, 1563, and 1575, declared themselves to be the owners, not only of the territory of Guayana but of all the islands of the West Indies, which, by "donation of the Holy Apostolic See and other just and legitimate titles, they were the lords of the aforesaid as well as of the islands and *terra firma* of the ocean discovered or that should be discovered, and which were incorporated into the royal crown of Castile."

This was long before the Dutch settled themselves on any part of the coast of Guayana, which, in reality, did not occur until after 1621. It must be particularly remarked that the Dutch had pretended to said rights under the allegations that they had come to America when they were subjects of the King of Spain, first discoverer and founder of the New World, and that the Spaniards ceded these rights to them by virtue of the Peace of Munster, in 1648.

It was not licit for the Dutch or for any others to come to America and effect occupation on her soil, and Spain constantly opposed them. It is true that by virtue of the aforesaid Treaty the occupations effected in Guayana, having the character of conquests by war, were legalized; but we have seen that the cession was limited to the occupations until then effected, which did not go beyond the mouth of the Essequibo, and did not authorize any new conquests except on the territory of Brazil.

From the foregoing remarks we arrive at the conclusion that outside of the possessions acquired prior to 1648, the Dutch did not validly effect colonization, and that therefore there can not exist any settled district in Guayana falling under the provision of the last part of Rule "*a*."

We have noted the differences between the settlements commencing by occupation on territory *nullius*, and prescription of these territories, in which there is a substitution effected of a negligent owner by another who takes advantage of his negligence.

CHAPTER XVII.

ARTICLE IV OF THE TREATY—RULE "*a*."

Rule "*a*" is as follows:

"Adverse holding or prescription during a period of fifty years shall make a good title. The Arbitrators may deem exclusive political control of a district as well as actual settlement thereof sufficient to constitute adverse holding or to make title by prescription."

This rule has two parts, differing the one from the other. The first is imperative; the second optional. If it is found that either of the two contracting parties has held, adversely, territory during a period of fifty years—the other requisites to prescription being fulfilled—the tribunal must consider such territory as being the property of the possessor who has enjoyed it for the requisite period. If what this possessor has effected is, to have exclusively and politically controlled a territory, or to have had settlements thereon, then it is left to the Arbitrators to decide whether this is or is not equivalent to prescription. We see by this that the limit of prescription has been extended, not in all cases, however, but in those cases only which, in the judgment of the Arbitrators, are susceptible of such assimilation as seems to have been newly introduced. Of course it is to be understood that this exclusive political control or settlement must have lasted fifty years. The second clause of the rule is not an isolated proposition complete in itself; it is connected with the preceding clause, the only object being to elucidate its meaning by making it more explicit.

According to the Civil Code of France and the commentaries thereon, "possession is the holding or the enjoyment of a thing or of a right that we have or that we exercise by ourselves or through another who exercises it in our stead." Prescription is neither true nor proper except when it implies jurisdiction, control over the thing, the holding of it in the capacity of owner. This is why those do not prescribe who hold or possess in the name of others, such as the depositary, the lessee, the usufructuary, or others who precariously retain the thing of the owner.

It is said that prescription can not take place if the one in whose name the property was possessed, precariously, or any other person pretending to be the owner thereof, effects a sale to the deforciant, or donates or transmits the property by hereditary succession, or, in short, makes a transfer of it by means of a transferable deed of property. The other case occurs whenever the precarious deforciant, either judicially or extra-judicially, resists by openly denying the exercise of such right by the one who was the possessor. For instance, when a lessee pretending to be the owner ejects the lessor from the part of the property which he used to occupy; when the lessee informs the lessor that he means to be the possessor on his own account, as he considers himself to be the sole owner of the property; when, on being sued for the payment of the rent money, answers that he does not owe any, as the property is his own. In these and similar cases there is manifestly an act of contradiction, and reckoning from this act the deforciant may prescribe. It is added, moreover, that this would not take place by the mere cessation of the payment of the rent money, as no matter how complete and prolonged this cessation should be, it could not be explained by ascribing it to patience or generosity on the part of the lessor; besides, this act not being in itself a contradiction to the right of property; that an act of resistance against the exercise of the right is needed, based on the denial of such right; that since the performance of said act, should it bear all the characteristics mentioned in Article 2229, the possession would be useful to prescription, which shall be consummated either in the period of from ten to twenty years or thirty years, according to the good or bad faith of the precarious ex-deforciant in his taking possession *animo domini.*

The Article 2229 establishes that in order to be able to prescribe, it is required *that the possession be continued and uninterrupted, pacific, public, and unmistakable, and in the capacity of an owner.*

For the ten to twenty years' prescription the French Civil Code exacts good faith and a good title.

Wharton's Lexicon of Jurisprudence says that "*Adverse possession is unmolested occupation of real and personal property against the person holding a lawful title thereof, such possession becoming in due time an unassailable title,*" and makes reference at this point to the Act of Limitations of Real Property, 1874, 37–38 Vict., chapter 57, by which it is resolved that "No person shall take possession or seize or shall sue for the recovery of any land or leased property but within the next twelve years following the time when the right was originated."

These doctrines show that adverse possession, in order to originate prescription, must have the characteristics alluded to exactly as if it were another kind of possession. Prescription, however, is such a grave and complex matter that we have thought it proper to devote to its discussion special chapters. In the present chapter we shall deal with the second sentence of Rule "*a* ."

Let us, then, discuss the exclusive political control of a district or its settlement in this rule assimulated to the title of prescription.

We can not fail to observe that, as before explained, prescription presupposes the possession of a thing acquired by some one in virtue of a transferable deed of property, such as a sale, exchange, donation, hereditary succession, and bequests. Thus, in cases such as when the alienor, aware or not of the fact, transferred as his own property something which turns out to belong to some one else, the possessor receives the property in ignorance of its vitiated or faulty title, and at the end of a certain time the legislator places him beyond an action for recovery by the despoiled owner. So far, we are able to understand the nature of the consequences of this system. What is not quite so clear is its analogy to prescription and the exclusive control over a territory. Perhaps the words may have been meant to designate the right exercised over a territory not materially possessed, but which, by its contiguity, is considered as part of the territory belonging to the same owner.

The contents of the preliminary statements in the Blue Book No. 3 (supplementary to No. 1), seem to give weight to this idea, as the main object of that statement is to show the extent to which the Dutch and the Spaniards, prior to 1796, exercised control over the territory lying between the Essequibo and the Orinoco, with reference to those acts by which the dominion and influence of a nation are ordinarily manifested, as, for instance, settlement, exploration, trade, dealings with native tribes, and general control.

The subject is divided into five articles, namely, settlement, post-holders, jurisdiction exercised by them, trade, and relations with Indian tribes. In considering these, it is stated in the Blue Book that the following principles should be kept in view, viz.:

"The territory which belongs to a nation in a country sparsely populated is not confined to the spots or areas which have themselves been the subject of occupation. It is well established by the law of nations that the extent of territory to which a nation can justly lay claim depends upon a number of considerations. Regard must be had to the physical features of the country itself and to the question whether the situation and character of the areas occupied would enable the nation to which the occupants belong to control the adjoining district, and to prevent, if necessary, hostile aggression.

"A familiar instance is afforded by the claims which

have frequently been put forward by various nations to the water-sheds of particular rivers of which they controlled the mouths and passage. Similarly the exercise of control over native races, the exploration of the country and the making of roads, the exercise of native ownership by the cutting of timber in parts of the forests, the controlling of the trade of a district, and the preventing of foreigners from taking part in it,—all these and other acts of similar description have been long regarded by international lawyers and by nations as founding a just claim to a district which has formed the scene of such operations. Moreover, the title so acquired has for many generations been recognized as being superior to a title claimed on grounds of any alleged discovery which has not been followed by similar acts of ownership."

After these remarks the Blue Book argues that this, and no other, was the situation of the Dutch in Guiana.

There is nothing to say against the principle of contiguity, also invoked by Venezuela, if a reasonable limitation be made to the extension of territory deemed indispensable to the convenience and integrity of the possession, or such as may not be separated from the whole. Thus, Solomon establishes the rule that the occupation of a coast involves the acquisition of the right of sovereignty over all the islands lying along the coast within the limits of the territorial waters; that in case of two States taking possession of two neighboring territories, all the intervening space which separates them being *a nullius*, and there being no agreement to the contrary, a line can be drawn equally distant from the two extreme points where their possession may be considered to cease to be effective; that the topographical features may furnish another means of settling the difficulty; that when a portion of a certain island is occupied it may not always be considered that the acquisition extends to the whole of it; that it is inadmissible that the occupant of the seacoast should also be *ipso facto* occupant of all the lands forming, with the seacoast, a natural aggregate or totality, a theory which has been called a theory of the natural limits and the necessary frontiers; that it is no less exorbitant to pretend that the possessor of the mouth of a river has any rights to the basin formed by its watershed and by its affluents, this being against the rights of whoever occupies the headwaters.

These doctrines, however, apply to nations having made discoveries of lands *á nullius*, and is foreign to the present circumstances. Guayana had been discovered and occupied by the Spaniards when the Dutch ships came there. The Dutch, though rebellious against Spain since 1579, did not constitute a free and independent nation until 1648, when Spain recognized Holland as such. In consequence, the States-General, which in 1621 granted to the Dutch West India Company certain trading privileges, had no legal right to authorize that corporation to acquire territory.

The Dutch landed in Guayana as domestic enemies of Spain, to make war against her in her colonial possessions in America, and succeeded in taking away from her certain territories. When peace was made, in 1648, Spain agreed to leave these territories to Holland. It has been ascertained that the Dutch possessions were then limited to the fort of Kykoveral, constructed on the remains of a building formerly erected by the Spaniards, and to the mouth of the Essequibo, without having extended to the west of said river. It is true that the restitution to the Dutch of that which the Portuguese had taken away from them in Brazil was stipulated in Article V of the Treaty, and also their right was recognized to the forts and places that the States-General might chance to conquer and possess after that time, without infraction of the Treaty. We have already seen, however, that this cession did not mention any Guayana territory, but Brazilian territory only, where the Portuguese (then also separated from Spain) continued to carry on war against Spain, in order to insure their independence. It would be strange indeed if Spain, upon entering into a treaty of peace with Holland, should authorize her to make *conquests* (this is the word used in the French text of the Treaty) in her own territory, as conquest presupposes a state of war, and such conquest could not have been foreseen. On the other hand, there is no necessity for the authority, this being a right of every belligerent by force of circumstances.

The United Netherlands lacking the faculty to increase their possessions in Guayana, we are compelled to admit that they were obliged to content themselves with their possessions of Kykoveral and Essequibo, ceded by Spain in 1648; and we must also admit that the increase of said possessions, either on the coast or inland, constituted a plain act of usurpation. In the extradition treaty of 1791, as we have seen, are named as Dutch the Colonies of St. Eustace, Curaçao, Essequibo, Demarara, Berbice, and Surinam. This last named was settled by the English, and by them exchanged with the Dutch for New York in 1667, and was included in the Treaty of 1670, by which Spain confirmed all that the Dutch had acquired in America.

The Dutch may have granted permission to cut wood on the Guaima; they may have had trading-posts at Pomorón, Moroco, and Cuyuni (although several of these assertions are only founded on their word); this, however, did not constitute them owners of those places.

Entering a territory for the purpose of trade does not constitute a right of domain, whether the entry be made with or without permission of the sovereign. In either case the owner may, at his option, allow them to remain or may expel them.

This is why we find in the treaties of friendship and commerce that there generally exists an indispensable clause by which the contracting parties reciprocally agree to grant to their citizens or their subjects the faculty to enter the coasts and lands of their respective possessions, to reside in them and to trade there or manufacture, it being understood that they are to remain subject to the laws and regulations relating to entry and permanency or residence in the country—taxes, the use of harbors or roads, the determination of the places where articles of commerce may be entered or disposed of, and of the places not accessible to foreigners, etc.

The fact of carrying trade into a territory does not presuppose dominion over it, but only the enjoyment of the faculty that the local sovereign, either by reason of a treaty or otherwise, grants to those wishing to engage in trade in that territory. The Spanish Government was so jealous with respect to their American possessions that not only did they prohibit foreigners from travelling through them, but also punished by death those who should trade in them.

As neighbors, the Dutch at Essequibo, making use of the rivers and creeks which connected their settlements with those of the Spaniards at Orinoco, used to go there more frequently to trade in the Indian settlements, and often surreptitiously. At times certain rules, less strict, were adopted and afterwards changed. If, at first, the Dutch went to Orinoco, the Spaniards afterwards went to Essequibo. To pretend that for these acts the Orinoco belonged to the Dutch, would, for the same reason, justify Spain in claiming the Essequibo, especially since she was the discoverer of the latter river and its affluents. Spain, also, from the commencement, opposed the Dutch, who endeavored to carry on trade, as can be proved by a number of instances.

On the other hand, the Dutch, at certain places had barracks, as described by Netscher, guarded by a few men, not as signs of ownership of those places; but to facilitate trade in trifles with the poor Indians, and to buy from the fierce Caribs the captives made by them among the other native tribes, and who were sold by them as slaves for the cultivation of the plantations of the Dutch Colony.

When, in 1758, the Spaniards destroyed the Dutch post at Cuyuni, and carried away as prisoners those found there, demand was made for their return. This the Spanish Governor refused, on the ground that they had been found violating a Spanish law within Spanish jurisdiction; and that was the end of it.

When, in 1768, Governor Centurion ordered the ejection of the Dutch traders, or, rather, smugglers, from Barima, the order was promptly executed. The Dutch had gathered there fugitive slaves from the provinces of Cumaná and Caracas, and had employed them as guides to indicate the disloyal Spaniards engaged in making secret shipments along the rivers and unknown landing places outside of the roads. Centurion based his orders on several laws and the latest Royal decrees issued by His Catholic Majesty, prohibiting that foreigners, under any pretext whatsoever, be tolerated or allowed to settle on Spanish domains or form new Colonies. It was declared, therefore, that the Dutch had committed a crime and incurred the penalty of seizure of their implements and of other property found with them, and the amount of 380 *pesos*, proceeds of the sale of the seized property, was adjudged to the Royal Treasury.

Not only in her laws, but in the Treaties with other nations as well, Spain always retained her exclusive right of trading with her Indians. Suffice it to recall that even in 1814, notwithstanding the great services obtained from Great Britain against the French invasions, the most that Spain did was to grant England, "in case that foreign nations be allowed to trade with Spanish America, His Catholic Majesty promises that England shall be admitted to trade with them as the most favored and privileged nation."

According to Mr. Burr, in his Report to the Washington Commission, the Dutch in Essequibo carried on trade in Guayana in three ways, viz.: By contraband ; By outside vagabonds ; and by means of the trading posts.

The first was a secret performance, by means of which an effort was made to escape the vigilance of the Spanish authorities, the payment of taxes, and obedience to the fiscal regulations. Thus evading revenue regulations, the smuggler could enter into competition with merchants who were honest and jealous of their good name, with injurious results to the latter, as the smuggler reaped all the benefits. Frequently no trace is found of their operations which remain in the dark. Such a trade is universally considered as a crime, punishable more or less severely by law. Even certain foreign countries which, in the preparation of his plans, the smuggler makes use of, although they have no interest in his proceedings, deem themselves under obligation, at least, to withdraw their concurrence in the consummation of such frauds as damaging to the interests of friendly nations.

Regarding the vagabonds particularly engaged in the slave-trade and also in smuggling, Mr. Burr thinks it is not possible to draw any inference from their wanderings as regards territorial boundaries ; because, in the first place, their routes are completely unknown, and in the second place, because they were irresponsible and did not care in the least about frontiers. In this manner, if some from the Essequibo crossed over the region extending toward the Orinoco, others went from Bérbice, from Surinam, from the French Colonies on the continent, from the British islands of the Barbados, from the Portuguese islands of Brazil, and from the Spanish coast islands. It seems, moreover, that some of these vagabonds changed their nationality at will.

It seems that Mr. Burr gives value only to the "posts," which he asserts were few, changeable, often ephemeral, and sometimes at fixed places. Some of these had a certain military and political as well as a mercantile character; that trade with the Spaniards of the Orinoco was through the territory now in dispute, by means of the pass from Moroco to Barima; that until about the middle of the eighteenth century this trade was in the hands of the Dutch, but fell, later on, into the hands of the Spaniards.

We shall study this point in connection with the British arguments based on the hypothesis that trading posts were a species of territorial occupation and settlement.

CHAPTER XVIII.

ARTICLE IV OF THE TREATY, RULE "b."

Rule "*b*" is as follows:

"The Arbitrators may recognize and give effect to rights and claims resting on any other ground whatever valid according to international law and on any principiples of international law which the Arbitrators may deem to be applicable to the case and which are not in contravention of the foregoing rule."

This rule authorizes the Arbitrators to apply any principle of international law which they may deem applicable, and not in contravention of the foregoing rule; that is, the rule "*a*" which declares a good title by adverse holding or prescription for fifty years, and also establishes title by exclusive political control of a district for fifty years.

The modes of acquisition common among nations, according to E. Ortolan, who has discussed the subject in a monograph, are occupation, modifications of the variable boundaries, such as changes due to water boundaries, rise of islands or islets, covenants of transfer of international domain, and possession such as cession, sale, compromise, demarcation of boundaries, partitions, etc., arbitral decisions, result of war, and prescriptive acquisition.

The last is the one especially selected to decide the question submitted to the Arbitrators, and of the other modes enumerated none has taken place that could be applicable to the present case.

Scarcely any mention has been made of the right of occupation which, as regards private individuals, will be treated in the discussion of rule "*c*." We shall, later on, consider whether public prescription can be invoked.

For the present we will remark that the principles of international law, included in rule "*b*," are undoubtedly those concerning prescription between States. We have already noted those principles which the law deems necessary, among which is the time of possession by the one who acquires. This is the only one which the treaty defines. Regarding the others, the Arbitrators are left the faculty to use them as a guide, and by so doing there will be no contradiction of the foundation of the rules, *i. e.*, the fifty years' possession. We have already stated that, beside the requisite of time, possession must be by the State, must be continuous, public, pacific, uninterrupted, and in the capacity of owner or sovereign. Phillimore shows that the proofs of *prescriptive possession* are, *principally*, publicity, continued occupation, absence of interruption, with the aid of employment of labor and capital by the new possessor during the time of silence or passiveness (*inertia*), or absence of any attempt to exercise proprietary rights by the former owner; and that the lapse of time, which can not be fixed in international as in private law, depends on circumstances, both variable and varying. In another place he expressed himself emphatically in reference to the actual enjoyment and pacific possession of the territory by the nation as necessary to produce the required effect. Should we put both propositions together, the doctrine will be complete and in accordance with those of other authors. Observe that Phillimore uses the word *principally* to express his idea, so that he admits the necessity of the convenience of the other condition, although he does not deem them of equal importance with those enumerated.

Nor should we forget what has already been quoted from English legislation respecting the conditions of prescription, which clearly shows how necessary they are to give semblance of justice to the system establishing them.

If by simply occupying the property of some one else the usurper may acquire it (said possession not having been pacific, public, continuous, uninterrupted and in the capacity of owner), what security is there for the domain of States, and what would be the difference between such institution of the principle of occupation by right of war sanctioned by Roman law and the principle of occupation by right of conquest that the progress of the world has suppressed among civilized nations? Why, then, when conquests are made in war, are they not deemed sufficient to give title to ownership, but a treaty of peace is needed; an act showing the consent; the cession of the dispossessed to confirm the rights of the conqueror?

"Were this otherwise there would be the necessity for legitimizing the most iniquitous acts. One nation might fall upon another to deprive it of its territory. It would not then be necessary to establish so carefully the cases where a first occupation may be just and to exact that such occupation should take place in territory without an owner, since the admission that conquest in itself could produce the transmission of property from one State to another.

"War must not be considered as means to extend one's power or increase one's domains; but as a fatal necessity the inevitable result of the right of independence; a necessity which would disappear were it possible to realize the project of universal congresses already suggested, it is said by Sully and Henry IV., by placing over the different States a common authority, and consequently blotting from the rights of nations the right of absolute independence existing at the present time.

"War is a procedure between powers which does not recognize a legitimate superior. A nation should not go to war except when compelled by violence or by the denial of any essential right, and when all the pacific means to prevent it have been exhausted."—[ORTOLAN.]

Phillimore, himself, who does not make any distinction between possessions, makes a point of not confounding occupation with conquest. In Paragraph D, xxvi, Vol. 3, Part XII, chapter 1st, he says in reference to the means by which war is terminated and peace re-established, as follows:

"It is now pretty generally acknowledged that there is both absurdity and iniquity in classing territory obtained by *conquest* under the category of *res nullius*, and of applying with unreasoning pedantry or sophistical injustice, not the spirit, but the letter, of the Roman law to a subject-matter which, like that of conquest, has necessarily undergone, in all its bearings, a most important change since the time of Justinian.[1]

"The shameless pretext of Frederic the Second for the invasion of Saxony in 1756 will not be alleged again by the most reckless despiser of international justice."

In consequence rule "*b*" can not have reference to conquests by war, notably so since after 1648 no war took place between Spain and Holland. Although the latter did not take part in the war of succession against the former in 1700, and for this reason also figured in the treaty of peace of 1714, which brought the war to an end hostilities were not extended to their respective colonies in America. In 1796 Spain appears united with Holland against the common enemy, England, who had taken possession of Surinam, thereby becoming a menace to the neighboring Spanish colonies. By the peace of Amiens the conquered Dutch possessions in Guayana were restored. In 1803 Great Britain retakes

[1] Various treaties of peace fortify the sound international doctrine that *conquest* and *occupation* of territory are distinct public acts, carrying with them very different consequences, both to the State and to the individual. The language of treaties which concerns the acquisition of conquered territory is that the subdued State *yields* or *concedes* (*cédera*) a certain territory to another; not that the conquering State *retains* or *keeps* possession of what it has seized, which would be the proper expression in the Treaty with respect to a State obtaining the recognition of an unoccupied territory.

"It is unquestionable," says Mr. de Rayneval, "that the word *concede* (*ceder*) means essentially the property; consequently neither war nor conquest destroys it. Thus practice denies the principle taught by the Roman law and the greater part of writers."

them, continuing the war against France and her allies, among them the Batavian Republic. In 1809 Spain becomes separated from this alliance and intimately united to the United Kingdom against the French Emperor, which Spain also effected in 1814 upon the fall of that Emperor.

From the period of 1796 to 1809, during which the Spanish and British crowns, with a brief interruption, were enemies, the state of possession was not changed in Guayana, so that no conquest took place.

Since no conquest occurred until the latter year, we do not deem it amiss to inquire whether any public possession of the nation took place, this sort of possession being the only one capable of producing legal effects.

All authorities agree that possession is a mode of acquisition between nations, only however when it is coexistent with the two essential conditions, viz.: 1st. That the territory does not belong to any one, *res nullius*. 2d. That the possession of the thing be effected *corporæ et ánima;* that is, materially and with intent to make it one's own.

Should either condition be lacking, the act does not originate acquisition.

The thing may be *nullius* either because no one has ever occupied it, or else because the former occupant has unmistakably abandoned it.

All authors agree that it is necessary in order to acquire by occupation—

1st. That the possession be effected without impairing another's rights.

2d. That the property occupied be susceptible of being possessed exclusively by a State.

3d. That this property, even when susceptible of being possessed exclusively, should have no owner, or have again become *res nullius*.

4th. That the taking possession of such property without an owner should have been effected with the well-defined intention to appropriate it permanently, no one being able to acquire it without his knowledge and involuntarily.

5th. That the intent to appropriate be accompanied or followed by an effective occupation, verified by the use of such measures as are needed to establish permanent control. In other words, "occupation, to be legitimate," says Klüber, "requires that the thing be susceptible of being owned exclusively; must not belong to any one; the nation must have the intention to acquire it and take possession of it; that is to say, to have it entirely at its disposal and under its physical power."

Let us study the concrete point whether Holland or Great Britain has been able to effect occupation in Guayana.

The first and third requisites above mentioned form one single rule, to wit: If the thing occupied be not *res nullius*, such occupation is detrimental to some one else's rights.

The second requisite presents no difficulty, as a nation is capable of possessing a territory exclusively.

Nor does the fourth point, if the intention of appropriating the thing has accompanied the possession of it.

The fifth demands effective possession.

We note that neither the first nor the third requisite has been fulfilled; in other words, that all the territory belonged to Spain. It belonged to Spain by right of discovery, followed by occupation, colonization, evangelization of the country where the nomadic tribes roved.

By right of the adjudication which, in conformity with the right generally recognized in those times, Pope Alexander VI. made, in 1493, to the King and Queen of Spain.

By virtue of the treaty concluded between the Kings of Spain and Portugal at Tordesillas, in 1494, to change somewhat the boundary line given in the Pontifical Bulls to their respective acquisitions.

By the ancient right, which invests the owner of a territory not only with the territory materially occupied, but also all that is essential to the real use of the colonizers, though this use be only inchoate and not fully developed; and moreover, all that is necessary to the integrity and security of the possessor such as can not be separated from the whole.

By the right of consolidation of the property based on the measures taken to defend it, exclude foreigners therefrom, eject them by force, involving expenditures and loss of life.

By the right acquired by the notification made to the world in the laws of the Indies and contained in the several treaties made by Spain with other nations.

It cannot be argued that Holland, Great Britain, and France did not attach much value to the rights attributed to Spain, the discoverer of the New World, and which did occupy some regions in America. Such arguments are valueless, and, since the Netherlands, who were subjects of Spain until 1648, by accepting the cessions of their new occupations in Guiana which Spain made them by the Treaty of Munster, did recognize Spain's pre-existing sovereignty over the ceded regions.

There is no force in the argument that by the 5th Article of the Treaty of Munster a grant was made by Spain to the States-General of all the forts and places which they might chance to *acquire* (conquer) and possess after this, without infraction of the present Treaty. It is plain, as we have elsewhere shown, that this clause did not refer to territory in Guayana, but to the Brazilian territory; and this by reason of hostility to Portugal, which, since 1640, had also struggled to break the Spanish yoke. Holland, by admitting the concession, acknowledged the right of Spain to dispose, not alone of the territory in Guayana, but of that acquired in Brazil, from the Indians and the Dutch as well.

The remarks in reference to the Netherlands also apply to the English, who, having acquired territory in America, did not deem their titles perfect unless strengthened by the consent of Spain. There remains not the slightest doubt in regard to this point after reading Article 7th of the Treaty concluded between Great Britain and Spain on the 18th of July, 1670, for the resumption of friendship and kindly intercourse with America, said article appearing also in the Treaties of 1713, 1763, 1783, and reads as follows:

"That all the offenses, damages, and injuries suffered both by the Spanish and the English nations reciprocally in America at any time in the past, for any cause or pretext whatever, by one or the other nation, be henceforth forgotten and entirely obliterated from memory as if they never had occurred. Moreover, it has also been agreed that the most serene King of Great Britain, his heirs and successors, shall enjoy, hold, and possess perpetually, by full right of sovereignty, property, and possession, all the lands, provinces, islands, settlements, and dominions in the West Indies, or those in any portion of America that the aforesaid King of Great Britain and his subjects may hold at the present time. So that, neither by reason thereof nor under any other pretext whatever, shall there be any further pretension allowed nor hereafter give rise to any controversy."

If, to calm her fears in regard to her acquisitions in America, Great Britain deemed it expedient to sign a treaty with Spain by which the latter confirmed said possessions, neither Phillimore nor any one else can claim that the Bull of Alexander VI. and the other titles were inefficient; as in such case, neither Holland nor Great Britain would ever have appealed to one who lacked good source of title. If America was the property of no one, notwithstanding its discovery by Spain, who also peopled it in part, whatever any other State should occupy with the same formalities would have been acquired by said State as fully as possible.

Nor does it impair Spanish title the fact of the difficulty of coming to an understanding with Portugal in the matter of the meridian which should separate their respective possessions, as, whatever these possessions may have been, there stands the incontestable truth fact, in their Treaties of 1750 and 1777, for the division of said possessions in South America, they ended all their disputes arising from that origin.

It is not known, moreover, that such possession ever extended further north than the boundaries fixed to Portuguese Guayana; both parties in reason thereof did reciprocally guarantee each to the other all the frontier and adjatcen territories of their domains in South America. This guarantee, as regards Portugal's possessions, extended as far as the margins of the Orinoco from one side to the other, being indefinite in the interior. Article 18 of the Treaty is worthy of note on account of the division of the waters established by it, according to which all the watersheds of the Marañon or Amazon should belong to Portugal, and those of the Orinoco to Spain.

The territory of Guayana was not an isolated possession taken by the Spaniards, but part of the continent of South America, almost totally colonized by Spain; it was part of the whole, forming the Captaincy-General of Venezuela and the new Kingdom of Grenada. In order to recognize its importance it is sufficient to recall what the English officer, Macrea, said, in October, 1802, to the commander of the forces of His Britannic Majesty in Essequibo, Demerara, and Berbice, viz.:

"Except the conversion of the aboriginal natives (which is certainly not the primary motive) the Spanish Government has, obviously, no other object in occupying the Orinoque than the very important one of excluding other powers from a river which runs along the rear of the Provinces of Popayan, Venezuela, Carraccas, Cumana, and Paria; which, therefore, in the hands of a commercial nation, would carry away from them the productions and monopolize the traffic of those rich territories, and which, if possessed by a warlike power, might immediately paralyze the authority and gradually destroy the tenure by which Spain holds her vast empire in South America. And on this account not only the cultivation of the fertile territory of the Orinoco is prohibited, the augmentation of its settlers in every manner discountenanced, but the very commerce of old Spain to that particular river, except to a degree indispensably requisite, is sedulously discouraged."

From this we infer that the Government of Spain, sovereign of all the mentioned provinces, was indisputably in *need* of the territory of Guayana watered by the Orinoco and its countless affluents, for the administration, vigilance, prosperity, and defense of said provinces. On this account (if for no other), all the lands within them belonged to Spain, and were not open to occupation by any other nation.

It is true that the Dutch, the French, and the English, envious of Spain's aggrandizement and desirous of participating in the benefits of the enterprise to which Spain owed the acquisition of the New World, began, from early times, to dispute it, sending expeditions to take possession at various times. It was thus that the British established the thirteen Colonies, which, near the end of the last century, shaking off the fetters of English rule, formed an independent nation; first, as a Confederation; later, as a Federal Republic, now so great and powerful.

It was thus that France also formed, chiefly in North America, a powerful colonial empire, of which she has now only very few possessions—among them French Guiana, lying between the Dutch of Surinam and the Brazilian, formerly of Portugal, and a few islands in the Caribbean sea.

It was thus that the United Netherlands rebelled against Spain, from whose dominion they were anxious to be free, undertook to establish, on the coast of Guayana, settlements, first, for trading purposes, and later on for agricultural purposes.

Upon the termination of that civil war the Treaty of Munster was concluded (30th of January, 1648). By its first article the King of Spain recognized the States-General and their respective provinces and all their associated territories, cities, and lands as States, provinces and countries free and sovereign.

Article V stipulated that the aforesaid King and States-General, respectively, should continue in the possession and enjoyment of such "lordship's cities, castles, towns, fortresses, commerce and countries of the East and West Indies, as also in Brazil and upon the coasts of Asia, Africa and America, respectively, that the said Lords, the King and the States-General, respectively, held and possessed, comprehending therein particularly the places and forts which the Portuguese had taken from the said Lords, the States, since the year 1641; as also the forts and places which the said Lords, the States, should chance to acquire (conquer) and possess after this without infraction of the present Treaty."

Article VI added that the subjects of said King should forbear sailing to or trading in any of the harbors, forts, lodgments, places or castles, or in any other places possessed by the other party; nor should the subjects of the said States do likewise in those held by the King; and that among the places held by the States, there should be comprehended the places in Brazil which the Portuguese had taken from the States, and had been in possession of ever since the year 1641, as also all the other places which they then possessed while they were occupied by the Portuguese.

By virtue of these provisions, concession was made to the Dutch of all they had acquired in the territory of Spain in Guayana during the war, and that was on the *coasts*, as expressed by the article cited. Holland could not grant to Spain anything in Guayana, because she did not possess any before; and only by reason of the cession in the Treaty did Holland acquire full title to the territory she then occupied there. There could be no reciprocity on this point; perhaps such may have existed in the Spanish and Dutch possessions on the coasts of Africa and Asia, mentioned in the Treaty, but not in America.

This Treaty forbids the subjects of the two powers to sail or trade from any of the places of one of the parties to those of the other, which implies prohibition to effect occupations in their respective possessions. To occupy and to possess is much more than to sail and to trade; if the latter could not be done, much less could the former.

The Treaty embodies the concession of a special favor to the Dutch, due to the generosity of Spain, who did not receive anything in compensation. This special favor consisted in authorizing the Dutch to acquire and possess places and forts thenceforth, provided such acts be not in contravention of the Treaty, besides Spain's consent to give back those which the Portuguese had taken from the States since 1641. Article VI insists upon this point; that is to say, the places which the Portuguese had taken from the States in Brazil are considered as property of the Dutch.

It is a fact that the Dutch did not colonize certain places in Brazil, as can be seen in the pamphlet written on the subject by General Netscher, the historian of the Colonies of the Essequibo, Demerara, and Berbice; they found, however, resistance on the part of the Portuguese, whose aspirations were to take possession of the country, and they at last succeeded. Portugal which, since 1580, had been part of Spain, broke, in 1640, the ties which united them. Spain, in her purpose to renew these ties, endeavored to reduce the Portuguese, and to this end strove to make enemies against them. This explains why, in 1648, when recognizing the independence of the Netherlands, she at the same time opposed Portugal's aspirations to the same end, and consented to give back the acquisitions made by the latter over the former, and even went so for as to endeavor to cause them further injury by encouraging the Dutch to undertake other conquests in Brazil. This has been clearly shown by the Washington Commission, through the report made by Professor Burr.

The consequence was that Spain authorized the Dutch, not to injure her rights in Guayana, which would have been not only unheard of, but absurd; but to acquire territory from the Portuguese, formerly her subjects, but at that time her enemies.

In this act Spain claimed a right of sovereignty over Brazil which, later on, she recognized as a Portuguese dependency, after she had recognized Portugal, in 1683, as an independent power

Nothing of that region remained to the Dutch who were at last definitively ejected therefrom.

Spain acted as she did with the purpose to maintain, as Venezuela, following her example, has done, that all the region of Guayana belonged to her, with the exception of what she ceded to the Dutch on the coasts by the Treaty of 1648, and what she left to the Portuguese by the Treaties of 1777 and 1790.

It is in vain to argue that Spain had no effective occupation but in some few places. As Twiss states, "in order to make an occupant the legal owner of the thing it is not necessary that he have possession of the whole; if he be in possession of a part that can not be separated from the whole, he is then in possession of the whole." If a nation has occupied a territory, that nation is entitled, as being one of its belongings, to everything necessary to the integrity and security of its possession. By an analogous principle, when a nation has discovered a country and made her discovery known, the presumption is that she intends to take possession of all the country within its natural limits, being essential to the independence and security of her establishment, and her right of discovery has the same extension of such limits.

On page 1 of the Blue Book No. 3, 1896, this principle is presented in the words we have quoted elsewhere.

Notwithstanding that authors demand the effectiveness of the occupation, the practice of nations in this regard has not strictly enforced this requisite.

We have already cited examples showing that in America large tracts of territory have been ceded which not only were the property of those making that cession, but that remained in the hands of the Indians.

In an article on "Occupations and Territories and the Procedure of Hinterland," by F. Despaguet, Professor of international law in the University of Bordeaux, published in the General Review of International Public Law, Paris, 1894, the following appears:

"The only thing to be observed, from the standpoint of international law, is that the legal considerations of occupation of a territory have been greatly modified, mainly since the second half of our century. By the Bulls of the Pope the countries were to be evangelized more than colonized—such as the Bulls of Clement VI., giving to Spain the Canary Islands, November 13, 1344; those of Nicholas V., granting to King Alphonse V., of Portugal, the Guinea, in 1491; and notably the famous Bull, '*Inter cætera*,' of Alexander VI., dividing between the Spaniards and the Portuguese the territory yet to be discovered. These Bulls are followed by the proper initiative by the more independent governments of the Holy See—France, the Netherlands and England—signally since about the middle of the fourteenth century. *But then, just as before, notwithstanding* some declarations which had no more than a theoretical value, occupation is effected in a fictitious manner. Any manifestation whatever, such as the erection of a monument, of a cross, the planting of a flag, was considered sufficient to realize the occupation of extensive territories, and this gave rise to numberless difficulties with the competitors for the exact demarcation of the share of territory appertaining to each."

It is necssary to come to contemporary epochs to demand practically effective possession of a territory in accordance with the rational and juridical notion of occupation, such as the publicists of the eighteenth century, and particlarly Vattel, had understood it.

It is well known that this new rule was formally accepted by the powers which signed the final act of Berlin on the 26th of February, 1885, article 35, for the future occupation on the coasts of the African Continent, and that the effective character of possession is, according to the same article quoted, indicated by the fact of establishing or *maintaining*, if such does not already exist, sufficient authority to make the acquired rights respected, and, should such case arise, the freedom of commerce and traffic. It is also known that Article 34 of the act of Berlin imposes upon the occupant the obligation to inform the other Powers of its occupation, sufficiently in advance to permit them to present any claims thereto should they have any. This notification is only demanded when, instead of an occupation properly, there is the intention to establish a protectorate.

Ch. Soloman, doctor of law, in his treatise on "Occupation of the Territories without an Owner," published in 1889, makes the following distinction of these historical periods, viz.:

"1st. The period during which the faculty of the Sovereign Pontiff to grant at will and with the character of a privilege the right to discover and occupy certain territories was recognized, and when he was considered sovereign of the whole world.

"2d. The period of the right of discovery proper, when the pretensions of the Pope seemed exorbitant even to the Catholic Powers which did not participate in his favors, and when priority and occupation, effected either by planting a flag on a desert shore or even looking through a telescope at indistinct shores of a far-off land, were sufficient to acquire territorial domain.

"3d. The period in which we find ourselves is the principle of *effectiveness, although it can not be said that such principle has attained complete success except in theory; the principle of effective occupation; the principle that labor or effective use in international* as well as private law, is the only legitimate cause of acquisition of a territory that does not belong to any one—a principle long ago proclaimed by some jurists, and definitely admitted as applicable to a portion of the world only in the conference of Berlin in 1884–1885."

The author quoted is of the opinion that the occupations effected in former times can not be considered by the standard of principles admitted in Berlin, but according to the principles ruling at the time; that the nation whose nominal and fictitious sovereignty was acknowledged up to 1884 has the right to demand from the other Powers continuance of said acknowledgment, though she do not make effective her sovereignty.

As an example, the author presents the case of the Caroline Islands, and asserts that the question was settled with as much wisdom as impartiality by the eminent man who at present occupies the Apostolic chair. Germany alleged the existence on the islands of commercial establishments of her subjects; the steps taken by the founders of such establishments to induce the German Government to establish a protectorate over the island; the absence of sovereignty of Spain, who did not have even subjects engaged in commerce in that region; the want of indications to the powers that there was a nation exercising right of sovereignty over the territory; and the participation of Spain in the Berlin Congress. The exceptions taken by Germany and Great Britain in 1875 were also alleged respecting the case of a consul having claimed as Spanish subjects some natives of the Caroline Islands, saved by an English vessel from a shipwreck, exception over which Spain remained silent as though she did not pretend to rights of sovereignty over those islands.

Spain alleged that effective occupation was not applicable to the Island of Tap—1st. On account of its geographical position; (2d) because it was not an object of new occupation. There had been a prior occupation; Spanish officers were on land engaged in building a small fort when the German officers arrived; the Spanish flag had floated over the Caroline Islands since 1526. From that time forward and in the sixteenth, seventeenth, and eighteenth centuries, Spain had sent to those islands a great number of military expeditions and many religious missions, and had made repeated attempts at colonization. In 1731 the Phillipine missionaries succeeded in reaching the Archipelago. Spain had the monopoly of missions, the diffusion of religion, and of the planting of civilization in those remote islands. In 1885 the frigate Velasco visited the Island of Tap, and the minister for the islands informed the Senate that it was the intention to renew those visits, and that the manifestation of sovereignty seemed expedient; that the natives knew the name of His Majesty Alfonso XII., and knew also that they were under Spanish control.

Appointed as a mediator, the Pope recognized the sovereignty of Spain over the Caroline and Palaos Islands, based on the fact of discovery, and the acts performed there by the Spanish Government through these acts did not give it the character of *effective* occupation.

From these Solomon concludes that when reference is had to occupation the validity of such occupation, although it may have been a fictitious one, is recognized if in conformity with the principles of international law in practice at the time the acquisition was made; that, on the other hand, the modern interpretation of the right of occupation being different from what it was in other times, Spain should make effective the control which until then may have been fictitious by establishing on the island a regular administration with a force sufficient to insure order and guarantee vested rights.

Both powers, Germany and Spain, accepted this decision in the protocol of December 17, 1885.

We must state again that the declaration of Berlin only affects the nations which took part in the conference and then approved its declarations; they refer only to future occupations and to the coasts of Africa, not to past occupations nor to countries not mentioned in the agreement.

It is a fact, moreover, that the United States, although represented at the Congress, have not yet ratified the project of declaration; that Sir E. Mallet, British Plenipotentiary, showed himself particularly anxious in accordance with his instructions that no retroactive effect should be given to the declaration; that the motion made that it should apply to the whole of the African continent failed; that Said Pasha, the Turkish Minister, declared that articles 34 and 35 were inapplicable to the possessions of the Sultan, although they are situated along the coast to the north, as well as to the east of Africa, and signally towards Cape Ras Hafon, which forms the eastern extremity of the Black Continent; that M. de Courcel, Plenipotentiary from France, declared on his part that the declaration had no other reference than to the littoral, and particularly indicated that Madagascar remained outside of its field of application, perhaps because he feared that this large island would be considered as a dependency of the continent.

The author we have quoted makes another remark that must not pass unnoticed, to wit, that if it is true that the dispositions concerning the *effectiveness* and notification are useful, moral, and general on account of their inherent nature, and shall possibly become uniform rules of conduct for the colonizing powers, and thus become an international doctrine—that still, though this may be recognized as a feature of modern progress, it is not yet a feature of conventional law. The declaration of the subject made by the Institute of International Law of Lausanne, on the 7th of September, 1888, with the character of universal doctrine, has not yet been adopted by the Powers, nor are there any hopes that it will soon be accepted.

Solomon does not think that the right of occupation of a nation ought to be limited to the territory that it may cultivate or settle if this possession is accompanied by sufficient force to repel outsiders.

This is the same principle laid down by Vattel, and adopted by Calvo, as already quoted, that when a State is in possession of a country, whatever lies within that country becomes the property of the State, even though its occupation be effective only with respect to a portion of the country; and should uncultivated places be left no one has the right to take these places without the nation's consent. It does not matter that the possessing nation should not actually use the places; they are hers; they are dependent upon her sovereignty; and she has an interest in keeping them for ulterior use. The nation has no need to account to any one for the use she makes of her property. This is particularly applicable to the case of the United States of North America and to the nations of South America, which possess large territories as yet either unpeopled or inhabited only by savage tribes.

Solomon is of the opinion that if the doctrine of discovery can be considered as antiquated, the same can not be said of the doctrine of priority of occupation, although he remarks that the English publicist, Twiss, gives great importance to priority of discovery.

Solomon also examines the point as to how far occupation extends, and in this connection says it is one of the most delicate points in the matter; that possession operates in a certain way by *reaction* on the territories adjoining the one which was the seat of the first establishment of the State: that this is the view taken by the greater number of writers who recognize the existence of a right of vicinage, priority, or preference, which the

English jurists call *right of contiguity*. He also recalls the fact that England has more than once disputed with other nations the right to establish themselves in the vicinity of any of her Colonies. Mention has been made already of the Treaty by which Great Britain and Spain stipulated, on the 28th of October, 1790, in reference to both the eastern and western coasts of South America and adjacent islands, that British subjects would not, in the future, settle on any part of said coasts and adjacent islands already occupied by Spain, although the said subjects should have the right to land on the coasts and islands thus situated for the purpose of fishing and erecting huts and other temporary structures serving only for those objects.

Solomon admits that the occupation of a coast embodies the acquisition of rights of sovereignty over all the islands situated along the coast within the limits of the territorial waters, although the occupation of every one of them does not partake of the character of effectiveness and is based on considerations derived from the necessity of defense of the new establishments.

He also admits that when two nations take possession of two neighboring territories, the space separating them being *res nullius*, and in the absence of an agreement to the contrary, in order to determine the boundaries of their respective occupations, a line may be drawn equidistant from the two extreme points from whence their possession may be considered to lose its effectiveness, adding that the geographical configuration of the territory might also permit of another solution.

He rejects the principle stated by David Dudley Field, that the occupation of any portion of a desert island must be understood as occupation of the whole island. He accepts only the case of the occupation embracing all the coast of the island, the interior portion of which will then be completely under control.

He more decidedly rejects the principle that the State occupying the seashore has, *ipso facto*, possession of all the portion of lands forming with the coast a natural *ensemble;* of what is necessary for the new colony to develop under the best possible conditions, which he says is the theory of the natural limits and of the necessary frontiers, applied not to a State already formed, but to an incipient colony.

The same writer also denies that a State settling on the mouth of a river has any right to the whole basin drained by it, and notes that this rule was presented by the American diplomatists as forming part of those unanimously acknowledged among civilized States.

Mr. Gallatin, one of the diplomats referred to, after referring to the occupation and cultivation of a country, said that two rules had been generally adopted, or rather sanctioned by the usage of nations, viz.: 1st. That first discovery gave right of occupancy whenever the occupation was effected within a reasonable time and ultimately followed by permanent settlement and cultivation of the soil; 2d, that the right of first discovery and first settlement was not limited to the place discovered or first settled, but that the extension of the territory so discovered and settled could not be precisely determined. But that the first discovery and subsequent settlements *of the mouth af a river*, within a reasonable time, particularly if none of its branches had been explored previously to such discovery, gave the right of occupation, and, in fine, the right of control over all the country watered by the said river and its various branches, had been generally admitted; and that, in a controversy between the United States and Great Britain, a successful appeal had *been* made to Great Britain's acts, showing that the principles upon which said acts were founded were in accordance with those of the United States, which invoked the language of old charters granted to companies of adventurers and individual explorers by European sovereigns, as showing the practice of European nations in regard to rights born of discovery.

The Plenipotentiaries of Great Britain replied that such charters had no force or effective value against the subjects of another sovereign; that they could only bind and restrain, *vigore suo*, those under the jurisdiction of the grantor; and that though they could well confer upon the grantees an exclusive right against the subjects of the same sovereign power, such right could only affect the subjects of other foreign powers, in so far as the common law of nations should compel the other powers to respect acts of discovery and occupation made by members of other political and independent communities.

Twiss finds that the principle of the United States is antagonistic to one of those upon which they based their pretensions against Spain in reference to the boundary of Louisiana in 1805, to wit: That the discovery and occupation of *an extension of sea coast* by a nation was understood to give her right of possession over the interior country *as far as the line of the watershed.* This principle, the United States Commissioners stated, had been fully established in the controversy between France and Spain on the one side and Great Britain on the other, which caused the war of 1775 between those nations.

The same publicist is of the opinion that the pretension to all the lands watered by a river and its affluents, based upon discovery and occupation of the mouth of the river, is antagonistic to the pretension to all the interior territory as far as the line of the watershed, based on the discovery and occupation of the seacoast—this being a principle of law, he states, over which there is no dispute among nations.

He thinks that such pretension is incompatible with the principles of law that the *de facto* occupation of one of the banks of a river and of the river itself by a nation does not establish a right of possession over the opposite bank so that it may preclude any other nation from settling thereon should it be *de facto* vacant.

The writer ends by stating that, in consequence of the doctrine of the Commissioners of the United States against which Great Britain deemed it her duty, as well as the duty of other powers to protest, may be considered as extravagant, as it is not based on the natural law, which considers the rivers as belonging to the land and not the land as an adjunct of the rivers; and that such doctrine can not be admitted without abrogating the rules of public law established by common consent of all nations.

Solomon can not understand why a State, establishing itself on the headwaters of a river, should not have the same right to all the country watered by said river as the State which takes possession of its mouth. The interest is the same in both; in the one case the intention is to penetrate to the center of the lands; in the other, to have free egress to the sea. As the publicists who admit it state that it could not be applied to the Mississippi, for example, Solomon asks who will decide the question whether the extension of territory through which the river runs is too considerable to apply to it the rule which it is endeavored to formulate?

He foresees that insolvable conflicts will take place between these two pretended principles. For instance, on a coast running from east to west, there empties into the sea a river, the general direction of which is from northeast to southwest. Two States have been established on that littoral; one of them possesses the mouth of the river, while the other has settled eastward of it. It is evident, he says, that the rule of the boundary line drawn perpendicularly to the coast and towards the interior, can not be reconciled with the one which gives to the State possessing the mouth of the river sovereignty over all the basin.

That same principle, admitted by Mr. Gallatin, and against which His Britannic Majesty protested in his own and in the name of other Powers, is, however, the same that Great Britain now wants to apply to Venezuela, as shown by the last paragraph of the preliminary statement of the Blue Book No. 1, page 42, which reads as follows:

> "The foregoing statement and the documents annexed to it establish that if the matter be treated as one of strict right, Great Britain, as the successor of the Dutch, is entitled to the territory extending to the Barima, including the watersheds of all the rivers of Guiana south of the Orinoco which flow into the Atlantic."

In the Blue Book No. 3, the Barima is no longer the terminus of the British domain, but it is affirmed that "for a period of upwards of two hundred years prior to 1796 the Dutch had control of the whole coast extending from the Corentin to the *Orinoco;* that they had the control of all the rivers flowing direct to the Atlantic between the *Orinoco* and the *Corentin;* that they had established settlements at various points on the coast and in the watersheds of these rivers, and notably far up the Cuyuni in close proximity to the territory afterwards occupied by the Capuchin missions."

Nor is this all. Lord Salisbury wrote to Dr. Rojas, Minister Plenipotentiary of Venezuela in London, under date of January 10, 1880: "The boundary which Her Majesty's Government claims in virtue of ancient treaties with the aboriginal tribes and of subsequent cessions from Holland, commences at a point at the mouth *of the Orinoco,* westward of Point Barima, proceeds thence in a southerly direction to the Imataca mountains, the line of which it follows to the northwest, passing from them by the Highlands of Santa Maria, just south of the town of

Upata, until it strikes a range of hills on the eastern bank of the Caroni river, following these southwards until it strikes the great backbone of the Guiana district, the Roraima mountains of British Guiana, and thence, still southward, to the Pacaraima mountains."

The line which Great Britain declared to be "indisputable," differs very slightly from the one here described, comprising the Cuyuni and its affluents and even the tributaries of the Orinoco, such as the Amacuro and the Barima and all the cross-channels and cañons, by which they communicate with them. These pretensions rest on no other foundation than that of the rejected principle that the (pretended) discovery of the mouth of a river and the subsequent (pretended) settlement by a nation on it gave to said nation the right of sovereignty over the whole country watered by said river and its watersheds.

We have already remarked that it was not Holland but Spain who discovered the mouth of those rivers, principally of the Essequibo which the British, notwithstanding, assert as belonging to them conjointly with all its tributaries. If Spain, who was unquestionably the proprietor of the *interior* lands watered by said rivers as well as of their mouths, abandoned that portion of them near the sea and even made cession of it by the Treaty of Munster, although leaving undefined the extent of transferred territory, did not by that act lose any other portion of her land in the interior of her domains.

If, as proved by Venezuela, neither the Amacuro nor the Barima ever belonged to or was ever settled by the Dutch, what reason is there for a divisional line to commence on the former, to follow its course and to endeavor to follow the course of other rivers towards the Cuyuni, following this to its headwaters, thus depriving Venezuela of the vast extent of territory lying west and south of that frontier?

He who advised the line of the Amacuro did not even affirm that Great Britain should have a right to it as the heir of Holland, but solely appealed to the pretext or convenience of having natural limits marked out. It is possible that such a "convenience" may exist in determining boundaries when it is not a question of *right* between parties to divide a thing in common, accompanied by the assignment of compensations to whomsoever should suffer damage by reason of such transaction. But this is not the mode of procedure to settle a dispute between adjacent neighbors according to the principles of law. The duty of the Arbitrators is to fix the dividing line between Venezuela and Great Britain in accordance with the law, and in conformity with the first of the three rules agreed upon, when its application be proper by virtue of adverse holding of fifty years' duration, in conjunction with the requisites established by the law of nations and after having studied the arguments, the proofs, and correspondence presented by both parties.

They will take into consideration that Spain possessed, besides the coast of South America, its *interior* countries, especially in Guayana, the Orinoco, and the other rivers flowing into the Atlantic, which were the easy and necessary means of communication between the Captaincy-General of Venezuela and the adjoining New Kingdom of Grenada, of the metropolis of which they were subjects together with the remaining Colonies of Spain, which constituted her empire in America. These colonies were naturally in communication among themselves; were obliged to be so in order to give mutual aid; had to be allied in order to strengthen themselves and contribute to the development and prosperity of their inhabitants, which formed but one people as a whole.

Consider what disputes might arise between Spain and the other nations, who, taking advantage of her discovery, should hasten to the coasts of America to dispute the benefits which might accrue to her from the free use of her rivers!

Lord Salisbury wrote to Sir Julian Pauncefote, under date of May 18, 1896, in reference to the different situation of individual and national rights as regards lands, that "*all the great nations in both hemispheres claim and are prepared to defend their right to vast tracts of territory which they have in no sense occupied and often have not fully explored.* The modern doctrine of Hinterland, with its inevitable contradictions, indicates the unformed and unstable condition of international law as applied to territorial claims, resting on constructive occupation or control."

To this the American Government replied that "spheres of influence" and the theory or practice of the "Hinterland" idea are things unknown to international law, and do not as yet rest upon any recognized Principles of either international or municipal law. They are new departures, which certain great European Powers have found necessary and convenient in the course of their division among themselves of great tracts of the Continent of Africa, and which find their sanction solely in their reciprocal stipulations."

A modern English writer on international law was cited, who discusses the doctrine of "Hinterland," and states that the accepted rule regarding the area of territory affected by an act of occupation on a land of large extent, has been that the crest of a watershed is the presumptive interior limit of the country, and that the flank boundaries are the limits of the land watered by the rivers debouching at the point of the coast occupied; that the extent of territory claimed in respect of an occupation on the coast has hitherto borne some reasonable ratio to the character of the occupation, and that asking what are the limits of the "Hinterland," adds: "Either these international arrangements can avail as between parties only and constitute no bar against the action of any intending stranger; or, might, indeed, is right." Mr. Olney, while not adopting this criticism and putting aside the question of whether the "spheres of influence" and the "Hinterland" doctrines be or not intrinsically sound and just, there can be no pretense that they apply to the American continents or to any boundary disputes that now exist there or that may hereafter arise.

Despagnet, in the work before mentioned, explains that in order to settle controversies relative to priority of occupation of *res nullius*, or to the establishment of a protectorate on barbarian domains, the process of the "Hinterland" (word meaning *back country*) is applied, this process being to fix, by international agreement, a topographical line beyond which each country has the right of occupation, or to establish a protectorate with exclusion of the other contracting State. This is his "Hinterland," or land back of the conventional line, which, in practice, becomes the prolongation towards the interior of the territory already occupied on the coast as far as the limit of the possessions of the other contracting State.

He finds that at bottom it is the repetition of ancient history having great analogy with the "spheres of influence" established in the fifteenth and sixteenth centuries among the colonizing nations of the Holy See and between Spain and Portugal by the Treaty of Tordesillas. The same writer is also of the opinion that, by means of such a process, Germany undertook to revive the process of fictitious occupation, by causing to be ascribed to her, by right and preference, vast territories of which she had occupied only certain points on the coast, thus reserving the freedom to make future extensions should she deem proper to follow up her first experiments. He thinks that the "Hinterland doctrine," being the result of a contract, can only be applied to the contracting countries.

The same writer also finds as a distinctive characteristic the acceptance of the conventional occupation, consequently fictitious, as regards large portions of land, which bring us back to the application of the right of contiguity, by virtue of which occupation of a point on the coast would give title to the region forming a geographical whole, according to its topographical and hydrographical characteristics.

What Great Britain pretends to claim in Guayana is no less than a "Hinterland," as though Spain had agreed to it at any time, while, on the contrary, she persistently opposed the advance of the Dutch on the province of Guayana.

No doubt of this will ever remain in the mind of whoever should carefully read the following words from Lord Salisbury's communication of the 26th of November, 1895:

> "It is of importance to notice that Sir R. Schomburgk did not discover or invent any new boundaries. He took particular care to fortify himself with the history of the case. *He had further, from actual exploration and information obtained from the Indians and from the evidence of local remains, as at Barima, and local traditions, as on the Cuyuni, fixed the limits of the Dutch possessions and the zone from which all trace of Spanish influence was absent.* On such data he based his reports."

Notwithstanding the fact that when Schomburgk visited Barima he did not find any manifestation of the presence of any sovereign power, but, at the most, alleged remnants of a former occupation, which, if it ever really existed, was as temporal and ephemeral as it was unauthorized (as we now know), Lord Salisbury wants, in the absence of vestiges of any Spanish influence thereon, to deprive Venezuela of a territory which, in the hands of Great Britain, as Schomburgk urged, would tend to secure the advantage of *controlling the mouth of the Orinoco*, as being in possession of it would be of great value in a *military* respect, as the peculiar configuration of the only channel (Boca de Navios) which admits vessels of some draught to the Orinoco passes near Point Barima. Major Macrea had already reported, in 1802, that entering the Orinoco by the southeast through the so-called Boca de Navios, Cape Barima is the southeastern point.

Spain never concluded with Holland treaties of this character, nor has Venezuela concluded any such with Great Britain. The pretension to apply such principles in this case is, therefore, without reason or justification.

No mention is made of any occupation existing when Schomburgk visited Barima. He states that he noticed there signs of former cultivation, and that the surroundings showed vestiges of ditches and some isolated yuca plants and annatto shrubs, which do not grow wild on lands subject to the influence of the tides. This stimulated his zeal in making inferences in support of the "indisputable" right of Great Britain to the Barima, and to all the rivers connected with it. That some Dutchmen went to Barima and began to cultivate the lands has already been mentioned, remarking on the subject that in 1768 Governor Centurion ejected them from the place, as Barima belonged to the Province of Guayana. *The Dutchmen never returned after this.*

If, for the reason that the Dutch were once there for a short time, as intruders, and were promptly kicked out by the Spanish authorities, England may now claim the Barima, how much more may Venezuela claim it, as the heir of Spain, who discovered it, and was there from 1530 onwards? Early in the sixteenth century Spain sent Caravals with 300 men, under the command of Pedro de Acosta (as stated by Rodway and Watt in their "Annals of Guiana," page 8), for the security of her possessions there. Its possession is now as indispensable to Venezuela as it then was to Spain.

It is pertinent here to repeat, with Monroe, that the American Continents, by reason of the free and independent state they had assumed and maintained prior to the declaration of 1823, are not to be considered thenceforth as subject to future colonization by any European power.

We must bear in mind what the "London Times" of November 11, 1896, said in reference to the acceptance of that doctrine in speaking of the terms upon which the United States had agreed upon for the settlement of the Venezuelan controversy, namely:

"It is to be remarked that Venezuela is not represented in the Tribunal which will decide upon her pretensions. The meaning and the importance of this settlement are obvious. It insures to this country (England) the practical advantage of dealing with a responsible and friendly Government, which has given evident proof of its desire to arrive at a friendly and lasting settlement. *From the point of view of the United States the arrangement is a most important concession made by Great Britain.* It admits the principle that, as regards the South American Republics, the United States not only can mediate in any dispute, but also can entirely substitute the primitive contending party and assume the exclusive direction of the negotiations. *Great Britain, of course, can not bind another nation by her conduct in this matter*, but she has also established a *precedent which, in the future, may be used against her with great effect*, and has strengthened the hands of the Government of the United States in any dispute that may hereafter arise between a South American Republic and a European power, and in which the United States may wish to interfere."

This is the acceptance of the Monroe Doctrine. Venezuela, however, *is* represented in the Arbitral Tribunal by Mr. Melville Weston Fuller, Chief Justice of the Supreme Court of the United States, whose appointment Venezuela made directly, and Mr. David Josiah Brewer, a member of the same Court, which appointed him as an Arbitrator at the request and with the concurrence of this Republic.

It is shown in a separate brief by Venezuela that the Cuyuni basin never belonged to Holland; that its countless cataracts served as an insurmountable obstacle to her extensions up the river; that the acts of Spain and the Netherlands establishes the title of His Catholic Majesty to the Cuyuni, notably, the act of expulsion of 1758; the continued and uninterrupted exercise of control there by Spain; the situation of the posts of the Dutch and their disappearance; the absence of occupation on that river; the acknowledgment of the Spanish possession; the erection of a Spanish fort near the mouth of the Curumo; the possession of the savannas by the missions; the legal status of an occupant coming after the first occupant to establish himself; the absurdity of the immense expansion that is now sought to give to the Dutch occupation; the meaning of Articles V and VI of the Treaty of Munster; the lack of foundation to the pretensions to Barima, etc.

From all that has been stated we conclude that Rule "*b*," by virtue of which the Arbitrators may recognize and give effect to rights and claims resting on any other ground whatever valid according to international law, and on any principles of international law which the Arbitrators may deem applicable to the case, and which are not in contravention of Rule "*a*"—that is, the rule which accepts as valid the title resting on adverse holding for fifty years, making equal to it the exclusive control or effective settlement of a district—does not nor can it be construed to refer but to the application of the rule of prescription which can not be separated from that of time, and without which this mode of acquisition by a State would not be justifiable.

CHAPTER XIX.

ARTICLE IV OF THE TREATY—RULE "c."

This rule is as follows:

"In determining the boundary line, if territory of one party be found by the Tribunal to have been at the date of this Treaty in the occupation of the subjects or citizens of the other party, such effect shall be given to such occupation as reason, justice, the principles of international law and the equities of the case shall, in the opinion of the Tribunal, require."

This rule was adopted as the result of the negotiations between the United States and Great Britain, looking to some just and equitable solution of the present stage of the controversy between the latter and Venezuela respecting their boundary line in Guayana. To this end, Lord Salisbury had proposed the creation of a Tribunal composed of four members, two of whom should be British subjects and two of whom should be American citizens, who should fix the dividing line between the two countries. Under his proposition, however, the proposed Tribunal would have been hampered by the condition that they could not include as Venezuelan territory any territory that on the 1st of January, 1887, should be found to be occupied *bona fide* by British subjects, nor as British territory any territory *bona fide* occupied by Venezuelan citizens on the same date.

Mr. Olney, after carefully considering this proposition, very wisely declared it to be unacceptable. (See his communication of June 12, 1896.) Venezuela had likewise used arguments on a similar basis to show that if such a contingency should arise she could not be held responsible for any indemnity that might be claimed on that account.

It was objected at the time that, even in case the Tribunal of four should find that a certain territory belonged to Venezuela, it would still depend upon the good pleasure of Great Britain, upon her generosity, her sense of justice, her caprice, or her view of expediency generally, whether Venezuela should really obtain that territory.

In a second communication, Mr. Olney insisted on the fact that in no way had even a clew been given for the determination of *bona fide* occupation. It could not be the occupation effected under a temporary or revokable mining license, beginning December 31, 1886; because the claims of Venezuela having been always matters of public notoriety, a British subject could not establish a *bona fide* domicile, as against Venezuela, by showing that, in point of fact, he had never heard of them.

The pointed objection of Mr. Olney was against the fundamental condition that the boundary line decided by the Tribunal to be the true one, could not operate upon territory *bona fide* occupied by a British subject on the 1st of January, 1887. The reciprocal application of this condition, such as Great Britain had asked and Venezuela had opposed, would inevitably result in the former's interest, while those of Venezuela would be sacrificed.

Mr. Olney said that the true solution would be found in some rule, just in itself, without reference to its actual working, so that Great Britain would not be able to impose her will upon Venezuela. He did not find any support to the proposed rule, either in any principle of international law or in any recognized international usage, it being a rule hardly to be insisted upon unless its practical application were supposed to extend to many persons and to cover large interests. Yet, if the facts were not to be ignored, nor the ordinary rules of law set aside, its scope should be limited. The so-called Schomburgk line had been proclaimed for the first time as an *ex parte* boundary in October, 1886; yet, in June, 1887, in contradiction to this, the Governor of British Guiana, by express instructions from the home Government, addressed the Court of Policy of the Colony of British Guiana in the following terms:

"Before we proceed to the order of the day I am anxious to make a statement with reference to the question of the boundary between this Colony and the Republic of Venezuela. Among the applications which have been received for mining licenses and concessions under the mining regulations passed under ordinance 16 of 1880, 16 of 1886, and 4 of 1887, there are many which apply to lands which are within the territory in dispute between Her Majesty's Government and the Venezuelan Republic. I have received instructions from the Secretary of State to caution expressly all persons interested in such licenses or concessions, or otherwise acquiring an interest in the disputed territory, that all licenses, concessions, or grants applying to any portion of such disputed territory will be issued, and must be accepted, subject to the possibility that, in the event of a settlement of the present disputed boundary line, the land to which such licenses, concessions, or grants applies may become a part of the Venezuelan territory; in which case no claim or compensation from the Colony or from Her Majesty's Government can be recognized; but Her Majesty's Government would, of course, do whatever may be right and practicable to secure from the Government of Venezuela a recognition and confirmation of licenses, etc., now issued."

From this Mr. Olney concluded that the equity of any British subject must have accrued during the eight months between October, 1886, and June, 1887; and he thinks that this *bona fide* on the part of a British subject is quite immaterial, since it is the *bona fide* of either *Government* that is important, and not that of private individuals. Assuming it to be true that there were British subjects settled in the territory which they may have had reason to believe to be British, the grounds for such belief were certainly not derived from Venezuela, but must have emanated solely from the British Government, and if British subjects had been deceived by the assurances of their own Government, that was a matter wholly between them and their own Government, and in no way concerned Venezuela. Venezuela was not to be stripped of her rightful possessions because the British Government had erroneously encouraged its subjects to believe that such possessions were British.

Mr. Olney held that there was but one possible contingency under which a claim of that sort by Great Britain could have even a semblance of plausibility; and that was, if it could be shown that the alleged assertion of jurisdiction, on the faith of which British subjects had made settlements in territory subsequently ascertained to be Venezuelan, could be shown to have been in any way assented to or acquiesced in by Venezuela. But the fact was notoriously the other way. Venezuela's claims and protests had been constant, persistent, and emphatic; and had been enforced by all the means practicable or possible within the reach of a weak power as against a strong one, even going so far as to break diplomatic relations. It was Mr. Olney's opinion, that only by being amended in certain important particulars could the proposal of Lord Salisbury be made to meet the equities and justice of the case. And he concluded his note by stating that the proviso by which the boundary line is not to include territory *bona fide* occupied by British subjects or citizens of either of the two parties on the 1st of January, 1887, should be stricken out altogether, and the following substituted for it:

"Provided, however, that in fixing such line, if territory of one party be found in the occupation of the subjects or citizens of the other party such weight and effect shall be given to such occupation as reason, justice, the rules of international law, and the equities of the particular case may appear to require."

Mr. Olney suggested the suppression of the proviso prepared by Lord Salisbury, after having made clear the reasons why it was inexpedient, viz., that no clew had been given to ascertain the *bona fide* of private individuals. *Bona fide* on the part of private individuals is immaterial. It is the *bona fide* of the Government that is important, because, otherwise, the results would depend on the generosity, sense of justice, caprice or convenience of Great Britain, being advantageous to her and detrimental to Venezuela; because there is no reason why Great Britain should impose her will upon Venezuela; because the rule is not based either on international law or on any recognized international usage, Her Majesty's Government having declared that neither the Home Government nor the Government of the Colony would recognize any claims for compensation in case that lands granted for mining purposes, etc., should be adjudged to Venezuela; because Venezuela never assented to the jurisdiction previously claimed by Great Britain on said territories, but, on the contrary, had protested repeatedly and had even broken diplomatic relations in consequence.

But if this be so, then justice and the rules of international law demand that no value whatsoever shall be given to such occupations.

There is something more, however. The British Government had actually notified its subjects that neither it nor the Colony would admit any claims for indemnification of the interested parties should such occupation be lost. How, then, can it be reasonably or justly contended that Venezuela should recognize such claims? She did not grant the licenses; she did not seduce the grantees or squatters or claimants into error. On the contrary, notwithstanding the repeated protests and admonitions of the Venezuelan Government, the British did not heed them; so British subjects exposed themselves deliberately to the consequences of their own conduct. What Great Britain declared not to be her duty towards her own subjects can not be made the duty of Venezuela toward British subjects.

There is no lack of arguments to show want of legality in such occupation as is here under discussion.

According to the publicists who have treated the subject of occupation, two essential conditions are required for it; one is that the thing, the acquisition of which is aspired to, should not belong to any one, should be *res nullius;* the other is, that possession must be taken *corpore et anima*, in order to become possessor of a thing in accordance to the legal requirements.

The present question deals with territories, and we have shown elsewhere that there was none open to occupation in the Guayana region.

Again, it can not be acquired but by whoever has legal capacity for so doing; and this legal capacity belongs to the State, not to private individuals.

International domain being the right of a nation to make use of, to take the products of, to dispose of a territory to the exclusion of other nations, to rule over it as a sovereign power independently of any foreign power, it is indispensable that such privileges be beyond the reach of private individuals. Even States themselves, when possessors of immovable property on the territory of another, hold such possession in the capacity of a private individual, subject to the local laws. They have no right of domain over property belonging to their subjects on foreign soil, such property being under the laws of the country where they are situated.

Solomon, in his work on "Occupation of Territories Without an Owner," discusses at length (Part 2d, Section III), "whether corporations or simple individuals are incapacitated to acquire rights of sovereignty, either by occupation or treaty," and concludes as follows:

"The principle, then, is this: when a private individual or a company settles in a desert country, not by order of a State, and not acting in the capacity of *negotio cum gestor*, the occupation insures them only title of private property; there is no principle of law which will prevent them from acquiring at length right of sovereignty. According to circumstances, a new Colony or a new State will be formed. Previous to becoming a State, it may fall under the colonial control of a State already formed, and become a *Charter Colony*, such as Borneo, or a *Crown Colony*, such as Assab. The Charter Colony is the Colony possessing a charter of protection, such as the German possessions in the east of Africa.

"When a State is the occupant, it will acquire either mere rights of property or right of control, or both, at one and the same time, according to the nature of the *animus domini;* that is to say, according to the intention. Acquisition of sovereignty may be followed by acquisition of property even in the absence of a special *animus*, and in conformity with a rule of public or private internal law."

Phillimore (Chapter XII), on the right of acquisition, affirms repeatedly the same doctrine. He says:

"Discovery, according to the acknowledged practice of nations, whether originally founded upon *comity* or *strict* right, furnishes an inchoate title to possession in the discoverer. *But the discoverer must either, in the first instance, be fortified by the public authority and by a commission from the State of which he is a member, or his discovery must be subsequently adopted by that State;* otherwise, it does not fall, with respect to the protection of the individual, under the cognizance of international law, except in a limited degree; that is to say, the *individual* has a *natural* right to be undisturbed in the possession of the territory which he occupies as against all *third* powers. It will be a question belonging to the municipal law of his own country whether such possessions do not belong to her, and whether he must not hold them under her authority and by her permission. Such would be the case with the possessions of an English subject."

* * * * * * *

And again—

"In the various discussions which took place between the United States and Great Britain with respect to title to the Oregon Territory, the title resulting from discovery was attempted to be pushed far beyond the limits of this doctrine, even to the extent of maintaining that first discovery by a *non-commissioned merchant-ship* gave priority to the claims of America to these regions. But such a position appears opposed to all the authorities upon International Law, and it was steadily denied by Great Britain."

"The *inchoate title*, then, must in the first place be fortified by the previous commission or confirmed by the subsequent ratification of the State to which the discoverer belongs."

The Institute of International Law agreed on the 7th of September, 1888, to the following project of international declaration relating to territorial occupation:

"Article I. Occupation of a territory in the capacity of sovereignty shall not be recognized as effective, unless it has the following considerations:

"1st. Possession of any territory within certain limits *effected in the name of the Government.*

"2d. Official notification of the effected possession."

* * * * * * *

In the "Theoretical and Practical Study of Occupation as a means of acquiring territories under international law," a book published in Paris in 1896, by Gaston Jèze, LL. D., we find the following (page 116, No. 1, Section II), "Who may experience the *animus domini?* The effect of occupation is acquisition of sovereignty. It is perfectly evident that the occupation can be effected by him who may be invested with a title of sovereignty, in a word, by him who may experience the *animus domini.*" By the Roman law only persons *sui juris* could acquire by themselves. The persons, *alieni juris* were incapacitated from holding their own patrimony, being, therefore, unable to increase it. Acquisition by occupation was forbidden to them at least on their own right. Those forming this class were: 1st, slaves and servants; 2d, minors; 3d, free persons admitted to any jurisdiction, *manus mancipium,* etc. Such persons could only acquire in behalf of those under whose jurisdiction they were submitted. We hold that public international law offers the same criterion. There are persons *sui juris* and persons *alieni juris*. To the first belong the States and the States alone; in the second, we must place the citizens of the different States and members of private societies."

"In other words, in order to be able to experience the *animus domini*, in order to be capable to occupy under international law, it is required to be a State, but this necessary condition is also sufficient in itself."

I. The condition is necessary. This is equivalent to saying:

"(1) *That a State may experience the animus domini.* (2) *That the State alone may experience the animus domini.*

"To state this, suffices: The notion of State and the notion of sovereignty are inseparable. *The State alone may experience the animus domini.* All others are incapable of it, whether private parties or commercial and colonization companies."

There is this note at the foot:

"*A priori*, if the legislature of the country of the private individual should forbid him to acquire in his own name rights of sovereignty. This is what takes place in England. This is, in fact, what Dudley Field states, § 77: 'When Englishmen settle in a country (be it civilized or barbarian), they must carry with them not only the right but the sovereignty of the State from whence they originate.' Cready, in his recent work on 'The Imperial and Colonial Constitutions of the British Empire' (page 66, *et seq.*), confirms this point: 'When British subjects take possession of a desert country, they effect it in virtue of powers derived from the State, and can not remain faithful to their duty as subjects should they take possession of a territory in virtue of an act emanating from their own will.' * * * 'Neither an English subject nor a company of English subjects can acquire for their own control, either by treaty or conquest."

Supposing there had been territories *nullius* in Guayana and that British subjects had settled thereon, *gratia argumendi*, the occupants would not have acquired for themselves, but for the Crown; and if this be the case, Great Britain would have no excuse for demanding an idemnification from Venezuela for what the British subjects might lose. Moreover, the British would lose nothing, because they had acquired nothing. And should they lose what the British Government, believing to be its own property had given to its subjects, it devolves upon that Government to bear the consequences. Should the British Government be deprived, by the verdict of the Tribunal, of any part of territory of which it had taken possession, by what principle, either of law or of reason, could Venezuela be held responsible for damages which England might have caused her subjects?

But there are no *nullius* lands in Guayana, although there are lands in dispute by Venezuela and Great Britain. In regard to these, the latter proposed, and her proposition was accepted by Venezuela in 1850, that neither of the two parties would occupy nor encroach upon these disputed lands. This shows clearly that no British subject could have legitimately settled on the disputed territory; and, if they settled there, it would have been an infraction of that Agreement, and instead of receiving a reward for such trespass, rather deserve punishment.

It was, perhaps, these persons to whom Lord Salisbury referred when he stated, in his note of November 26, 1895, addressed to Sir Julian Pauncefote, British Embassador in Washington (to be communicated to the American Government), the following:

"The Venezuelan Minister replied in February, 1881, by proposing a line which commenced on the coast a mile to the north of the Moroco river, and followed certain parallels and meridians inland, bearing a general resemblance to the proposal made by Lord Aberdeen in 1844. Señor Rojas' proposal was referred to the Lieutenant-Governor and Attorney-General of British Guiana, who were then in England, and they presented an elaborate report showing that *in the thirty-five years which had elapsed since Lord Aberdeen's proposed concession natives and others had settled in the territory under the belief that they would enjoy the benefits of British rule and that it was impossible to assent to any such concessions as Señor Rojas's line would involve.* They, however, proposed an alternative line, which involved considerable reductions of that laid down by Sir R. Schomburgk."

Here, it is admitted that from about 1850 to 1881, and also thereafter, both foreigners and British subjects have been settling on territory within the projected line of Lord Aberdeen; thus constituting a flagrant violation of the Agreement proposed by Great Britain and accepted by Venezuela, notwithstanding the former's solemn promise neither to order or sanction such occupations. And it is one of these same authorities, the Governor of British Guiana, to whom, first of all, the aforesaid orders were sent, who comes to oppose obstacles to the proposition of Señor Rojas, because occupations which he had been positively commanded *not* to sanction had been effected.

Lord Salisbury closes his note by stating that Her Majesty's Government "can not consent to entertain or to submit to the arbitration of another power or of foreign jurists, however eminent, claims based on the extravagant pretensions of Spanish officials in the last century, and involving the transfer of large numbers of British subjects (who have *for many years enjoyed the settled rule of a British Colony*), to a nation of different race and language, whose political system is subject to frequent disturbance, and whose institutions as yet too often afford very inadequate protection to life and property."

So, then, Great Britain may take possession of any uninhabited lands of Venezuela that she may see fit, settle them with English subjects, and then refuse to give them back on the plea that these subjects had remained there for say thirty-five years under her rule, and that Venezuela was a country of different race and language, and subject to frequent political disturbances? Such aggressions justified by such a plea would unsettle titles to half the American Continent.

It might not be amiss to recall here what Lord Macauley says in his "History of England" in reference to the Scotch expedition of Patterson in 1699 to the Spanish Isthmus of Darien, because of his opinions on this point. His remarks, though severe, fit the present case precisely. But we forbear.

In the banquet speech, already referred to, Lord Salisbury, speaking of the Agreement with the United States relative to the Guayana controversy, said:

"But, as you know, in the discussion we have had with the United States in the name of their friends, the Venezuelans, the question has been, not if there would be arbitration, but if arbitration could have application without obstacle; and we have always claimed that those who, leaving aside the historic rights, had the inherent right to establishments already formed to colonize districts, ought to be excluded from the arbitration. Our difficulty during many months has consisted in finding the way to define the colonized districts, and a solution has been found—I believe it has come from the Government represented by Your Excellency (the United States Minister), and it is, that we must treat the Colonial Empire just as we treat individuals; that the same lapse of time protecting individuals in civil life from the attacks against their titles should protect the English Colony from the attacks against her. *And besides this, that where no claims could be laid to the lapse of time, even when the title was examined, concession would be made in equity in consideration of the inchoate right. This is a very simple solution.*"

This would seem to indicate that the occupation to which the speaker referred will have the effect of prescription, even though it lack the period of fifty years agreed upon.

But rule "c" does not admit of the extension that it is pretended to give it. International prescription being a mode of acquisition from one State to another is not applicable to *private individuals.* This is just the same as in the case of occupation.

Let us consider what Ortolan says in his work frequently mentioned (Chapter IV), in reference to prescriptive acquisition: "By analogous reasons in international law prescription must be held in the capacity of owner and sovereign of the territory. *It would not suffice, for instance, that some individuals belonging to the nation should have in their own name performed acts of private ownership in that territory; it is necessary that possession be effected in the name of the State, and accompanied by such acts of enjoyment, dominion and jurisdiction as constitute the exercise of international dominion.*"

In the case under consideration the British subjects whose occupancy the Lieutenant-Governor and the Attorney-General of British Guiana reported to Her Majesty's Government, not only lacked authorization, but they were acting in their own name and in opposition to the solemn obligations of their sovereign; otherwise, their sovereign would not have been kept in ignorance of their proceedings.

"The attempts to recover, in fact, possession of the disputed territory," says the writer cited, "would, with greater reason, be a cause for the interruption of prescription, even though they may not have succeeded; *it is required that the attempts should have been made in the name of the State as a public undertaking so recognized by it, and not by mere individuals acting without authority and in a private capacity.*" Private individuals are not competent by international law, either to acquire title by prescription or to interrupt it.

To bring this point to a close we will quote other doctrines of E. Ortolan, found in the pamphlet already alluded to. He says:

"Private occupation, moreover, has at present scarcely any occasion to be applied to the soil. Even in America the lands that the colonists will clear and cultivate are either sold to them at a nominal price or are granted to them by the Government of the country; theirs is the right of concession and not the right of first occupation. What we have just said in reference to this means of acquiring land, as regards private property, exists in theory, so to speak, or may be found in primitive times, of which we only speak by conjecture."

This coincides with Article 453 of the Civil Code of Venezuela, according to which "all the lands lying within its territorial limits and having no other owner belong to the private domain of the nation," and also agrees with Article 1st of the law relating to public lands, by which it is stated that public lands are those lands which, lying within the limits of the nation, have no legitimate owner; that is to say, that do not belong to citizens individually or to corporations.

It also agrees with the principle in force in Great Britain where, by the Constitution, title to all such lands is considered as invested in the Crown as the representative of the nation, for in the nation resides exclusively the faculty to grant them as a branch of the Royal prerogative. The same principle has been recognized in the United States.

In France all territory not susceptible of private ownership is considered as public property, as well as all the vacant lands without owners, and those of deceased persons without heirs, or whose successions are abandoned. (Articles 538 and 539 of the Civil Code.) The same in Italy. (Articles 427, 428 and 429, Civil Code.)

Mr. Delavan says: "It is a principle of law that only the States can exercise sovereign rights, the most important of which being the right of territorial possession, which can not be called by a more exact name than right of sovereignty, the corollary of which is the right of annexation. This right belongs exclusively to the State."

Jèze, in quoting this passage, adds that such opinion has in its favor the authority of Bluntschli, who declares (in § 278 of his work) that "The sovereignty over territories not forming part of any State is acquired through the taking possession thereof by a *determinate State.*" "From this we may infer," he continues, "1st, that the territory occupied by a private individual or a private corporation, whatever be their claims to sovereignty, is *nullius;* 2d, that the occupation can not emanate from a private individual or a private company." On the other hand, § 279 leaves no doubt in this regard: "The taking possession can be effected *in the name and by express authority of the State,* but on condition that" * * * "if the colonists have acted without authority their acts must be ratified by the State upon which they depend. In §§ 280, 281 *et seq.*, the eminent jurist supposes that the subject of the occupation is a State."

The paragraphs which Dudley Field devotes to occupation are conceived in the same spirit. They always deal with a State which takes possession of a territory not subjected to another State's control.

Tèze, in several other places in his work devoted to occupation, deals with the same doctrine. For instance, on pages 204 and 205, he treats of the hypothetical case of a private individual, with a certain number of companions that land in a country occupied by a barbarian State. He falls upon the occupants, destroys their army, overthrows their government, and either reduces them to subjection or exterminates them, and finally proclaims himself sovereign of the country.

Jèze asks: "What is the value of this claim?" He answers: "There is a certain point, to wit, that the territory becomes *nullius* from the standpoint of public international law. An occupation is then possible. But, can this be effected by an individual acting in his private capacity? No; because he is incapable of having *animus domini*. Let us recur to the first hypothesis, and the country will not cease to be *nullius*, but the very day when the collectivity becomes a State, the title of acquisition of sovereignty will be occupation. We have arrived at this conclusion: Private individuals and private societies, being incapable of having *animus domini*, can not acquire in their own name rights of sovereignty over territories. What part does the *animus domini* play in this matter of occupation, judging from the standpoint of international law? In the hands of the powerful it is an instrument for acquisition."

On page 205 of Jèze, from which we have made the foregoing extract, there is a foot-note reading as follows:

> "The principles developed in the text are a condensation of the claims presented by certain adventurers on territory over which they proclaim themselves as sovereigns. (See the very recent case, August, 1895, of Baron Harden-Hickey in regard to an island called Trinidad.)"

Baron Harden-Hickey had taken possession of the island, and, calling himself its sovereign, addressed several Governments, soliciting their recognition of him as such. Of course, no one paid any attention to this request.

This is the same island of which Great Britain also took possession in 1895, with the object of making fast a submarine cable; it had been discovered in the sixteenth century by Portuguese sailors. The British occupied it temporarily in 1782, abandoning their pretensions later.

All the attempts made to cultivate and settle it being fruitless, it was, to all appearances, abandoned. But, as the Brazilian Government had always maintained its intention to hold possession of it as part of the Brazilian domain, it was thus recognized by Lord Salisbury in 1896, through the Cabinet of Lisbon, which had mediated in the question.

This brings to mind the ridiculous attempt of M. de Foumens, who, in 1860, went to Araucania, held conference with the savage chiefs, caused himself to be proclaimed as "King" of Araucania and Patagonia, appointed ministers, formulated a constitution, and gave himself the title of Orllie Antonio I., all under the pretext that the tribes of both regions were independent. But the Government of Chili, to whom he had the effrontery to notify his advent to the throne he had just established, shut him up in prison.

A similar farce was attempted in 1886 by the French journalist, Jules Gros, who caused himself to be appointed President of the Republic of Cumania, endeavored to take immigrants there, and who, according to the newspapers, had also instituted an order of chivalry, for which a reasonable amount was paid, in order to defray expenses of the enterprise. But it seems that France, in 1887, in concert with Brazil, put an end to the farce.

In his work on "Codified International Law," Fiori says (No. 352):

"The discovery of a desert and unoccupied country, made by private individuals, without order of their Government, without their support or approval, can not be considered or effected in the name of the State to which the explorer belongs, neither as giving right of preference in regard to any other State. If this Government, however, being informed of the discovery made by one of its subjects, has notified, through the diplomatic channels, to the other Government its intention to profit by the discovery and to effect occupation, its rights to the country must be recognized in preference to any other, whenever its passivity be not prolonged during a period sufficient to give rise to the presumption that said Government is not able or does not wish to make effective its projects of occupation."

Let us now present some remarks derived from the Venezuelan, French, and Italian legislations, According to the Civil Code of Venezuela (Article 469), "the owner of the piece of property upon which another person has, with his own materials, either built, sowed, or planted has a right to make such improvements his own, or to compel the party who made them to destroy them. Should the owner elect to use the first of the rights above mentioned, he must either pay the value of the materials and labor or for the increase in value attained by the property. *Should the owner elect to make use of the second right, the destruction of the improvements are to be made at the expense of the person who made them, who is liable for damages by reason of the damages the property may have suffered.*"

Article No. 686: "The *bona fide* possessor makes the profits his own, and is under obligation to restore only what he receives in this respect after he has been made cognizant of the suit against him."

Article 687: "The possessor, though he be so in good faith, can not claim any indemnity whatever by reason of the improvements he has made if such improvements do not exist at the time of the eviction."

The French Code (Article 555) and the Italian Code (Article 450) both make the same provisions.

According to Articles 362 and 363 of the Spanish Civil Code, "Whoever builds, plants, or sows in bad faith on a territory of some one else forfeits whatever he may have built, planted, or sowed, and the owner of the land on which such building, planting, or sowing in bad faith has been effected, may demand the demolition of the buildings or the destruction of the plantation, restoring everything to its primitive state at the expense of the one who so built, planted, or sowed."

Article 451. "The *bona fide* possessor makes the profits his own while such possession is not legally interrupted."

Article 452.' 'If at the time the good faith ceases there should be forthcoming some natural or industrial products, the possessor shall be entitled to the expense incurred by him for their production and to a share besides of the net proceeds of the crop in proportion to the time of the possession."

Among the Romans, whoever built with his own materials on some one else's ground, if he be a *bona fide* possessor and the building were in his possession, he could retain it until the owner of the ground paid him the price of the materials; if he were a possessor in bad faith, he received nothing for the materials, losing his control by reason of his fraud, which consisted in building in bad faith in full knowledge that it was some one else's ground.

Pradier-Fordére, in his unfinished work, "A Treatise on European and American International Law," Vol. II, No. 866, asserts that the same principle has been adopted by the law of nations. He says:

"International domain may be recovered against any and all possessors, even the possessor in good faith, without there being any need for reimbursement of the price paid for acquisition. 'From the things existing in nature,' says Grotius, 'springs the obligation incumbent upon the possessor of a thing belonging to us to do all in his power, so that it may come back to us.' * * * Property always carries with it such things as are natural to it, among which is found *that every possessor is under obligation to restore to its owner everything of which he is possessed. The profits must also be restored after deducting the expenses.* Heffter states that, while adopting Grotius' opinion in that respect, he only takes notes of the principles of justice approved by all leading nations, possession not being able to take the legal character or control, at least in an absolute manner. He then concludes that the necessary and useful expenses made by the possessor in good faith to the benefit of the thing not compensated by the profits thereof must be reintegrated. The *bona fide* possessor receives the benefit of the profits made by him before the suit, when the owner has been silent, as it is surmised by reason of his passivity that he has ratified the possession and can not impugn acts accomplished by reason of said passivity. This is really a theory in conformity with the principles of justice which is one for private individuals and the States. But in applying it in practice we must not lose sight of the fact that there are no judicial means to compel States to fulfill their obligations. The success of the recovery will depend, after all, upon the material force of the one who recovers."

Upon invoking this authority, it is well to state that it can not be imputed to Venezuela that she has been inactive in the present case, as it has been shown that she was not aware of the occupation referred to, and it seems that even Great Britain did not know of it. In the passage already quoted of Lord Salisbury's communication, explaining the reason why the proposition made in 1881 by the Venezuelan Minister, Doctor José Maria Rojas, was not accepted, notwithstanding its similarity to the one made to Mr. Fortique, in 1844, by Lord Aberdeen, it is stated that, after consultation with the Governor and the Attorney-General of British Guiana, who were then in London, they submitted an elaborate report that "*in the thirty-five years which had elapsed since Lord Aberdeen's proposed concession, natives and others had settled in the territory under the belief that they would enjoy the benefits of British rule, and that it was impossible to assent to any such concessions as Señor Rojas' line would involve.*"

It is evident, then, that had not the Governor and the Attorney-General of British Guiana (who were in London during the negotiations of Doctor Rojas and Lord Granville in 1881) made that report, her Majesty's Government would have continued to be unaware of the colonization made by her subjects and others on districts which the British had agreed to maintain closed to all occupation pending the boundary controversy.

It is proper to remember that Doctor Rojas' requests to continue the discussion of the question were not heeded; the British Foreign Office stating (under date of April 23, 1880) that the Attorney-General for British Guiana, being expected shortly in that country, "Her Majesty's Government would prefer to postpone the discussion of these questions until the arrival of that officer."

The arbitrators, in applying Rule "c," must not lose sight of the opinion of the British Cabinet in this matter, as expressed in the Memorandum sent to Doctor Pulido (page 442, of the Blue Book No. 1), namely, that "Her Majesty's Government in offering that certain portions of their claim beyond that line should be submitted to arbitration, expressed their willingness to exclude from the proposed reference those valuable districts in the neighborhood of Guacipati, which, although falling within their claim, have for some time been in Venezuelan occupation, *and in regard to which an Arbitral decision adverse to Venezuela might have caused her considerable embarrassment, and would have involved heavy pecuniary claims on the part of Great Britain on account of revenue received in past years.*"

This is equivalent to maintaining that whoever has enjoyed the possession of a territory subsequently found not to be his, must indemnify the owner for the benefits derived from its enjoyment, instead of having a claim against the owner for indemnification for the losses to which he has voluntarily exposed himself.

In short, English subjects who may have occupied territories in dispute between Venezuela and Great Britain, whether they have acted knowingly or in error to which they were led by their Government, notwithstanding said Government's solemn Agreement of 1850 to respect said territory and command that it be respected, such English subjects, we say, have committed an evident violation of such obligation, and so have been incapacitated for acquiring any rights on lands forbidden to their access. Nor can they merit the protection of their Cabinet, which by not compelling their subordinates, either natives or foreigners, to abide by the Agreement entered into earnestly and spontaneously, has taken upon itself the consequences of the act.

We are confident that the Arbitrators will rule that neither "reason" nor "justice," nor "the principles of international law," nor "equity" can give the British any right to claims against Venezuela should the contingency alluded to arise.

APPENDIX I.

List of Accompanying Documents.

1st. Copy of the document in regard to the Orders issued by the Spanish Government to prevent the French from extending their possessions in the Province of Guayana.

2d. Royal Decree of the 1st of October, 1780, in regard to the inspection and colonization of the eastern part of the lower Orinoco.

3d. Dutch documents relating principally to the Moroco.

4th. Acts of jurisdiction exercised by the Spanish authorities in Barima and Guayana.

5th. New documents found in the archives of Caracas, relating to the fort of Cuyuni.

6th. Lists of the maps relating to the Guayana boundary question, classified according to the lines which they indicate.

CARACAS, November 10, 1897.

Royal Decree of the 1st of October, 1780, on the Inspection and Colonization of the Eastern Part of the Lower Orinoco.

Although the papers on board the brig "Nuestra Señora del Rosario" were lost, as well as the other two ships that escorted her from the port of La Guaira, bound for Spain, the captain of the above-mentioned brig, Don José Felipe de Inciarte, was able to save the letter of the 12th of last April, which Your Excellency gave him to present to me and inform me of the result of his commission with regard to the inspection and colonization of the lands in the eastern part of the lower Orinoco; all of which he has done verbally, besides delivering to me the original drafts (which he also saved) of the diary, map, and report which your Excellency made on the 27th of November of the past year. And, having informed the King of the contents of these documents, His Majesty has resolved that the above-mentioned Inciarte shall return with the object that you shall, when you so find it convenient, commission him again for the same end of inspecting and colonizing the places specified in your mentioned report of the 27th of November ult.; also to erect two provisional forts, which Your Excellency thought necessary—one for the protection against any attempt at insult from the Hollanders of the Essequibo to the Colony about to to be founded, as proposed in said report, to be erected near the inlet of the small river or stream of Moruca, at the distance of a quarter of a league from the post or guard of the Hollanders, advanced about eighteen leagues from Essequibo, towards the Orinoco, said first fort to be situated at the highest point and overlooking the spot to be occupied by the settlement and its suburbs; and the second fort, with four or six cannons, to be situated on the same inlet of the river Moruca, in order to bar the way to any of the vessels of the enemy; eject the Hollanders from said post or guard which they have there erected, it being well understood that, should the Director-General or Governor of Esquibo complain of this act, he shall be answered to the effect that this method of procedure has been and is in accordance with general laws and instructions for the good administration of our Indians, which does not allow the intrusion of foreigners on Spanish domains, for the same would be said here should any complaint or claim be made by the States-General of Holland.

Five hundred *pesos sencillos* have been delivered to the before-mentioned Inciarte, which he stated were necessary for the voyage; and, that he might depart more honored, the King has deigned to confer upon him the rank of Lieutenant of Infantry of the army, the commission of which has been issued and delivered to him, together with this Royal Decree, that he may place them in the hand of Your Excellency with the enclosed letters of instruction for that Captain-General and the Governor of Guayana, in which they are charged to aid, with the utmost despatch and efficiency, Your Excellency, as well as your Commissioner, in order that the objects of this commission may be completely fulfilled with that promptness and exactness so much to be desired in the service of His Majesty. All of which I inform Your Excellency, by his royal command, for Your Excellency's information and fulfillment of the part corresponding to Your Excellency.

May God save Your Mercy many years.

SAN ILDEFONSO, October 1, 1780.

JOSÉ DE GÁLVEZ.

To the Intendant of Caracas.

Dutch Documents Principally Relating to the Moroco.

INTRODUCTION.

I.

We confirm by these presents the orders already given several times to cultivate friendly feelings with the Indians, which same may be of great service in recovering fugitive slaves, and as it appears to the Representative and Directors to be most necessary to attract the Indians and maintain friendly feelings in them that they may be always at the service of the Government, upon which the security of both Colonies so greatly depends, it has been deemed necessary to order this by these presents to you very earnestly.

We believe it to be the more necessary to repeat these orders, in that they have been so badly fulfilled that even the staffs with silver knobs, which were sent to be presented to the chiefs of the Indians, have not been distributed to them, notwithstanding the express orders of the Representative and Directors, as seen in the inventory corresponding to the year 1776, which has been sent to us.

Besides this, the Representative and Directors are informed that the Indian chiefs never, or at least rarely, present themselves, because they are not invited to do so, this being, nevertheless, very necessary, and that for this reason the trifles (or toys) sent remain for the greater part in the shops (according to the inventory sent), while it would be expedient to present, from time to time, these trifles to the Indian chiefs in order to stimulate them to present themselves.

From a letter sent by the Representative and Directors of the West India Company, in the Council of Zeeland, dated from Middlebourg, on the 20th of June, 1777, and addressed to the Director-General and Council of the Colony of Essequibo.

II.

(*Translation.*)

Whereas the Representative and Directors in their resolution passed in the last meeting of the Ten, on the 25th of June, 1778, after having seen the letters of Director-General Trotz and Council, dated November 11, 1777, and a separate one from Director-General Trotz, dated the 8th of January, 1778, and from the Commanding Captain Severyn, dated November 22, 1777, have resolved and decreed that in the western part of the stream or river Moroco a post shall be established, fitted with four or five cannon, of eight pounds caliber, with the necessary ammunition, and held by a trustworthy corporal, an artilleryman and three soldiers detached by the Commanding Captain according to orders of the Director-General, and supplied monthly with the necessary provisions from the stores of the Company in Flag Island, and supplied daily with necessary water from the old post or trading station of Moroco.

That, whereas, the Representative and Directors, in the supposition that said post has been or will be very shortly established (in accordance with the plans sent from Demerara), are willing to allow a cannon to be placed on the point of the Island Arovabisi and another on the point of Hammack, to the effect that in case of flight of any slaves that proper notice of the same shall be given to the garrison, above-mentioned, of Moroco.

And that the Representative and Directors have agreed also to give to the person that the Director-General and Council should deem proper, the title of Titular Official of the Militia, that he may take command of a Burmudian sailing vessel, fitted out with a crew of ten mulatoes, and armed with six two or three-pounders, which vessel shall remain in the vicinity of the new post of Moroco, in order to pursue the slaves in their flight, providing that the costs, arming and maintenence of said vessel shall be defrayed by the product of gavels and minor taxes of the Colony.

It has been deemed expedient to ask for a report from the Director-General and Council of Essequibo, and of the Commander and Council of Demerara, minutely detailed, as to whether there is need of establishing at the west of Essequibo, on the seacoast, any military posts between Hammack Point and the river or creek of Moroco, where, at times, the slaves pass who are fleeing in boats towards the Orinoco.—(From the minutes of the meeting of the Directors of the West India Company, Friday, May 7, 1779.)

III.

(*Translation.*)

List of the districts of the public highways in Essequibo, 1808 :

1. Eastern part of Leguan Island.
2. Western part of Leguan Island.
3. Eastern part of Wakenam.
4. Western part of Wakenam.
5. West coast from the !Supenam creek to the Oena creek.
6. West coast from the Oena creek to the Manistáy plantation, inclusive.
7. West coast from the Manistáy plantation to No. 1, on the Arovabisi coast.
8. On the new western coast of Arovabisi from the plantation No. 1, inclusive, to where the public highways stop.

(Decree of Lieutenant-Governor Robert Nicholson, in regard to the division of the Colony into districts for the keeping of the public highways and bridges.)

IV.

(*Translation.*)

To the Governor-General of the river and lands of Orinoco and other establishments of His Catholic Majesty the King of Spain on the Guayana coast, etc.

Most High, Noble, and Just Sir :

Whereas our Sovereign, the High and Mighty Lords, the General States of the United Netherlands have, on the 23d of June of the past year, made an Agreement in Aranjuez with His Catholic Majesty the King of Spain, with regard to the extradition and deliverance of fugitive slaves from the Spanish Colonies and of our own in the West Indies: and whereas the confirmation of said Agreement has been sent to us, we have the honor to inform Your Excellency of the same and to send you a copy thereof.

We have no doubt, however, that Your Excellency shall have received already the necessary notice in regard to this matter; and in this belief we hope that the bearer of this letter will receive from Your Excellency all the facility and aid to recover several negro slaves who have fled from Essequibo and Demerara to Orinoco, for which purpose he has received our order to observe the stipulations in the mentioned Agreement.

We are disposed, on our part, to strictly fulfill the abovementioned Agreement, and the first claim made by His Catholic Majesty's subjects in the West Indies in regard to fugitive slaves shall be attended to with all consideration to facilitate the recovery in conformity with the stipulations of the Agreement.

By which same we commend, Most High, Noble, and Just Sir, Your Excellency to God's holy protection, and remain, Most High, Noble, and Just Sir, Your Excellency's most servant.

(Signed.) A. BACKER.

Drawn in Demerara, 9th of June, 1792.

Sealed and countersigned.

M. DIEZ TANGE,
Secretary.

V.

(Translation.)

You are hereby most rigorously commanded to take the greatest care that the Indians shall not suffer injury under any pretext, nor maltreatment; but rather that they shall be shown the same justice as shown to other free people, and, as far as possible, that the friendly feelings of the natives shall be cultivated by every suitable means.

[*Article 29 of the instruction for the Director-General and Council on the river Essequibo, given by the meeting of the Ten of the West India Company, on the 22d of March, 1773, and approved by High Mightinesses the 7th of the following April, and which same is to be observed by Señor Jorge Enrique Trotz, the above-mentioned Director, and by the Council as well.*]

VI.

Translation.

But the slaves who run away to Orinoco are always those of the better class of a plantation; are active and skillful in everything and are instigated to go to the

Spaniards only in the hope of obtaining their liberty. By experience it is known that the bad negroes make no effort to run away, except when their masters are sleeping; they have to collect their small belongings and some provisions, so that as the night is so far advanced that they have not sufficient time to get *to the eastern coast of the Essequibo* without being arrested in their flight by the post above mentioned and established there to pursue them.

[*Orders and extracts from the minutes of the Neerlandisa West India Company, addressed to the Commander and Court of Demerara, February to May, 1776, page 248.*]

VII.

Translation.

Means must be devised to get possession of such negroes as have suffered most in Orinoco, and who have been there a long time, that they may inform their companions of these circumstances, and discourage them by these means.

For this purpose it would be necessary to make a fund (of about 10,000 francs), with the object of persuading some Spaniards of the lower classes to endeavor to procure some negroes like those already described, * * * and in order that by this means not to give to the Spaniards any opportunity of having much communication with our negroes in the Colony, it would be expedient to give orders to said Spaniards, who might have any negroes (like those before mentioned), to bring them to the post of Moroco, and there to deliver them to a person appointed for that purpose, giving them a fixed sum.

[*Orders and extracts from minutes taken from the West India Netherland Company, addressed to the Director-General and Court of Essequibo, 1783–1791, pages 34–35, in the office of the Secretary of the Government, Georgetown.*]

XV.

Translation.

List of the number of employés and clerks, salaries, table expenses and rations for the higher and lower officials, officers, soldiers, and other employés in Essequibo.

	Monthly salary.	Table expenses.	Rations.
One Director-General	*f.* 150	**f.* 1,200	6
One captain commandant of the militia	50	....	2
One sutler	25	....	1
One auctioneer and collector of taxes	Nothing.		
One secretary and bookkeeper	50	....	3
One preacher	*400	....	3
One first amanuensis of the secretary's office	30	....	3
Six assistants, each one	20	....	1½
One lieutenant	40	....	2
One ensign	35	....	1½
One nurse for the sick	12	....	1½
One distributer and inspector of stores	16	....	1½
Three directors in the three plantations of the Company, each.	30	....	
One sexton, first precentor and undertaker	8		1
Beadles, each one	12	....	1½
One head servant in the Fort of Zelandia	15	....	1½
One surgeon	20	....	1½
One carpenter	30	....	1½
One mill-builder for the plantations of the Company.	36	....	1½
One blacksmith	24	....	1½
One butcher	16	....	1½
Sergeants, each one	12	....	1½
Corporals, each one	9	....	1
Drummers, each one	8	....	1
Soldiers, each one	8	....	1
One gunner	12	....	1½
One watchman in "Brandwag"	18	....	1
One "post-holder" in Moroco	14	....	1½
One watchman in Moroco	8	....	1
One "post-holder" in Arimba	14	....	1½
One watchman in Arimba	8	....	1
One "post-holder" in Maycouny	14	....	1½
One watchman in Maycouny	8	....	1
One "post-holder" in Cajoene	14	....	1½
One first watchman in Cajoene	10	....	1
One second watchman in Cajoene	8	....	1

(Extract from the Register of Resolutions of the Noble-Lords, the Representative of His Illustrious Highness

* Per year.

and the Director of the States-General West India Company, in the respective Chamber commissioned for the meeting of the Ten, held at Amsterdam, Wednesday, March 26, 1773.)

(Register of Resolutions of the Directors of the West India Company, 1773–1776, pages 4 and 5, in Registrar-General's Office, Georgetown.)

XVI.

Translation.

(From the Instructions given to the "post-holder" of Wacupo and Morocco, by L. Storm van 's Gravesande, dated October 7, 1767.)

He must watch with great care, as far as possible, all that takes place in Barima, and give written information of the same, as well as of all other extraordinary occurence at the "Post."

(Registrar-General's office, Georgetown.)

XVII.

Translation.

Year 1781.

Register of the Plantations on the River Essequibo.

	Plantations.
On the Bonasique Creek	2
On the Upper Essequibo	1
On Masseroeni	1
On the west coast of Essequibo	65
On the Island of Legnuan	49
On the Island of Wakhanaam	26
On the Island of Avocabisi	6
On the Island of Carabara	5
On the Island of Trooljes Grande	7
Opposite, on Tierra Firme	2

On the Island of Abrejaboenaboe.................. 1
On the Island of Benabanabo 1
On the Island of Verkken..... 11
On the Island of Loulonu.......... .. .. (one brick yard.)

(From a list in the Public Register, Georgetown.)

XVIII.

Translation.

(Court of Policy.)

Jaques Donaq is elected "post-holder" in the post of the Noble Company on the Upper Essequibo, to replace J. van der Burg, deceased, with a salary of *f.* 14 monthly.

(Ordinary session held in the New Fort on the 6th of December, 1739.)

(Extract from the minutes of the Court of Policy 1730–1743, page 112, in Registrar-General's office, Georgetown.)

XIX.

Translation.

Whereas there is such general ruin wrought in the defense of the Colony; and whereas the native Indians of this country for a long time since have been at odds, which necessitates devising a means of making them useful in the service of the Colony, since the state of defense requires it so strongly;

And desirous to repair said ruin, the Court has thought well and has resolved that there shall be a post established on the lower part of the river with forty or fifty Indians, the command of whom will be given to José Bartholy;

To which end said Bartholy shall be notified that he shall personally present a plan indicating the spot where said post ought to be established, and the other appropriations and expenses necessary for the same, so that at the meeting on the 1st of November next the Court may pass a resolution.

* * * * * * *

In consequence of the resolution passed by this Court on the date of October 15th, with regard to the formation of a plan for the establishment of a post on the lower river, José Bartholy appeared, and presented to the Court a plan indicating the spot and the means most conducive to its realization, which plan, after being duly examined by the Court, was approved of, and it was resolved that the post should be established in the lower part of Moroco, where there was formerly a post on lands belonging to Frederico Beystendeyfel, and that José Bartholy should be appointed Commandant, with the rank of Ensign and a yearly salary of *f.* 800, besides his rations as Ensign, and a premium of *f.* 100 for each slave or fugitive that shall be arrested, apprehended, and brought to this fortress by the men under his command; advising him, however, that of these *f.* 100 only *f.* 50 should belong to the Commandant or to whoever should occupy that position, and that the other *f.* 50 shall be distributed among the Indians employed in the service of the post. Besides, it is resolved, for the establishment of this post, that the convict slaves shall be made use of for the digging and building of a dam; also a house and dwellings, and for the same purpose twelve hatchets, twelve spades, twelve knives, and one grindstone.

The garrison for the post shall consist of six mulatoes, with a salary of *f.* 25 each, monthly, and one soldier's ration for each one, and that they shall exact nothing of the *f.* 50 before mentioned, which shall serve as payment and incentive to the Indians. Said Bartholy shall press into service besides, 25 or 30 Indians to serve at the post, and whose maintenance is to be at the expense of the Colony of the Noble Company. The post shall be provided with one flag, two fusees, two cannons, two swivel guns, six lombards, six muskets, six swords, one pair of pistols, together with ammunition, powder, and balls, and whatever else may be necessary. There will be also a small vessel, with four swivel guns, its flag and pendant, one Indian canoe, and two small boats (curiaras). Besides this, the said Bartholy shall receive his uniform and sword according to his rank, and letters patent shall be given him to press into service the six mulatoes, and also the instructions, which he is to follow exactly.

Thus it was resolved.

(Signed) AM. V. DOORM, M.
M. GEELHOED.

(Minutes of the Court of Policy, Friday, November 5, 1784, pages 764, 765, 805, 806, Public Register, Georgetown.)

XXI.

Translation.

SIR: Having received repeated advices from the Island of Barbados with regard to the arrival of a body of troops at Trinidad, and of their destination and departure for the Orinoco, as well as of the preparations made by your orders in Cumaná and in other places, and of the plan to make an invasion into lands of my Government, I feel myself constrained to send you these presents by special messenger to manifest to you my surprise, and to ask you the motive for all these preparations while in the enjoyment of full peace in our territory.

I have tried, as far as was in my power, to preserve friendly relations with my neighbors, and not to fail in any way to fulfill the treaties between His Catholic Majesty and my Sovereigns, the States-General of the

United Netherland Provinces, and I am resolved not to transgress them in any particular, but to conform to them religiously in every particular, as I have always done.

But I am constrained to inform you, and I feel indispensably obliged to do so, that in case others should transgress, I am resolved, to my utmost power, to maintain my Sovereign's right. I have advised and armed all of our Indian allies, who only await my orders to begin their march, and to send special messengers to all our neighbors. In short, I have done my duty.

On informing you of this, and asking for a positive answer from you, Sir, I shall not have to reproach myself in any way for the misfortunes that may be the outcome of this, and shall have a free conscience before God and my neighbors. Once more, I assure you that I shall strictly observe the agreements, and that I shall be happy to promote and preserve the old friendship of our good neighbors. I shall contribute to this as far as I am able; but, while fulfilling this duty, I shall not cease to avail myself of the [information] that I have received, and shall make all the preparations necessary.

I close this letter by assuring you that I shall be (as long as I shall be allowed to be so), with all esteem and consideration, Sir, your very humble and obedient servant,

(Signed) L. STORM VAN 'S GRAVESANDE.

ESSEQUIBO, *September* 12, 1754.

According to the original Eseq., 12th of September, 1754. Quod attestor.

(Signed) ADRIAAN SPOORS.

XXII.

Translation.

1. Having seen the petitions of the captains of the militia for the establishment of a post on this side of

Moroco, for the purpose of preventing the desertion of slaves, the counsellor, E. Pypersberg, is commissioned to make a personal visit, together with the aforementioned gentlemen, to the proposed spot, and further arrangements will be made after having received their report.

(Court of Justice at Essequibo, January 7, 1754.

2. Mr. E. Pypersberg, who at the last meeting was commissioned to visit, together with the captains of the militia, the spot near Moroco which had been proposed as a fit site for the establishment of a post, with the object of preventing the flight of slaves from here to Orinoco, has presented his report at the present meeting, stating that a post might certainly be established on the proposed site, although some difficulties presented themselves; but that, in his opinion, the site in no way answered the requirements of the purpose for which it was intended, for reasons alleged.

Which, on being duly considered, and seeing that the expenses of the Colony are already very great without increasing them, it is resolved to take no further steps in the matter for the present.

(Court of Justice, April 1, 1754.)

3. The respective officers of the militia, having presented a petition with a certain plan by means of which they believe that by moving the trading post of the Company at Moroco, the slaves deserting from this river might be prevented from passing so easily to the Orinoco, and since the Colony will bear the expenses of the same, it has been resolved to discuss with the captains of the militia the means by which they believe that the necessary slaves may be procured from the Colony for this purpose, the Company meanwhile to defray the expenses of the "post-holder" and contributing, as far as may be convenient and to the purpose, to the building of the houses.

(Court of Justice, 6th and 7th of October, 1755.)

XXIII.

Translation.

1. Abraham van der Cruyso cedes to Abraham Couzzni certain lands situated in Mazaruni, from the river Cattony to the Asakuruku creek, of 250 " roeden " (1 roede, 3,75^{m}) in width.

(Court of Policy, Zealand Fort, April 1, 1759.)

2. The following neighbors have asked for lands, to wit:

Esteban Gerardo van der Heyden, the Acajoe Island in Cuyuni; granted, providing that after examination it shall not be found too large.

Christiano Finct and Daniel Couvreur, both having asked for the same lands on the upper Mazaruni, have been notified to first come to a mutual agreement.

(Court of Policy, January 3, 1745.)

3. Pedro de Wind has asked for 400 "roeden," from Hayaroa to Barima Cabrera; granted.

(Court of Policy, January 3, 1745.)

4. Surgeon Juan Pedro Bolle has asked for the deserted stubble land in Cartabo; it was granted with the condition that the Noble Company shall reserve the right to build thereon at least those houses which it shall deem necessary.

(Court of Policy, January 3, 1746.)

5. Pedro Marchial has asked for and obtained 1,000 " roeden " of land on the river Mazaruni, from the river Tawnery upwards.

(Court of Policy, July 2, 1747.)

6. To Pedro Marchall is granted his petition for the Island of Koeyball on the upper Mazaruni.

(Court of Policy, July 1, 1753.)

7. Simonson Swarts and Eduardo Ling, in company, have asked for the privilege of cutting wood on the river Weyne, which petition has been granted, provided that they pay, as they have promised, 2½ per cent. to the

Noble Company, and that they shall make a sworn statement of each embarkation.

(Court of Policy, January 6, 1754.)

8. To Francisco Appelhans has been granted, on the upper Mazaruni, according to his petition, the island called La Quemada, and on the borders of the river, 500 "roeden" of land above the lands of Daniel Couvreur.

(Court of Policy, October 6, 1754.)

9. Jacques Salignacy and Isaac Knott have petitioned for the former to be allowed to plant and export annatto, and the latter to cut wood on the river Bouweron and Weyne, promising to pay, for a period of six, eight, or more years annually to the Noble Company, a sum of 1,000 florins outside of the taxes and ordinary duties.

These petitions, after having been duly considered, are sent to their Highnesses, that they may resolve as they see fit; and since the letter of the Council has already been signed, the Director-General is asked to forward the above-mentioned petition, by copy, to their Highnesses by the vessel "Essequibo Welvaeren," which is about to sail.

(Court of Policy, July 4, 1756.)

10. The site and deserted lands of Calekkoe in Mazaruni are granted to Jan Heraut.

(Court of Policy, July 1, 1759.)

11. To Federico Beysantoufel is granted 1,000 acres on the western shore of the Moroca from the new garrison on the coast up the river, and also some lands for yuca plantations, providing that the Indians be not injured.

(Court of Policy, January 6, 1760.)

12. P. A. Schoneman, who has petitioned for lands at the mouth of the Wacquepo to make thereon a ranche, is informed that, in regard to the permit, he must apply to His Excellency the Director-General.

(Court of Policy, October 5, 1760.)

13. Mr. Abraham van der Crugese grants to Esteban Gerardo van der Heyden part of his lands on the river Mazaruni from the river Simery to the river Caura, to wit, the lands lying in front or cane-fields (?), reserving for himself the lands at the back or yuca plantation.

(Court of Policy, April 5, 1761.)

14. To Christian Crewitz 200 " roeden " are granted on Cuyuni, from the limits of the lands of Esteban Gerardo van der Heyden, or the border of the old indigo plantation, upwards.

(Court of Policy, October 4, 1763.)

15. To E. Palmer is granted his petition for 500 acres of the lands of Negerkop downwards, on the Mazaruni.

(Court of Policy, January 1, 1769.)

16. The petition being read of H. T. de Fousche for 1,000 acres of land on the lands fallen into disuse on the upper shore of the Esequibo, he has been granted the lands on the west side, near the mouth of the Cuyuni, where lie the lands fallen into disuse, which belonged to Ab. Cousin.

(Court of Policy, July 2, 1769.)

17. To H. T. de Fousche has been granted 1,000 acres of land situated on the mouth of the Cuyuni, to wit, the lands of A. Cousin, fallen into disuse commencing from the sugar plantation of the former Counsellor van der Heyden, and downwards.

(Court of Policy, October 1, 1769.)

18. To the former Counsellor S. G. van der Heyden, are granted the lands belonging to the widow van der Wehe, situated on the Mazaruni.

(Court of Policy, March 4, 1770.)

19. The petition of Pedro Kerks has been granted for 1,000 acres of the lands fallen into disuse of Daniel Couvreur, on the Mazaruni, beginning wherever he chooses.

(Court of Policy, July 1, 1770.)

IV.

Copy of the document in relation to the Measures that were dictated by the Spanish Government to prevent the French from extending their Possessions in the Province of Guiana.

With the object of encouraging agriculture and increasing the population in French Guiana, a Company has been formed in France, the promoters of which have been granted by the Government of France the territory lying between the rivers Oyapoco and Aprorak. This project has had great success, persons of high rank becoming associated in the enterprise on account of the great benefits expected from it. And it being necessary that we should prevent the progress of the French settlements in the aforesaid province by occupying, at this side, such places and territories as are proper for this object, the Intendent of those provinces is directed to take such steps as he may deem necessary (with all due secresy, so that the cause for such steps may not transpire) to call settlers who will establish themselves in the aforesaid places, effecting at once their occupation, in charge of the Governor, Don Antonio de Pereda, and the Commissioner that he should select to assist him; of which I inform Your Excellency, by order of the King, so that Your Excellency may assist the aforesaid Governor and help to make effective whatever measures the Intendent may deem proper in the matter.

God preserve Your Excellency many years.

SAN LORENZO, October 20, 1778.

(Signed) JPH. DE GALVEZ.

To the Governor of Caracas.

V.

New copy of the acts of Jurisdiction exercised by the Spanish Authorities in Barima and Guayana.

1785 and 1786.

[L. S.] Seal of the third class, one real. The years one thousand seven hundred and eighty-four and eighty-five.

To the Governor and sub-Delegate of the Intendency :

I, Don Gil Baz, a resident of this city and captain and owner of the scooner "Nuestra Señora del Carmen," before Your Excellency do appear and declare that I am one of those who, for the support of my family (as others do for theirs), make voyages with cargoes of beasts to friendly colonies; but that at the present time I am in great perplexity and know not what to do in order to meet my most pressing engagements, owing to the fact that there are so many navigators from this province, as well as from the neighboring ones, there is little use or value for the animals which we export to the above-mentioned Colonies. For this reason, being well convinced of Your Excellency's goodness, and to the end that I may not be, as up to this present time, lacking in anything towards my family, I pray Your Excellency to grant me Your Excellency's gracious permission to take cargoes of letter-wood in the creeks of this river Orinoco, and to export the same to the aforementioned Colonies; as by this I hope to be able to earn a little; for, in addition to our sufferings, in regard to the small value of the animals we carry, our losses are still greater on account of their dying on the voyage, and hence when the royal dues and other indispensable expenses are deducted, we hardly get enough to cover actual cost. Therefore I ask and pray Your Excellency to consider me as having appeared before you and presented a truthful account, and to provide for me what I plead for, that I may receive this favor from the noble and meritorious office which Your Excellency holds, which I, being duly sworn, do implore.

(Signed) GIL BAZ.

No. —.

The Governor and sub-Delegate of Guayana informs you of the abundance of woods existing on the creeks and mouths of the Orinoco for the building of houses, and the furtive removal of these woods by foreigners, without being able to prevent the same, and the utility of exporting these woods to the friendly Colonies by these residents, under certain regulations, with a prohibition for the construction of vessels, together with other matter contained in the two memorials and two copies of documents annexed.

CARACAS, August 12, 1786.

Let it be submitted to the assessor for advice.

SAAVEDRA L.

MY DEAR SIR: By the two annexed memorials Your Excellency will be informed of the pretension of the interested parties and of the motives upon which they are founded, to undertake a branch of trade unknown till now to the merchant residents of Orinoco, notwithstanding the abundance of luxuriant groves which they possess on the vast extent of the creeks and mouths by which the river empties into the sea, foreigners taking advantage of this same bounty which nature offers us, there being no way to prevent them from this furtive and continuous removal of our wood, which they practice at will on account of the proximity of their Colonies to our possessions, which are completely open, with no proper

The assessor, Your Excellency, being informed of the prohibition to remove woods from the places mentioned by the sub-Delegate, and of the efficacious measures which Your Excellency has ever taken to prevent the same; and since the petition of the sub-Delegate might bring about many abuses, he postponed the dispatch of this measure for others of greater importance, and which necessitated speedy and efficacious measures; being of the opinion that the extraction of said woods should not be allowed with all the latitude solicited, alleging for this that the rules which should be fixed never are, but that Your Excellency will grant that privilege in certain cases, under the conditions which Your Excellency will indicate, provided they be not in opposition to whatever orders in the matter may have been communicated to Your Excellency by His Majesty.

CARACAS, April 15, 1788.

ALCALDE.

CARACAS, April 15, 1788.

Let the foregoing report be sent to the sub-Delegate means for guarding them, it being difficult to have any.

I am informed of the little value of cattle on the islands, on account of the abundance and superior quality of those from North America, by reason of which our residents have suffered more losses than gains since the declaration of peace; and as this Province does not produce beasts of burden, and not every one has the means to purchase in the neighboring provinces, they are greatly troubled to maintain or support the industry by which they live and help towards the increase of the community, as well to agriculture as to commerce, which is the source of the Royal Exchequer.

in reference to what has been already communicated to him on the matter under date of the 7th inst.

SAAVEDRA.

From the castles of Guayana to the mouth of the sea, which is about seventy leagues according to the general opinion, there is found a desert place filled with heathen Indians; and as there are a great number of creeks crossing each other, it is very easy for foreigners to go in or come out at will when they wish to go woodcutting or fishing or to engage in the abominable traffic of Indians, whom they carry away and enslave in their colonies, as has recently occurred, and from which Your Excellency will deduce the instructions which I gave to Matheo Beltrán, whom I dispatched with information that I had received, in order to prevent this, which I enclose in copy, together with a diary which he made on his journey. From which Your Excellency will infer that when the news of these events arrives here it will be at a time when the blow will have been struck and they having returned to their former places, unless they should not chance to stay longer than usual.

This vast expanse which forms a long peninsula, is filled with luxuriant forests of many different kinds of trees; the greater part of which are woods useful in the building of houses. These woods are useless to us here, as we have such an abundance in the immediate vicinity, of which the residents make use when there is need for so doing; and for this same reason, besides the woods carried away by the foreigners, the rest are uselessly lost, and by this also a branch of industry that might well bring great advantages in commerce and in general to the residents permitting them to export these woods to the islands, under certain rules which would prevent the abuse that they might commit by this privilege, and by forbidding the use of implements for the building of national vessels, it being well to encourage the residents, and is recommended by the Sovereign: besides barring the way to transgressors, this will afford the relief which these merchants solicit.

Notwithstanding my knowing the favorable results to the royal service that would accrue in case of granting this petition, I have not wished to do it myself, in consideration of the fact that by the instructions given to the Intendency that office has the faculty only of delivering such permits; in virtue of which Your Excellency will, as always, deliberate upon the more expedient course, giving the orders that may so please you in this particular, the communication of which I await.

God save Your Excellency many years.

GUAYANA, 12th of December, 1785.

I kiss Your Excellency's hand.

Your Excellency's most trusty servant,

MIG[l] MARMION, G.

Señor Don Francisco Saavedra.

Instructions to be followed by Mateo Beltran, the commander of the revenue boat in this river, on his voyage to reconnoiter the Barima creek and other points, as instructed:

1st. Sailing from this point he will steer in a straight

course, not stopping anywhere, to the great mouth of the Orinoco at the sea, when he will enter, with all caution possible, the Barima creek to intercept two foreign vessels which, according to reports received, are cutting wood there.

2d. Before boarding them he will examine the tonnage and armament they carry; and if such are judged to be of such superiority that, notwithstanding the advantages of a row-boat in a river or creek, and the impossibility of the adversary to manœuver or use all his artillery, as when at sea, he should consider that he would fail in the attempt to capture them, on no account shall he expose our arms to failure, and in this case he will observe them from a safe distance, noting all their movements and the cargoes they carry away.

3d. If it should happen that, when these two or more vessels referred to are leaving, one should become separated from the rest in such a manner that the others could not assist her, he will plan her capture, if circumstances be favorable, but must not attack unless with a probability of victory.

4th. In case of capturing one or more of said vessels referred to, he will bring them to this capital, together with their cargoes, sealing these in the holds and securing the crew by whatever means possible, sailing with the greatest caution, to the end that any plan which the crew might form might be defeated, and for greater caution the boat will follow in the wake, at a proper distance, until the arrival at this port.

5th. Should he not find any vessel, either in or out of the aforesaid creek, he will ascertain whether there are any signs that the vessels have been there, or that wood has recently been cut there, or about what length of time has elapsed since it was cut, and what kind of wood may have been taken therefrom, and what was its quality and quantity.

6th. Should he find on land any Europeans, of whatsoever nation they may be, he will arrest them and seize all their belongings ; but he shall molest no Indians, nor shall he commit any act to exasperate them, and shall only examine them in a friendly way to obtain all the information possible in regard to whether vessels enter there to cut wood or for any other furtive trade.

7th. Having carried out the principal commission of reconnoitering the vessels, ascertaining in regard to wood-cutting, and other orders before mentioned, and should it result that he return to this capital empty-handed, he will endeavor to find out a place, river, or creek in our territory where any considerable number of runaway negroes may have settled themselves with Carib Indians; and being well assured of the information which, by much tact and suavity, he will obtain from the Guaraunos and Aruacas, he shall then consult with Silvestre Rodriguez, who, with this view, accompanies him, to find out the surest means for discovering this place and learn how they are situated, what are their means of defense, what is their number, more or less, negroes as well as Indians, and with what arms they are provided; and should they be situated in simple ranches, without other preparations which indicate a disposition for resistance, he shall try, by means of a flatboat, to find out how the negroes are disposed; and should he find that they are willing to come to this capital, he will bring them on his vessel and boats that he may have, guarding and defending them should the Caribs show any opposition to their departure.

8th. Whenever the number of Caribs and blacks should be superior to his force, or in case they should be defenseless, or in case the negroes should show unwillingness to come to this capital, he will try to induce them to do so, and, failing in this by gentle means, he will seize them and take them away, securing them well ; and in case of resistance by arms, he will make use of his own in defense, according to circumstances, always avoiding, however, as far as possible, the use of force if he be able to persuade them by peaceful and kind measures.

9th. Lastly, in the principal commission as well as that in regard to the negroes, on recognizing superiority of forces, which prudence would suggest could not be defeated, he will withdraw, not allowing the object of his commission to be known, and without giving any motive to their taking steps to fortify themselves more or to make such provisions for defense that should make their capture more difficult; and if all that shall. occur and of whatever observations he shall make, he must give an exact account to this Government.

Guayana, June twentieth, in the year one thousand seven hundred and eighty-five.

MIGUEL MARMION.

This is a *verbatim* copy from the contents of the original, to which I refer.

GUAYANA, 16th of September, 1785.

(Signed) MARMION.

GUAYANA, *June* 23, 1785.

Diary, 23d day. Having left this capital by order of the Governor and Commander-General Don Miguel Marmion, steering in a straight course to the great mouth of the Orinoco, from thence passing into the Barima creek, on the same day, at ten o'clock at night, we arrived at the Port of San Miguel.

Diary, 24th day. At dawn we took on board the cassave, and at that same hour we left the said port, and at twelve o'clock we arrived at Presidio, and I began to put the (launch) or barge in order.

Diary, 25th day. At daybreak we put our arms in order and made the cartridges for the cannon and for the swivel gun; and, on the same day, at two o'clock in the afternoon, we set forth on the way to our destination, with four Indians, three being mine and one being given to me by the Commander, Don Antonio de Perello, because those whom I brought from the capital went away, and although the Commander wrote to the "father" he would not send them back.

Diary, 26th day. Daybreak found us at the Portuguese Islands, and at eight o'clock in the morning we found two "curiaras" (boats) belonging to the Guarauno Indians, who informed me that there was a schooner fishing on the mouth of Guiama (Waini), and I steered straight ahead; the same date, at eleven o'clock at night, we slept at the Vuleta del Diablo.

Diary, 27th day. At three o'clock in the morning I weighed anchor, and at eight o'clock we found four "curiaras" of Carib Indians, belonging to the mission of Morocure at the month of the Arature, with the gunner, Josef Maria, by order of the Commander; the said gunner, with two Guarauno Indians and a pilot, going to said creek; they were from a hut on the mouth, and they informed me that there were three negroes inside living with some Indians, for which reason I prevented them from going into the hut until my return from the trip, and I took the two Indians from them. The same day, at three o'clock in the afternoon, we met three Carib Indians from the village of Cumaco of the mission of the Catalan Capuchin Fathers and they informed me that they had come down from the river head of the Barima creek in bark canoès, and no permit was found on them, and having asked them for news of the Barima creek they told me they had seen nothing, and nothing was found in the curiara but nine hatchets and one *Mapire de totumo* (water-gourd) and that same night we slept at Cangrejos.

Diary, 28th day. At ten o'clock in the morning I weighed anchor, and at two o'clock in the afternoon we arrived at the mouth of the Macuro, where I waited for the tide to go on my way; meanwhile I sent for the three chieftains, one of whom lived at Amacuro in the dwellings that belonged to the Caribs in the past time, and the other two lived at the mouth of the sea, between Barima creek and Amacuro, and I made them ask whether there were any negroes living at Amacuro with Carib Indians and they said there were none, nor even any Carib Indians there.

Diary, 29th day. I weighed anchor at eleven o'clock at night, and at two o'clock in the morning I anchored at the mouth of the Barima, and at daybreak I sent the coxswain in a "curiara," with eight spies, up the creek, and at five o'clock in the afternoon he returned, saying that all he had seen was one dug-out and two "curiaras" concealed in the bushes, where some Carib Indians had a hut inland; and a short time after that some Guarauno Indians appeared in two "curiaras" and we made them come on board, and they told me that they were Indians from Sacaupana fleeing from the Carib Indians, and that on Barima creek and Amacuro there were 3,000 Indians fleeing from the severity (the floods?) of the Orinoco, and being asked by the Indian interpreter of the same nation, named Afortunado, as to whether there were any vessels on the river Barima or any negroes living with Indians in the woods, they replied that there were none, and that only in Guima did any schooners enter from Demerara and Essequibo for fishing purposes and to cut timite to cover and build their dwellings.

Diary, 30th day. We slept on the mouth of the Mura.

Diary, 1st day of July. At five o'clock in the morning we crossed the mouth of the Guima, and after visiting every part of it nothing has been found but the places where the Dutch were fishing and salting fish (and this agreed with the information given by the Indians), and that the last day there were two schooners loading "timite" and one fishing, and that they had gone; and I asked Silvestre Rodriguez whether he might know of any other place where we might fulfill the commission given to us, and he answered that he did not, for the chieftains of Amacuro had said that there were no negroes there, neither Caribs; that those that were in this capital were ordered to be taken away, and since then there had been none, and on that same day I returned to the capital.

Diary, 2d day. I left Guayna[1] and came to the Barima creek.

Diary, 3d day. At five o'clock in the afternoon I sailed to the mouth of the Barima, and on the same day in the afternoon there came some Guaraunos in four "curiaras," who were returning from crabbing, and they said that their chiefs were making ready to come to this capital. I enquired once again whether they knew of any negroes dwelling in Amacuro, or whether they knew if there were any in the neighboring creeks, and they said no, that some days previous some Hollanders had come down with a few Poytos to the head waters of the Barima, and that they had taken them to Esquivo; that same day, at seven o'clock in the evening, I sailed off to said mouth.

Diary, 4th day. At daybreak I was at the mouth of the Aratures, and I dispatched the coxswain in a curiara, manned with some sailors, to a hut of Guaraunos, that was inland, with orders to bring the chief to me, and they returned with him at eleven o'clock in the day, and when he came on board I had him interrogated as to whether he knew of any negroes living with Carib Indians, either at Arature or Amacuro, and he answered that he had neither seen nor heard of any; and at the same hour I went on my way and slept in the "Pasa de Tuncos."

Diary, 5th day. At four o'clock in the morning I weighed anchor and slept that night in the Lloran creek, as there was no wind.

Diary, 6th day. At four o'clock in the morning I weighed anchor and slept at the mouth of the Sacopana.

[1] Variously spelled Guayna, Guima, Wayni, Weyne, and Waiui.

Diary, 7th day. In the morning I sent off the coxswain to an Indian hut, which was up the creek, to get information. He found them empty, and came back on board, and then I set sail for the capital, and that same night I slept off the Portuguesa, because the wind died out.

Diary, 8th day. I weighed anchor at five o'clock in the morning and arrived at Presidio at eight at night.

Diary, 9th day. I awaited the letters from the Commandant.

Diary, 10th day.

Diary, 11th day. We left Presidio and arrived at daybreak at the mouth of the Caroni.

Diary, 12th day. We went up to San *Joaquin* for some tobacco, which was at the port for the "Administration." The same day we slept in said mouth.

Diary, 13th day. I weighed anchor at daybreak, bound for the capital.

This is a *verbatim* copy of the contents of the original, which is filed in the archives of the Secretary of this Government.

GUAYANA, September 16th, 1785.

(Signed) MARMION.

Among other points which the Governor of Guayana treats of in his report of the 3d of this month, No. 113 there is an item of expense of fifty-one *pesos*, which he found himself obliged to make in the reconnoitering which he ordered on account of repeated and confirmed information which he received, to wit, that there were some foreign vessels at the Guayana point, there anchored (and said to be English); he taking this step in consideration of the King's order, to be watchful and cautious and to be on the alert in case the English should undertake any attempt before the opening of the war. Said Minister refused the reimbursement under the pretext of lack of authority and other formalities, and taking into consideration that said expense was incurred for so urgent a matter, it seems very proper to approve of it, and I therefore hope that Your Excellency will attend to this matter, issuing orders to the end that whenever the Governor may find it convenient in extraordinary cases to take secret steps, the expenses should be reimbursed, as His Majesty has repeatedly ordered; for he who orders the payments to be made must be aware of the legitimate cause producing them, and will at all times be responsible to the King for his operations.

God save Your Excellency many years.

CARACAS, December 22d, 1786.

(Signed) PEDRO CARBONELL.

Intendent-General of the Army and Royal Treasury.

VI.

New documents found in the Archives of Caracas, relating to the Fort of the Cuyuni.

No. 63.

To His Excellency the Intendent of Caracas:

Enclosed, as promised, is the certificate and other documents relating to the building of a stronghold or sentry box, and the establishment of a Spanish town on the fork or meeting of the rivers Curiamo and Cuyuni of the Province of Guayana.

In my very private report of the 29th of September ult., No. 1, advising Your Excellency of the resolution I had taken to order a stronghold and sentry box to be built, and to establish a Spanish town on the fork or meeting of the rivers Curiamo and Cuyuni of the Province of Guayana, which empty into the Essequibo, in the Dutch Colonies, I indicated that I would forward to Your Excellency a certified document which had been drawn up for other reasons, and which agrees on the point of said establishment and of that of the town or mission of Tumeremo.

In effect, I enclose to Your Excellency, with No. 1, the certification of said document which I promised, and also Nos. 2 and 3, copies of my dispatches and order to the Reverend Father Prefect of the Capuchin and Catalonian Missions and Ministers Plenipotentaries of the Royal Treasury, in order that, being informed of all that has occurred, Your Excellency may approve of my resolution; it being understood that as regards the military point of this new fortress and the separation from it of the Major-Adjutant of the Veteran Companies of Guayana, Don Antonio Lopez de la Puente, I will report to the Most Excellent Count of Campo de Alange as my belief it behooves me.

May God save, etc.

CARACAS, October 25, 1790.

Index of the reports remitted to His Excellency Don Pedro de Lerena by the Intendent of Caracas, Don Julio Guillelmicon, under date of October 25, 1790:

No. 59.

Acknowledging receipt of the Royal Order, communicating the Royal Decree that henceforth, that in America as well as in Spain, all vessels destined for the Royal Service are to be careened and made ready by account of the navy.

No. 60.

Acknowledging receipt of the Royal Order, by which the yearly salary of the Minister of the Royal Treasury of Coro, Don Joseph de Navarrette, is to be increased ten pesos.

No. 61.

Answering the Royal Order communicating His Majesty's Royal Resolution that hereafter the treasury of Guayana should be served by a Royal Official, with the salary at present enjoyed, and a clerk with 500 pesos, and that when there be a vacancy he will give places to the Royal Official and clerk who by this are unemployed.

No. 62.

Acknowledging receipt of the Royal Decree to the effect that the amount of six and one-half pesos be deducted from the salary of Agustin Indo, overseer of the naval storehouses at Puerto Cabello, by account of the Royal Treasury, which sum began to be paid to his wife since the 1st of February of this year.

No. 63.

Acknowledging receipt of the Royal Decree, ordering the Treasury of Cumaná to pay to the children of Don Pedro * * * storekeeper and majordomo of the distillery of sugar-cane rum, who was * * * Province, the sum of 300 pesos, from the 1st of March, of '88, until his death.

No. 64.

Asking that the Minister of the Royal Treasury of La Guaira, Don Antonio * * * shall apologize for the insult he offered, not only to him but also to the Superintendent-General sub-Delegate of the Royal Treasury, calling him unskillful in matter of accounts.

No. 65.

Enclosing, according to promise, the certificate and other documents relating to the construction of a stronghold and sentry-box and establishment of a Spanish town on the fork or meeting of the rivers Curiamo and Cuyuni of the province of Guayana.

No. 66.

Enclosing invoice and bill for wood for gun-carriages and artillery mountings embarked on board the frigate "La Concepcion," of the Shipmaster Don Tre. Antonio Garay.

No. 67.

Enclosing and approving the request of Don I° Antonio Careaga, Commander of the Maritim Guard of those provinces, requesting a hearing before an impartial judge in case that it be true that the Governor of Margarita has made a complaint against him in regard to his proceedings in the commissions he held there.

No. 68.

Enclosing and supporting petition of Don Pedro Urrieta, who is in prison at the barracks of the white militia of that city, for debt to the royal tobacco revenue.

No. 69.

Enclosing statement of the funds of the tobacco and playing cards revenue of the district of said Intendency, corresponding to the first six months of this year.

No. 70.

Asking amount of 8 pesos worth of fine Seville seed of the make of Don Pedro Alonso Guines and Ciaraco for the stock of the tobacco warehouses of the district of that Intendency.

No. 71.

Enclosing and recommending documentary petition of Don Antonio Pablo Gonzalez and Peraga, under administrator of the Royal Treasury of the district of Capaya of that province, asking that adequate place be given to him, either in La Guaira or in the capital.

No. 72.

Enclosing memorial to the King praying to be relieved from the Intendency and Superintendency-General sub-Delegate of the Royal Treasury, a position which he temporarily holds.

No. 44.

The temporary Governor of Guayana, informing of the trouble occurred on the river Cuyuni and of the revolt or flight of the Indians of the town of Curauno, which belongs to the spiritual jurisdiction of the Catalonian Capuchin Fathers.

By the copy which I hereby send to Your Excellency (as I also do to the Captaincy-General), Your Excellency will be informed of the trouble occurring on the river Cuyuni, which flows into that of the Colony of Esquivo; the news of the gathering of the Indians provided with firearms and protected by an entrenchment of stakes on the island further down on the mouth of the river Masaruni, which flows into the Cuyuni, lacks confirmation; but, notwithstanding, for the sake of precaution and for fear of what might happen, I have made my provisions for aiding, in case of need, as far as circumstances will allow, the Sergeant-Commander, who is detached in the stronghold or sentry-box on the Cuyuni river, charging him to ascertain the truth of the matter. In case our fears are realized it will be necessary to strengthen that stronghold, it being an open avenue for the Colony of the Esquivo and a road for the fugitives and for others who are not fugitives and wish to travel by the river to leave the place; it is also indispensable that some means should be devised for the subsistence of the troops who man this place, and to this end I make a suggestion to the Father Prefect of the Catalonian Capuchins of these Missions, in a letter dated February 22d ult.

Although the same Prefect advised me of the flight of the Indians from Pueblo del Cura, without informing me of their numbers, I have had private information that there were over eight hundred of them, together with others who joined them from the Missions in the vicinity —Sergeant Bommon having set forth to pursue the fugitives, aided by such of the residents of the town of Upata as could be collected at that time by the lieutenant, and also the militia of this capitol, and who served as a guard, dispersed in various distant towns. Up to the present time I know nothing of the results of the steps they have taken.

This is the state of affairs, as shown by the letters, copy of which is enclosed, and according as events transpire I shall keep Your Excellency promptly advised of the same.

God save Your Excellency many years.

LOUIS ANT° GIL.

GUAYANA, March 1, 1692.

(Copy.)

Superintendent-General sub-Delegate of the Royal Treasury.

By Your Excellency's note of May 10th ult., No. 44, and copies of notices addressed by the Prefect of the Missions of the Capuchins of that province, and the Sergeant-Commandant detached to the fort of the river

Cuyuni, I am in receipt of the information of the flight of the Indians of Pueblo del Cura and the neighboring missions, in number 800 or more, and I hope that the wise provisions you have made for their restoration to my respective dwellings shall meet with the success they so well deserve and is so much to be desired; but, in order to calm the anxiety of these people living in the obscurity of their origin, I would advise it as very expedient that Your Excellency should persuade some European families or creoles to establish themselves in the Indian towns in numbers in proportion with those in each one, to the end that, by contact with the former, they may learn the Spanish language and the civilization which they lack.

God save, etc.

CARACAS, April 11, 1792.

I enclose to Your Excellency a note of the establishment of Spanish towns on the fork or union of the rivers Cuyuni and Curiamo, having for defense a stronghold or fort and a town of Guaica Indians, which Your Excellency asked of me in Your Excellency's [note] of the 4th of the present month.

God save, etc.

CARACAS, October 8, 1796. (Flourish.)

President-Governor and Captain-General.

The documents were filed.

I hereby return to Your Excellency the dispatch which Your Excellency enclosed in the note of the 8th in regard to the establishment of the town of Cura and stronghold on the fork or union of the rivers Cuyuni and Curiamo, in the province of Guayana, which I asked for on the 4th inst.

God save Your Excellency many years.

CARACAS, October 14, 1796.

JOACHIM DE TUBILLAGA.

Intendent-General of the Army and the Royal Academy.

(Copy.)

Statement of the effective force of the troops in arms at this present day and date in this province of Guayana, and where destined. No. 2.

Companies.	At the capital.							At Fortresses of Antigua, Guayana.							At Rio Negro.				At Sacaripoma.			At Cuyuni.			Par-ime.	Ca-ura.	Misi-ones
	Captains.	Lieuts.	Ensign.	Sergeants.	Drummers.	Corp. and soldiers.	Total.	Captains.	Lieuts.	Ensigns.	Sergeants.	Drummers.	Corp. and soldiers.	Total.	Ensigns.	Sergeants.	Corp. and soldiers.	Total.	Sergeants.	Corp. and soldiers.	Total.	Sergeants.	Corp. and soldiers.	Total.	Corp. and soldiers.	Corp.	Soldiers.
Co. of R. C. of Art'y.	1	......	......	......	......	1	1	1	1	......	2	1	26	29	......	......	1	1	......	......	......	......	......	......	......	......	......
Co. of veterans........	2	1	1	1	......	1	2	1	2	1	3	5	62	70	1	2	16	18	1	10	11	1	......	1	9	1	2
Co. of white militia.	1	......	......	3	1	64	68	......	......	......	......	......	2	2	......	......	......	......	......	......	......	......	......	......	......	......	......
Co. of quadroons.....	......	......	......	......	......	......	......	1	1	......	2	1	90	94	......	......	......	......	......	......	......	......	8	8	......	......	......
Co. of mulattoes......	......	......	......	......	......	......	......	1	1	......	3	......	38	40	......	......	......	......	......	......	......	......	......	......	......	......	......
Total..........	4	1	1	4	1	66	71	4	5	1	10	7	218	235	1	2	17	19	1	10	11	1	8	9	9	1	2

(Copy of the original. Guayana, October 16, 1800.)

GUAYANA, October 14, 1800.

(Signed) INCIARTE.

FRANCISCO PIRARES.
FRANCISCO OROSCO.

Index of the official correspondence between the Intendent of Guayana, at this date and the Superintendency:

No. 252. One note; received Royal Order for the observance of law 45, title 4, Book 8, and Royal Decree of 5–7 of November, 1790, for the better administration of the Royal Treasury.

No. 253. Another; received Royal Order, informing of the inauguration of the Council of Admiralty for the fulfillment of the prescript in the Royal letters patent of February 27, 1807.

No. 254. Another; enclosing state of tobacco for July.

No. 255. Another; soliciting approval for expense of building barracks for the troops of the detachment of the Cuyuni.

No. 256. Another; recalling that of January 27th ult., No. 165, asking approval of the post of watchman held by Domingo Antonio de la Torre.

No. 257. Another; accompanying duplicate copies of the statement of the Royal Treasury for the end of July.

GUAYANA, August 17, 1807.

INCIARTE.

Listas de los mapas relativos á la cuestión de límites de Guayana, encontrados por la comisión de Venezuela y la de Washington, clasificados según las líneas que senalen:

Nota de los Mapas que Señalan el Esequibo como limite, sacada de la lista Publicada por la Comisión Investigodora de Washington.

Autores.	Fecha de publicación.	Lugar de su publicación.	Nombre del mapa.	Notas.
Jacobz (A.)	1621	Amsterdam	Indias Occidentales	Vease la posición de los nombres.
Lucena (T. Paluzie)	1895	Barcelona	Am[a] Sept[nd] y Me[nal]	Se envió.
Niles (T. M.)	1838	Hartford	Sud América	Id.
Reichar (C. G.) (C. Compe Ed[or].)	1832	Nuremberg	.....id	Id.
Russel (T.)	1794	Londres	......id	Id.
Tanner (H. T.)	1836	Filadelfia	Brasil	No se envió éste sino uno de 1829. (Suraname) que da Nassau.
Mentelle (S.) Instituto Geog[co] Weimar.	1804	Weimar	Guayanas Hold[a] y Fransa	Se envió.
Id	1814	......id	Id.	
Gío Mazzajoli			América	Se envió pero fué una idición de Roma.
Hall (Signey)	1825	Londres	Colombia	Id.
Le Sage (C. de las Casas)	1812	París	América Meridional	Se envió pero con fecha de 1814.
Martin (Robert Montgomery)	1839	Londres	Colonias Gran Bretaña	Límite por color.
Reid (John)	1796	New York	Sur América	Límite por la posición del titulo.
Tomlins (Fred Guest)	1842	Halifax	......id	Id.
Arowosmith (Aaron)	1817	Edinburgo	Id.	
Bianconi (F.)	1888	París	E. E. N. U. de Venz[la].	
Carey Cellatrew	1823	Filadelfia	Colombia.	
Otro......id	1814	......id	Caracas.	

Mapas enviados por la Comisión de Venezuela á la de Washington que señalan el Esequibo y que no se hallan enla lista publicado por ésta.

Autores.	Fecha.	Lugar de publicación.	Nombre del mapa.	Notas.
Villemin	1830 á 40		América del Sur	Dice en la nota de la Comisión, qúe es modificación de Cruz Caño.
Restrepo (T. M.)	1825	Londres	Colombia.	
Holmes Laurie (editor)	1829	id	Hemf[rio] Occid[tal] Colom[a].	
Purdy (John)	1832	id	Carta del Mundo.	
Lincobi y Edmand		Boston	Sur América.	
Anónimo			Provincias de Venezuela, de Caracas, etc.	

Lista de los nuevos mapas encontrados que dan el mismo límite.

Autores.	Fecha.	Lugar de publicación.	Nombre del mapa.	Notas.
Houzé (A.)	**1846**	**París**	**América Meridional**	**Acompaña los viajes publicados por W. Smith.**
Monaldi (A.) atlas	**1840**	**Roma**	**Globb terrestre**	**Certificado por Urdaneta.**
Manuel Mª Paz	**1882**	**Bogotá**	**Colombia y Venezuela**	**En el Alegats de Colombia ante S. M. Alfonso XII.**

Mapas que siguen la linea de Cruz Caño ósea el Cabo Nassau.

Autores ó editores.	Fecha.	Lugar de publicación.	Nombre del mapa.	No. de mapas.	Notas.
Anónimo—G. Cowic & C^a	1824	Londres	Colombia.		
Anónimo—Coleografia Camerale.	1896	Roma	Tierra firme y Guayana		*Enviado* por la Comisión clasificadora (de 1798).
Arowosmith (A.)	1811	Londres	América del Sur		Id.
Bache (Richard) Capit^o	1827	Filadelfia	Colombia.		
Bell (James)	1834	Glasgow	Brasil y Paraguay.		
Bellin (Jacques Nicolas)	1760	París	Costas de Guayana	2	De S. Bellin de 1709. *Se envió* y este de 1760 esdel mismo.
Codazzi (Agustin)	1740	Caracas	Colombia.		
Cradoc y Joi	1808	Londres	Sur América		*Se envió.*
Cruz Cano y Almedilla	1775	Madrid	América Meridional		Id.
Anónimo—Ed^o Baldwin Cradoc y Joy.	1823	Londres	Colombia.		
Luis Stanislas Darcy de la Rochette.	1807	Londres	Colombia Prima		*Se envió* la edición de 1820.
Depons (J. R. J.)	1805	París	Caracas		Dice Nassau—*Pero el titulo Guayana Holana no pasa el Esequibo.*
Dirwald (J.)	1823	Viena	Sur América.		
Ducondray Holtein	1829	Londres	Colombia.		
Dufourtd (A.)	1830	París	América del Sur		Hay otro en los viajes á América, Africa, Asia, etc.
Duvotenay (Th.)	1839	Forino	Colombia y Guayana	2	Se envió el sin fecha.
Faden (W.)	1799	Londres	América Meridional.		
Fer (N. de)	1719	París	Tierra firme		No tiene límites.
Finley (Anthony)	1826–29	Filadelfia	Sur América	2	

Mapas que siguen la linea de Cruz Caña ósea el Cabo Nassau—Continued.

Autores ó editores.	Fecha.	Lugar de publicación.	Nombre del mapa.	No. de mapas.	Notas.
Vrijlink (H.)	1854	Amsterdam	Id		Se envió—Atlas 1855 que señala á Nassau.
Geografia Annal	1854	Filadelfia	Brasil, etc., y otro Colombia	4	En el de 1835 "Venezuela y Guayana Británica" y en el sud América Barima.
Guocchi Giacomo	1859á64	Milan	América Meridional		Se envió.
Giusseféld (J. L.)	1796	Nuremberg	América.		
Guttrie (W.)	1803	Roma	Amª Meridional y Nuevo Reyno de Granada.	2	Se envió.
Hall, Sidney	1857	Londres	Hemisferio Occidental de Colombia diversos nombres.		*Se envió uno de* 1825 *de Cochrane "Colombia" que da el Esequibo.*
Humboldt (Alejandro de)	1830	Viena			Se envió.
Lapié (P.)	1809á28	París		9	Se enviaron.
Le Sage A. (Conde de las Casis.)	1827	París	América histórica		Se envió—También otro de 1812 "América moderna" que da el *Esequibo*.
Cary y Len (editores)	1823	Filadelfia	Sur América		Se envió uno de 1827.
Instituto Geográfico	1828	Weimar	Guayana.		
Mälte Brun	1837	Filadelfia	Colombia y Guayana	2	Se envió.
Masmert	1803	Nuremberg	Sur América		Algo variada.
Michelena y Rojas	1867	Bruselas	América del Sur.		
Mollien (G. Th.)	1824	Londres	República de Colombia.		
Murray (Hugh)	1834	id	Brasil, Paraguay y Guayana.		
Cª del Orinoco (Fitzgerald)	1896	Nueva York.			
Pinkerton (J.)	1804	Paris	América Meridional	4	Todos señalan el Cabo Nassau—Se envió.

Poirson (J. B.)	1802	París	Guayana Francesa y Holandesa.	5	Se envió 1802—Los de 1803–14 y 21 también.
Reichard (C. G.)	1832	Nuremberg	Sur América	....	dice modifica á C. Cano—Se envió por señalar á *Esequibo*.
Regnena, Francisco	1796	Filadelfia	América Meridional	....	Se envió.
Restrepo, José Manuel	1827	París	Departamento de Orinoco	....	Se envió el de 1825 por señalar á *Esequibo*.
Rosa (R.)	1865	Nueva York	Estados Unidos de Venezuela.	....	Se envió.
Rossi (Luigis)	1821	Milán	América Meridional	....	Se envió como del Editor Sasso (G.) y Bonattil (M.) con alguna modificación.
Schlieben (W. E. Av.)	1830	Leipzig	Guayana	2	
Schumith (J. M.)	1820	Berlin	América.		
Smiley (Th. F.)	1830	Filadelfia	Sur América.		
Stedman (J. G.)	....	París	Guayana	....	Se envió.
Streit (J. W.)	1842	Leipzig	Sur América	2	Se envió el 1832.
Turville (L. de)	1778	Madrid	Nueva Andalucía	....	Se envió con la obra de Canlín.
Tanner (H. S.)	1829	Filadelfia	Sur América	6	Se envió.
Tardien (Pierre)	1833	París	América	....	Se envió.
Tegg (Th.)	1826	Londres	Sur América.		
Thomas y Andren	1812	Boston	Caracas con Guayana	....	Se envió copià.
Thompson (T. F)	1817	Edimburg	Caracas y Guayana.		
Vallardi (Anto.)	....	Milán	América Meridional	....	Se envió con el nombre del Autor Sergen.
Vandermaelen (Ph.)	1827	Bruselas	Parte de Colombia	....	Se envió.
Vivien (L.)	1825	París	América Meridional	....	Se envió.
Villemin	1830	....	America del Sur	....	Se envió por señalar á Esequibo—Dice la comisión que modifica á Cano.
Wild (J.)	1830	Londres	Sur América	....	} Colombia prima—Se envió.
Otro	1820 y 29	id.	id.	....	

Mapas enviados por la Comisión de Venezuela y que no figuran en la lista anterior.

Antores ó editores.	Fecha.	Lugar de publicación.	Nombre del mapa.	Notas.
Renard (L.), editor	....	Amsterdam	Nueva Vranchryck, Nueva Inglaterra, Nueva Holandor, Nueva Andalucía, Guayana, Venezuela.	
Buchon (J. A.)	1825	París	Atlas geográfico, cronológico, estadístio de las dos Américas.	
L. Renard	1745	Amsterdam	....	Editado por Reinier y Ottens—Atlas el número 14.
P. Angrand	1835	....	Colombia y las Guayanas	Colección.
G. Sasso y M. Bonattil	1821	Londres	América Meridional.	
Marchal, editor	18 3	Bruselas	Atlas histórico, general, cronológico, etc.	
Rainal (G. F.)	1780	Ginebra.		
Anónimo	1864	Londres.		
Levy Alvarez	....	París.		
Andrwea Gonyon	1845	París.		
Newtons	1836	Londres	....	Espera.
A. Dufour	1856	Barcelona	....	Acompaña al viaje pintoresco á las dos Américas por M. M. A. D'Orbigny y J. B. Eyries.
Juan Oliveres	1863	......id	América Meridional	En la obra "Historia general de las Misiones."

VIII.

LISTS of the maps relating to Guayana boundary question found by the Venezuela and the Washington Commission, classified according to the lines they show.

Note of the Maps which show the Essequibo as a boundary, taken from the list published by the Investigating Commission of Washington.

Authors.	Date of publication.	Place of publication.	Name of map.	Remarks.
Jacobz (A.)	1621	Amsterdam	West Indies	See position of names.
Lucena (J. Paluzie.)	1895	Barcelona	North & South America.	Was sent.
Niles (T. M.)	1838	Hartford	South America	Do.
Reichar (C. G.), C. Campe Pubª	1832	Nuremberg	do	Do.
Russel (T.)	1794	London	do	Do.
Tanner (H. S.)	1836	Philadelphia	Brazil	Was not sent, but one of 1829, Surinam, which gives Nassau.
Mentelle (S.) Geograp.[l] Institute Weimar.	1804	Weimar	Guayanas, Holland, and France.	Was sent.
Do	1814	do	Do.	
Gio Mazzajoli			America	Was sent, but it was a Roman edition.
Hall (Signey)	1825	London	Colombia.	Do.
Le Sage (C. de las Casas)	1812	Paris	South America	Was sent, but with date of 1814.
Martin (Robert Montgomery)	1839	London.	Colonies of Gr. Britain.	Boundary indicated by color.
Reid (John)	1796	New York	South America	Boundary by the position of title.
Tomlins (Fred. Guest)	1842	Halifax	Do	Do.
Arrowsmith (Aaron)	1817	Edinburgh	Do.	
Bianconi (F.)	1888	Paris	U. S. of Venezuela.	
Carey Cetlatrew	1823	Philadelphia	Colombia.	
Do	1814	do	Caracas.	

Maps which follow the Cruz Caño line, or be it Cape Nassau.

Authors or publishers.	Date.	Place of publication.	Name of map.	Nos. of maps.	Remarks.
Anonymous—G. Cowie & Co.	1824	London	Colombia.		
Anonymous—Coleographic Camera Co.	1796	Rome	Terra firma and Guiana		Sent by the Committee of Classification (of 1798).
Arrowsmith (A.)	1811	London	South America		Do.
Bache (Richard), captain	1827	Philadelphia	Colombia.		
Bell (James)	1834	Glasgow	Brazil and Paraguay.		
Bellin, Jacques Nicolas	1760	Paris	Coasts of Guiana	2	Of S. Bellin of 1709. Was sent, and this one of 1760 is the same.
Codazzi (Agustin)	1740	Caracas	Colombia.		
Cradoc & Ivi	1808	London	South America		Was sent.
Cruz, Caño and Olmedilla	1775	Madrid	do		Do.
Anonymous—Ed Baldwin, Cradoc & Ivy.	1823	London	Colombia.		
Luis Stanislaus Darcy de la Rochette.	1807	do	Colombia Prima		Was sent. Edition of 1820.
Depons (T. R. T.)	1805	Paris	Caracas		Says Nassau; but the title is Dutch Guiana. It does not pass the Essequibo.
Dirwald (T.)	1823	Vienna	South America.		
Ducoudray Holtein	1829	London	Colombia.		
Dufour (A.)	1820	Paris	South America		There is another in the Travels to America, Asia. etc
Duvotenay (Th.)	1859	Forino	Colombia and Guiana	2	The one without any date was sent.
Faden (W.)	1799	London	South America.		
N de)	1719	Paris	Terra firma		Has no boundaries.
Finley, Anthony	1826–29	Philadelphia	South America	2	

Vrylink (H.)	1854	Amsterdam	South America		Atlas of 1855 was sent, showing Nassau.
Annual Geography	1854	Philadelphia	Brazil and another of Colombia.	4	In that of 1895, Venezuela and Guayana Británica, and in that of South America, Barima.
Guocchi, Giacomo	1859–64	Milan	South America		Was sent.
Giussefeld (J. L.)	1796	Nuremberg	America.		
Guthrie (W.)	1803	Roma	South and New America, Kingdom of Granada.	2	Was sent.
Hall (Sidney)	1857	London	Western Hemisphere		*One of Cochrane's Colombia was sent, date* 1825, giving the Essequibo.
Humboldt, Alexander de	1830	Vienna	Colombia		Was sent.
Lapié (P.)	1809–28	Paris	Different names	9	Were sent.
Le Sage, A. (Count of las Casas.	1827	Paris	Historical America		Was sent. Also another of 1812, "Modern America," giving the Essequibo.
Cary & Len, publishers	1825	Philadelphia	South America		One of 1827 was sent.
Geographical Institute	1828	Weimar	Guayana.		
Malte Brun	1837	Philadelphia	Colombia and Guayana	2	Was sent.
Masmert	1803	Nuremberg	South America		Slightly changed.
Michelena & Rojas	1867	Brussels	South America.		
Mollieu (G. Th.)	1824	London	Republic of Colombia.		
Murray (Hugh)	1835	do	Brazil, Paraguay & Guayana.		
Company of the Orinoco, Fitzgerald.	1896	New York.			
Pinkerton (T.)	1804	Paris	South America	4	All show Cape Nassau. Were sent.
Poirson (T. B.)	1802	do	French and Dutch Guayanas.	5	1802, was sent. Those of 1803–14 and '21 also.
Richard (C. G.)	1832	Nuremberg	South America		Says that C. Caño is modified. Was sent to show the Essequibo.
Requena, Francisco	1796	Philadelphia	South America		Was sent.
Restrepo, José Manuel	1827	Paris	Department of the Orinoco		That of 1825 was sent to show the *Essequibo*.

Maps which follow the Cruz Caño line, or be it Cape Nassau.

Authors or publishers.	Date.	Place of publication.	Name of map.	Nos. of	Remarks.
Rosa (R.)	1865	New York	United States of Venezuela		Was sent.
Rossi (Luigi)	1821	Milan	South America		Was sent as from publisher Sasso (G.) and Bonatil (M.)
Schlieben (W. E. A.)	1850	Leipzig	Guiana	2	With some changes.
Schumith (T. M.)	1820	Berlin	America.		
Smiley (Th. F.)	1830	Philadelphia	South America.		
Stedman (T. G.)		Paris	Guiana		Was sent.
Streit (T. W.)	1842	Leipzig	South America	2	That of 1832 was sent.
Turville L de	1778	Madrid	New Andalusia		Was sent with Conlin's work.
Tanner (A. S.)	1829	Philadelphia	South America	6	Was sent.
Tardien (Pierre)	1833	Paris	America		Was sent.
Tegg (Th.)	1826	London	South America.		
Thomas & Andrew	1812	Boston	Caracas with Guayana		A copy was sent.
Thompson (T. F.)	1817	Edinburgh	Caracas and Guayana.		
Vallardi Ants		Milan	South America		Was sent with the name of the author, Sergen.
Vandermaelen (Ph)	1827	Brussels	Part of Colombia		Was sent.
Vivien, L	1825	Paris	South America		Was sent.
Villemin	1830		South America		Was sent to show the Essequibo. The Commission says that Caño is modified.
Wild (T.)	1830	London	South America		Colombia prima was sent.
Another	1820–29	do	do		

Maps sent by the Venezuelan Commission to that of Washington, showing the Essequibo, and which is not found in the list published by the latter.

Authors.	Dates.	Place of publication.	Names of maps.	Remarks.
Villemin	1830–40		South America	In the note of the Commission it says that this is a modification of Cruz creek.
Restrepo (J. M.)	1825	London	Colombia.	
Holmes Laurie (editor)	1829	do	Western Hemisphere of Colombia.	
Purdy (John)	1832	do	World's map.	
Lincobi and Edmund		Boston	South America.	
Anonymous			Provinces of Venezuela, Caracas, etc.	

List of the new maps found which show the same limits of boundary.

Authors.	Dates.	Place of publication.	Names of maps.	Remarks.
Houze (A.)	1846	Paris	South America	Accompanied by the Travels published by Smith.
Monaldi (A.), atlas	1840	Rome	Terrestrial Globe	Certified by Urdaneta.
Manuel Maria Paz	1842	Bogota	Colombia and Venezuela.	In the charge by Colombia before His Majesty Alfonso XII.

Maps sent by the Venezuelan Commission, and which do not show in the foregoing list.

Authors and publishers.	Date.	Place of publication.	Name of maps.	Remarks.
Renard (L.), publisher		Amsterdam	New Vranchrych, New England, New Holland, New Andalusia, Guayana, Venezuela.	
Buchon (T. A.)	1825	Paris	Geographical Atlas, chronological estadistical of the Two Americas.	
L. Renard	1745	Amsterdam		Published by Renier and Ottens, Atlas No. 14.
P. Augrand	1835		Colombia and the Guayanas.	Collection.
G. Sasso and M. Bonatil	1821	London	South America.	
Marchal, publisher	1853	Brussels	Historical, general, chronological, etc., Atlas.	
Reimal, G. F	1780	Geneva.		
Anonymous	1864	London.		
Levy Alvarez		Paris.		
Andrwea Gonyon	1845	Paris.		
Newtons	1836	London		(Sphere) Globe.
A. Dufour	1856	Barcelona		Accompanies the Illustrated Travels in the Two Americas, M. M., A. D'Orbigny and T. B. Eyries.
Juan Oliveres	1863	do	South America	In the work, "General History of the Missions."

www.ingramcontent.com/pod-product-compliance
Lightning Source LLC
LaVergne TN
LVHW052110210926
848482LV00024B/535
9798891849266